# Personal Influence

# Personal Influence

The Part Played by People in the Flow of Mass Communications

# Elihu Katz & Paul F. Lazarsfeld

With a new introduction by Elihu Katz and a foreword by Elmo Roper

Transaction Publishers
New Brunswick (U.S.A.) and London (U.K.)

New material this edition copyright © 2006 by Transaction Publishers, New Brunswick, New Jersey. Originally published in 1955 by The Free Press.

All rights reserved under International and Pan-American Copyright Conventions. No part of this book may be reproduced or transmitted in any form or by any means, electronic or mechanical, including photocopy, recording, or any information storage and retrieval system, without prior permission in writing from the publisher. All inquiries should be addressed to Transaction Publishers, Rutgers—The State University, 35 Berrue Circle, Piscataway, New Jersey 08854-8042. www.transactionpub.com

This book is printed on acid-free paper that meets the American National Standard for Permanence of Paper for Printed Library Materials.

Library of Congress Catalog Number: 2005043945
ISBN: 1-4128-0507-4
Printed in the United States of America

Library of Congress Cataloging-in-Publication Data

Katz, Elihu, 1926-
    Personal influence : the part played by people in the flow of mass communications / Elihu Katz & Paul F. Lazarsfeld ; with a new introduction by Elihu Katz and a foreword by Elmer Roper.—2nd ed.
        p. cm.
    T.p. verso: "Originally published in 1955 by The Free Press."
    Includes bibliographical references and index.
    ISBN 1-4128-0507-4 (pbk. : alk. paper)
        1. Public opinion. 2. Mass media. I. Lazarsfeld, Paul Felix. II. Title.

HM1236.K38   2005
303.3'8—dc22                                                2005043945

To Ros[e]

**And to Ruth—for more than fifty years**
**—2005**

"And what is a still greater novelty, the mass do not now take their opinions from dignitaries in Church or State, from ostensible leaders, or from books. Their thinking is done for them by men much like themselves, addressing them or speaking in their name, on the spur of the moment. . . ."

JOHN STUART MILL
*On Liberty*

# Contents

[ vii ]

# PART TWO

# THE FLOW OF EVERYDAY INFLUENCE

# IN A MIDWESTERN COMMUNITY

### Section One: *Locating Personal Influence*

# Acknowledgments

THE FIELD STUDY reported in the second part of this volume
owes a great deal to a variety of collaborators. We shall not try
to rank the importance of their contributions. In some cases it
is the amount of attention and energy spent on the collection
and analysis of data which deserves thanks. In other cases the
contribution consisted of a specific idea or a helpful preliminary draft on a specific topic. We shall list the names of our
associates in the sequence in which they worked on the various
phases of the study.

The statistical work which led to the selection of the town
and the sampling within the town was supervised by Bernard
R. Berelson.

The whole organization of field work for the study was in
the hands of C. Wright Mills.

The field staff was trained and supervised by Jeanette Green.
The first perusal of the material was done by a group of ana-
lysts who wrote a series of memoranda on various topics of
immediate interest. Especially valuable were the many contributions of Helen Dinerman and Thelma Anderson. Leila A.
Sussmann and Patricia L. Kendall contributed early analyses
of the marketing and movie materials.

When it came to the drafting of a text for publication, the
component sections were entrusted to several associates. It is
to these colleagues that our greatest debt is due:

David B. Gleicher
Peter H. Rossi
Leo Srole

Messrs. Srole and Gleicher prepared drafts for the section on
the characteristics of opinion leaders and Mr. Rossi's work was
primarily in the section on the impact of personal influence.

Through all the varying phases of analysis and writing the
advice of C. Wright Mills was extremely valuable, often opening up completely new perspectives on the data.

For reading drafts of the manuscript of Part One and making helpful suggestions, we are indebted to Edmund deS. Brunner, David Riesman and M. Brewster Smith. Patricia Kendall read each new version of Part Two sympathetically but critically and contributed clarity, caution and good sense right through to the final proofreading.

The index is the contribution of Alberta Curtis Rattray; the charts are the work of Seymour Howard. The major portion of the typing of the final draft was done by Robert Witt, and the service staff of Columbia University's Bureau of Applied Social Research did the difficult job of coding and tabulating with its usual efficiency.

To Everett R. Smith of Macfadden Publications, and Jeremiah Kaplan of The Free Press we owe thanks for a degree of patience considerably in excess of that which one has a right to expect even from sponsors, publishers and friends.

# Introduction to the Transaction Edition
# Lazarsfeld's Legacy:
# The Power of Limited Effects*

IN THE FAMOUS debate between Emile Durkheim and Gabriel Tarde (Clark, 1969), Durkheim argued that sociology was about the compelling power of social norms, while Tarde, the ostensible loser, gave priority to the study of aggregation, how communication from person to person to person contributes to the formation of these norms. In designing "The Decatur Study"—on which this book reports—Paul Lazarsfeld sided with Tarde. He admired Tarde's (1898) brilliant study of the role of conversation in the aggregation of public opinion. Tarde's observation that "if no one conversed, the newspapers would appear to no avail...because they would exercise no profound influence on any minds" is the classic precursor of Lazarsfeld's "two-step flow of communication."

"The Decatur Study" is an empirical validation of Lazarsfeld's serendipitous discovery, dating to *The People's Choice*, his 1940 study of voting decisions. He found that messages from the media may be further mediated by informal "opinion leaders" who intercept, interpret, and diffuse what they see and hear to the personal networks in which they are embedded. Together with the concept of "selectivity" in exposure, perception, and recall of media messages, the "two step" hypothesis points to a shift in the balance of power between media and audiences, at least as far as short-run persuasion is concerned. There was talk of "limited effects," and anticipation of the "active audience." It was implied that media effectiveness was somehow dependent on "supplementation" by interpersonal influence (Lazarsfeld and Merton, 1948; Katz and Popescu, 2004).

The hypothesis evoked interest. In addition to Decatur, it spawned a number of subsequent studies at Columbia University's

---

* Thanks to Jatin Atre, Jeff Pooley, and Peter Simonson for their advice and to Irving Louis Horowitz, Michael Delli Carpini, and Peter Bearman for their encouragement.

[xv]

Bureau of Applied Social Research, notable among which were Robert Merton's (1949) study of how "cosmopolitan" opinion leaders relayed the content of newsweeklies to their constituents, Bernard Berelson et al's (1954) sequel to the 1940 voting study, and Daniel Lerner's (1958) effort to identify opinion leaders in the process of modernization. Objections came from irate advocates of "powerful effects," such as Gitlin (1978), who argued that the opinion leader idea was mere camouflage for the direct effects of the media, and from researchers such as Lang (1981), Adorno (1969), and McLuhan (1964), who insisted that the power of the media lay in slowing change or in "long-run" effects and not in short-run "campaigns" to affect voting or buying behavior.

## *II.*

Conceptually, the Decatur study began as a partnership between Lazarsfeld and C. Wright Mills (Sterne, 2005). But the two men soon agreed to part. Methodologically, it is pure Lazarsfeld, expanding the innovative design of his voting study to other arenas of decision-making. By means of his "panel method" of repeated interviews with the *same* sample of respondents, it became possible to observe the interactions of mass media and interpersonal influence in the making of these everyday decisions. Taking a step beyond the voting studies, the Decatur study constructed influential-influencee dyads by "snowballing" from members of the original sample to the persons whom they had implicated in their decisions. This was a first step toward the incorporation of sociometric methods into large-scale opinion research. Note also Lazarsfeld's belief that the study of media effects might better be served by proceeding "backward," so to speak, from response to stimulus, rather than "forward."

These few paragraphs testify to the character—not just the extent—of Lazarsfeld's contributions to communications research. Noteworthy are (1) his theoretical explorations and his incisive questioning of basic assumptions; (2) his effort to examine media effects in real life, outside the laboratory; (3) his commitment to continuity and cumulation from study to study; (4) his methodological prowess and innovative designs for large-scale survey research; and not least, (5) the building of university institutes—or laboratories—for the conduct of such research (Barton, 2001). One might also add (6) his belief that applied research—the kind that is commissioned by government or business—need not detract from its academic usefulness and respectability. In a nod to the Frankfurt School, Lazarsfeld (1941) distinguished between "administrative" and "critical" research, acknowledging that the former conceptualized problems from the client's point of view while the latter took the "client" as part and parcel of the problem itself. To critics who complained that the downgrading of media power by the Columbia studies were allowing the media to shirk their social responsibilities, Lazarsfeld might have referred to his own map of media effects, in which the study of short-run persuasion occupies only one corner (Klapper, 1960; Katz, 2001). It is true, nevertheless, that this is the corner in which he was most active.

Work on this scale cannot be done alone, of course, as the Decatur study well exemplifies. In addition to the early contributions of Mills, and his overseeing of the elaborate fieldwork, Peter Rossi, David Gleicher, and Leo Srole made major contributions to the analysis. Their work is duly noted—but understated—in the Acknowledgments and at the relevant sections. Almost a decade after the fieldwork, the project was still deemed unfinished by Lazarsfeld, who asked me—in 1954—to try my hand. I also undertook to prepare an essay exploring the unlikely-sounding possibility that small-group research had some bearing on mass communication research in view of the two-step flow of communication. This essay became my doctoral dissertation, and Part One of the book.

*III.*

Lazarsfeld's importance to communication research extends far beyond the Decatur study, even beyond the sum of his work in this field. Indeed, it extends beyond his lifetime in ways he could not have anticipated. He presaged the ways in which the field would develop, and perhaps even the ways in which it will fall apart.

As noted above, the empirical work of the Columbia group led to the conclusion that the media have only "limited effects" in the process of mass persuasion, in contrast to the debate that accompanied the early days of radio. That conclusion was based on repeated evaluations of intensive attempts to change opinions, attitudes, and actions in the relatively short-run. Seeking explanations for the absence of powerful effects, the Columbia group identified a number of "intervening variables" that come between media and audiences.

Two of these are noteworthy. One is the "selectivity" in exposure and perception used by individuals to "protect" their preexisting cognitive structures from the challenges of dissonant messages. The other is "interpersonal relations"—also a kind of selectivity, but at the group level—whereby messages are filtered through social networks and vetted in the light of group norms. These two, and their expansion in the "two-step flow" of media-conversation-opinion, allow us to assess the progress of communication research since the '50s and '60s, and not incidentally, to uncover Lazarsfeld's footprints.

Let us consider these three strands in turn. We will first show how the selectivity that empowered the audience converged with the study of "uses and gratifications," and in turn, with the currently fashionable study of reception. Then, we will show how the influentials who mediate between messages and opinion led to the study of social networks and the diffusion of innovation. Finally, we will trace the nexus underlying the "two-step flow" to current theories of the public sphere of participatory democracy, and thus, to the reunion of Tarde, Lazarsfeld, and Habermas. Each of these routes, and some others, along which communication research has proceeded are marked on Lazarsfeld's map.

First, let us tell the stories of the two intervening variables.

1. *Selectivity.* The introduction of selectivity into the persuasion paradigm helped to explain why media campaigns fall so far short of expectations. The observation that a campaign of persuasion is more likely to reinforce than convert—because the non-believers have departed or misinterpreted—led to a keen interest in other forms of self-selection based not only on defensiveness but on interests and role-obligations. This thinking converged with another Columbia tradition called "uses and gratifications," which shifted attention from the question of direct effects ("What do the media do to people?") to the question, "What do people do with the media?" Herta Herzog (1941) asked

early what radio listeners take from soap operas and quiz shows; Matilda and Jack Riley (1951) compared the ways in which isolated and integrated children used action-adventure programs; Edward Suchman (1941) discovered the kinds of listeners who were attracted to classical music on the radio. By the same token, because of the roles they played, those Decatur women who were sought out for advice about marketing, fashion, or politics were more knowledgeable in their fields than those whom they influenced.

Knowledge-gap studies—more European than American—argued similarly that prior cognitive structure or differing degrees of interest selectively affect the likelihood of absorbing additional information on a particular subject (Tichenor, 1970). Thus, information campaigns designed to *reduce* differences among the information-rich and the information-poor often achieve the opposite result. Even when everybody learns something, those who start with more will gain disproportionately.

But the ultimate blooming of selectivity is to be found in the current practice of reception research whose focus is on the way in which different "readers" decode the "same" text. Some of this research centers on varieties of decoding while other work considers the match between the "implied reader" of the text and the "real reader." More sociologically oriented studies (e.g. Liebes and Katz, 1990) aim to discover relationships between types of readers and types of readings. Like the study of gratifications, this work posits the relative autonomy—the power—of the reader. Various strands of postmodern scholarship have taken up this pursuit with only grudging acknowledgment of gratification studies. With respect to the difference between them, one can say, with Livingstone (2003), that gratifications research deals in "uses," while reception studies are concerned with "meanings." It is ironic that reception scholars, anchored in so-called cultural studies, renounce this; James Curran (1990) has tried to right the record on this point. A further irony of reception research is its gradual disconnection from the media. Everything is text—from a love letter to the Berlin Wall—and media are just another supplier of texts. Some theorists even postulate that there is no text and that the reader him/herself is the author. More sober theorists describe reading as a negotiated interaction with a text. It seems fair to say that the media are lost in the thicket of selectivity, and that reception theory has no special interest in finding them. Yet recent calls from receptionists for an ethnography of communication—for study of the reception "context"—sound like an opportunity to reintroduce both small groups and mass media; we'll see.

2. *Interpersonal Relations.* The same sort of losing-touch-with-origins may be said to characterize the other major hurdle in the persuasion process. First notice of the (unexpected) relevance of small groups to mass communication came in the 1940 voting study, which found high homogeneity in the political orientation of friends and family, and the observation that such primary groups exert normative pressure on their members' decisions. Then came the opinion leader idea that refocused media research on the nodes that connect the media and interpersonal networks. This is how the norms and networks of primary groups insinuated themselves into the Columbia studies of mass communication, including this one.

The limited-effects paradigm that led from *The People's Choice* to Decatur found its next iteration in "The Drug Study," which sought to trace the progress of a new antibiotic as it spread among physicians in four towns via salesmen, advertising, medical journals, and interpersonal influence (Coleman, Katz, and Menzel, 1966). More than a "decision" study—of the kind that occupied Lazarsfeld from Vienna to New York—this was a study of flow, or "diffusion," that is, of a cascading sequence of decisions.

By challenging the assumption that messages are received and acted upon simultaneously, it widened the gap between a paradigm of powerful effects based on (1) the everybody audience, (2) simultaneity of reception, and (3) unmediated contact between senders and receivers, and a paradigm based on (1) audience selectivity, (2) a sequence of adoptions over time, and (3) the mediation of influentials and social networks. Thus, while the "decision" studies discovered selectivity and personal networks, "diffusion" studies discovered time (even if the panel method and the turnover tables of the voting studies hover at the brink of the time dimension).

There are important differences between "decision" and "diffusion." The decision model, at least in Decatur, is indifferent to

time and indifferent to the object of change (Ms. A may be changing from fashion x to y, while Ms. B may be going from y to x).
Its primary interest is in "why," that is, in the intrinsic attraction
of an item, in the extrinsic sources of influence that recommended
it, and in the fact of adoption. There is equally strong interest in
the identities of the "who" and "whom" of the influence dyad in
order to chart the direction of flow.

The diffusion model is also interested in adoption, but it is in
the cumulative growth of adoption by a collectivity, as some
specified item moves through its ranks over time. For example,
the sociometric mapping of physicians' relationships made it
possible to follow the new antibiotic as it traveled through their
interpersonal networks, revealing changes in the rate of adoption at each point in time. Diffusion research asks the question
"when," without being able to do much more than surmise the
sources of influence on individual decisions or the changing roles
of these sources over time. Unlike the decision model, the diffusion model attempts to obtain adoption data "objectively," independent of the adopter's ability to recollect.

Comparing "decision" and "diffusion" unveils an even more
fascinating difference between the two. Decision research, based
on the introspective ability of respondents, is associated with
"persuasion," where both influential and influencee can confirm
that influence has, indeed, been transacted. However, persuasion is not the only form of influence; in fact, there are at least
three other types of influence, which might be called "imitation,"
"manipulation," and "contagion." Contagion best defines diffusion studies—as in spread of the measles, for example—in that A
may influence B without either of them knowing it, and the dif-
fusing item is merely relayed rather than negotiated. By the same
token, there are situations in which only one of the parties is
aware that influence has been transacted. In "manipulation," it is
the influential who is aware, while his/her victim is not. In "imitation," as in fashion, the reverse is true—i.e. the influencee may
be aware of having been influenced, while the influential may be
innocently unaware. In fact, all four types of influence have a
place in the paradigm of diffusion, while only "persuasion" (and
perhaps "imitation") applies to Lazarsfeld's study of the role of
personal influence in decision-making.

The drug study makes clear how difficult it is to specify the points of contact between interpersonal networks and the media. Medical journals and drug-company salesmen fed into physicians' decisions and into conversation with colleagues, but it was not easy to treat these external influences systematically. This problem is nicely reflected in Gladwell's (2000) popularization of diffusion research in that television does not appear in the index, as if to imply that interpersonal networks themselves are sufficient for the take-off and spread of an innovation. Methodologically, only new combinations of the two models—decision and diffusion—can hope to overcome this problem.

By now, there is a flourishing field of research on social networks (Watts, 2003), inspired, in part, by the Columbia tradition (Kadushin, 1976; Burt, 1999). While diffusion is one of the applications of this work, even here—as in reception studies—only little effort is being made to bring the media back in. It is interesting to note, again, how the media have almost dropped out of sight: compare the evolutionary course that led from selectivity to gratifications to reception with the course that led from interpersonal relations to diffusion to social networks.

## *IV.*

Let us turn now to consider the bearing of *Personal Influence* on the public sphere. The "two-step flow of communication" means more than that interpersonal relations intervene in the process of mass persuasion. Lazarsfeld's hypothesis rescued communication research from the psychologism of message and response. In a larger sense, it situated the media in a societal context, and enlisted society in the process of transmission and reception. Or, to invoke some classic theory, it saw society itself as a system of communication. By proposing the role of "opinion leaders" it raised the larger question of how to conceptualize the linkage between the media system and the social system.

In the Decatur study, the "public affairs leaders"—like the influentials in the other areas—enlisted other members of their personal networks in the polity. In the 1940s, for example, it was clear that husbands influenced the vote decisions of their spouses, and were more likely to follow politics in the media.

Politics was the one area in which influence crossed class lines, and where a hierarchy of personal influence was discerned.

But the public sphere of deliberative democracy has a place for the "two-step flow" that extends far beyond individual decision-making. Both Tarde (1898) and Habermas (1989) may be said to have theorized a public sphere based on the sequence media-conversation-decision-action. In Tarde's scheme, the media deliver a menu of political issues to the cafes and coffee shops and salons. Discussion of these issues percolate more "considered opinions." These opinions circulate from café to café until they crystallize into Public Opinion, which feeds back to government, the media, and individual decisions. As already noted, it is obvious that the "two-step flow"—media to conversation to opinion—has a major presence in these theories. Even here, among students of deliberative democracy, the role of the media is often overlooked, or understated. Putnam (2001), for example, despairs of the media as agents of information; even worse, they keep people home. Civic affairs rest on the shoulders of television's escapees. Others, like Mutz (1998), disagree, pointing out that democracy requires knowledge of oppositional ideas and that political talk engages only the like-minded. The media, therefore, are our only recourse to what others think. Schudson (1997), too, finds little use for political conversation.

Had Lazarsfeld remained in the field of political communication, he might have turned his attention from the immediate circle of the individual voter (or shopper or movie-goer) to the larger public sphere in which these social and political molecules are embedded. The combined methodologies of decision and diffusion might help to explain the dynamics of deliberation and aggregation, where the media come in, and how binding social norms emerge.

*V.*

It is ironic that theory and research on "reception," on "networks," and on "public space" are still struggling over the relative power of the individual, the media, and interpersonal influence (Chaffee and Mutz, 1988). The same thing holds true in the realms of marketing and fashion, where advertising is contrasted with the power of "buzz."

By now, we *know* that the media have only limited effects, as far as short-run persuasion is concerned. Even (well-hidden) advertising research will confirm this. We know, since Plato, that personal influence is persuasive. We also have learned that there is little use in asking which medium is more important because each may serve different functions—at different times—both in decision-making and in diffusion.

The question to ask is how do mass media and interpersonal influence interact at the individual level of decision-making and at the collective level of diffusion. *Personal Influence* represents first steps toward connecting a paradigm of decision-making—which had occupied Lazarsfeld since his earliest work in Vienna—to a paradigm of diffusion. This was accomplished via the addition of personal networks and the direction of flow ("who to whom"). Now it is clear that the diffusion model should combine with the decision model rather than displace it. The interaction of interpersonal influence and the media are central to both.

## *VI.*

Standing on the shoulders allows us to look a little further:

1. The leadership of "opinion leaders" is spelled with a small "l." As everyday influentials, they are ubiquitous; it has proven of little use to single them out one by one. The secret is to locate those segments of a population that influence other segments in each particular domain. For example, if it is still true that husbands influence the way their wives vote, and if you know how to reach husbands, the reward is two for the price of one.

2. Even when horizontal influence within a segment seems to prevail, watch for evidence of vertical flow across boundaries—of gender, class, ethnicity, age, etc.

3. Opinion leaders perform different functions. Sometimes they are mere conduits. At other times, they select, interpret, or advocate. Sometimes, they follow.

4. Where you find an opinion leader, you are bound to find a conversation—about politics, fashion, marketing, movies, education, sports, etc. Studying conversations is a better way to understand persuasion than simply nominating leaders and followers.

5. Try to identify the points at which media enter the conversation.

6. Interpersonal influence comes in chains longer than two.

7. Don't ask, "Which of the sources you have mentioned had the most influence on your decision?" Different sources—interpersonal or mediated—serve different functions at various stages in decision-making. In general, consider the patterning of interactions among the different sources.

8. Instead of "snowballing" from a decision-maker within a sample to an influential outside, first build a social molecule around each atom in the sample. That allows both for the representativeness of the sample, and the sociometry of a personal network.

9. The flow of influence is not limited to persuasion. Distinguish among persuasion, imitation, manipulation, and contagion.

10. Consider the challenge of aggregation, i.e. tracing the process of how opinions diffuse, and how they coalesce into Public Opinion.

In the prophetic tradition, Lazarsfeld foresaw that the institutions of politics, fashion, marketing, etc. may be conceptualized as communications systems: He gave us a glimpse and a go-ahead and a good-bye. The Decatur study left it to us to reconnect the media with the engines of stability and change implicit in the sociology of communication and diffusion.

Elihu Katz

Philadelphia and Jerusalem
February 2005

## Bibliography

Adorno, T. (1969). "Scientific Experiences of a European Scholar in America." In D. Fleming and B. Baylin (eds.), *The Intellectual Migration: Europe and America 1930-1960*. Cambridge: Harvard University Press.

Barton, A. (2001). "Paul Lazarsfeld as Institutional Inventor." *International Journal of Public Opinion Research, 13*, 245-269.

Berelson, B., Lazarsfeld, P., and McPhee, W. (1954). *Voting: A Study of Opinion Formation in a Presidential Campaign*. Chicago: University of Chicago Press.

Burt, R. S. (1999). "The Social Capital of Opinion Leaders." *Annals of the American Academy of Political and Social Science, 566*, 37-54.

Chaffee, S. and Mutz, D. (1988). "Comparing Mediated and Interpersonal Communication Data." In R. P. Hawkins, J. M. Wiemann, S. Pingree (eds.), *Advancing Communication Science: Merging Mass Media and Inter-Personal Processes*. Newbury Park, Cal.: Sage Publications.

Clark, T. (ed.) (1969). *Gabriel Tarde on Communication and Social Influence*. Chicago, University of Chicago Press.

Coleman, J., Katz, E., and Menzel, H. (1966). *Medical Innovation: A Diffusion Study*. Indianapolis: Bobbs-Merrill.

Curran, J. (1990). "The New Revisionism in Mass Communication Research: A Reappraisal." *European Journal of Communication, 5 (2-3)*, 135-164.

Gitlin, T. (1978). "Media Sociology: The Dominant Paradigm." *Theory and Society, 6*, 205-253.

Gladwell, M. (2000). *The Tipping Point: How Little Things Can Make a Big Difference*. Boston: Little, Brown and Company.

Habermas, J. (1989). *The Structural Transformation of the Public Sphere: An Inquiry into a Category of Bourgeois Society*. Cambridge: MIT Press.

Herzog, H. (1941). "On Borrowed Experience: An Analysis of Listening to Daytime Sketches." *Studies in Philosophy and Social Science, 9(1)*, 65-95.

Kadushin, C. (1976). "Networks and Circles in the Production of Culture." *American Behavioral Scientist, 19*, 769-784.

Katz, E. (2001). "Lazarsfeld's Map of Media Effects." *International Journal of Public Opinion Research, 13*, 270-279.

Katz, E. and Popescu, M. (2004). "Narrowcasting: On Communicator Control of the Conditions of Reception." In P. Golding and I. Bondebjerg (eds.), *European Culture and the Media*. Bristol: Intellect.

Klapper, J. (1960). *The Effects of Mass Communication*. New York: The Free Press.

Lang, G. and Lang, K. (1981). "Mass Communications and Public Opinion: Strategies for Research." In M. Rosenberg and R. H. Turner (eds.), *Social Psychology: Sociological Perspectives*. New York: Basic Books.

Lazarsfeld, P. (1941). "Administrative and Critical Communications Research." *Studies in Philosophy and Social Science, 9*, 2-16.

Lazarsfeld, P., Berelson, B., and Gaudet, H. (1944). *The People's Choice: How the Voter Makes Up His Mind in a Presidential Campaign*. Columbia University Press: New York.

Lazarsfeld, P. and Merton, R. (1948). "Mass Communication, Popular Taste and Organized Social Action." *The Communication of Ideas*. New York: Institute for Religious and Social Studies.

Lerner, D. (1958). *The Passing of Traditional Society: Modernizing the Middle East*. Glencoe: Free Press.

Liebes, T. and Katz, E. (1990). *The Export of Meaning: Cross-Cultural Readings of "Dallas."* New York: Oxford University Press.

Livingstone, S. (2003). "The Changing Nature of Audiences: From the Mass Audience to the Interactive Media User." In A. Valdivia (ed.), *The Blackwell Companion to Media Research*. Oxford: Blackwell.

McLuhan, M. (1964). *Understanding Media: The Extensions of Man*. Toronto: McGraw-Hill.

Merton, R. (1949, 1968). "Patterns of Influence: Local and Cosmopolitan Influentials." *Social Structure and Social Theory*. New York: Free Press.

Mutz, Diana C. (1998). *Impersonal Influence: How Perceptions of Mass Collectives Affect Political Attitudes*. Cambridge: Cambridge University Press.

Putnam, R. (2001). *Bowling Alone: The Collapse and Revival of American Community*. New York: Simon & Schuster.

Riley, M. and Riley, J. (1951). "A Sociological Approach to Communication Research." *Public Opinion Quarterly, 15*, 445-460.

Schudson, M. (1997). "Why Conversation is Not the Soul of Democracy." *Critical Studies in Mass Communication, 14*, 297-309.

Sterne, J. (2005). "C. Wright Mills, the Bureau for Applied Social Research, and the Meaning of Critical Scholarship." *Cultural Studies/Critical Methodologies, 5(1)*, 65-94.

Suchman, E. (1941). "An Invitation to Music." In Lazarsfeld and Stanton (eds.), *Radio Research 1941*. New York: Duell, Sloan and Pearce.

Tarde, G. (1898, 1989). *L'opinion et la Foule*. Paris: Presses Universitaires de France.

Tichenor, P. et al. (1970). "Mass Media Flow and Differential Growth in Knowledge." *Public Opinion Quarterly, 34*, 159-170.

Watts, D. (2003). *Six Degrees: The Science of a Connected Age*. New York: W.W. Norton & Co.

# Foreword

Over the past 20 years a good deal of light has been shed on the tastes, preferences, and behavior patterns of the American people. We have begun to build a significant body of knowledge about how people change some of their tastes, preferences, and behavior patterns. Research-wise, we have, for years, been able to take the still portrait, and, in recent years, we have begun to introduce some measure of animation.

But we have developed very little documentation about the entire area of what are the forces that have a bearing on helping to shape people's basic attitudes on the one hand, and in changing these attitudes on the other. We know even less about the degree to which various forces have influence. One first step in approaching this important area of knowledge about human behavior is that of learning how attitudes and opinions are transmitted: the study of communications.

When we speak of studying communications, we must immediately face up to the transmission of ideas. We have, in the past, tended to think of idea communication as primarily a function of the printed word—or certainly of the formal mass and selective media, since radio and television have become so important. Perhaps we have given an over-emphasis to this formal mode of transmission of ideas—or at least not understood the level at which it works.

As the result of my own research into public attitudes I have come to the tentative conclusion that ideas often penetrate the public as a whole slowly and—even more important —very often by interaction of neighbor on neighbor without any apparent influence of the mass media.

Let us examine this conclusion further. I have outlined elsewhere[1] the hypothesis that, insofar as the flow of ideas is concerned, the entire American public can be stratified into six groups. In the inner concentric circle is the smallest group,

---

1. *Saturday Review*, July, 1954.

which I described as the "Great Thinkers." Even when one
considers the many fields in which great thinkers could exist,
there probably aren't more than a half a dozen of these in
the world at any one time, and usually the perspective of
history years later is necessary to give them full recognition
and evaluation. They are not necessarily widely known by
their contemporaries. In fact, on the contrary, in many cases
they are rarely and little known by those who live in the
same period with them.

By way of illustration, let us name a few Great Thinkers
(no doubt we have a number now living, but to avoid con-
troversy—with one exception—all I shall name here shall be
dead). In the field of economics, Adam Smith and Karl Marx
would qualify. (A Great Thinker does not always have to
develop "good" philosophies!) In the field of politics, Plato
and Thomas Jefferson would definitely qualify as Great
Thinkers.

The ground common to all Great Thinkers is that all have
evolved important philosophies or major theories which at
some point in history have gained wide acceptance. Among
the living I would venture to name only Einstein as a Great
Thinker in the field of science. I name this one living example because he also illustrates the important point that a
Great Thinker might be a leader in one field, but a comparative novice in another. Einstein is a comparative novice
in the field of political science, even though he brings to his
views in this field the enormous weight of his achievements
in the natural sciences.

After the Great Thinkers comes the next group of those
who may be called the "Great Disciples." There might be as
many as a dozen of them in any one country at any one time.
They are the people who do not think out great theories or
philosophies, but they have a sufficient understanding and a
close enough mental association with those who do to become most effective advocates and protagonists for an idea
or a philosophy. In the field of religion, for instance, St. Paul
would be a Great Disciple. In the field of philosophy, Spi-
noza. In the natural sciences, Thomas Huxley. In politics,
Abraham Lincoln. The common denominators are a great

pcwer of expression and a forum from which the ideas can be expressed, along with a mind that can apprehend the social consequences of the theory evolved by a "Great Thinker."

A third group as we move outward in our scheme of concentric circles in the evolution and transmission of ideas would be the "Great Disseminators." There might be as many as 1,000 or as few as 250 in America today. Here we can give illustrations of contemporary Americans. Great Disseminators are people who have an important forum—national or international—and who are respected and listened to by a number of people. The United States Senate might be an illustration of such a forum, and as widely separated as Senator Ralph Flanders and Senator Joseph McCarthy might be on many points, they are together in that both are "Great Disseminators"—under this theory. In his capacity as president of the CIO, Walter Reuther would qualify. Because they have wide reading and listening audiences on a national basis, Elmer Davis, Robert Sherwood, Walter Lippmann, Westbrook Pegler and George Sokolsky would qualify. Because he owns a chain of powerful magazines, so would Henry Luce qualify. We could go on to Edison and Marconi in the field of science and technology. To be sure, sometimes the Great Disseminators advocate "good" and sometimes "bad" philosophies. However, we are not drawing moral judgments in defining their role. The single criterion is simply whether or not they reach large numbers of people who regularly listen to them—and, to some degree, are impressed with them.

In a fourth group come people who might be called the "Lesser Disseminators." There might be as few as 15,000 such people, or perhaps as many as 50,000 in this country. These people also have a forum and are listened to—but their forum is more limited. For instance, a national labor leader might have the role of Great Disseminator, but the president of a local union would be a Lesser Disseminator—listened to, but in a more localized and more limited area. Other illustrations would be a minister in a small town, the editor of a country weekly, or a purely local news commentator.

Moving outward in our concentric circles is a fifth group, which might be called the "Participating Citizens." These people might number as many as 10 to 25 million Americans today. They vote with some regularity, contribute money or work in local and national campaigns, belong to organizations active in civic or public affairs, write letters to Congressmen and public officials, are active in discussions on current affairs and problems. They are members of a multitude of organizations that dot the American scene. They are alert citizens who strive to fulfill their obligations to society by performing the simple democratic function of voting and of joining with others in groups in the expectation of making their voices more clearly heard. They are generally the more articulate citizens in our midst, are better educated, and take a higher degree of interest in the world around them.

Many of them become the "experts" to whom a sixth group turn for guidance in formulating their own ideas of what is good or bad politically, economically, or socially. One of them has a little group of fifty to whom his word on whether Middleville can afford a new school is law. Another has a hundred people whose ideas about whether it was right or wrong to go into Korea seem much clearer after he speaks. In short, they and their opinions are respected by their neighbors who are less at home in the world of ideas.

This sixth group I have labelled the "Politically Inert." These are people generally who are not very much at home in the world of ideas, at least when ideas are presented to them in raw or undiluted form. They seldom are active in their communities, and they rarely speak out on any subject. They are not vocal about what they believe in. But they are extremely important. For they come to easily the largest number of people in the country—at least 75 million; and if they are aroused, and enough of them vote, they can determine in a basic sense the political and economic and sociological outlook for some time to come. Finally, even though they rarely express their views, they do indeed pass judgment on many ideas. They are, in a sense, the broad audience to whom the vast chain of communications of ideas is ultimately directed—at least one end of the spectrum.

These six groups are loosely formed groups. They are not mutually exclusive. A Great Disseminator in one field may be Politically Inert in another. The hypothesis I outlined—and there is some evidence to support it—is that however else ideas may be disseminated, one effective way follows the pattern just described—from the Great Thinker to the Great Disciple, to the Great Disseminator to Lesser Disseminator to Participating Citizen to Politically Inert—with, of course, sometimes a hurdling of one or more groups entirely.

There is some evidence that ideas can be communicated to the Politically Inert by way of the mass media. But I think it is an assumption worthy of greater research that the Politically Inert come to accept ideas more readily from their Participating Citizen neighbors and that, in turn, the Participating Citizen neighbors are more apt to accept ideas from the Lesser Disseminators, who in turn are swayed by the Greater Disseminators and the Great Disciples.

This book raises the interesting question as to whether or not there is not a sharp distinction between the role of the Great Disciple or Great Disseminator, for example, in the permeation of ideas for a basic philosophical concept and their role in influencing opinions on the more "every-day matters" such as preferences in food, clothing, movies, etc. Not only does this book raise this question but goes a long ways towards answering it in the affirmative. On these matters the authors make a strong case that the movement of ideas in what might be called the "lesser concepts" or "every-day life" problems is more horizontal than vertical.

In their book Katz and Lazarsfeld have done something which is as unusual as it is useful. They have carefully taken stock of much of the work which has gone on in the field (useful to students and indispensable in making systematic progress in research) and then have gone on to make a new and positive contribution of their own to the existing body of knowledge. All too often, the reader of any book is left with the uncomfortable feeling that he is unable to evaluate just where in the literature a particular work belongs. This book places a number of other significant contributions in their proper focus.

The Decatur study itself is a most important work in the field of the communication of ideas and of the measuring of inter-personal influence. An especially refreshing part of the study is that it deals in several dimensions. While much has been achieved in the field of political research, the authors in their study have gone into such areas as fashion influence, movie attendance, and others—moving into the social as well as public affairs fronts. And they have contributed much in describing the inter-play of influence and informal communication in one area with another area. This contribution is not only valuable for the student or academician but has very concrete practical value for those who have goods and services to sell. As such it is a striking illustration of a contention I have long made that the so-called "practical" people have much to learn from the so-called "academic" practitioners—just as the reverse is also true.

Just as Lazarsfeld has pioneered the way in the use of the panel technique and, in so doing, unlocked for all of us a whole new dimension of analysis, he has here brought us a new supply of integrated data on the effect of communication *between* people as distinguished from the better known effect of mass media *on* people.

This book by Katz and Lazarsfeld is an admirable effort to explore the transmission of ideas to the participating citizens and the politically inert. As such, it is one part of the larger framework of the general theory which I have briefly described here. This book—a pioneer effort—is certainly making tracks in a direction long needed. It is my hope that this study, penetrating as it does one area of the above described hypothesis, can help chart a new course for social research, and in so doing, will enhance our understanding of human behavior, especially the transmission of ideas. This, after all, is the objective of social science research, and it is the real reward for those of us who engage in it.

Elmo Roper

New York, New York
January, 1955

# Introduction

ALTHOUGH mass communications research is a recent development, it has already acquired a definite structure, which is often expressed in the well-known organizing formula, "Who says what to whom and with what effect?" The first volume in the series devoted to this field and edited by Paul F. Lazarsfeld and Bernard Berelson dealt with content analysis. Other volumes will be concerned with audience research, with the structure of the communications industry, and with the effect of mass media on various sectors of contemporary American life. These are units which, in their general outlines, are familiar to all students of mass communications. In recent years, however, the organizing formula referred to above has acquired a larger meaning. When it was first stated by Lasswell it was intended to indicate that a radio station or newspaper could be likened to a person who was communicating a flow of messages. But in the meantime we have once again become interested in person-to-person communication and it now has become increasingly clear that the individual person who reads something and talks about it with other people cannot be taken simply as a simile for social entities like newspapers or magazines. He himself needs to be studied in his two-fold capacity as a communicator and as a relay point in the network of mass communications. It therefore seems appropriate to include a volume on personal influence in the present series.

Because the investigation of personal influence is quite new, it has not yet been possible to develop a unified approach. The present volume consists of two parts. In the first, a large number of studies conducted by social psychologists are organized in a way which points up their relevance to the analysis of personal influence. The second part contains the main findings of an investigation conducted in Decatur, Illinois. The relation of these two parts to each other can best be understood if we start out with a brief history of our field study.

Just before the last war the executives of a national news magazine wanted to give a new twist to a familiar research story. They had found repeatedly that their magazine was read by people who held important positions in the business community like bankers, lawyers and industrialists. But were they actually influential in the sense that they affected other people's decisions either by their example or their advice? Called on to suggest a procedure by which this possibility might be investigated, one of the authors of this volume suggested the following design: A sample of persons in a moderate-sized community were to be asked who had influenced them in any of a number of areas; the individuals who were most often designated as influential in this first step were then to be asked which magazines they read.

As can be readily seen, two research ideas were merged in this suggestion. One came from the field of sociometry: the relative position of different community members was to be ascertained by asking them about the kinds of interrelations which existed between them. This is exactly the kind of characterization which the sociometrist makes; he asks the members of a group with whom they would like to talk or work and, from that information, determines which individuals are isolated and which are sought after. But the sociometric choice proposed here was not to be an abstract or artificial one: it was to be the report of a choice already made. This was to be done by inquiring into actual decisions which a sample of persons had made, and the influences which they had experienced in connection with their decisions. Whether or not a particular individual was to be considered influential would be determined by the number of people whose decisions he had affected in some concrete manner.[1]

1. A trial study along these lines was actually conducted under the direction of Robert K. Merton. Individuals who were named by others as influential in public affairs were classified according to whether their influence had to do with "local" or "cosmopolitan" matters. It was found that the "cosmopolitan" leaders, in disproportionately large numbers, were in fact subscribers to national news magazines. See Merton's "Patterns of Influence: A Study of Interpersonal Influence and of Communications Behavior in a Local

Simultaneously, another study[2] had focused attention on what were then called "molecular leaders," or persons who were influential in their immediate environments, but not necessarily prominent within the total community. The importance of this kind of leadership was discovered almost accidentally. During the 1940 presidential campaign the effect of radio and print on developing vote decisions was investigated in an Ohio community. The findings of that study indicated that the effect of the mass media was small as compared to the role of personal influences. Voters made up their minds in such a way that, in the end, they conformed closely to the political climate of their social environment. And there was ample evidence that these decisions were strongly influenced by the advice and suggestions of others whom the voters met in the course of their daily lives. For it develops that, in all walks of life, there are persons who are especially likely to lead to the crystallization of opinion in their fellows.

This finding came to the attention of Mr. Everett R. Smith, research director of the Macfadden Publications, Inc. He felt that it might have important implications for his firm, many of whose publications are aimed at reaching readers in the wage-earning class. It had been generally assumed previously that opinions were formed by the elite of the community, and then percolated down from one social stratum to the next until all followed the lead of the conspicuous persons at the apex of the community structure. But the 1940 election study seemed to indicate the parallel existence of what was then called horizontal opinion leadership. Each social stratum generated its own opinion leaders—the individuals who were likely to influence other persons in their immediate environment. In addition, the investigation seemed to indicate what was called a two-step flow in the effect of the mass media. In each social stratum, these "molecular"

Community," in Lazarsfeld and Stanton, eds., *Communications Research 1948-49* (New York: Harper and Brothers, 1949). An earlier exploratory study was conducted by Frank Stewart, "A Sociometric Study of Influence in Southtown" (*Sociometry*, Vol. 10, pp. 11-31, 273-286).

2. Lazarsfeld, Berelson and Gaudet, *The People's Choice* (4th ed.; New York: Columbia University Press, 1954).

opinion leaders were more likely to expose themselves to magazines and broadcasts especially tuned to their level of education and interest. This seemed to suggest that influences stemming from the media make contact with opinion leaders who, in turn, pass them on to other people. An obvious question to raise was whether these findings could be corroborated in another investigation more carefully centered around the problem of personal influence.

The design for the present study begins with a cross-section of women and then proceeds to identify the persons who are influential for these sample members in the pursuit of their daily activities. Four areas were chosen for special investigation: daily household marketing; the area of fashion as represented especially by dresses, cosmetics and various beauty treatments; attendance at movies; and the formation of opinions on local public affairs which happened to be under discussion at the time of the study. Each respondent was asked whether she had recently made a change or reached a decision in any of these four areas. If she had, she was asked a large number of questions in an effort to find out which media and what individuals had influenced her. By an inverse procedure, we also identified those individuals who, according to a number of criteria, seemed more likely to be sought out for advice by other persons in their immediate environment.

The locale of the study was selected by a number of objective indices. For cities with approximately 60,000 population, all available census information was collected. A small number were found to be most typical in terms of their average characteristics. By adding some further considerations, Decatur, Illinois, turned out to be the obvious choice. The whole selection procedure is reported in an appendix.

Five main problems were singled out for investigation; in the second part of this book the data collected in Decatur are selected and organized around them. For the guidance of the reader, the problems may be described briefly in the following terms:

1. How is the notion of personal influence, as implicitly defined by our procedure, related to similar concepts such as prestige, persuasion, and so on? (In Merton's preliminary study,

a careful analysis of a variety of concepts was made. In our study, comparative data were provided for some of these.)

2. The application of sociometric methods to a community of 60,000 people was to be tried out. Heretofore the study of mutual choices had been largely confined to small groups like school classes or boy scout troops. In those cases everyone who was interviewed and everyone who was chosen belonged to the same group. But only a small portion of a total city population can be questioned. The persons they designate (in the present study, those chosen as influentials) are most likely to fall outside the sample; they therefore had to be located and investigated in separate follow-up interviews. In order to single out the influential people within the original sample, we had to make use of techniques of self-designation. Because different approaches were required, the various procedures had to be checked against each other.

3. Once the influential persons were spotted—they were called opinion leaders in our study, and most of them were located through procedures of self-designation—we wanted to find out what kind of people they were. This was to be done in terms of their social and demographic characteristics, their interest in the area under investigation, and their position in the network of mass communication. We also wanted to find out how they were related to the persons for whom they were influential: Were they older or younger; were they richer or poorer; were they family members, friends, neighbors, or co-workers?

4. For all of our respondents, and this was the crucial issue, we wanted to know how influences stemming from other people compared with the mass media influences in their decision-making experiences. This led us to a detailed discussion of what we have called "impact analysis." The problem is whether, under proper interviewing conditions, external factors such as advertising or another person's advice can be traced into a decision made by a particular respondent. Both authors of the present volume have carried out a number of studies in which this kind of question was raised; but this book offers the first detailed analysis of pertinent procedures.[8]

3. For further discussion on this point, see Lazarsfeld and Rosenberg, eds., *The Language of Social Research* (Glencoe: The Free Press, 1955)

5. At the beginning of the study it was hoped that follow-up interviews with advisers could be made in more than two steps, so that a chain of impact leading from one person to the next could be traced. Because of budget limitations only token data could be collected. But these data, which are presented here, point to a very promising area for future research.

From the last section of our report the reader will see that the existence of horizontal opinion leadership in many crucial areas of people's daily lives becomes clearly established. This does not mean, of course, that like always influences like. Even in our own study we find areas where vertical opinion leadership plays a considerable role and it is not quite absent anywhere. So the problem then arises of how the different modes of personal influence are interlaced. When it comes to choosing a movie, young people influence older people. When it comes to buying small consumer goods the older housewife influences the younger. The actual vote of a person in a presidential campaign where major social allegiances are involved is established within a social stratum rather independently of the choices made by people considerably higher or lower on the social scale; but when it comes to making up one's mind on local affairs where party tradition doesn't matter and where more need is felt for specific information, then the wage earner is more likely to take advice from the better educated white collar person. The original sponsor of the study will be pleased to learn that horizontal opinion leadership is most clear-cut in the field of small consumer purchases; in this realm, influence rarely crosses from one social stratum to another. However useful and informative such findings are, it should not be overlooked that they don't settle, but rather open up, an interesting and complex topic of inquiry.

This might be a good point to take a stand on an issue which is sometimes debated among social scientists. Many of them make a distinction between dignified and undignified topics of research. How college students choose their dates is considered a dignified topic for a Ph.D. dissertation. The study

---

Section 5, especially the paper by Peter Rossi. This is a study of residential mobility in Philadelphia, and the "impact analysis" carried out there is an improvement and extension of the work done in Decatur.

of the effect of advertising on purchases is frowned upon in spite of the fact that the empirical study of human action could hardly find better material than this to develop systematic knowledge. At another place, one of the authors discusses this matter in considerable detail.[4] There seems to be no point in repeating the argument here, for it can be hoped that the results reported in our study will by themselves show that the analysis of consumer actions goes far beyond its commercial implications into general problems of human behavior.[5]

Preparations for our study began in the fall of 1944, and field work was started in the spring of 1945, just as the European war ended. Analysis of the large mass of data which was collected proceeded slowly, because of the heavy work load imposed on the universities during the years following demobilization. As will be seen from our Acknowledgment, a number of colleagues who were associated with the study in its early phases moved to other positions, and could not maintain their affiliation with our inquiry. By the time our findings were ready for publication, an important new trend in social research had become so widespread that it had to be considered in connection with our approach. This required additional time.

Stemming from a number of intellectual sources, the study of small groups had almost reached the status of an independent discipline. In many ways, the rapidly accumulating findings in this field were relevant to our own problem. For example, if one looked at a person in isolation or as simply an element in a statistical aggregate, something was left out of the picture. It had become obvious that the influence of mass media are not only paralleled by the influence of people; in addition, influences from the mass media, are, so to say, refracted by the personal environment of the ultimate consumer. Whether one person influenced another did not depend only upon the relation between the two, but also upon the manner in which they were imbedded into circles of friends, relatives

---

4. In *The Language of Social Research*. See previous footnote.
5. As a matter of fact, the present book as a whole is so much oriented toward the interests of social scientists that it seemed wise to point up its usefulness for the world of affairs. Mr. Elmo Roper was kind enough to do this in a special preface. He there has added his own more general reflections on the dissemination of ideas. This helps to emphasize again how much further empirical research is needed in this field.

or co-workers. While we had a large collection of data of relevance to this new approach to the problem, we certainly had not worked with a basic theory of "group dynamics" in mind.

At the same time, as we started to examine the growing literature on the role of small groups, we also made an inverse observation. Authors in this area had paid little attention to the way in which their work was related to the large body of knowledge concerning the mass media; nor had they questioned how the results of experiments could be related to findings of large-scale field surveys and to techniques which aim at tracing influences through direct interviews with people affected in the normal course of their daily lives. It therefore seemed that, as a natural and necessary complement to our study, we should attempt a systematic integration of the two developments which had grown rapidly and simultaneously, but which had not taken account of each other: Small group research, on the one hand, and the study of mass media and personal influence through broad-scale survey techniques, on the other.

As a result, one of us undertook the task of providing such an integration. This new sort of overview, which took the better part of two years to ready for publication, now forms the first part of the present volume. It begins with a short historical review which makes it evident that the "discovery of the small group" came about simultaneously in several areas of social research. The pertinent findings are organized into two major categories: those which trace influence within the group, and those which study factors impinging upon groups from the outside.

As far as "communications *within* the group" are concerned two major sets of findings current in small group research are of considerable relevance:

(a) Ostensibly private opinions and attitudes are often generated and/or reinforced in small intimate groups of family, friends, co-workers. Opinions are more stable if they are shared by a group, and, under pressure of a "campaign," people are more likely to change opinions jointly than individually.

(b) Families, friendships, work-groups and the like are interpersonal communications networks through which influences flow in patterned ways. The leader is a strategic element in the formation of group opinions: he is more aware of what the several members think; he mediates between them; and he represents something like the "typical" group-mind.

Then we consider what small group research has contributed to an understanding of "communication *to* the group"—that is, to the problem of how groups keep in touch with their environments, and how influences stemming from outside make their way into the group. It is especially in connection with this second line of inquiry that the intertwining of personal influence and the mass media becomes evident. Here, however, small group research can contribute only a little, since so much of this work has been carried out in laboratories where the natural environment is intentionally eliminated. But if small group research cannot serve so well at this point, we are reminded that other fields of social research can. In underdeveloped areas, for example, face-to-face contacts probably play a more important role than they do in Western society. As modern mass media gradually make their way into Middle and Far Eastern countries, our main topic can be studied under very promising research conditions. As a matter of fact, we soon realized that there is a great deal of material which deserves scrutiny from our special point of view. There is rapidly accumulating a fund of anthropological data in which the interplay between mass media and personal contact has come to the attention of the field worker. Even in our own society there are situations which deserve re-analysis from this point of view: for instance, the role of the agricultural agent and of fellow farmers who interpret for farmers materials which they can obtain over the radio and through government pamphlets.

These are the main considerations which lay behind the organization of our book in its present form. Originally, a third section was contemplated; it should at least be mentioned so that the reader can see the problem of personal influence in its total context. The way in which people influence each other is not only affected by the primary groups within which they live; it is co-determined by the broad institutional setting of the American scene. Some influence is exercised by the concentrated efforts of pressure groups. In recent years these efforts have been extended in several dirctions: It is not only the legislator, but also public opinion at large, which is being influenced; and the target is not only legislation, but also the choices and general attitudes of the ultimate consumers. Whole new professions, such as advertising and public relations, have grown up in this connection. But purposive activities of this kind are not the only ones which are relevant for our topic. The beauty parlor, the disc jockey, the department store, while intended as means of selling commodities become, derivatively, agencies which affect the styles of life and ways of thinking of those whom they influence. Some social theorists like David Riesman are inclined to feel that the whole intellectual climate in modern industrial society is permeated by the "advertising spirit." In the course of our field work, we collected a considerable number of interviews and observations pertaining to the more institutionalized sources of personal influence: beauty parlor operators, columnists who give advice in Decatur newspapers, lawyers, and others who are at the service of local businessmen and political figures. It turned out, however, that this material was too sketchy to permit a coherent presentation; it therefore is not included in our report.

One more word is needed regarding the decision we made as to which of our own empirical data to include in the present publication. From the questionnaire reproduced in the appendix the reader will gather how many topics were included in the original plan of the study. He will notice, for instance, that the respondents were, on many topics, interviewed twice. The original plan was to analyze the changes in their answers, a procedure which is now generally known as the panel technique.[6] In recent years, however, so much more extensive panel data have become available that it did not seem worthwhile to publish one of the earlier efforts. It will be seen that we asked our respondents a large number of questions regarding details of their reading and listening habits. Their answers are likely to be pretty much out of date by now.

Inversely, however, we have included data even when they

6. A review of the present state of this technique has been made by the Columbia University Bureau of Applied Social Research under the sponsorship of the Social Science Research Council. It is to be published in the near future by the Free Press.

were not very impressive statistically in cases where they could exemplify a more important research idea. Thus, for instance, we have information on conversations by two partners, the one who gave advice and the one who got it. For a variety of reasons, discussed at several points in the report, the number of cases is small. But this type of information was not only new at the time it was collected; no other study to our knowledge has provided it since. It therefore seemed desirable to bring it to the attention of our colleagues in the hope that other students would subsequently find the report and try it out on a large scale.[7] We have attached a rather lengthy technical appendix where the short-comings as well as the promises of some of our efforts are candidly discussed.

The place of this volume in a series on communications research can thus be summarized as follows. We are presenting the results of an empirical study which was intended to extend the scope of traditional communications research by taking into account some specific notions about the role of people. Behind the design of this study was the idea that persons, and especially opinion leaders, could be looked upon as another medium of mass communication, similar to magazines, newspapers and radio. We could study their "coverage," their effect, and, in a way, their content.[8] The Decatur study did

---

7. On the basis of preliminary reports of our materials, various studies already under way have incorporated some of these ideas. Peter H. Rossi, who contributed much to the early analysis of our data, has applied some of these ideas in his study of a Massachusetts community and Robert D. Leigh and Martin A. Trow have developed an extensive study of media and personal influences relevant to public affairs opinions, in Bennington, Vermont. Neither of these studies has reached publication stage as yet. Other authors who have drawn explicitly on the idea of "opinion leadership" in their work include Matilda and John Riley, "A Sociological Approach to Communications Research," (*Public Opinion Quarterly*, Vol. 15, Fall, 1951); S. N. Eisenstadt, "Communications Processes Among Immigrants in Israel," (*Public Opinion Quarterly*, Vol. 16, Spring, 1952); David Riesman, *The Lonely Crowd* (New Haven: Yale University Press, 1950); Leo A. Handel, *Hollywood Looks at Its Audience* (Urbana: University of Illinois Press, 1950); Berelson, Lazarsfeld and McPhee, *Voting* (Chicago: University of Chicago Press, 1954); Lerner, Berkman and Pevsner, *Modernizing the Middle East* (tentative title, forthcoming).

8. The "content" of persons as a method of communication was to be their conversations. In subsequent studies of the 1948 presidential campaign, it was possible to collect statistical data on conversations: who initiated them, what the relative status of the participants was, to what extent the conversations involved an exchange of factual information or opinion, and so on. See Berelson, Lazarsfeld and McPhee, *Voting, op. cit.*

indeed provide supporting data for such an approach. But it turned out to be too narrow. The individual person, whether as a generator or as an object of influence, must be studied in the setting of the primary group within which he lives. Studies in the newly developed tradition of small group research turned out to be amenable to re-organization and re-interpretation along the lines of this broader problem. The results of our secondary analysis of such material is also presented in this volume. There remains the corresponding task of relating both parts of the book to the work of students who have concentrated on broad social analyses. This, for the moment, must be left to a future endeavor.

E.K.
P.F.L.

Chicago, Ill.
Palo Alto, Calif.
May, 1955

**Part One**

**THE PART PLAYED BY PEOPLE: A NEW FOCUS
FOR THE STUDY OF MASS MEDIA EFFECTS**

CHAPTER |

# Between Media
# and Mass

WHEN PEOPLE first began to speculate about the effects of the mass media, they showed two opposite inclinations. Some social commentators thought the mass media would do nothing less than recreate the kind of informed public opinion which characterized the "town meeting," in the sense that citizens would once again have equal access to an intimate, almost first-hand account of those matters which required their decision. People had lost contact with the ever-growing world, went this argument, and the mass media would put it back within reach.[1]

---

1. Robert E. Park, pioneer American sociologist, and a former journalist himself, attributes this motivation to journalists in his 1925 essay on the newspaper: "The motive, conscious or unconscious, of the writers and the press in all this is to reproduce as far as possible, in the city, the conditions of life in the village. In the village everyone knew everyone else. . . . In the

Others saw something quite different. In their view, the mass media loomed as agents of evil aiming at the total destruction of democratic society. First the newspaper, and later the radio, were feared as powerful weapons able to rubber-stamp ideas upon the minds of defenseless readers and listeners. In the 1920's, it was widely held that the newspapers and their propaganda "got us into the war," while in the 1930's, many saw in the Roosevelt campaign "proof" that a "golden voice" on the radio could sway men in any direction.[2]

From one point of view, these two conceptions of the function of the mass media appear widely opposed. From another viewpoint, however, it can be shown that they are not far apart at all. That is to say, those who saw the emergence of the mass media as a new dawn for democracy and those who saw the media as instruments of evil design had very much the same picture of the *process* of mass communications in their minds. Their image, first of all, was of an atomistic mass of millions of readers, listeners and movie-goers prepared to receive the Message; and secondly, they pictured every Message as a direct and powerful stimulus to action which would elicit immediate response. In short, the media of communication were looked upon as a new kind of unifying force—a simple kind of nervous system—reaching out to every eye and ear, in a society characterized by an amorphous social organization and a paucity of interpersonal relations.[3]

---

village gossip and public opinion were the main sources of social control." Similarly, in his 1909 classic, *Social Organization*, C. H. Cooley writes rhapsodically on this subject. ". . . In a general way they [the changes 'in communication and in the whole system of society' since the beginning of the 19th century] mean the expansion of human nature, that is to say, of its power to express itself in social wholes. They make it possible for society to be organized more and more on the higher faculties of man, on intelligence and sympathy, rather than on authority, caste and routine. They mean freedom, outlook, indefinite possibility. The public consciousness, instead of being confined as regards its more active phases to local groups, extends by even steps with that give-and-take of suggestions that the new intercourse makes possible, until wide nations, and finally the world itself, may be included in one lively mental whole." See Park (1949), p. 11 and Cooley (1950), p. 148.*

*Note: Citations appearing in the text and in footnotes will contain only author's name and a date of publication, e.g., Park (1949). The appended bibliography should be consulted for the full reference.

2. Berelson (1950), p. 451.

3. For a comparatively recent statement of this point of view, and for a vivid portrayal of the traditional image of the mass audience, see Wirth

This was the "model"—of society and of the processes of communication—which mass media research seems to have had in mind when it first began, shortly after the introduction of radio, in the 1920's. Partly, the "model" developed from an image of the potency of the mass media which was in the popular mind. At the same time, it also found support in the thought of certain schools of social and psychological theory. Thus, classical sociology of the late 19th century European schools emphasized the breakdown of interpersonal relations in urban, industrial society and the emergence of new forms of remote, impersonal social control.[4] Later, random sampling methods, opinion and attitude testing techniques, and a discipline based on an approach to "representative" individuals lifted from the context of their associations link the beginnings of communications research to applied psychology.

## Mass Media Research: The Study of "Campaigns"

These were some of the ideas with which mass media research began. And as it proceeded, it became traditional to divide the field of communications research into three major divisions. Audience research—the study of how many of what kinds of people attend to a given communications message or medium—is, historically, the earliest of the divisions, and still the most prolific. The second division is that of content analysis, comprising the study of the language, the logic and the

---

(1949). Wirth also deals with the two kinds of mass media impact which we have just described—the "manipulative" and the "democratic"—assuming the inherent potency of the media which underlies both. An equally clear statement is Blumer (1946).

4. In "The Study of the Primary Group," Shils (1951) discusses this main trend in 19th century European sociology which was reflected in the notion that "any persistence of traditionally regulated informal and intimate relations was . . . an archaism inherited from an older rural society or from a small town handcraft society." Discussing early American sociology, Shils indicates that there was a comparatively greater interest in the primary group as a subject for study. He points out, however, that Cooley's well-known contribution and the interest displayed by American sociologists in voluntary associations, pressure groups, etc. were counterbalanced by an emphasis on the disintegration of the primary group in urban society such as may be found in the work of W. I. Thomas, Park and his associates, and others. Several sections of this and the following chapter will draw extensively on Shils' excellent essay.

layout of communications messages. And finally, there is what has been called effect analysis or the study of the impact of mass communications.

For some purposes, this three-way division is useful. For other purposes, however—and, notably, for the purpose at hand—it is misleading because it obscures the fact that, fundamentally, all of communications research aims at the study of effect. From the earliest theorizing on this subject to the most contemporary empirical research, there is, essentially, only one underlying problem—though it may not always be explicit —and that is, "what can the media 'do'?" Just as the "model" we have examined poses this question, so too, do the "clients" of mass media research. Consider the advertiser, or the radio executive, or the propagandist or the educator. These sponsors of research are interested, simply, in the effect of their message on the public. And if we find that they commission studies of the characteristics of their audience, or of the content of their message, clearly we have a right to assume that these aspects are connected, somehow, with effects.

Moreover, if we reflect on these patrons of research and their motivations for a moment longer, we can sharpen this notion of effect. We have been talking as if effect were a simple concept when, in fact, there are a variety of possible effects that the mass media may have upon society, and several different dimensions along which effects may be classified.[5] Now of all the different types of effects which have ever been speculated about or categorized, it is safe to say that these sponsors of research—whose goals underlie so much of mass media research—have selected, by and large, just one kind of effect for almost exclusive attention. We are suggesting that the over-

---

5. Lazarsfeld (1948), for example, has distinguished sixteen different types of effects by cross-tabulating four types of mass media "stimuli" and four types of audience "response." The responses are classified along a rough time dimension—immediate response, short term effects, long term effects and institutional change. This classification makes clear, for example, that an investigation of the effect of *Uncle Tom's Cabin* on the outbreak of the Civil War calls for particular kinds of concepts and particular research tools and that this kind of effect must be distinguished from a study of the effect of print on Western civilization, on one hand, and a study of the effect of a subway car-card campaign on prejudiced attitudes, on the other. Many of the substantive statements about mass media research findings in this chapter are based on this paper and on Klapper (1950).

riding interest of mass media research is in the study of the effectiveness of mass media attempts to influence—usually, to change—opinions and attitudes in the very short run. Perhaps this is best described as an interest in the effects of mass media "campaigns"—campaigns to influence votes, to sell soap, to reduce prejudice. Noting only that there are a variety of other mass media consequences which surely merit research attention but have not received it,[6] let us proceed with this more circumspect definition clearly in mind: Mass media research has aimed at an understanding of how, and under what conditions, mass media "campaigns" (rather specific, short-run efforts) succeed in influencing opinions and attitudes.

## Intervening Variables and the Study of Effect

If it is agreed that the focus of mass media research has been the study of campaigns, it can readily be demonstrated that the several subdivisions of research—audience research, content analysis, etc.—are not autonomous at all but, in fact, merely subordinate aspects of this dominant concern. What we mean can be readily illustrated. Consider, for example, audience research—the most prolific branch of mass media research. One way of looking at audience research is to see it only as an autonomous research arena, concerned with what has been called fact-gathering or bookkeeping operations. We are suggesting, however, that audience research may be viewed

---

6. The Lazarsfeld (1948) classification cited in the footnote above indicates quite clearly that the study of "immediate" or "short term" responses to concerted mass media "campaigns" is only one of many different dimensions of effect. There are, furthermore, several effects which have been speculated about which do not fall readily within Lazarsfeld's classification. Lists of several such effects—predominantly of a long term sort—which seem accessible to, and deserving of empirical investigation—may be found, for example, in McPhee (1953) and in the appendix to Katz, E. (1953). It is important to note that some of these longer range effects which have barely been looked into promise to reveal the potency of the mass media much more than do "campaign" effects. The latter, as we shall note below, give the impression that the media are quite ineffectual as far as persuasion in social and political (i.e., non-marketing) matters is concerned. The reasons why marketing influences are so much more effective and therefore more easy to come to grips with than other mass media influence attempts are discussed by Wiebe (1951), and under the heading of "canalization" by Lazarsfeld and Merton (1949). Wiebe's paper will be discussed below, p. 29. See also Cartwright (1949).

more appropriately as an aspect of the study of effect, in the sense that counting up the audience and examining its characteristics and its likes and dislikes is a first step toward specifying what the potential effect is for a given medium or message. In other words, if we do not lose sight of the end problem which is clearly central to this field, audience research falls right into place as an intermediate step.

And so, it turns out, do each of the other major branches of mass media research. One might say that the intellectual history of mass media research may, perhaps, be seen best in terms of the successive introduction of research concerns—such as audience, content, and the like—which are basically attempts to *impute* effects by means of an analysis of some more readily accessible intermediate factors with which effects are associated.

However, these factors serve not only as a basis for the indirect measurement or imputing of effects: they also begin to specify some of the complexities of the mass communications process. That is to say, the study of intermediate steps has led to a better understanding of what goes on in a mass media campaign—or, in other words, to an understanding of the sequence of events and the variety of factors which "intervene" between the mass media stimulus and the individual's response. Thus, each new aspect introduced has contributed to the gradual pulling apart of the scheme with which research began: that of the omnipotent media, on one hand, sending forth the message, and the atomized masses, on the other, waiting to receive it—and nothing in-between.

Now let us turn to document these assertions somewhat more carefully. A brief view will be taken of each of four factors that come in between—or, as we shall say, that "intervene" —between the media and the masses to modify the anticipated effects of communications. We shall consider four such intervening variables: exposure, medium, content, and predispositions. Each of these has become one of the central foci of research attention (audience research, media comparison studies, content analysis, and the study of attitudes). Each contributes to our understanding of the complexity of mass persuasion campaigns. Treating these factors will set the stage for the introduction of another (the most recently introduced) of these intervening variables, that of interpersonal relations, with which we shall be particularly concerned.

## Four Intervening Variables in the Mass Communication Process

The four variables we shall consider contribute, under some conditions, to facilitating the flow of communications between media and masses and, under other conditions, to blocking the flow of communications. It is in this sense, therefore, that we call them intervening.[7]

First, there is the variable of "exposure" (or "access," or "attention") which derives, of course, from audience research.[8] Audience research has shown that the original mass communications "model" is not adequate, for the very simple reason that people are not exposed to specific mass media stimuli as much, as easily, or as randomly as had been supposed. Exposure or non-exposure may be a product of technological factors (as is the case in many pre-industrial countries),[9] political factors (as in the case of totalitarian countries), economic factors (as in the case of not being able to afford a TV set), and especially of voluntary factors—that is, simply not tuning in. In the United States, it is, typically, this voluntary factor that is most likely to account for who is in the audience for a particular communication message. Perhaps the most

7. Our use of this phrase should not be confused with the technical usage in the methodology of survey analysis where "intervening variable" refers to a "test" factor which is introduced to "interpret" a correlation between two factors to which it (the "test" factor) is related. See Lazarsfeld and Kendall (1950) for a full discussion of this usage. For a discussion of the widespread usage of this term in psychology, see Tolman (1951), pp. 281-285.

8. For reviews of some of the major findings of audience research in radio, newspapers, movies and television, see Lazarsfeld and Kendall (1948), Minnesota (1949), Schramm and White (1949), Handel (1950), Meyersohn (1953), Lazarsfeld (1948). It is needless perhaps to reiterate that the findings of audience research have an intrinsic value other than the one here discussed, and that the motivation to do audience research is not exclusively to impute effects. Research on, say, the likes and dislikes of an audience may be motivated by a desire to understand what an audience wants in order to pitch a "campaign" in the right way, and/or by a desire to study the characteristics of audience "tastes" for the sake of testing some hypothesis in this realm.

9. See Huth (1952) for a discussion of such factors as barriers to international technical assistance and informational programs.

important generalization in this area—at least as far as an understanding of the process of effective persuasion is concerned—is that those groups which are most hopefully regarded as the target of a communication are often least likely to be in the audience. Thus, educational programs, it has been found, are very unlikely to reach the uneducated; and goodwill programs are least likely to reach those who are prejudiced against another group; and so on.[10] It is in this sense that we consider the mere fact of exposure itself a major intervening variable in the mass communications process.

A second focus of mass media research which developed very early was the differential character of the media themselves. The research which falls into this category asks the general question: What is the difference in the effect of Message X if it is transmitted via Medium A, B or C? The appearance of Cantril and Allport's (1935) book, *The Psychology of Radio,* called attention to a whole set of these "media comparison" experiments. Here, type-of-medium is the intervening variable insofar as the findings of these studies imply that the process of persuasion is modified by the channel which delivers the message.[11]

Content—in the sense of form, presentation, language, etc.—is the third of the intervening variables on our list. And while it is true that the analysis of communications content is carried out for a variety of reasons, by and large, the predominant interest of mass media research in this area relates to the attempt to explain or predict differences in effect based on differences in content. To be more precise, most of the work in this field imputes differences in intervening psychological processes—and thus, differences in effects—from observed differences in content.[12] Content analysis informs us, for example,

---

10. Examples of this phenomenon are documented in Lazarsfeld (1948) and Klapper (1950).

11. In a sense, one of the later sections of this book, "The Impact of Personal Influence," (Part Two, Section Two) contributes to this tradition by comparing the relative effectiveness of personal influence with the influence of radio, newspapers and magazines. See also Lazarsfeld, Berelson and Gaudet (1948). Chaps. 14 and 16.

12. The authoritative work in this field outlining the technique of content analysis and the several uses to which it can be put is Berelson (1951); this book also contains an extensive bibliography of content studies. For a report on the most important series of *experimental* studies to date which,

of the psychological techniques that are likely to be most effective (e.g., repetition, appeal to authority, band-wagon, etc.); the greater sway of "facts" and "events" as compared with "opinions"; the cardinal rule of "don't argue"; the case for and against presenting "one side" rather than "both sides" of controversial material; the "documentary" vs. the "commentator" presentation; the damaging effect of a script at "cross-purposes" with itself; etc. Important techniques have been developed for use in this field, and the controlled experiment has also been widely adopted for the purpose of observing directly the effect of the varieties of communications presentation and content. The characteristic quality of these techniques is evident: they concentrate on the "stimulus," judging its effectiveness by referring either to more or less imputed psychological variables which are associated with effects or to the actual "responses" of those who have been exposed to controlled variations in presentation.

A fourth set of mediating factors, or intervening variables, emerges from study of the attitudes and psychological predispositions of members of the audience, insofar as these are associated with successful and unsuccessful campaigns. In this area, mass media research has established very persuasively what social psychologists have confirmed in their laboratories—that an individual's attitudes or predispositions can modify, or sometimes completely distort, the meaning of a given message. For example, a prejudiced person whose attitude toward an out-group is strongly entrenched may actively resist a message of tolerance in such a way that the message may even be perceived as a defense of prejudice or as irrelevant to the subject of prejudice entirely.[13]

---

instead of *imputing* effects from content, attempt to measure the relationship between content variation and variation in effects *directly*, see Hovland, Lumsdaine and Sheffield (1949). Statements of some of the "principles" of effective propaganda can be found in the publications of the Institute for Propaganda Analysis, e.g., in Lee and Lee, eds. (1939), etc. For further discussion of "principles," see Krech and Crutchfield (1948), Chapter 9.

13. This motivated missing-of-the-point is documented in Cooper and Jahoda (1947). For an illustration in the realm of public opinion on international affairs, see Hyman and Sheatsley (1952) where the ineffectiveness of providing favorable information to people with initially unfavorable attitudes is demonstrated. For a purely theoretical treatment of this same theme, see Katz, D. (1949).

Just as prior attitudes on issues must be studied, so attitudes toward the media themselves must be accounted for if we are fully to understand the role of psychological predispositions in modifying the effectiveness of communications. Here research on predispositions joins with the previous subject of media differences. Thus, many people regard the radio as more trustworthy than the newspaper, and others have the opposite opinion. In the same way, in many of the highly politicized countries abroad, there is a great intensity of feeling about the relative trustworthiness not just of the several media in general but of each newspaper and each radio station.[14] Similarly, attitudes toward the sources to which information and news are credited are likely to affect the acceptance of a mass media message. The very large number of studies which fall under the heading of "prestige suggestion" bear on this problem.[15]

So far, then, we have examined four intervening factors—exposure and predisposition from the receiving end, media differences and content differences from the transmission end—and each gives a somewhat better idea of what goes on in between the media and the masses to modify the effects of communications.[16] That is, each time a new intervening factor is found to be applicable, the complex workings of the mass persuasion process are illuminated somewhat better, revealing how many different factors have to be attuned in order for a mass communications message to be effective. Thus, the image of the process of mass communications with which researchers set out, that the media play a direct influencing role, has had

14. Attitudes toward the comparative trustworthiness of the media were investigated as part of a study by the Social Science Research Council (1947) and in communications studies in the Near and Middle East by the Bureau of Applied Social Research (1951).
15. For a review of these studies, see Asch (1952B).
16. As has been noted earlier, together with the greater precision and increasing predictive power of mass communications research where it takes account of such factors, there has come an increasing skepticism about the potency of the mass media. As research becomes bolder, it becomes increasingly easy to show that—outside the range of marketing influences—mass media influence-attempts have fallen far short of the expectations of the communicators. This is notoriously the case with regard to persuasion attempts in the civic and political areas. It would be a mistake, however, to generalize from the role of the mass media in such direct, short-run effects to the degree of media potency which would be revealed if some longer-run, more indirect effects were conceptualized and subjected to study.

to be more and more qualified each time a new intervening variable was discovered.

We propose now to turn to the newly accented variable of interpersonal relations. On the basis of several pioneering communications studies, and as we shall see later, on the basis of an exploration of the bearing of the field of small group research on the field of mass media research, it appears that communications studies have greatly underestimated the extent to which an individual's social attachments to other people, and the character of the opinions and activities which he shares with them, will influence his response to the mass media. We are suggesting, in other words, that the response of an individual to a campaign cannot be accounted for without reference to his social environment and to the character of his interpersonal relations. This is the matter which we want to consider most carefully for the reason that it promises to be a key link in the chain of intervening variables, and because it promises also to promote the convergence of two fields of social science research—the one dealing with macroscopic mass communications, the other with microscopic social relations.

## *Interpersonal Relations: The Discovery of "People"*

How, it will be asked, can quite casual and seemingly irrelevant social ties have anything to do with the way in which an individual is affected by what he sees or hears? We shall attempt to answer this question in the following way: *First*, we shall cite several case studies in which interpersonal relations appear to be relevant for the mass communications process. *Second*, we shall try to point out the way in which research —which began with an image of the atomized individual on one hand, the mass media on the other, and nothing in between— happened to hit upon the idea that interpersonal relations might be relevant. *Third*, we shall look at several parallels in other fields of social science which also have recently "rediscovered" the relevance of interpersonal relations. These three items will constitute the remainder of this chapter and the whole of the next. Then, in the following section, too, we will continue with exactly the same problem in mind—that is, with the hypothesis that interpersonal relations must be taken into account if the mass communications process is to be properly understood—but our approach there will be quite different.

Our first task, then, is to examine several illustrations of the relevance of interpersonal relations which have emerged, sometimes unexpectedly, from communications research of the last few years:

(1) A study which takes as its problem the extent to which children are integrated into groups of their peers and the relationship between such integration and utilization of the mass media provides an excellent illustration of what we are trying to say. In a paper reporting this study, Matilda and John Riley (1951) demonstrate very well one of the ways in which interpersonal relations, as an intervening variable, is relevant for the mass communications process.[17] Consider just one of their examples: Those children who had only weak social relations with other children reported that they liked action and violence programs on the radio somewhat more than those who were well integrated with their peers. But while this is a suggestive finding, the authors take us much further. They examine all the children who report equally high liking for programs of action and violence, and discover that what the peer-group "members" (the well-integrated children) like in these programs is often very different from what the "non-members" like. The "non-members" seem to enjoy the "creepy," "hard-to-get-out-of-your-mind" excitement of the stories, while the "members" report much more often that these very same stories give them ideas for group games—a new way for playing "Cowboys and Indians" with their friends, for example. The authors suggest that peer group "members" judge the media in terms of contribu-

---

17. It should be noted here that this study—and some of the others that will be cited at this point—does not actually deal with "campaign" effects. The present study, for example, deals with what McPhee (1953) and Katz, E. (1953) call "uses" or "gratifications." Because there are so few mass media studies which have actually taken interpersonal relations into account we have decided to include here the most interesting of available illustrations; each of them, however, also has manifest implications for studying the kinds of effects with which we are specifically concerned.

tions to their social life, while "non-members" more often turn to the media for fantasy and escape. Apparently, then, differences in the relationship between children and their peers may be an important determinant of the effect which the very same communication will have upon them.[18] And the point for us is that these differential effects could not have been accounted for except by examining the varying interpersonal contexts in which these children were involved.

(2) But having friends or not having them is not the whole story of the influence of interpersonal relations on mass communications. Equally important for understanding communications behavior (and behavior in general) are the opinions, attitudes and values—the norms—of the *particular* friends and family members who constitute one's interpersonal relations. Thus the *extent* to which two individuals are integrated into their respective groups may be equal, but the norms of the two groups may be different. A study by Suchman of the influence of radio on serious music listening illustrates the way in which the opinions of others are likely to affect media behavior.[19] Those whose taste for serious music was created by radio listening were compared, by the author, with those music listeners whose interest in music was developed apart from radio. He asked both groups, "Can you tell us how you *first* became interested in serious music?", and discovered that almost half of those who credited radio as the major factor in their musical development said that "friends" had given them the initial impetus for their interest, while only 26% of those whose interest developed apart from radio named "friends."

This finding suggests the importance of social pressures in motivating people to expose themselves and to be receptive to the influence of communications.[20] It appears from this study that a communication will be "effective" for an individual when

18. Thus, group relations has bearing on exposure, liking and effect. W. S. Robinson (1941) reports a parallel finding in his "Radio Comes to the Farmer." He notes that there is a high correlation between listening to serious programs on the radio and attendance at club meetings among rural farm women. Here the "use" value of this listening is articulate, as "over half the women belonging to these groups reported using the radio in connection with their club work."

19. Suchman (1941).

20. This study, then, illustrates the role of interpersonal relations in mak-

it aids him in rising in the esteem of his friends. An individual seeking acceptance in a new, more "cultured" group, for example, may listen to serious music on the radio in order to achieve the group norm in this matter. "The main importance of the radio," the author concludes, "does not lie in its ability to create interests, but in its effectiveness as a follow-up for forces quite detached from it."

(3) Or consider another example. We have learned over the last decade that there is good reason to suspect—though there is really no empirical evidence available—that some of the most effective radio broadcasts involve the presence of planned listening groups rather than isolated individuals. Father Coughlin's radio success, for example, appears to have been built on group listening.[21] And we know from a recent study of communications in Soviet Russia that the channels of communication there depend heavily on in-person presentations to organized groups and that mass communications are superimposed upon this interpersonal framework.[22] A related point —that individuals will reject a communication which seeks to separate them from their group—is a central finding of Shils and Janowitz (1948) in their study of allied propaganda to German troops during World War II.

(4) With the beginnings of international communications research, we have become aware once more of such primitive phenomena as the one-radio village and the no-newspaper town. Studies of the flow of news and influence in such social situations add not only to our knowledge of communication in pre-industrial communities but, given our present concern with the connection between interpersonal relations and mass media effectiveness, point out some of the communications

---

ing for effects, and also its role in making for exposure. Another interesting aspect of the role of interpersonal relations in inducing exposure is reported by Freidson (1953B) whose research on the media habits of children would seem to indicate that these habits correspond to the varying social settings which children of different ages prefer. Thus, the youngest children prefer the family setting to the company of their peers and seem also to like television because it is viewed in the family setting, while somewhat older children, preferring to associate with their peers, like movies more than television—apparently because movie-going is a peer activity.

21. Lazarsfeld (1941) discusses the rationale for this point and speculates further on it in Lazarsfeld (1942).

22. See Inkeles (1950), especially Chapter 8, "Oral Agitation and the Soviet System."

roles played by *people* which may be relevant even in a mass media society such as ours. We shall say more about this below, referring in particular to studies in international communications.

(5) The much-discussed problem of why the mass media are more effective in merchandising commodities than they are in "merchandising" good citizenship and democratic action has been soundly thought through in two recent articles by G. D. Wiebe.[23] Successful commodity advertising, Wiebe points out, contributes a last push to people's motivations and then directs them to an appropriate "social mechanism" (usually a retail store) for the expression of these motivations. This "social mechanism" must actually be both physically and psychologically "nearby" and must be appropriate to the particular demand. In terms of this very plausible model for social action, Wiebe goes on to examine several successful and unsuccessful mass media campaigns. He finds, for example, that a radio documentary which concluded by urging listeners to form neighborhood councils to combat juvenile delinquency, was asking, in effect, nothing less than for listeners to erect their own "social mechanisms"—with no blueprints provided. What we learn from Wiebe is that variations in the effectiveness of a communication may be related to the character of the connections between an individual and those particular others who constitute an appropriate "social mechanism." Good intentions are not translated into action, we can conclude, when the individual is not "near" enough to an appropriate "social mechanism"—where "near" (we are assuming) often must mean a relatedness to other people.[24]

There are very few such examples, but their import should be clear. They imply that there are consequences for the transmission of communications first, in the mere frequency of association with peers; second, in association with others who share a particular norm or standard; third, in being a member

---

23. Wiebe (1951) and Wiebe (1952).
24. Although Wiebe does not say this explicitly, it is clear from several of the case studies he presents that a personal relationship with somebody else who shares a similar value may often serve to overcome the distance between an individual and the "social mechanism" which represents action, or, in fact, may be prerequisite for the establishment of a "social mechanism" in the first place.

of a group which supplements and reinforces the mass media message; fourth, in belonging to a social group which has "hooked up" a human communications system of its own with that of the mass media; and finally, in being "near" enough to an appropriate social outlet to give expression to a motivated social action.

In sum, these studies are among the very few that we know of which point to the possible relevance of interpersonal relations as an intervening variable in the mass communications process. Of course, not all of them were designed explicitly to demonstrate that such is the case; as a matter of fact, several of these findings are afterthoughts or speculations, while the others of more recent date were motivated, in part at least, by an initial "discovery" of which we have not yet spoken.

# CHAPTER II

# The Part Played By People

DURING THE COURSE of studying the presidential election campaign of 1940, it became clear that certain people in every stratum of a community serve relay roles in the mass communication of election information and influence.[1]

This "discovery" began with the finding that radio and the printed page seemed to have only negligible effects on actual vote decisions and particularly minute effects on *changes* in vote decisions. Here, then, was another of those findings which reduce belief in the magic of mass media influence. But the authors were not content to report only this unexpected negative finding. They were interested in how people make up their minds, and why they change them, and in effect, they asked, if the mass media are not major determinants of an individual's vote decision, then what is?[2]

---

1. Lazarsfeld, Berelson and Gaudet (1948).
2. The authors could ask themselves this question because they were equipped with more than just the standard gear of mass communications research. They were equipped to study both mass communications effects and what we might call "decision-making." There is an interesting difference between these two approaches: Communications research begins with a communication and then attempts to track down the influence it has had, while a decision-making study begins at the other end with an "effect," that is, with a decision—about a career, about moving from one house to another, about marketing and fashion purchases, etc.—and tries to locate all of the influences—whatever they happen to be—that went into the making of that decision. *The People's Choice*, the study which we are discussing, seems to have been the first academically legitimated report of the wedding of these two traditions of social research: the tradition of mass media research and the tradition of decision-making studies.

## The Opinion Leader Idea and the
## Two-Step Flow of Communication

To investigate this problem, particular attention was paid to those people who changed their vote intention during the course of the campaign. When these people were asked what had contributed to their decision, their answer was: other people. The one source of influence that seemed to be far ahead of all others in determining the way people made up their minds was personal influence. Given this clue from the testimony of the voters themselves, other data and hypotheses fell into line. People tend to vote, it seems, the way their associates vote: wives like husbands, club members with their clubs, workers with fellow employees, etc. Furthermore, looked at in this way, the data implied (although they were not completely adequate for this new purpose) that there were people who exerted a disproportionately great influence on the vote intentions of their fellows. And it could be shown that these "opinion leaders"—as they were dubbed—were not at all identical with those who are thought of traditionally as the wielders of influence; opinion leaders seemed to be distributed in all occupational groups, and on every social and economic level.

The next question was obvious: Who or what influences the influentials? Here is where the mass media re-entered the picture. For the leaders reported much more than the non-opinion leaders that for them, the mass media were influential. Pieced together this way, a new idea emerged—the suggestion of a "two-step flow of communication." The suggestion basically was this: that ideas, often, seem to flow *from* radio and print *to* opinion leaders and *from them* to the less active sections of the population.

The study presented as the major part of this volume represents an attempt to test and further extend these ideas. Other studies with similar bearing, and the ways in which they are linked to one another, are set forth briefly in the Introduction.

These studies all tend to bear out the validity of the opinion leader idea, in one way or another, and to make quite explicit that the traditional image of the mass persuasion process must make room for "people" as intervening factors between the stimuli of the media and resultant opinions, decisions and actions. These studies contribute not only to the validation of the apparent relevance of this new intervening factor, but also to a more fruitful formulation of the opinion leader idea itself. We might say, perhaps, that as a result of investigating and thinking about the opinion leader, mass communications research has now joined those fields of social research which, in the last years, have been "rediscovering" the primary group.[3] And if we are correct, the "rediscovery" seems to have taken place in two steps. First of all, the phenomenon of opinion leadership was discovered. But then, study of the widespread distribution of opinion leaders throughout the population and analysis of the character of their relations with those for whom they were influential (family, friends, co-workers) soon led to a second idea. This was the idea that opinion leaders are not a group set apart, and that opinion leadership is not a trait which some people have and others do not, but rather that opinion leadership is an integral part of the give-and-take of everyday personal relationships. It is being suggested, in other words, that all interpersonal relations are potential networks of communication and that an opinion leader can best be thought of as a group member playing a key communications role. It is this elaboration—that is the tying of opinion leaders to the specific others with whom they are in contact—that completes the "rediscovery."[4]

---

3. The "rediscovery" of the primary group is an accepted term by now, referring to the belated recognition that researchers in many fields have given to the importance of informal, interpersonal relations within situations formerly conceptualized as strictly formal and atomistic. It is "rediscovery" in the sense that the primary group was dealt with so explicitly (though descriptively and apart from any institutional context) in the work of pioneering American sociologists and social psychologists and then was systematically overlooked by empirical social research until its several dramatic "rediscoveries." As Merton (1948B), pp. 66-7, points out, and as we shall demonstrate below, it was essentially the "latent functions" of primary groups which were "rediscovered." For an account of early interest in the primary group as well as some of the stories of rediscovery and of present-day research, see the aforementioned Shils (1951) paper.

4. The idea that the model of the mass communications process must abandon its image of a totally atomized audience is discussed along some of the lines presented here in a thoroughly independent appraisal of the concept of "mass" in mass communications by Freidson (1953A). The convergence of our review and Freidson's seems to us noteworthy.

This "rediscovery" of the primary group, if our model turns out to be anywhere near the truth, has a series of parallels in social science over the last three decades. And, of course, it is not strange that communications research—predicated as it is on the non-existence, or at best, on the irrelevance of inter-personal relations—is among the last to announce that it has stumbled onto the small group.

We want to digress somewhat now from our concern with mass communications to note the occurrence in several completely different fields of this very same pattern of primary group "rediscovery." The next several pages, to the end of the chapter, will be devoted to this digression.

## The Rediscovery of the Primary Group: Case Histories of an Intervening Variable

The "rediscovery" of the primary group is one of the achievements of empirical social science. We have been telling the story of "rediscovery" in one field, pointing out how researchers happened to hit on the idea that primary interpersonal relations might be an important intervening variable in the mass communications process, and how that idea is now beginning to be applied. Similar stories can be told in other major fields of social inquiry and we propose to reproduce some of them to illustrate what we mean. An examination of each of these cases will reveal, we think, that researchers were forced, as a result of empirical findings, to amend their images of the fields they were studying in order to make room for the intervening role of primary group relations.

In very broad strokes, let us review the story of the "rediscovery" of the small group in industrial sociology, by now a near-famous event, with far reaching implications; then, we shall look into the wartime researches reported in the volumes of *The American Soldier* for a second case of "rediscovery"; and for a third case, we shall consider the account of the small group in a community context given by W. L. Warner in the first volume of his *Yankee City* series.

In each of these three contexts—in the factory, the army, and the urban community—it is the *pattern* of rediscovery that in-

terests us most of all. We are concerned with *the way in which*
the primary group as a relevant factor was hit upon in each
case, and, if it is so important, how it happened to be overlooked in the first place. This is exactly what we have been
trying to point up in the account of our own experience in mass
media research and it strikes us, in comparing the four cases,
that the rediscovery of the primary group has a specificiable
pattern. In each case, as we shall see, research began with a too-
simple "model"; and then, at a given point, the "model" did
not quite explain what was going on; at this point, typically,
clues which pointed to the primary group were unearthed; and,
finally, the relevance of interpersonal relations was "rediscovered." We shall elaborate on the common elements in the
pattern below, but first let us consider the three cases:

## (A.) THE GROUP IN AN INDUSTRIAL CONTEXT:
### THE HAWTHORNE STUDIES

The classic rediscovery of the primary group, as a factor to
be reckoned with in mass society, is a central theme in the
best known contribution of industrial sociology, the Hawthorne studies.[5] What began as a study of the effect, on productivity, of changes in working conditions—such as variations
in illumination, wage plans, rest periods, working hours, etc.
—resulted in the finding that *however conditions were varied,* whether they were made "better" or "worse," the productivity of the specially selected test group increased. Over
a period of several years of work, the puzzle got bigger, and
it became quite clear that the response of the workers was
not related to the experimental variables at all, but to some
other factor; and the search for the mysterious factor led to
an answer.

As a matter of fact, statements made by the test group girls
themselves furnished the clue. They said "it was fun"—by
which they seemed to mean that they were a cheerful intimate
group who had become good friends and who were responding
with gratitude to the avalanche of attention they had begun

5. Roethlisberger and Dickson (1939). We shall base our account of
those aspects of this study relevant to our interest on the review in Homans
(1952).

to receive from management and researchers as soon as the experiments began. Each time an experimental variable was introduced—whether it improved work conditions or made them worse—the group would express its collective high spirits and involvement in the experimental task by increasing production. But this is not yet the main point.

The experience in the artificially created test room was a strong enough stimulant for the researchers to ask themselves whether it was not possible that informal groups arose *naturally* within the larger factory itself (i.e., without the isolated test room and the extraordinary recognition which the first test group had) and, if this were true, whether such group formations might not also have an effect on productivity. This time, the investigators set watch on some workers in their natural habitat, more or less, and readily found that they constituted just such an informal group. And when they studied this group, they discovered that it had a decided influence on production. But where the influence of the first group had acted to *increase* production, here the investigators found a group norm which *depressed* production. The workers had organized on their own, so to speak, to resist management's individualistic incentives to greater productivity which the prevailing "piece rate" represented. Very simply, they decided to enforce what amounted to their own idea (within management's broadly acceptable limits) about what an average day's production should be, and this is the production norm they held each other to.

Here is the point: Just as in the study of mass communications and voting intentions where the research blueprint gave no inkling of the possible relevance of interpersonal relations, so here, in the case of the mass production factory—the very core of industrial society—nothing less than a *discovery* that the "model" was wrong, could have revealed that primary relationships were in operation and were *relevant to productivity*.

### (B.) THE GROUP IN THE CONTEXT OF THE ARMY: THE AMERICAN SOLDIER

In several much more recent works, we find other examples of the unanticipated emergence of the primary group within the framework of large, formally organized social structures.

One of the best known of these is *The American Soldier,* a study of attitudes of soldiers in the American Army during World War II.[6] Several different sections of this study employ the idea of primary group attachment as a major explanatory variable.

That part of the investigation which focuses on the underlying motives for willingness to fight is an interesting example for us to consider. The authors report their finding that combat motivation was associated with attachment to an informal group. The protection of friends, for example, or the need to conform to primary group expectations was often given as the most important reason for willingness to enter battle. Here, again, it seems to have been something of a surprise to find that motives associated with interpersonal relations were consistently reported as more important than motives related to hatred for the enemy or the political and ideological goals of the war, or the coercion of discipline and of formal orders from above. This is our pattern again—here, too, the primary group was not at first conceived of as *relevant.*[7]

The data in the Hawthorne studies were largely observational, and could focus easily on the *interaction* of individuals. In *The American Soldier,* however, data were gathered from an atomized cross-section of individual soldiers responding to a questionnaire. In this particular regard, *The American Soldier* is much closer to the studies of communications effectiveness than are the industrial studies. The kinds of data with which communications research stumbled upon the primary group are very much like those that were available in *The American Soldier,* that is, the reports of isolated individuals in a cross-sectional sample. The primary group had to be imputed, so to speak, in both these studies.[8]

6. Stouffer *et al.* (1949). Our remarks are based on Volume II of this work, entitled *Combat and its Aftermath* and on the summary and analysis by Shils (1950) of material in both volumes bearing on the primary group.

7. Shils (1950), p. 17. It is interesting to note, parenthetically, that the Army seems to be trying to find applications for these and other social science studies of military life. *The New York Times* for Sunday, July 5, 1953, carried the following headline over a page one story: "Army to Let G.I.'s Pick 'Buddies' to Live and Fight in 4-Man Teams." A subsequent announcement, however, reportedly indicates some change in this declared policy.

8. But the central theoretical problem raised by the discovery of the group in industry and in the army is similar: how the group functions relative to the

## (C.) THE GROUP IN A COMMUNITY CONTEXT:
### THE YANKEE CITY SERIES

There is another broad area of studies which came latterly to the idea that the informal group was worth reckoning with. The concern of these researches—the urban community—is also the locale in which mass communications research is particularly active.

Most important, for our purpose, is the series of studies by Warner and his associates, the Yankee City series.[9] The evidence that Warner, too, did not set out to study the primary group as an important element in the community is made quite clear; he even uses the language of "discovery." Warner reports that "the *discovery* of the clique and the determination of its great significance as a social and structural mechanism came rather late in our field investigation in Yankee City. . . . We eventually became convinced that the cliques were next in importance to the family in placing groups socially." Once more the clue seems to have come from the very people being studied. About this, Warner says:

. . . We had long been aware of the importance of such designations as "our crowd," "our bunch," "the Jones's gang," "the ring we go in," "our circle," but we had not focussed our attention on the theoretical implications of such terms as descriptive of a special type of social relations. It soon became apparent, however, that such statements as "that crowd's snooty as hell," "she's not so hot, she goes around with the X crowd," or "he thinks he rates because he plays with that Y gang," and other evaluations derisive or laudatory, and all referring to particular cliques, were of the highest importance in assigning people to their actual social position in the hierarchy of the city. . . .[10]

Here again we see interpersonal relations "rediscovered." This case, of course, is different in many ways from the preceding two and yet it shares with them, and with mass media

---

formally prescribed goals of an organization. Other studies of formal organizations have hit upon the relevance of interpersonal relations, too. See especially the studies cited by Shils (1951). We must again reiterate our indebtedness to this paper.

9. Warner and Lunt (1941).
10. *Ibid.*, p. 110.

research, the discovery that interpersonal relations are *relevant* to an understanding of a problem in social research. Here the problem is to understand the workings of the status system of a community and the criteria by which people assign prestige to one another, and to themselves. The investigators' early image of what was relevant included such things as income, neighborhood, family, etc., but the idea that informal friend-ship cliques might be a basic factor for conferring status, and that "mobility" might be characterized as moving from one clique to another simply did not appear. Thus, as Warner says, the clique was discovered. In our sense, that is, it was "redis-covered."

## The Common Elements in the Pattern

We now have examined four cases of "rediscovery"—our own mass communications story and the case of the factory, the army, and the urban community. For each, we have tried to trace the research steps that led to the recognition that interpersonal relations—the primary group—was a relevant "in-tervening variable": for production in the factory, motivation for combat in the army, social mobility in the urban community and for response to mass media influences. It is very apparent that there are *common elements* in this pattern of "redis-covery," despite the widely different substantive areas in which the discoveries took place. Roughly, the pattern seems to be as follows:

(1) First of all, it is possible in each case to reconstruct assumptions about what was expected to be relevant. In other words, it is possible to specify the "models" of how things would work—which were in the minds of those concerned as research got under way. In industry, where factors affecting productivity were under study or, in the case of the army, where the problem was to specify the determinants of morale, researchers had particular expectations as to what was im-portant and what was not. In each case, the image in the minds of researchers had no place for the primary group, or interpersonal relations, as a *relevant* factor for production, say, or for combat willingness.

That is the first element in the pattern. We might speculate for a moment on why this should be the case. Why should the factor of interpersonal relations—which turns out at the end to be so important—have been systematically overlooked? The answers, case by case, again seem to have common roots. Consider the imagery associated with the notions of the mass in the phrase *mass* production, *mass* communication, *mass* society of the city. In each case, the idea of the mass is associated with the newly "independent," newly individuated, citizen of the modern industrial age and, at the same time, for all his individualism, the person who is subject to the remote controls of institutions from which he and the myriads of his "unorganized" fellows feel far removed. The individual who comes to mind—and the one whom researchers seem to have had in their minds—is a worker attuned to individualistic economic incentive in the competitive race for maximizing gain; an anonymous urban dweller trying to "keep up" with anonymous Joneses; a radio listener shut in his room with a self-sufficient supply of the world outside.[11] These were standard images of individual behavior in realms where intimate interpersonal ties were thought anachronistic—and they are not altogether wrong, of course. But they are wrong enough to have furnished inadequate assumptions upon which to build empirical research.

(2) There is a second step in the pattern of "rediscovery" which is typical, too. At a given point in each study, a halt was called—figuratively, at least—because the variables which were taken into consideration still left too much unexplained. This led to the suspicion that perhaps there was something wrong with the "model" of what was relevant. In the case of the factory, physical and economic variables clearly were not the whole story; in the army, discipline and the ideals of the war could not fully account for combat motivation; in the city, social mobility seemed to be something more than mere eco-

---

11. The case of the army is somewhat different, obviously. Here, research assumptions had to do with the discipline of the army, identification of the men with the nation's goals, hatred for the enemy, etc. Yet, the parallel is evident here, too. The soldier is typically conceived as a social atom operating in response to the formal, impersonal controls of the military organization and its aims.

nomic advancement; and in mass communications, direct exposure to the media could not fully account for the observed differences in changing vote intentions. It was at this point of recognition, that the investigators began to become receptive to *new* ideas about what might be relevant; in effect, they became sensitized to the possibility that some other factor might be operative.

(3) It is noteworthy that the people being studied themselves furnished the major clue. In each case, when expectations about what would be relevant were frustrated, the investigators turned to their subjects and *asked them*, in effect, how they explained what was happening. In the factory, this is literally what took place, and the girls in the first test room told of the fine *esprit de corps* that had grown up among the teammates and how they enjoyed consistently increasing production. In the urban community, repeated allusions to the relationship between social status and clique membership attracted the researchers' attention. In the army, there were striking references to the role of primary group allegiance and support in answer to subjective questions about willingness for combat, while the effect of hatred for the enemy, identification with patriotic goals, fear of disciplinary action, etc. were not much mentioned. Finally, in the interview study of the effect of mass communications in the presidential election, those who had changed their vote intention during the course of the campaign were asked to try to point out what had influenced them. In reply, they referred to personal influences much more than to mass media influences.

(4) Then came "rediscovery." Each time attention was redirected, in a similar way, to the possibility that the primary group—interpersonal relations—was *relevant*. For, obviously, it was not simply the fact that the primary group *exists* that was discovered, but the fact that it is *relevant* to an understanding of the workings of each of these areas. Thus, the discovery was not that workers often form friendships in the factory, or that soldiers develop intimate ties to their buddies, or that city dwellers belong to cliques or that radio listeners have families but, rather, the fact that these alliances are

*relevant* (where previously no thought had been given to their relevance) for mass production, combat morale, class status and mobility, and communications behavior.[12]

---

12. These chapters intentionally omit all references to two social science traditions which not only "rediscovered" the small group many years ago, but have been using it, along with other relevant societal factors, as a basis for studying and administering communications programs! We refer to the diffusion and acceptance of new farm practices in rural sociology, and to the colonial administration and technical assistance concerns of applied anthropology. The conceptual framework and the empirical findings of these two traditions have the most manifest bearing on the kinds of communications research concerns expressed in this and the following chapter. While we shall make mention below of several studies in international communications research which come close to the haunts of the anthropologist, we avoid making any explicit connections because we feel that a separate study devoted to this matter alone is indicated. Such a study, along with the present effort, should aim at effecting a convergence of the communications concerns of mass media research, small group research and applied anthropology (and rural sociology). Recent examples of the communications aspects of the latter realm can be found, e.g., in Brunner (1945) and Mead (1953), and in the journals *Rural Sociology, Human Organization, Economic Development and Cultural Change,* and others.

CHAPTER **III**

# An Essay
# in Convergence

THE PREVIOUS CHAPTERS make two basic assertions: First, that communications research, to date, has been studying short run mass media *effects;* second, that the intellectual history of this research is best characterized as a successive taking account of those factors which *intervene* between the mass media and their audience and, thus, which modify mass media effects. The central focus of Section One had to do with the introduction of the intervening variable of interpersonal relations.

In the four chapters of the present section we want to scrutinize this notion of interpersonal relations, asking ourselves which elements of such social ties have most bearing on communications effectiveness. We shall try, in other words, to single out and examine those ingredients of informal primary groups which are, so to speak, the "active ingredients" as far as the mass communications process is concerned.

Our purpose, of course, is to try to point the way for the planning of research on the transmission of mass persuasion via the mass media—and, particularly, for the incorporation of a concern with interpersonal relations into the design of such research. By attempting to specify exactly which elements of person-to-person interaction might be relevant for mass media effectiveness, and by exploring what social science knows about the workings of these elements, we shall contribute, perhaps, to a more complex—yet, more realistic—formulation of a "model" for the study of mass persuasion campaigns.

Let us take as our starting point the several illustrations from mass media research set down above, and the thinking and research which constitutes the opinion leader tradition. If we reflect on these, and try to speculate about the specific ways in which interpersonal relationships might be said to affect the response of an individual to a communications campaign, we are led to two characteristics of interpersonal relations, each one of which seems to be a major key to our problem:

1. Interpersonal relationships seem to be *"anchorage" points for individual opinions, attitudes, habits and values.* That is, interacting individuals seem collectively and continuously *to generate* and *to maintain* common ideas and behavior patterns which they are reluctant to surrender or to modify unilaterally. If this is the case, and if many, or most, of the ostensibly individual opinions and attitudes which mass media campaigns seek to modify are anchored in small groups, then the bearing of this aspect of group relations on the effectiveness of such campaigns will be well worth our attention.

2. Interpersonal relationships imply *networks of interpersonal communication,* and this characteristic seems to be relevant for campaign effectiveness in several interlocking ways: The "two-step flow" hypothesis suggests, in the first place, that these interpersonal networks are linked to the mass media networks in such a way that some people, who are relatively more exposed, pass on what they see, or hear, or read, to others with

whom they are in contact who are less exposed. Primary groups, in other words, may serve as channels for mass media transmission; this might be called the *relay function* of interpersonal relations. Secondly, it is implied, person-to-person influences may coincide with mass media messages and thus either counteract or reinforce their message. This might be called the *reinforcement function;* and, there is substantial reason to suspect, when the reinforcement is positive, the communication in question is likely to be particularly effective.[1]

It is our guess that these two characteristics of small, intimate groups—(1) person-to-person *sharing of opinions and attitudes* (which we shall often refer to as "group norms") and (2) person-to-person *communications networks*—are the keys to an adequate understanding of the intervening role played by interpersonal relations in the mass communications process.

We propose now to turn to contemporary social science research to look for corroborating evidence for these hypotheses, and, in general, to see whether we might not in this way achieve a better understanding of just what such social relations have to do with the effectiveness of mass communications. Those who are acquainted with the compartments of social research will know that there already exists some modest theory plus a body of experimental findings which may take us a long way toward a more basic understanding of the problems we have raised; these are in the compartment called "small group research." This is one case where the much-discussed, sometimes confusing, division of labor in the social sciences seems to pay off very well. For while some sociologists were just discovering that the informal group intervenes almost everywhere, other social scientists—particularly the experimental social psychologists—were devoting themselves to a wide variety of investigations on the effect of "other people" on individual behavior.[2] Putting this somewhat differently, we

---

1. Lazarsfeld (1942) calls this "supplementation."
2. While the very basis of social psychology is rooted in a rejection of the possibility of a psychology based only on the study of an individual abstracted from his environment, nevertheless it seems legitimate to propose that even in social psychology there appears to have been a belated "discovery" of the primary group. This seems to have happened in two different ways. For some experimenters, interest in the small, informal group resulted

might say that while sociologists were finding that the effects of the institutional order of mass society are mediated by interpersonal ties, psychologists were finding that everyday psychological processes, such as perception and judgment, and everyday behavior, such as an individual's performance on a test, are markedly influenced by interpersonal relations. Out of this combination of interests grew small group research.[3]

Our purpose here will be to propose a framework for the organization of the findings of small group research in a way which will be meaningful for mass media research. Of course, we shall make no attempt to report on the entire field of small group research. But that does not mean that we shall report only those small group studies which have immediate implications for mass media campaigns. Rather, we shall report studies which seem to have some sort of relevance, or which may provide some sort of lead, for the possible application of the principles and conclusions of small group studies to research in communications effectiveness.

Here, then, is the plan for the section:

In the following chapter, Chapter IV, we shall seek evidence for our hypothesis that small groups are anchorage points for opinions, attitudes and values. And if we are persuaded on that point, we shall inquire further into the effect

---

simply from an attempt to create "social" situations (characterized by the presence or absence of anonymous "others"); for these experimenters, the "discovery" consisted of the recognition that the small group *per se* merits study as a natural unit of social structure in which individuals are tied to each other through patterned interactions and sentiments. A second group of experimenters, notably Kurt Lewin and his associates, had been dealing from the first with such patterns of interpersonal interaction and sentiment but here, one senses, the concern with small groups was a concern with the construction of small scale-models for the purpose of studying the properties of large social structures. If that is so, then the later interest of Lewin and his disciples in small groups *per se* seems also to be a reorientation of interest— and, in our sense, a sort of "discovery." Evidence on these matters may be obtained by comparing, for example, the number of studies dealing with small groups *per se*, and the character of the interest in small groups, in Newcomb and Hartley (1947) with the revised Swanson, Newcomb and Hartley (1952); some support for our hunch concerning the Lewinians may be found in Lewin (1951), p. 164.

3. Shils (1951) in his excellent discussion of the antecedents, as well as the contemporary flowering, of small group research credits the pioneering work of three men each of whom established a small group research tradition: Mayo (the "human relations" approach in industry); Moreno (sociometry—for the mapping and analysis of patterns of attraction and repulsion in interpersonal relations); and Lewin (the "group dynamics" tradition).

that such shared norms would be likely to have on the response of an individual to an influence-attempt stemming from outside his group—whether from the mass media or elsewhere. Thus, Chapter IV will be concerned with the evidence for the existence of group-shared norms, the origin of such norms, the reasons and the dynamics of their enforcement and then, in Chapter V, we shall see the bearing that they may have on an understanding of the process of effective communication.

In Chapter VI, we shall review the teachings of small group research concerning the processes which are involved in the interpersonal transmission of a communication. We shall want to explore the conditions making for the effectiveness—or for the lack of it—of personal communication and, generally, to ask what accounts for the substantial influence that people in face-to-face contact seem to have over each other. We shall want to know, too, which people will be influential for which others and under what circumstances. When we arrive at some understanding of the flow of influence *within the group,* we shall then, in Chapter VII, turn to inquire about how such networks of intragroup communication are linked up with the world *outside* the group. Specifically, we shall want to know whether there is any evidence for our hypothesis that there is a linkage between these small group networks and the mass media. Let us call this second step communication *to the group.*

If we succeed in this exploration, we shall have made a contribution not only to our own understanding of the mass communications process, but also to the possible convergence of two areas of substance and of method which have been almost completely unrelated to date. The study of mass communications, on the one hand, with its global reach and its image of an atomized society, and of the small group, on the other, with its therapeutic and psychologistic concerns, now seem to have something to say to each other. A large part of what follows is an attempt to spell out that something.

CHAPTER IV

# Norms and Small Groups: The Shared

# Character of Opinions and Attitudes

OUR FOCUS is the primary group. We are thinking specifically
of families, friends, informal work teams, etc., as well as those
relatively more formal groupings of clubs and organizations
of all kinds within which individuals are likely to form what
we might call sociometric connections, that is, mutual attractions for each other as personalities. Such groups are usually
characterized by their small size, relative durability, informal-
ity, face-to-face contact and manifold, or more or less un-
specialized, purpose.[1] We shall refer interchangeably to primary groups, small groups, intimate social ties, interpersonal
relations or sometimes just to "others," with no attempt to be
prematurely precise in our definitions. Our aim now is to see
whether those who have studied such interpersonal relations
can assist us in developing an idea of how to account for the
role of *people* in the flow of mass media influence in modern
society.

Our chief concern is with the hypothesis that such groups
actively influence and support most of an individual's opinions, attitudes and actions. The evidence on this point is not
yet very abundant, but what there is, is persuasive. We know,
for example, from several studies that the members of a family
are likely—except under certain conditions—to share similar
attitudes on politics, religion, etc., and the same thing is true,
we know, for most friendships.[2] We know from a set of pio-

---

1. From Cooley's (1909) classic definition. For the contrast of secondary
groups, see Davis (1949), Chap. 11.
2. Empirical evidence for the homogeneity of family opinion can be found
in Newcomb and Svehla's (1937) study of parents' and children's attitudes,

[ 48 ]

neering studies (which now constitute the core of what is called "reference group theory") that individuals seem often to have particular groups "in mind" when reporting their opinions.[3] Here, then, is the suggestion that opinions are originated and maintained by an individual in common with specifiable others of his associates.

The fact that interacting individuals influence each other, or that an individual entering a new group is likely to adopt the thinking habits of that group is not an easy thing to prove because it almost always involves *disproving* the alternate hypothesis that individuals in a similar situation are each responding independently to the same external stimuli. Thus, even when it is demonstrated that Northern students attending Southern universities become increasingly prejudiced toward the Negro with each succeeding year at school (although never quite so prejudiced as the Southern students themselves), the authors cannot permit themselves to assert that the Northerners are adopting the attitude of their Southern classmates, because they must also show (and their data do not permit them to) that whatever it is that has caused prejudice in the Southerners is not also at work directly on the Northerners.[4]

But although we do not yet have a mass of statistical evidence to demonstrate the *fact* that opinions, attitudes, decisions and actions are rooted in relatively small groups, we can feel much surer than we ordinarily might because we know

and in Lazarsfeld, Berelson and Gaudet (1948), pp. 140-145. Evidence for the homogeneity of friends' political opinions is reported by Berelson, Lazarsfeld and McPhee (1954). See also Fisher (1948) and the bibliography contained therein. While knowledge of the family as a primary group exceeds our knowledge of any other primary group, it is interesting that contemporary social scientists (unlike their more theoretically oriented predecessors) rarely attempt to generalize from the family to other intimate groups, though a recent, very notable exception is Homans (1950). Some parallels between the family and other primary groups will be implicit—though not spelled out —in this chapter. For example: it will be shown that there are mechanisms in every group for indoctrinating newcomers in the ways of the group, and bringing deviates back into line; it will be shown that individuals picture themselves much as others around them picture them; it will be shown that intimate groups of all kinds affect the opinions and attitudes of their members in spheres of thought and action that often go far beyond the group's immediate concerns. All these (and many more) are just what the family does.

3. See the writings on reference group theory, notably Merton and Kitt (1950), and Newcomb (1952).

4. Sims and Patrick (1947).

from careful case studies some of the *reasons why* we are warranted in our expectation that this is the case. Several reasons have been put forward quite convincingly.

## The Instrumental Function: The Benefits of Conformity

First of all, we might consider what can be called the *instrumental value*—the "benefits"—that can be derived from sharing the opinions and attitudes of those with whom an individual desires to be identified. We may cite here, as an illustration, Newcomb's well-known study of the political attitudes of a class of Bennington College girls.[5] By beginning his study in the freshman year and recording changes in attitudes over the four-year period of college, Newcomb was able to show that those students who were postively oriented toward the college community and who aspired to be accepted or to achieve leadership tended to assimilate the liberal attitudes and sentiments which prevailed on campus, despite the strongly conservative family background from which they had come. On the other hand, Newcomb demonstrates, a major factor associated with non-acceptance of the prevailing political climate was a strong positive identification with the family group. Thus, the family group, on the one hand, and the small college community, on the other—each serving as "positive" or "negative" reference points of varying intensity—seemed to be associated with the steadfast conservatism of some of the girls and the increasing non-conservatism of the majority. In Newcomb's own words,

In a membership group in which certain attitudes are approved (i.e., held by majorities, and conspicuously so by leaders) individuals acquire the approved attitudes to the extent that the membership group (particularly as symbolized by leaders and dominant subgroups) serves as a positive point of reference.[6]

In other words, to the extent that a group is attractive for an individual, and to the extent that he desires acceptance as a

5. Newcomb (1952).
6. *Ibid.*, p. 420.

member of that group, he will be motivated—whether he is aware of it or not—to accept that group's outlook.

Another set of findings supports the implications of New-comb's study very neatly. In *The American Soldier*,[7] Stouffer *et al*, compare the attitudes of those "green" soldiers (no combat experience) who had been sent as replacements to divisions composed of combat veterans, with the attitudes of equally "green" soldiers who were members of divisions composed only of others like themselves. Noting that 45% of the latter but only 28% of the former express attitudes reflecting a "readiness for combat," the authors indicate that this difference may derive from the two different social contexts in which these otherwise indistinguishable "green" troops were placed. It is suggested that those troops who found themselves in veterans' divisions were strongly influenced by the attitudes they encountered there since the combat veterans' own response to the same set of questions was overwhelmingly negative (only 15% indicated readiness for combat). The new men were seeking acceptance, it is argued, and they adjusted their opinions accordingly.

Conformity is not exacted from "new" members or potential members alone. Even long-time members who "deviate" too far from group opinion lose status, or may even lose membership in groups to which they already belong. Several recent experimental studies demonstrate this everyday fact quite well. In one study of a housing community by Festinger, Schachter and Back—(we shall refer repeatedly to this "Westgate" housing development study and to others by these authors and their associates)—it was found that those who conformed least to the opinions of their immediate neighbors (as far as the particular item being studied was concerned) tended also to be the ones who were "underchosen" when people were asked in an interview to name their three best friends.[8] From another study by one of this same team of

<hr>

7. Stouffer *et al*. (1949) Vol. II, p. 244. See Shils' (1950) summary and analysis of this subject, and in the same volume, the treatment of the same subject by Merton and Kitt (1950).

8. That is, they were not named as frequently as they named others. This is one of the standard sociometric procedures employed in Festinger, Schachter and Back (1950).

authors, we learn that when participants in clubs were asked, following their initial discussion periods, who among the participants they would like to see dropped from the club, those who had maintained extremely deviant opinions (these extremists were in the employ of the experimenter) were named most of all.[9]

Individuals conform, we have seen so far, and obtain acceptance and friendship in return. In order to become a *leader*, too, one must share prevailing opinions and attitudes. Merei demonstrates this very vividly in his study of leadership in children's groups.[10]

Children were observed at play in a day nursery and those children who displayed leadership qualities were singled out and separated from the other children. The remaining children were formed into twelve groups, homogeneous as to age and sex, comprising three to six members each. Each of these twelve groups met separately over a period of several days and very soon each developed group "traditions" with regard to its activities, most of which centered about an experimentally prescribed task. The author reports that it took from three to six meetings (35 to 40 minutes each) for the development of group "traditions" such as permanent seating arrangements, permanent division of objects (who plays with what), a stable sequence of games, preference for certain activities rather than others, group jargon, etc. Then the original leaders, who had not been included in these twelve groups, were reintroduced. In every case, when an old leader attempted to assert authority which went contrary to a newly established "tradition" of the group, the group did not respond. Some of the leaders, as a matter of fact, never returned to power. Others, who were successful, did achieve leadership once more but only after they had completely identified with the new "tradition" and participated in it themselves.

In sum, all these studies seem to indicate that if an individual desires to attain, or maintain, an intimate relationship

---

9. Schachter (1951).

10. Merei (1952). For confirmation, with case study illustrations, of the relationship between social status and degree of conformity to group norms, see Homans (1950) on "social ranking and norms."

with others, or if he wants to "get somewhere" either within a group or via a group, he must identify himself with the opinions and values of these others. That does not necessarily mean that this identification is therefore rationally calculated. It may be quite unwitting. But conscious or not, the *consequences* of conformity or non-conformity which we have noted will remain the same.

Thus, from the "instrumental" point of view, we are led to expect that an individual's opinions will be substantially affected by the opinions of others whose company he keeps, or whose company he aspires to keep.[11]

## Providing a Social Reality

Let us now consider another of the reasons which may help explain our confidence in the assertion that individuals very largely share their opinions with other people who surround them. Here, we are thinking of the group not in instrumental terms (that is, not in terms of the "benefits" of conforming) but rather in terms of the function of the group as a provider of *meanings* for situations which do not explain themselves. Experimental social psychologists concerned with the impact of the group on perceptual processes,[12] and particularly the

11. Warner and Lunt's (1941) "discovery" of the clique in Yankee City indicates that upward mobility in the social status system of a community involves being accepted by (and presumably, therefore, conforming with) small groups which personify each successive step on the status ladder. A whole series of such examples—cutting across traditionally rigid boundary lines in sociology—are provided by Merton and Kitt (1950) in their reference group paper. They begin with data from *The American Soldier* to indicate that army privates who at Time A have attitudes more closely resembling those of non-commissioned officers than other privates, are more likely at Time B to have attained a higher rank than other privates. Generalizing from this finding, they say: "An army private bucking for promotion may only in a narrow and theoretically superficial sense be regarded as engaging in behavior different from that of an immigrant assimilating the values of a native group, or of a lower-middle-class individual conforming to his conception of upper-middle-class patterns of behavior, or of a boy in a slum area orienting himself to the values of the street corner gang, or of a Bennington student abandoning the conservative beliefs of her parents to adopt the more liberal ideas of her college associates, or of a lower-class Catholic departing from the pattern of his in-group by casting a Republican vote, or of an eighteenth century French aristocrat aligning himself with a revolutionary group of the time."

12. For an interesting formulation of the contributions of gestalt psychologists to the study of group processes as these influence perception, judgments, motivations, etc., see Katz, D. (1951).

late Kurt Lewin and those who continue in his tradition, have studied this phenomenon. The Lewinians have named it "social reality" and they explain it as follows:

Experiments dealing with memory and group pressure on the individual show that what exists as "reality" for the individual is to a high degree determined by what is socially accepted as reality. This holds even in the field of physical fact: to the South Sea Islanders the world may be flat; to the European it is round. "Reality," therefore, is not an absolute. It differs with the group to which the individual belongs.[13]

This concept provides an alternative or better, a supplementary, explanation for the soldiers' attitudes we reported above. Instead of attributing the attitude of the replacements (compared with their peers in all-"green" divisions) simply to their motivation to be accepted in the veterans' outfits, we might have suggested there, as we shall here, that the "reality" of the combat experience toward which attitudes were being expressed might well have been different for those who were in daily touch with combat veterans as compared with those who were not. The Westgate study makes this point very well:

The hypothesis may be advanced that the "social reality" upon which an opinion or an attitude rests for its justification is the degree to which the individual perceives that this opinion or attitude is shared by others. An opinion or attitude which is not reinforced by others of the same opinion will become unstable generally. There are not usually compelling facts which can unequivocally settle the question of which attitude is wrong and which is right in connection with social opinions and attitudes as there are in the case of what might be called "facts." If a person driving a car down a street is told by his companion that the street ends in a dead end, this piece of information may easily be checked against physical "reality." . . . The "reality" which settles the question in the case of social attitudes and opinions is the degree to which others with whom one is in communication are believed to share these opinions and attitudes.[14]

This is the way that stereotypes develop; and it is one of the

---

13. Lewin and Grabbe (1945). The notion of "social reality" has an important parallel in Harry Stack Sullivan's (1953) "consensual validation."
14. Festinger, Schachter and Back (1950), p. 168.

reasons why ideas about what is real in religion or in politics vary from group to group. So many things in the world are inaccessible to direct empirical observation that individuals must continually rely on each other for making sense out of things. Several experimental studies illustrate this. For example, there is Sherif's now classic study which is perhaps the best single beginning point for a review of the twenty or so years of attention in experimental social psychology to the role of the small group as an influence on opinions, attitudes and actions.[15] Sherif constructed experiments using the "auto-kinetic effect" which is the name given to the illusion of movement created by an actually stationary pinpoint of light when it is flashed on in a totally darkened room. He first tested each of his experimental subjects singly, asking them to make judgments about the number of inches the light "moved" each time it was lit. After each individual had developed a personal "norm"—that is, a modal number of inches—around which his judgments centered, Sherif brought his subjects together in groups of twos and threes, and asked them to repeat the experiment once more. Each of the subjects based his first few estimates on his previously established standard, but confronted, this time, with the dissenting judgments of the others each gave way somewhat until a new, group standard became established. Thus, knowing what each individual brought with him to the situation, Sherif was able to show how the effect of the judgments of others resulted in the convergence of substantially different private standards and the emergence of a shared norm. When the experiment was reversed—that is, when the group situation came first and the private situation second—individuals accepted the group standard as their own and carried it away with them into the private situation. The group norm thus became the norm of each group member. Interaction had given rise to a definition of "reality" which each participating individual retained.

Such laboratory experiments are sure to encounter a barrage of critical objections concerning the dangers of generalizing laboratory findings to "real life" situations. Often these

---

15. Sherif (1952).

warnings are very sound. Often, however, they are not more than pat pronouncements about the impossibility of studying human behavior in a laboratory. It may be interesting, then, to digress for a moment to consider some of the possible objections to the study we have just reported. Consider, for example, the arguments that (1) the situation was completely *unstructured* and therefore unreal, for, after all, nobody could know that the light did not move at all; (2) it was completely *without emotional affect* for the participating subjects—that is, they could not have cared much about the validity of their judgments; and (3) it was a situation where people were *forced* to make a decision in response to the artificial demands of the experimental situation. In short, these three objections taken together would imply that Sherif's experiment can be legitimately generalized only to situations where individuals are (1) forced to make decisions (2) about something they know nothing about and (3) about which they care not at all. The critic of laboratory experimentation too often retires at this point; but we shall continue. Let us suppose, now, that these objections are in fact valid and do limit the generalizability of Sherif's finding, as in fact they probably do. Still, that leaves us with a question: are there any real-life situations that resemble this laboratory one? And our answer happens to be —yes. Consider one: For very large numbers of people the presidential voting situation can be characterized as a situation where social pressures (1) force people to make a decision they would not otherwise make (2) between two candidates about whom they may know nothing and (3) about whom they may care not at all. In such a situation, for such people, we may expect informal groups to play a large part in defining the situation, and in influencing decisions. And let us add, that it would be wrong—in the case of almost any of the complex issues on which people in our society are expected to have opinions—to overestimate the objective verifiability of any social situation.

## Interaction: *The Process of Convergence*

If we recall now that we are still engaged in the task of reasoning out the thesis that the opinions and attitudes of individuals are rooted in the social spheres to which they belong, we will find something more in the Sherif study. The Sherif study points out for us two basic ideas: first, that individuals turn to and depend on others, when they have to form opinions or make decisions in unclear situations—this we have called the "social reality" function of groups; and secondly, that individuals interacting with each other relative to a particular problem which concerns all, will develop a collective approach to that problem and thus create an opinion, an attitude, a decision, or an action which they then will grasp in common.

Here, then, is another "reason" why we can have confidence in the contention that opinions, attitudes and actions of individuals are likely to be connected with interpersonal relations. For, in Sherif's experiment, we find an early attempt to meet the problem of *the way in which* shared norms are created and we are offered the suggestion that when individuals interact with each other relative to a problem they have in common they begin to "see" things in the same way and consequently create a social norm. If the "benefits" of conformity and the "social reality" function of groups begin to answer the question *why* individual opinions and attitudes are so often anchored in groups, then the observation that norms arise from the interaction of individuals begins to answer the question *how*. We shall consider now the way in which individuals, interacting together, simultaneously *create* a shared way of looking at things or of doing them.[16]

The Westgate study presents an opportunity to watch norms arise in the "real-life" context of a newly-built housing community for married veterans who had come to study at a large Eastern university.[17]

The community was made up of residential courts, each court consisting of several buildings and each building of several apartments. Apartments were assigned at random and

---

16. In an essay on "Social-Psychological Theory," Newcomb (1951) remarks that it is "to Sherif's eternal credit that he . . . formulated the problems of social norms in terms of perceptual processes." "Norms," Newcomb says, "represent shared ways of perceiving things (or, more exactly, shared frames of reference in which things are perceived)."

17. Festinger, Schachter and Back (1950).

none of the residents seems to have known each other prior to moving in. Research began just as the project was completed and the residents arrived. The researchers opened their investigation by focusing on factors which were influencing the growth of friendships; and we are told that friendship ties—at least in this homogeneous population[18]—can be related directly to factors like physical proximity and functional proximity (where your daily route takes you by someone's door). Thus, the largest share of all friendships grew up among people living in the same court or the same building. "These ecological factors," say the authors, "determine not only specific friendships but the composition of groups as well." Stated otherwise, it is quite clear that contact—or interaction—was the basis for the formation of social groups. Now let us see about the rise of norms.

Friendships and informal groupings were mapped by means of a sociometric questionnaire which requested each member of the entire community to name the three people "whom you see most of socially." Then, some time following this sociometric questionnaire, an attitude questionnaire was administered in order to study the distribution of attitudes for and against a newly-formed Tenants' Council. In the majority of cases, the attitude of an individual was found to be identical with the prevailing attitude of the other members of the court in which he lived. And since we know that contact centered primarily around the residential court—and since the attitude toward the Tenants' Council varied from court to court—we may conclude, as the authors do, that the shared opinions of the members of each court arose out of their mutual contacts and interaction.

Variations in group "cohesion" from court to court were also examined by distinguishing the extent to which sociometric choices were confined to fellow court members by the residents of each court. They report that the greater the cohesiveness (and thus, the interaction) the greater the uniformity of attitudes. And furthermore, by studying the sociometric choices

---

18. These were all young married couples, of about the same age and similar social and economic status. The husbands were all veterans of military service in World War II, and were all students at the university.

of those individuals who did *not* share the attitudes of their courts, the authors discovered that often these non-conformists were residents whose friends and social life were centered not only outside the court in which they lived but outside the housing community altogether.

What we learn is that individuals who were randomly assigned to apartments throughout a housing community quickly formed themselves into friendship groups and once formed, these groups of friends adopted shared ways of thinking and judging things to which their members adhered. Here are real-life groups and real-life evidence for our contention that ostensibly private opinions and attitudes are often, in fact, opinions and attitudes which are generated and maintained in interaction with small groups of other people.[19]

## *The Attraction of Shared Values*

Now that we have talked about propinquity and motivated interaction as a basis for the collective creation of norms, we should point to one other factor which will also help us to explain how it happens that an individual's opinions are likely to be liked with the opinions of those around him. The phenomenon to which we refer now is the tendency of people with like opinions and values *to seek each other out* as companions. In a forthcoming study, Robert K. Merton will call this notion "value homophily" and will deal with its as a central concept for the study of interpersonal relations.[20]

"Value homophily"—or, mutual attraction on the basis of shared values—is a difficult problem to study empirically because one must demonstrate, to do the job thoroughly, that

19. In Chapter V, below, some of the processes of interpersonal communication are explored in greater detail. Here, we are concerned with the fact that interpersonal communication—or interaction—seems, somehow, to lead to shared opinions and attitudes and with some of the reasons why we might expect this to be the case. The "how" of the case is also implicit, of course, but while it is touched on at various points in this chapter, it will be given more attention later.

20. Merton *et al.* (forthcoming). Merton deals also with "status homophily," that is, mutual attractions based on similarities of social class, religion, nationality, etc., but we are concerned here only with "value homophily." Another study which will treat the relationship between friendship and like-mindedness is the study by Lipset, Trow and Coleman (1955) of a printers' union.

common values *precede* rather than follow from interaction. Thus, research must begin where aggregates of individuals with a variety of values come into contact with each other for the first time within a situation which is conducive to the formation of friendships and primary groups. A recent research on the borderlines of this problem seems worth reporting here.[21] The study we have in mind does not quite solve this problem nor does it pretend to, but it is an interesting step in this direction.

The problem for this study occurred as a by-product of another assignment. The author, Joseph A. Precker, had been asked to determine which criteria the students and the faculty of Bard College considered fundamental for the proper evaluation of a student's overall educational achievement at the college. The 242 students and 42 faculty members (the entire college population) offered some 1,300 criteria which they considered important, following which three judges condensed these into 39 categories. Everybody was then asked once more to rank the new list of 39 categories according to their individual judgments of the relative importance of each of the criteria. At the same time, each student was asked (1) to name the three students he would most like to keep in touch with after graduation and (2) to name the member of the faculty whom he would most like to have as faculty adviser. By means of a coefficient of rank-order correlation the author compared the evaluation rankings of each chooser with the rankings of the three students he chose and similarly, for each chooser

21. Precker (1952). It is curious that so little work has been done on this problem of the mutual attraction of similar values. Other than the present study which is on the borderline of the problem, and the Merton and Lipset studies which attack it directly, we know of no other work in this area. Yet, in *Social Organization* (1909), C. H. Cooley cites one of two prevalent notions about the effects of the new communications media: ". . . If there are in the civilized world a few like-minded people it is comparatively easy for them to get together in spirit and encourage one another in their peculiarity." And Cooley further remarks that "modern conditions . . . tend to make life rational and free, rather than local and accidental." The new voluntary associations of the gesellschaft society which would be based on mutual interest rather than propinquity also aroused considerable attention some years ago; for references see Shils (1951). Giddings (1896) concept of "consciousness-of kind" is obviously related, too—though its use refers now to the consequences and now to the antecedents of interaction. Obviously the two uses must be distinguished and only the latter is in point here. But despite all this, no empirical research has been done.

and the faculty member he chose. He found that students tended to select associates—both as post-college friends and as faculty advisers—whose values (as reflected in these educational criteria for the evaluation of students) resembled their own. Furthermore, Precker is able to indicate that, among peers, the greatest similarity of values tended to occur in those cases where friendship choices on the sociometric questionnaire were *mutual* rather than unilateral.

Of course, it is not easy to interpret these data definitively. On the one hand, we can say simply that this case appears no different than some of the previous ones we have seen, that is, that interaction leads to friendship which leads both to shared values and to a desire to continue the friendship. Precker himself offers data which would support this conclusion.[22] On the other hand, however, this argument which derives from mutual friendship choices cannot explain why those whose choices were not reciprocated should have selected individuals whose values resembled their own. It does seem, therefore, that a seeking-out process, based on "value homophily" is at work here, and in all probability, was at work in the initial formation of the mutual friendships. The conditions under which shared values are operative in friendship formation, as compared with other possible factors—such as propinquity or interdependence—would seem to warrant intensive research.[23]

---

22. He finds that the evaluational criteria ranked by seniors correspond more closely to the rankings of their actual advisers (regardless of the adviser they chose on the sociometric questionnaire) than did the rankings of freshmen with their actual advisers.

23. Empirical beginnings, and some debate, on this matter can be found in Lundberg and Beazley (1948), Lundberg, Hertzler and Dickson (1949) and Maisonneuve (1952). These studies compare the relative importance of propinquity with various dimensions of "status homophily," as friendship determinants in a small college, a large university and a French boarding school, respectively. Also see the review of Homans (1950) by Rogers (1952) which represents the stand of the sociometrists—who emphasize the role of choice in human relations and invoke the somewhat mystical concept of "tele"—as opposed to the "interactionists" who tend much more to emphasize proximity. And see, too, the Merton *et al.* (forthcoming) and Lipset, Trow and Coleman (1955) studies. Of course, this is not an either-or situation. It demands the specification of conditions under which one or another of these several factors is more likely to be operative.

## *Interdependent Individuals*
## *Demand Conformity of Each Other*

The instrumental value—the "benefits"—of conformity tells us that individuals will generally *desire* to adhere to the opinions, attitudes and habits of those with whom they are motivated to interact. The "social reality" aspect of group life tells us that individuals influence each other's perceptions, so that an individual's way of *"seeing"* things, may be limited to a large degree, by the extent of his social ties. Now, there is an aspect of interpersonal relations—the last one we shall discuss here—which is, in a sense, the obverse of these two, and it, too, contributes a "reason" for believing that interacting individuals will be homogeneous in their thinking and behaving. It is that groups *require* conformity of their members.

Some of the reasons why group members demand conformity of each other are worth looking into. First of all, individuals do not like to find their associates departing from a traditional way of "seeing" something. It is a very discomfiting experience for individuals to discover that one of their number proposes to "see" something in a new way. Consider, for example, the consequences of believing that witches do not exist, in the context of a witch-hunting Puritan community.

Secondly, groups like to preserve their identities, and one of the chief ways a group can make its boundary lines clear is by the requirement of uniform behavior on the parts of its members.

Third, and most important perhaps, is the fact that groups, like individuals, have goals; and group goals often cannot be achieved without consensus. That is to say, uniformity of opinion may be a *pre-requisite* for group action. In this connection, Festinger observes that "pressures toward uniformity" of opinion or attitude among group members "may arise because such uniformity is desirable or necessary in order for the group to move toward some goal."[24] Clearly, if individuals cannot agree on "what should come next," they cannot take collective action.[25]

---

24. He calls this "group locomotion." In Festinger (1950).
25. All this presupposes that an individual is motivated to retain his asso-

To this point, we have indicated a series of "reasons" which can be located in the literature of theory and research in the social sciences to account for the primarily social character of ostensibly individual opinions, attitudes and actions. We began, first of all, by pointing to the "benefits" for the individual of conformity to the opinions of others in terms of the satisfactions that come with acceptance and achievement of desired status. Next, we spoke about the manner in which groups function as providers of standards and meanings for their members, and consequently the dependence of an individual on those about him for the definition of "social reality." In the course of our discussion we looked, too, at some fundamentals in the process of norm formation, and we saw how interaction among individuals operates to produce shared standards of judgment, opinions, and ways of behaving.[26] We suggested, in the following section, that interaction is not the only way to explain why members of groups typically possess shared ways of thinking and acting, for initial attractions based on similarity of values may often *precede* regular interaction. And, finally, we indicated some of the reasons why groups are likely to insist on uniformity of opinion.

Thus, we have tried to make clear, primarily from the literature of small group research, why we are convinced that studying the relatively small groups of people to which an individual is attached, is a major key to understanding the content and the dynamics of individual opinions and actions. This is an appropriate point to hoist some warning signals for

ciation with this group. Such motivation may be a purely voluntary matter or may, perhaps, be a consequence of the need for solidarity in a dangerous environment, or of the need to attain some goal which requires collective action. It should be clear, furthermore, that we are more concerned here with the "automatic" controls implicit in the aspects of group life we have been discussing than in coercion or any other "special" measures which groups may take to enforce conformity. Thus, in everyday life, individuals do not depart from group norms because they do not want to surrender the "benefits" of conformity (acceptance, friendship, leadership, attainment of private goals, etc.); because they do not like to threaten their own mental security by permitting themselves to "see" what others do not see; and the like. This is what we mean by "automatic." On this point, see Homans (1950) on "social control."

26. Of course, the *processes* of interpersonal influence and communication have barely been hinted at up to this point. Much more of this subject can be found in Chapter V below on "Interpersonal Networks."

the reader, particularly relating to the oversimplifications we are employing.

## Some Hasty Qualifications

We sometimes talk as if people belong to only one group; or we may imply, at other times, that only the groups to which an individual *belongs* influence his opinions, though we are fully aware that the study of "reference" groups is a primary focus of current research; and at still other times, we may talk as if we had established beyond doubt that individuals take their standards only from small groups of others with whom they are personally acquainted and never from people whom they don't know personally or from mass media. Sometimes, too, we talk as if no other structure except the informal group exists in the world and as if no mechanisms of control or sanctions other than interpersonal influence and ostracism were operative. Very often, we sound as if all standards, judgments, values and ideas which govern an individual's thinking and acting *originate* within the small groups in which they are "anchored" (maintained and enforced).[27] For all these, we plead over-simplification.

And let it be noted, again, that we are aware of the sometimes misleading connotations of the word "group." It is the role that *other people* play in the communications process in which we are interested, and the use of the word "group" is often simply a shorthand device to connote the significant "others" with whom an individual associates. Which kinds of "others" are significant, is a problem we shall attempt to tackle

---

27. It is well worth noting here that reference group theory and research and small group theory and research have not yet been conceptually integrated. Merton and Kitt's (1950) analysis of the implications of data from *The American Soldier* for reference group theory suggests many points at which a knowledge of the small membership groups of the respondent is basic to the reference group concept. Some of the questions we raise at this point can be found in Merton and Kitt, e.g., do individuals relate themselves only to others whom they know personally or also to impersonal status categories such as, say, 'all draft-exempt war workers,' or 'high society.' If the latter is the case as well, then, our present interest immediately directs us to inquire into the mechanisms by which one establishes 'contact' with such anonymous others. Opinion leader research can make a major contribution at this point.

from time to time, although not in a systematic way. For it still will not serve us well to tangle either with precise definitions of different kinds of groups or with complex speculations concerning the actual interplay of groups in the lives of actual individuals. Let us suggest only that at this point in our knowledge, precise definitions, learned speculations, or "answers" of any kind are all considerably less helpful than the kinds of questions which we have seen—and which we shall continue to see—emerge at every turn, for questions will point the way to empirical research.

Finally, a word about "conformity." Our discussion of the consequences of deviation and the "benefits" of conformity, etc., is on the level of agreement or divergence of opinion among intimately interacting individuals. Obviously, this is quite a different level from the one on which current political discussions concerning conformity and orthodoxy in American thought are taking place. The only implication in this text for the latter discussion is the following: A non-conformist on the level of the larger society is likely to be in close touch with another, like-minded non-conformist with whom he conforms.

Now that we have explained ourselves, we shall conclude this chapter. In closing, however, we should reiterate that we have *not* been trying to establish simply that individuals in primary group interaction develop norms governing their interaction. That is a well-established proposition, which the studies reported here certainly support. What we *have* been trying to say is that even an individual's seemingly personal opinions and attitudes may be by-products of interpersonal relations. The evidence strongly suggests that opinions and attitudes often are maintained, sometimes generated, sometimes merely enforced, in conjunction with others. In short, we have attempted to marshal evidence for our contention that the individual expression of opinions and attitudes is not strictly an individual affair.

# CHAPTER V

# The Role of the Group in Influencing
# Change: Implications for
# Mass Media Research

IT FOLLOWS from what we have said so far that a *change* in an individual's opinion or attitude must be something more than it appears to be. For if opinions and attitudes are created and maintained in association with others, then a change in these ideas obviously cannot be a purely individual matter either. There surely must be social repercussions.

Now, the problem of mass media effectiveness, which was the starting point for our present interest in small group research, focuses directly on *change*. We are trying to learn more about the effect of mass media attempts to influence people to change their ways of thinking and behaving. And since we have now established that the opinions and attitudes which are the targets of mass persuasion campaigns may well be anchored in interpersonal relations, our next move is evident. We will want to inquire into whatever evidence is available in small group research for dealing with the problem of how individual opinions and attitudes are changed, given the fact that the individual himself is not so free to change unilaterally as we used to think.

Of course, some of the ideas we have encountered thus far should be directly applicable to the study of change. The idea that there are "benefits" to be derived from conformity, or that individuals will be influenced to "see" things in the same way that others around them do, clearly imply that individuals who change their opinions or attitudes will be likely to change them in the direction of a group norm. Let us examine some of the studies that illustrate this.

## The Group as a Medium of Change

First of all, there is the kind of change in opinions, attitudes or values which may accompany a motivated move from one group to another. That is to say, seeking acceptance in a new circle may lead an individual to bring his opinions and attitudes into line with the new group, and may, in turn, result in group support for him. This is a basic proposition which has guided applied work and research in various fields of re-education and re-habilitation, leadership training, prejudice reduction, etc. That part of Bales' (1945) study of Alcoholics Anonymous which analyzes the process through which a new member becomes integrated into the group, is a good case in point. According to the analysis, the initiate in this fraternity of reformed alcoholics first obtains recognition and response—in place of the condemnation to which he is accustomed—"through the admission of thoughts and activities which, before, he had been desperately trying to hide." And soon he begins to feel that he actually has the power to resist drink. When that happens, a second and perhaps more important step is scheduled. He is asked to take part in a program of activity which puts him in the role of advice-giver, teacher, and protagonist of the norms, for still newer members than himself. At this point, according to Bales, the ex-alcoholic begins to feel not only that he can resist, but that the craving has *left him.* The group thus serves not only as a support for the goal that membership itself signifies, but as the *medium* for an actual change in an emotional drive. More recent examples of this same sort of therapeutic work via the introduction of new members (returning prisoners of war, the chronic unemployed, etc.) into transitional therapeutic "communities" can be found, particularly in the work of a group of English social scientists and psychiatrists.[1]

---

1. See, for example, Wilson *et al.* (1952) and Jones (1953). References to other applications of these ideas may be found in Roseborough (1953).

In other words, seeking and gaining acceptance in a new circle seem to lead an individual to bring his opinions and attitudes into line with the new group. If our review of the Newcomb study at Bennington College, and our first interpretation of the item cited from *The American Soldier* (concerning the assimilation by "green" replacements of the attitudes of combat veterans) are recalled in this connection, the point we are making should be clear.[2] This kind of change corresponds to the type we have described under the heading of the instrumental function, or the "benefits" of conformity.

Another type of change which corresponds somewhat to the instrumental function, but most of all to the "social reality" aspect of conformity can be examined in some of the studies which constitute the tradition of research in prestige suggestion. A moment's reflection on the basic model of prestige suggestion studies is enough to indicate in what way these studies belong here. The typical experiment in this tradition is an attempt to change a previously expressed, or taken-for-granted, set of opinions, by attributing contrary opinions to presumably prestigeful figures or groups. Implied here is the importance of knowing exactly how "prestigeful" a given figure or group happens to be for each experimental subject, before the effect, or lack of effect, of a specific suggestion can be understood.[3] For example, an early study by Asch demonstrates that experimental groups of individuals were much more influenced to change their opinions (in this case, rankings of different professions in order of importance) when they were told of the opinions of a group which they consid-

2. These studies, as we have remarked, are the core of reference group theory. The principles involved obviously pertain also to small group studies, and since the latter have been so much confined to the study of one group at a time, the impetus to socio-psychological thinking is a very healthy one. Research on the process of 'moving' from one group to another would be a logical problem for the agenda of a combined investigation in small group and reference group theory. The studies cited here are Newcomb (1952) and Merton and Kitt (1950).

3. A recent review of some of these studies of the last 10 to 15 years concludes that the effectiveness of suggestion seems to depend on (a) the degree of clarity in the situation and (b) the relative congeniality of the prestige figure or group. Berenda (1950), Chapter 1. See also Miller and Dollard (1941) for reports of experiments in prestige suggestion from the point of view of learning theory; this volume also contains a synopsis of various views of "imitation" as a social process.

ered congenial than when they learned of the opinions of a group which they considered antagonistic.[4] Suggestion is not simply a bandwagon device. Only when a figure or a group is particularly prestigeful for the subject will there be reason to expect that suggestions attributed to that figure or group will influence changes of opinion.

The study of how such changes come about, and to what extent they really are changes, was almost completely ignored, and apparently misunderstood, until gestalt psychologists began to investigate what went on in the subjects' minds when they responded to prestige suggestion.[5] We shall not deal with that subject here—except insofar as it also seems to have led the way to the study of the effects of prestige suggestion in *actual group situations.* In a study of the experimental modification of children's food preferences through social suggestion, Karl Duncker (1938) discovered that children were more likely to follow the lead of other children than to follow adults in making food choices from among several alternatives with which they were presented.[6] Thus, when an adult chose first, only 4 in 17 children followed suit; when other children were predecessors, these same children made 17 in 20 identical choices. In other words, although these children regarded adults as authorities, authority alone was not enough. They followed their peers, it seems, because they identified themselves with them. The most striking proof of this is that among children known to have a high degree of mutual friendship, there was complete agreement on the foods that were selected.

A recent study by Berenda (1950) tells much the same story. Using a pattern of experimentation devised by Asch—which we shall report immediately below—she discovers that classmates are more influential on their peers than their teach-

4. Asch (1940), cited in Berenda (1950), Chap. 1.
5. Interviewing subjects in order to discover what pressures they were responding to resulted, first of all, in increasing specificity concerning the kinds of "authorities" which were prestigeful and this led, apparently, to a consideration of the possibility that one's own peer group might be highly prestigeful. Secondly, it led to the discovery that apparent changes of attitude are often really not changes at all. For discussion of this second point, see Lewis (1952) and for a theoretical presentation within the framework of a discussion of cognitive organization, see Krech and Crutchfield (1948), Chapters 3, 4 and 9.
6. Cited in Berenda (1950), Chap. 1.

ers are. Thus, we have some indication from this branch of research that "authority" figures may have less influence over opinions than congenial groups have.

The current leader of this research tradition, Solomon Asch (1952), decided "to study the social and personal conditions that induce individuals to resist or to yield to group pressures when the latter are perceived to be contrary to fact."[7] In effect, this is a study of the ability of the group to force changes in opinions from "right" to "wrong."

The procedure was as follows: Each experimental subject was placed in a group of seven others, who—unknown to him —were collaborating with the experimenter. All the members of the group were then asked to match an ordinary line several inches long with one of a set of three other lines, only one of which was equal in length to the test line. The judgment of the naive experimental subject was called for last—that is, following the intentionally incorrect judgments of each of the seven others. These intentional errors of the majority were large and very obvious, yet fully one-third of the experimental subjects capitulated in one-half or more of their trials. In contrast, a control group which had not been subjected to the experimental situation made virtually no errors at all. Commenting on the strong impact which the distorted estimates of the majority achieved, Asch points out that "the critical subject— whom we had placed in the position of a *minority of one* in the midst of a *unanimous majority*—faced possibly for the first time in his life, a situation in which a group unanimously contradicted the evidence of his senses."[8]

---

7. Note that Asch demonstrates aspects of group pressure and of group-engendered "social reality" even in an empirically verifiable situation. In other words, the unstructuredness and ambiguity which were considered inherent conditions for the operation of social pressures (as in the Sherif experiment discussed above, pp. 45-48) are here completely absent.

8. Asch reports that in his experiment there are apparently three kinds of yielders: Those whose *perceptions* are actually changed by the majority and who are not troubled at all by doubt; those whose *judgments* are distorted (this is the largest category), that is, they imagine that their perceptions are somehow incorrect and that they had better follow the majority judgment; and finally, those who know that the majority is wrong, but who follow "because of an overmastering need not to appear different from or inferior to others, because of an inability to tolerate the appearance of defectiveness in the eyes of the group." One quarter of the subjects remained unyielding throughout.

Perhaps we should anticipate an objection here, as we did in the case of the Sherif experiment, that no real-life situation could possibly match such a preposterous experimental situation. Our mass communications experience tells us otherwise, however, for we have reason to believe that one of the major keys to the high degree of communications effectiveness within totalitarian states is media "monopolization." That is to say, when there is no possibility of counterpropaganda, or an overt show of resistance, chances for the success of a propaganda effort based, even, on a manifest "lie," are very good.[9] By introducing a slight variation into the experiment itself, Asch provides us with the most striking support for the analogy just proposed. In this variation, the naive subject is confronted with a majority of *all but one*. This is accomplished either by the addition of another naive subject or by instructing one of the collaborators to depart from the majority mis-estimate and make correct judgments. In such a situation, the number of errors of the experimental subjects drops dramatically.

The studies we have seen so far all illustrate the way in which the group functions as a medium for changing individual opinions, attitudes and habits. It would follow that if motivated group membership is really so closely linked with pressures toward conformity, then group pressures on opinions and attitudes should be most strongly felt by those who are most attached to the group. That is precisely the point of one final study which we should like to report here. It deals with the relationship between conformity and group cohesiveness. A measure of cohesiveness is, in reality, a measure of the strength of the ties holding the people in a group to each other. Back (1952) created groups (two members each) of

---

9. Actually, in any situation where propaganda is unopposed, there is reason to look for comparatively greater effects. For some examples, see Lazarsfeld (1942). One is tempted to note, in passing, that the best known of all experiments in prestige suggestion was reported sometime ago by Hans Christian Anderson in *The Emperor's New Clothes*. This is a report which tells of how word went round, one day, that "only wise men" would be physically capable of seeing the beautiful new clothes that the Emperor had chosen for the parade. So everyone, including the Emperor, praised the great beauty of the Emperor's clothes, despite the fact that the Emperor, in "reality," was stark naked. Only a little child who, apparently, was not "suggestible" because he did not aspire to the company of the wise, disturbed the peace with a brutal attack on this manifestation of "social reality."

high and low cohesiveness by using a set of instructions designed to make individuals more and less attractive for each other. Each group member was asked, first, to write a preliminary interpretation of a set of photographs and then, to confer with his partner in order to see whether the story of either member could be improved. Unbeknown to the subject the set of pictures that each partner received (and saw only once before they were removed) contained slight differences which would allow for different interpretations. Thus, when the partners confronted each other they also met, necessarily, with each other's somewhat different interpretations. The low-cohesive groups, it was found, tended to react passively to the realization of difference while high-cohesive groups tended to set about reconciling their differences. In addition to the observational evidence from the final stories which makes this clear, the subjects, also, were able to report what happened. Thus, in answer to the question, "Did you think that your partner tried to influence you?" less than half of the members of low-cohesive groups, but more than two-thirds of the high-cohesive groups, answered that they had felt the pressure of their partner's attempt to influence them.

Furthermore, Back tells us, influencing in the high-cohesiveness situation met with greater success—i.e., was more effective —than in the situation of low cohesiveness. But that is something to which we will return in a later section.

To this point, then, we have attempted to illustrate by reference to several studies stemming from two different research traditions ("group dynamics" and "prestige suggestion") how interpersonal relations tend to be much more than passive social signposts pointing to the probable location of a shared set of opinions, attitudes, or actions. We have tried to show that interpersonal relations, to the extent that they are positively motivated, are continuously *active* in the preservation of group norms, in the disciplining of deviates, and in the exertion of influence toward conformity.

## *The Group as a Target of Change*[10]

Now that we have seen that people, in close personal con-act, are partners not only in creating and maintaining each other's ideas, but also in changing them, we must ask—for this was our motive in the first place—how this knowledge has been or might be applied to the study of influence attempts which originate *outside* the group. Translated into mass media language, this problem might read: Is there evidence that interpersonal relations act also to modify the effect of mass media campaigns on individuals?

Perhaps we can begin best with a negative statement: Everything we have seen so far would lead us to expect that an attempt to change an individual's opinion or attitude will *not* succeed if his opinion is one which he shares with others to whom he is attached, and if the others do not go along with the change. Kelley and Volkart (1952) in a study of Boy Scout troops, are able to demonstrate this proposition very clearly.

Two kinds of scouts were identified on the basis of an atti-tude questionnaire: those who valued their troop membership highly and those who did not. The authors set out to study whether those who valued their troop membership highly would show greater resistance to an attempt to change atti-tudes connected with Boy Scout life than those who did not feel strongly about their membership. This hypothesis was put to the test by introducing to the Boy Scout troop a guest speaker who, in his speech, implicitly attacked the worthwhile-ness of camping and of woodcraft, two of the chief concerns of Boy Scout lore. Following the speech, a questionnaire was

---

10. To order the material in this chapter, we are employing, though per-haps with a slight shift in usage, a distinction suggested in Cartwright (1951). Reviewing some of the principles associated with group-anchored changes of opinion and attitude, Cartwright divides change studies into those where the group is a "medium" of change, and those where the group is a "target" of change. If it is borne in mind that the subject under examination is, in both cases, the individual (and not a group), we can identify "medium" studies by the fact that the pressure for change arises *within* the group and aims at particular members, while in "target" studies, the pressure for change originates *outside* the group but seeks to reach individuals most effectively by first influencing their groups. "Target" attempts, in other words, presuppose and build on the strength of the group as a "medium" of change.

administered to determine the degree to which the communication was effective in changing attitudes toward the two
activities as they had previously been recorded in a "before"
questionnaire. And the conclusions that were reached bear out
the hypothesis, namely, that members of a group can be influenced to deviate from group-centered values to the extent that
their group membership is less important for them. And the
converse, of course, is evident: Those who do value their
group membership highly will resist outside attempts to change
the opinions which they share with their group.

Unquestionably, when what is communicated assails prevailing opinions, attitudes or habits that are shared with highly
valued others, then that influence attempt will surely be re-
sisted. Here, then, is concrete evidence for one of the ways in
which interpersonal relations intervene in the mass communications process to modify the effects of communications.

In the same way, it follows that an individual will more
readily respond to an influence-attempt if he perceives that
others support him in a proposed change. This hypothesis
underlies the well-known "group decision" experiments pioneered by Kurt Lewin and his associates.[11] Each of these
studies is concerned with inducing change in individual behavior and, basically, each attempts to demonstrate the effectiveness of group discussion (followed by "group decision")
for achieving change.

One of these studies compares the effectiveness of group
discussion and decision with private instruction:[12] At a certain
maternity hospital, it was customary to give instruction in
child-care to new mothers before they were discharged, and
this instruction was customarily given privately to one woman
at a time. An experiment was devised to compare the relative
effect of such individual instruction with group discussion. To
do this, some mothers were given individual instruction as
before, and others were formed into groups of six and guided

11. It would not be quite accurate to say that these studies pose a clear-
cut hypothesis and then set about testing it rigorously. As we shall note
below, these studies may all be criticized for the haziness with which they
are formulated and the alternative interpretations which are permitted by
their findings.
12. Lewin (1952), p. 467.

in a discussion which culminated in a "decision"—that is, participants were asked to indicate, by a show of hands, whether they had decided to comply with the suggested program. The time devoted to the group discussion was not more than that devoted to a single mother in individual instruction, and the subject matter was the same in both situations. Follow-up interviews after two weeks and after a month, indicated that participants in the group discussion adhered much more closely to the child-care program than did the mothers who had received individual instruction.

Other experiments compare the effectiveness of a lecture with that of group discussion and decision. In the earliest experiment in this series, for example, an expert on nutrition lectured to three groups of club women on the nutritional and patriotic justifications for the wartime food campaign to buy and serve "unpopular" cuts of meat.[13] Another three groups were involved in a discussion of these same problems as well as of the obstacles confronting "housewives like ourselves" who might consider cooperating with the campaign. The discussion groups were also asked at the end of the session who among them would be willing to try the suggested foods, and hands were raised and counted. A follow-up sometime later showed that only three per cent of the women who heard the lecture, but thirty-two per cent of those who participated in the group discussion and decision, had actually served the meats.

In this experiment, the lecturer and the group discussion leader were two different people, and no attempt was made to match the content of the lecture and of the discussion. A subsequent experiment, however, which was aimed at increasing the home consumption of milk, did take these variables into account.[14] Six small groups of housewives living in the same neighborhood were divided between lecture and group discussion situations. This time, however, the lecturer herself also served as discussion leader and the content transmitted at both types of sessions was comparable, we are told. A check-up after two weeks, and again after four weeks, revealed that the group decision which followed the discussion was consider-

13. *Ibid.*, p. 463.
14. *Ibid.*, p. 466.

ably more effective in increasing milk consumption—that is, in changing family food habits—than the lecture.

A more recent example from a different substantive area into which this experimental technique has been extended, may prove illuminating.[15] The twenty-nine foremen in a factory of 400 men were randomly divided into three groups—a lecture group, a discussion group, and a control group. The lecture and discussion groups (but not the control group) were confronted with the results of the semi-annual foremen's ratings on which are recorded a foreman's impression of the performance of the men under him in terms of such things as willingness to cooperate, accuracy, effective use of work time, etc. The results indicated that foremen tended to give higher ratings to the performance of men in higher-grade jobs than they gave to men in lower-grade jobs. There was substantial reason to believe, management felt, that this resulted from a kind of halo effect associated with the higher-grade jobs. The lecture group was told about the results and instructed in how to go about the task of assigning truly equitable ratings. The discussion group, in its characteristic way, considered the facts and arrived at the same unanimous "decision" to change the rating practices (in the same way that had been prescribed to the lecture group). In both cases, the time allotted was the same, and the subject considered was the same: "how to rate the man, not the job." The greater effectiveness of the discussion group was clearly demonstrated in the next rating period: the foremen who had participated in the discussion and decision substantially revised their rating habits, while those in the lecture group, and in the control group, did not.

The importance of these studies for an adequate understanding of the role of interpersonal relations in the mass communications process is quite evident. Apparently, something about interacting with others relative to a proposed change, compared with the isolation of the individual in both lectures and private instruction, produces a marked behavioral change. It is not at all evident, however, exactly which element or ele-

---

15. Levine and Butler (1952). Other studies of the effectiveness of this method of achieving change in industry are Marrow and French (1945) and Coch and French (1952).

ments in the discussion do the trick. There are two reasons why we say this: First of all, because there are unfortunate experimental flaws in every one of these studies; secondly, because assuming even that the experimental tests were more carefully controlled, it is by no means clear from these studies what accounts for the "reception" that the groups accorded these influence-attempts. Let us spend a moment with each of these problems.

(1) The experimental design of these studies is by no means satisfying. In some of the studies, the *content* of the lecture and of the discussion seems to have been different; in others, we are not informed whether the *time* factor was controlled or not; in still another, the discussion group was *forewarned* that there would be a follow-up, while in the lecture no such information was given; and so on. But these are relatively simple matters—and they are generally taken into account in the more recent studies (though there are still flagrant exceptions).

More important, however, is the fact that the several key elements — for example, discussion, decision, perception of others' opinions—have not been experimentally isolated.[16] Thus, it might be that the mere fact of discussion and the greater "involvement" that comes with discussion is enough to account for the observed effect. Or it might be that it is simply the "decision" that makes the difference. Again, it may well be that the key factor here is perception of the willingness of others to go along with the proposed change.

In our opinion, it is this last factor that seems most important. Support comes from a recent dissertation by Bennett (1952) which reports on an experimental investigation of these problems and points to "decision" and "perceived group unanimity" as the key factors. The fact that this research confirms the importance of perceiving the support of others gives weight to the interpretation we offer here. Thus, Bennett

---

16. Lewin (1952), p. 465, seems to suggest that the combination discussion-decision is what is important. If that is so, one wonders, at the very least, why it could not have been tested by requesting this same sort of "decision"—raising hands in affirmation—following the lecture as well.

reports that "the factors of decision and perceived unanimity of such decision were found to be significantly related to the carrying out of the specified action. Group discussion, other things equal, was not more effective than lecture, nor did public identification of individuals' decisions contribute appreciably to obtained differences."

It seems, then, that individuals are more willing to accept and implement a proposed change when they perceive that others are also willing to go along with it. Thus, the new mothers, the club women, the housewives and the foremen could more readily accept the influence-attempt which was aimed at them when they had the assurance that they were doing so in the company of other group members. We are assuming, in other words, that the individuals in the lecture and private situations might even have been as "motivated" to change as were those in the discussions, but that the chances of translating their motivations into action were considerably reduced when the action demanded unilateral departure—as far as these individuals knew—from some socially acccepted way of doing things. But all this is far from being experimentally established.

(2) There·is a second problem that emerges in connection with this series of "group decision" experiments which has important implications for the problem of this chapter. Specifically, we are given almost no indication, even of a speculative sort, to account for the cordial "reception" which the discussion groups seem to have accorded the influence-attempts which were aimed at them. As a matter of fact, we have already seen—for example in the Boy Scout study (p. 73)— how an influence which seeks to change some shared way of behavior is likely to encounter very strong resistance. What, then, explains the collapse of group resistance before an influence which contradicts group norms? In what way does the influence make its way into the group; does someone change first, for example, and then influence the others from "within"? At what point do members begin to perceive that the group standard is beginning to change? What kinds of changes will be accepted by what kinds of groups—or is it conceivable that

any influence whatsoever can be communicated to individuals so long as they are sitting with their peers? And most important, perhaps, what is the difference, for which kinds of influences, if the group is a durable, intimately interacting set of individuals or if it is composed of individuals brought together for the specific influencing session and then dispersed again?[17]

Such questions demand answers because scientific thinking can never be content merely with the knowledge that something "works." We cannot report any comprehensive answers here, simply because none exist; however, a review of the studies in this field and a reading of the several tentative summaries[18] of the principles which appear to be involved in this kind of change leads us to single out the following three generalizations:

(a) Many of these studies gives us reason to suspect that the influence directed at the group to change an attitude or a way of behaving consists, in part, at least, of an appeal to more deep-lying values which *also are part of the group's norms.* Thus, what appears as a simple substitution of one way of thinking or behaving for another may not be so simple after all. For it may well be that the success of this method of group influence depends upon wiring up the new norm to a basic value which also is shared by the group; then, the group change is not a simple substitution of one norm for another, but a change of the frame of reference within which a particular area of behavior or thinking is perceived. For example, the success which followed the attempt to overcome the resistance of housewives to the use of "unpopular" foods may have been the product of guiding the group to the recognition that this particular behavior belonged within the framework

---

17. This, for example, was the case with the groups at the maternity hospital. In the other experiments cited here, the groups tended to know each other more or less well before the meetings, and expected, presumably, to see each other again afterwards. All of these factors, however, must be varied in order to really understand the principles involved here.

18. The few statements that deal explicitly with the principles underlying these change studies come, naturally, from Lewin himself and also from two of his major associates. See Lewin and Grabbe (1945), Cartwright (1951), and Festinger (1950). It may be that the aforementioned Bennett (1952) does contain some of the "answers."

of another of the group's valued norms, namely, the norm of patriotism. The group then proceeded to affirm the new behavior with reference to the old value.[19]

(b) A second characteristic of these studies is the "objectification" of the problem. The very use of fact-finding techniques, the discussions of what "housewives like ourselves" would do in a similar situation, etc., may be clues to the puzzle of locating the *wedge* via which a new influence makes its way into a group despite a contrary norm. This goes a little distance toward answering the question of "how" an influence manages to receive the consideration of what might otherwise be a highly resistant group.

(3) A third element which seems to figure in most of these studies is "catharsis." The group discussion is conducive, apparently, to "talking out" the emotional insulation surrounding a given attitude or way of behaving, and the removal of this wrapper seems to make the norm more vulnerable to the influence of a counter-proposal.[20]

These are only three interesting possibilities to account for some of what goes on in these change studies.[21] There are

---

19. This *technique* of changing attitudes is well discussed in Newcomb (1950), Chap. 7. It is also reminiscent of the justification that Gunnar Myrdal (1944) offers for his optimism about the possibility of changing attitudes toward the Negro by appealing to the basic values of The American Creed. Neither of these works has *groups* specifically in mind, of course. Why, then, should we find that changing opinions and attitudes is more successful when the change is incorporated into the norm framework of a *group?* Our guess is that the only difference here between the group and individuals is the perception of the *social support* of significant others and the *enforcement* which interacting individuals require of each other particularly when important group values are concerned. As Cartwright (1951) suggests: "In attempts to change attitudes, values or behavior the more relevant they are to the basis of attraction of the group, the greater will be the influence that the group can exert upon them."
20. Discussed in Kagan (1952).
21. An additional explanation which seems to be particularly plausible has been suggested by Benjamin B. Ringer, of the Bureau of Applied Social Research. Noting the fact that some of these studies do not involve real-life groups at all, but rather individuals brought together specifically for the occasion, Ringer suggests that the success of these experiments and the "receptivity" of these groups to the influence-attempts directed at them, results from the fact that a *new group norm* is being established for the first time and that only the old, private standards of the separate individuals are being changed thereby. In fact, this suggestion directs us to propose that even those experiments which were conducted with real-life groups (the wartime food experiments, for example) may not have involved changing a norm that was already anchored in the group (since these groups, *qua* groups,

many others. Thus, for example, our opinion leader interest would lead us to ask whether it might not be that particular members—opinion leaders—in every kind of group tend to be more responsive than their fellows to extra-group suggestions and more influential, in turn, in effecting a change of group standards.

In any event, the bearing of these studies on our own problems should be clear. We have come to small group research to learn something about the ways in which interpersonal relations might "intervene" in the mass communications process, particularly in the communication of influence via mass media "campaigns." In this chapter we have focused on the fact that shared opinions and attitudes go along, hand in hand, with interpersonal relations. In this way we found that interpersonal relations "intervene" by inducing *resistance* to those influences which go counter to those ideas that individuals share with others they hold in esteem; and, on the other hand, we found that when individuals share norms which are in harmony with an outside influence or when they are willing to incorporate a proposed change into group norms, then interpersonal relations may act as *facilitators* of change.

---

may have had no felt standard relative to food) but may instead have served to introduce a norm relative to food for the first time. It is possible then that if the influence-attempt was really directed at a group norm of a real-life group which related, say, to some salient group concern, the resistance to an outside influence-attempt would be particularly strong.

# CHAPTER VI

# Interpersonal Networks:

# Communicating within the Group

IN THE INTRODUCTION to this Section, it was suggested that there were two "active ingredients" which might contribute to an explanation of the intervening role played by interpersonal relations in the mass communications process. The first of these, the group-anchorage of opinions and attitudes, was the subject of the preceding section.

The second "ingredient" which demands attention is person-to-person communication. Interpersonal communication is simply another name for interaction, and by definition, communication is, of course, a component of all interpersonal relations. Now, we want to look again into small group studies to inquire in what ways informal interpersonal communication might account for the success (or lack of success) of an influence-attempt stemming from the mass media. The illustrations from mass media research reported in Section One as well as some of the studies cited in the preceding chapters suggest the following:

1. Some individuals seem to serve as personal transmitters for others. Without these relay individuals, messages originating from the mass media might not reach otherwise unexposed people. This, of course, is the major part of the opinion leader idea; we call it the *relay function* of interpersonal relations.

2. Furthermore, personal influence seems to be singularly effective. When a mass media influence-attempt coincides with an interpersonal communication, it appears to have much

greater chance of success. We call this the *reinforcement function.*

We shall be concerned here with the processes by which individuals in primary relations communicate among themselves. We want to know, for example, what uniformities have been observed in interpersonal communications; we want to know who—in what situations—is likely to wield influence over others; we want to know whether the individuals who introduce communications to their groups are marked by any special characteristics; we want to know where in a group to look for the first signs that a proposed change in opinion or attitude will be acceptable. And once we have learned something about the characteristics of interpersonal communication and the networks of person-to-person influence, we shall want to know in what ways influences stemming from the mass media might be hooked up with these interpersonal networks.

Specifically, our plan is as follows: We shall devote the major portion of this chapter to an examination of studies which treat various aspects of communication *within* a group of interacting individuals. Having done that, we shall turn, in Chapter VI, to the problem of communication *to* the group in an attempt to indicate some of the ways in which influences stemming from outside the group—such as mass media influences—might make effective contact with individuals via their interpersonal networks of communication. Given the sheltered character of small group research, it is easy to understand that the material available for a discussion of communication *to* a group from outside, is very sparse, while the material bearing on communication *within* a group is much more abundant.

This subject of intra-group, or interpersonal, communication divides naturally into two roughly delineable compartments corresponding, we think, to two major approaches in small group research. One approach considers the *patterns* of interpersonal transmission and the links which hold communicating individuals together. The other, a more diagnostic approach, attempts to single out key roles—what we shall call *strategic points*—which are crucial for the flow of information and influence within a group. Thus, one approach emphasizes patterns and networks on the level of the group as a whole, while the other spotlights strategic points and is concerned with various communication roles, particularly the role of group leader or influential. Variations in both patterns and strategic points are associated, we think, with three major factors which we call (a) group *structures,* (b) group "cultures" or *climates,* and (c) group *situations.*

To recapitulate: We shall report first those studies which deal with the *patterns* of interpersonal communication, dividing these into three: patterns influenced by the *structure,* the *climate,* or the *situation* in which a group finds itself. Then, we shall do the same with studies dealing with *strategic points.* Having considered these two aspects of communication *within* the group, we shall turn, in Chapter VI, to the handful of studies which provide evidence on how these interpersonal networks link up with influences—such as mass media influences—stemming from "the world outside"; that is, we shall inquire into the part played by people in the transmission of communication *to* the group.

## The Patterns of Transmission

We are interested here in what holds people together in an interpersonal communications network, and we are interested in the variety of communications patterns that take shape under different social conditions. As has been announced, we shall consider these matters under three separate headings, the first of which is concerned with the influence on interpersonal communication of the structure of social connections among individuals.

### (A.) STRUCTURAL CONNECTIONS: THE NETWORKS
#### OF COMMUNICATIONS FLOW

Differences in the degree of mutual attraction among individuals, differences in the degree of their interdependence, differences in status, and, of course, mere differences in such things as propinquity or group size will make for significant differences in the rate of contact and communication and often, too, in the content of what is communicated. These are some of the elements of group structure, and there are a variety of studies to show how they are related to interpersonal communication.

Festinger *et al.* demonstrate, for example, how friendship ties operate as links in a communications network, in their studies of the transmission of rumors in two communities.[1] In "Regent Hill," a rumor spread to 62 per cent of those who had close friends in the community, to 42 per cent of those who had only acquaintances and to 33 per cent of those who claimed no friends at all in the neighborhood. In their Westgate study of the students' housing development, sociometric friendship choices accounted for the direction taken by almost half (six of fourteen) of the instances in which a planted rumor was passed on. Moreno (1953), too, studied a rumor and found that it followed very closely the path he had predicted for it in terms of the "psycho-social networks" which he had mapped out.[2] "Friendship between two people," says Festinger, "implies the existence of an active channel of communication."[3]

The sociometric method permits the study of communications flow in terms of an objectively delineable pattern of individual relationships. Thus, a rumor or a bit of news or an action-stimulant introduced into a social group whose sociometric connections are known, can be watched almost the way the doctor watches the flow of chalky liquid introduced into the human body during a fluoroscopic examination.

Rumor is not the only kind of interpersonal communication that has been studied this way. Jennings (1952), for example, tries to trace the transmission process by which relevant knowledge about girls running for election was spread among the 400 occupants at the New York State Training School for Girls. Jennings puts the problem this way: "Without a certain minimum publicity being spread to others by those who know and approve the individual's 'way of leading,' no individual can have a leadership position beyond his immediate interrelationships." She observes that the mechanism for publicity of this

---

1. Festinger, Schachter and Back (1950), Chap. 7.
2. For an interesting discussion of these networks and their relationship to both flow-of-influence and individual and group action, see Moreno's (1953) statement, pp. 440-450.
3. Festinger, Schachter and Back (1950), pp. 125-127.

sort is the immediate friendship group—"an interpersonal structure where the uniqueness of the individual as a personality is appreciated. . . ."[4] Now, when the overlap of these groups is extensive, that is, to the extent that individuals belong to more than one such group, there will be considerable shared knowledge; but we are told, where it is not well developed, shared knowledge will be restricted. Festinger's finding that rumors do not usually travel outside of self-contained clique structures is another way of expressing this same observation.[5]

An approach which examines *variations* of structure in the small group and the effect these have on the character of communications can also be singled out from the prolific work of Festinger and his associates. Here the key variable is the degree of group cohesiveness; and cohesiveness, one might say, is the cement of sociometric structure. In an experiment by Kurt Back (1952) which we have already mentioned, we learn that when people are more attached to each other, they exert greater influence over each other's opinions and, moreover, are more effective in their influencing. Thus, it will be recalled, when the groups were highly cohesive, the number of attempts at changing a partner's opinion were both greater in number and more successful than when the interpersonal relations were less cohesive. Similarly, the Westgate study demonstrates that there is greatest uniformity of opinion in those residental courts that are most cohesive, thus implying that there is more, and more effective, communication among the members of these courts.[6] Cohesiveness in this case was judged from the allocation of intra-court friendship choices.

In addition to friendship channels, there are of course other sorts of interpersonal channels. Back, *et al.* (1950), for example, studied the processes of rumor transmission in an industrial organization. The factory's hierarchy consisted of five levels and a total of 55 members. Information was obtained from the director and from several others about the formal and the informal structures that existed within the organiza-

4. Jennings calls this the "psyche group," contrasting it with a larger, more goal-oriented, more formally organized "socio group." The "psyche group" would seem to correspond, generally, to our idea of the primary group.
5. Festinger, Schachter and Back (1950), p. 127.
6. *Ibid.*, p. 92.

tion, and on the basis of this information, a small number of strategically placed "cooperating observers" were recruited by the experimenters. These observers were pledged to secrecy regarding their part in the study and were instructed to make a careful record of the content and the transmission channels of every rumor—planted one at a time by the experimenters over a four month period—that was passed on to them or that they overheard being told to others.[7] In this way, there were recorded 17 acts of communication resulting from several rumors whose content related to the entire organization. Of these, 11 were directed upward in the status hierarchy, four were directed to peers in the hierarchy, and only two communications were directed downward.

This study, it is important to remember, is concerned with informal communication patterns in the setting of a highly formal organization. It is interesting to speculate whether these upward-directed acts of informal communication reflect the more formally prescribed work-interaction patterns, or mobility aspirations, or perhaps, friendship patterns which cross status lines. To what extent would communications which are not directly relevant to the organization—say, communications about presidential elections, or World Series scores—flow in the same way? To what extent do communications beween, say, social classes in a community or between more and less prestigeful members of a small group parallel this case of the factory?[8]

---

7. By interviewing the entire membership of the organization at the end of the experimental period, the authors were able to ascertain that these cooperators had failed to record only 22 per cent of the communications that occurred; in other words, this method yielded 78 per cent of the desired information.

In general, there was not a great deal of communication concerning these rumors. The authors discuss several reasons for this including their suspicion that the cooperators themselves—who were chosen because of their key locations but who were not permitted to pass on anything they heard—may under ordinary circumstances have been important transmitting agents. Back's brief discussion of the assets and liabilities of several of the methods that have been used, or might be used, for the study of rumor transmission is very valuable.

8. These questions, of course, are raised again in later parts of this book. Specifically, it is asked whether interpersonal influencing in an urban community tends to take place between individuals of like status (or age, or gregariousness) or between individuals of differing status. And, again, it is asked whether the channels of interpersonal communication on one subject

All these are questions for which we do not have simple answers. But since we are concerned specifically with communication in informally organized small groups, perhaps we should attempt, at least, to place these problems in the small group context. If we ask whether communication even in small groups tends to be directed upward (from lower status to higher status members), the answer seems to be yes—but the yes needs considerable elaboration. Homans' analysis of this matter, for example, leads him to suggest, first, that "any single person interacts most of all with his equals."[9] At the same time, however, the higher a person's status, the more people will seek to communicate with him. In other words, higher ranking individuals are targets for communications from those below them in rank. Homans adds that these high ranking members, in turn, tend to address themselves to a larger number of group members than do lower ranking individuals.[10] Bales' studies at Harvard seem to corroborate these observations, though it is not quite clear to what extent his findings— which are based on discussion groups and problem-solving conferences—are generalizable to the more informal influencing that goes on between friends and neighbors, husbands and wives, workers on the job, etc.[11] Using a device for recording

---

—say, fashions—are the same as those employed for another subject—say, politics. See Part Two, Section Three. Later parts of the present chapter, too, treat the question of multiplicity of channels (see the "situational" aspects of communications, p. 94 ff. and p. 100 ff.). For discussion of content factors in upward and downward communication in informal organizations, see, e.g. Homans (1950), particularly p. 461, Kelley (1950), Thibaut (1950). These latter two are important studies of the relationship between membership in one or another of several hierarchically arranged groups (experimentally induced) and the frequency and content of communications behavior.

9. Homans (1950), p. 184.

10. *Ibid.*, pp. 182-3. In Homans' own words: "The higher a man's social rank, the larger will be the number of persons that originate interaction for him, either directly or through intermediaries . . . (and) the larger the number of persons for whom he originates interaction, either directly or through intermediaries." Authority for substituting "communication" for "interaction" will be found, *Ibid.*, p. 37.

11. Bales (1952) summarizes major findings from his studies which seek to describe uniformities of the following three kinds: (1) "Profile"—the relative frequency of different sorts of substantive acts during the course of a discussion—the ratio of questions to answers, for example; (2) "Phase Movements"—the distribution through time of the group's attention to three qualitative areas of discussion, namely, Orientation (what is it), Evaluation (how do you feel about it) and Control (what shall we do about it); and (3) "Who-to-Whom Matrix"—who says what and how often to whom.

interaction, Bales is able to show that if the members of a group are ranked in order of the frequency with which they speak to others, then it turns out that this same rank order holds for the frequency with which others speak to them. But the most frequent speakers tend to address themselves to the entire group; indeed, it turns out others tend to talk to them as individuals, but their own talk is more often directed to the group as a whole. Furthermore, it is important to note, popularity in the group is also distributed according to the rank order of frequency of speaking, so that the most frequent speakers are also most popular. It follows that person-to-person messages are directed at the most popular group members and thus may be said to move upward in the hierarchy, while communication from one person to several others tends to flow down.

To his analysis of the direction of flow, Bales adds an analysis of content. It becomes evident that the high ranking people —those who are most popular and most frequent talkers—are also likely to say different things than the low ranking people: The former tend to offer information and proffer opinion, while the latter typically request information and opinion, and express agreement or disagreement. The infrequent speakers, in other words, tend to "react" rather than "initiate," while the more frequent speakers seem to make more influence-attempts.

These studies show that social stratification—status and rank —plays an important part in channeling communications flow in small, informal groups, just as it does in more formally organized groups. But now that we have seen something of the influence of formal and informal hierarchies and of mutual attractions (friendship, cohesiveness) in making for variations in the networks of interpersonal communication, let us consider the consequences for communications behavior of another of the important dimensions of group structure: group size. Again, Bales talks to our point. As groups get larger (in this case, ranging from 3 to 8 people) he finds that more and more communication is directed to one member of the group (the most frequent communicator), thus reducing the relative amount of interchange among all members with each other. At the same time the recipient of this increased attention begins to direct more and more of his remarks to the group as a whole, and proportionately less to specific individuals. "The communication pattern," says Bales, "tends to 'centralize,' in other words, around a leader through whom most of the communication flows."[12]

But though the discussion in the larger group tends to focus more around one individual, it does not necessarily follow that the degree of consensus achieved will be greater. Quite the contrary, according to one experiment on this subject, which compared five-man and twelve-man discussion groups.[13] The discussants were Boy Scouts who came together to iron out differences in opinion regarding the relative merits of various types of camping equipment, and it was found that the five-man groups achieved a significantly greater degree of consensus than the twelve-man groups. Furthermore, the author reports—on the basis of a questionnaire—that there was greater dissatisfaction with the meeting expressed among members of the larger groups. There is evidence, too, that the dissatisfaction was due to the lower level of participation that was imposed on the larger groups by the time limit. This leads the author to suggest that lowered participation results in lowered consensus.[14]

Here, then, are a few brief illustrations of the ways in which different structural "arrangements" affect the patterns of inter-

---

12. *Ibid.*, p. 155.
13. Hare (1952).
14. This same study informs us that leaders in the large groups had less influence over the opinions of their groups than leaders of the small groups. Confronting this finding with Bales' report that leaders in larger groups tend to command a position of "centrality" in the communications channels of their groups, seemingly we are led to the conclusion that as the leader gains in centrality he loses in influence. As we shall see later below (p. 108 ff.) when we consider the relationship between social "location" and influence, this is not necessarily so. Intuitively, we may suggest that the extent to which there is a "pressure toward uniformity" in the group—that is, the extent that members are dependent on each other for the solution of some problem, or the attainment of a goal—is an important variable here. In the present experiment, a group vote was required, but there was no call for unanimity, or what's more (and this is a point we shall see illustrated below) no interdependence among group members was required insofar as obtaining an "answer" was concerned. Our suspicion is, therefore, that where there is strong pressure toward uniformity and/or considerable interdependence the more central role of large group leaders is also more influential, whereas under conditions where there is little pressure toward uniformity, the influentiality of the large-group leader is reduced.

personal communication. In our discussion of the strategic points of communication below, we shall return to a consideration of how "location" within a given communication structure constitutes one of the major keys to the study of strategic communications roles—particularly those of leaders and influentials. The concept of "centrality," which has already been touched upon, will be found to play a major role.

### (B.) COMPARATIVE CLIMATES: GROUP CULTURE AND COMMUNICATIONS

The idea that varying the links between the members of small groups might also result in significant variations in the patterns of communications flow, the volume of communication and even the content has occurred to different researchers in different ways. The studies we have just finished reporting were primarily concerned with the structure of the group. Here we shall turn to consider the effects on interpersonal communication of varying the "climate," or "culture," within which a group of individuals meets, and the first study we shall report is a well-known one by Kurt Lewin and his associates.

Together with Ronald Lippitt and Ralph K. White, Lewin set up what is perhaps his most famous experiment—that on "experimentally created social climates": "democratic," "authoritarian" and "laissez faire."[15] We shall not enter into a detailed discussion of the experimental design, except to indicate that each of four matched clubs of 11-year-old children were subjected, in varying sequences, to each of the three "climates," and that these "climates" were determined primarily by the carefully rehearsed behavior of the adult group leader. Moreover, the variations that might be products of the leader's personality were controlled by assigning more than one group to each leader and making him responsible for creating more than one kind of "climate." Each club met in the same clubroom setting and each engaged in the same activity. Records of all kinds were kept, including a minute by minute analysis of subgroupings, a quantitative running account of the behavior of the adult leader and of all group interaction, and a continuous stenographic record of all conversations.

---

15. For a summary of these studies, see Lippitt and White (1952).

Although this study was not formulated by its authors in terms of communications problems, many of its results will be of direct import for us. We learn, for example, that the sheer volume of conversation among group members was more restricted in the authoritarian atmosphere[16] than in the democratic or the laissez-faire situations.

The more interesting communications data, however, must be described in somewhat more substantive terms. Thus, in the authoritarian groups there were more attempts to attract and hold the leader's attention, although the character of the interaction with the leader was relatively less confiding and less "personal." In the democratic and laissez-faire atmospheres, on the other hand, members made more requests for attention and approval from fellow members than in the authoritarian climates. The laissez-faire groups exceeded the other groups by far in the category of requesting information of the leader, while the democratic groups were freest of all in making suggestions to the leader about group policy.

This evidence implies that the democratic group, by virtue of the processes of interchange and decision which were part of its group "climate," probably went much further than the other groups in establishing group-enforced norms of behavior, independent of the adult leader. The pattern of communication determined by the democratic "climate," in other words, did not center exclusively on the leader. This interpretation seems to be supported by the results of one of the "test episodes" in this experiment, whereby the leader was summoned from his group unexpectedly, and the reaction, in each "climate," to the leader's sudden departure was observed. When the leader left the authoritarian groups, the authors tell us, "'working time' dropped to a minimum . . . and most of what was done was in the minutes just after the leader had left the room . . . (but) in the democratic atmosphere the absence or presence of the leader had practically no effect."[17] Primarily, of course, this is evidence that the authoritarian groups depended completely on the leader's direction and lacked any

---

16. Actually, the authoritarian groups did not all behave alike. Some behaved very aggressively during the experiment and others apathetically, but we shall not go into the details of this distinction.

17. Lippitt and White (1952), p. 348.

sort of productive initiative except when the leader was present. Apparently, the group was not strictly a group—or at least a production group—except when cemented together by the leader. The democratic group, on the other hand, seemed to be able to function as an interacting goal-oriented unit without the adult leader. There seems to be evidence here that as a result of group-derived decisions which were the basis of the democratic group "climate," the group had transmitted to its members a set of shared "traditions" which became group property and were maintained even when the leader was absent.

Another climatic difference built into an experimental situation can be examined in Festinger and Thibuat's (1952) study of the effect of varying the "pressure toward uniformity of opinion." We know, for example, that some cultures more than others demand unanimity of opinion in their members; and we know, too, that even a single group in a single culture experiences some situations as permissive and others as demanding, as far as homogeneity of opinion is concerned. The authors "created" three different kinds of experimental "climates." One set of groups was told that the experimenter's interest was in observing "how a group went about coming to a unanimous decision." Thus, a "high" pressure toward uniformity of opinion was induced in these groups. A second set of groups was informed about the solution that some experts had proposed for a particular problem and were told that the group would be rated according to the number of its members who arrived at the "correct" solution; these instructions were designed to introduce "medium" pressure toward uniformity. The third set of groups was merely informed that the experimenter wanted to study a problem-solving group, and thus no external pressure toward uniformity was introduced. The results of the study clearly demonstrate the authors' hypothesis that "as pressure toward uniformity increases, both pressure to communicate and readiness to change also increase. Since both of these factors are conducive to change, there should be increasing change toward uniformity of opinion as the pressure toward uniformity increases."

By means of these studies we have tried to show that the "climates" or "cultures" within which individuals find themselves, influence the patterning of interpersonal communication. Like the structural characteristics of interpersonal relations, "climatic" characteristics must be accounted for if we are properly to analyze the varied character of the channels of flow of information and influence among interacting individuals.

### (C.) SITUATIONS: COMMUNICATIONS CONTENT
### AND INTERPERSONAL RELATIONS

Individuals in modern society are usually members of more than one group, and have interpersonal ties in different sorts of situations. Groups of individuals, furthermore, share certain interests on the level of the group as a whole, and divide into sub-groups, as far as certain other interests are concerned. Therefore, the very same group may engender quite different communications networks relative to different interests and different situations. Important questions emerge from this situational approach to interpersonal relations: How do communication patterns change in different social situations? What kinds of communication content flow through which kinds of interpersonal networks? For example, is the family group important in generating or transmitting political opinions or is it the work group—and for which kinds of people?

Because most small-group studies are conducted in laboratories, there are very few answers for this kind of question in actual research reports. Some leads, however, are available to us, notably from those who have stepped outside the confines of the small-group laboratory to study "natural" groups.

The cardinal principle that emerges from all work in this area is that shared interest in a given subject is the basis for interpersonal networks of communication. In other words, as Allport and Postman (1947) put it in their study of rumor, "A rumor public exists wherever there is a community of interest." For example, financial rumors circulate among those who are likely to be affected by financial ups and downs.[18] Festinger and his associates (1950) provide several illustrations for this principle in their studies of housing communities.[19] When a

---

18. Allport and Postman (1947), p. 180.
19. Festinger, Schachter and Back (1950), Chap. 7.

rumor concerning the future of the children's nursery school was circulated, these investigators were able to ascertain that it had reached 62 per cent of the people in the community with children of nursery school age, and only 28 per cent of the people who had no children of that age. When a rumor hostile to the existence of the Tenants' Council was "planted" in Westgate, it tended to reach people who were particularly associated with the organization and among those who heard it, it was passed on, in turn, only by those who were active participants in the organization, or who were members of a family with active participants, but not at all by any others. Similarly, in the study of "planted" rumors in an industrial organization, Back *et al.* (1950) find that when a rumor pertained specifically to a small group, it tended to spread very quickly to the members of that group and not to go beyond the few people who were vitally concerned.

Here, then, it appears that networks of communication exist not only within the web of friendship networks but within the web of shared interests and concerns as well. Festinger *et al.* (1950) however, suggest several important amendments to this conclusion, though their proof for these is not quite conclusive. In terms of their Westgate study of attitudes toward a Tenants' Council, they tell us, first of all, that information favorable to the Tenants' Council was much more actively communicated within those residential courts whose members were favorable to the Council than those courts which were unfavorable. Secondly, they say that there seemed to be little or no communication on matters relevant to the Tenants' Council between members of courts which had conflicting court attitudes toward the Council. On a more abstract level, these findings seem to point to the generalization that there will be a greater amount of communication concerning a given matter among people who share a concern in the matter when (a) their point of view on a particular concern is homogeneous and (b) when the content of the communication is favorable to their shared point of view.[20]

20. Festinger, Schachter and Back (1950), p. 129. We are not told, however, that communications unfavorable to the Council were more actively spread in the unfavorable courts. Moreover, what we *are* told is that com-

That the contents of interpersonal communications tend to harmonize with opinions and attitudes and to flow among similarly minded people is interesting, too, because it is a conclusion which corresponds so closely with what is known of people's mass media habits. Research in mass communications has shown that people tend not to "expose" themselves to communications which conflict with their own predispositions, but instead to seek support for their opinions and attitudes in favorable communications. Examples in Chapter I indicate this at several points, and there is substantial evidence for the role of mass media as "reinforcers" rather than as "converters" of opinions and attitudes. Now we find that this is the case for interpersonal communications, too.

Here, let us turn from our discussion of the role of mutual interest as a basis for the establishment of networks of communication in varying situations, to the closely allied topic of the multiple networks to which individuals belong and the varying communications functions of each. Sociometric studies show that when individuals are asked different sorts of questions such as "with whom would you most like to work?" for example, and "with whom would you most like to spend your leisure time?"—they name somewhat different people.[21] Reference group studies contend, too, that individuals use different groups as points of reference for different matters.[22] These traditions make plain that among the topics that deserve empirical study are the different sorts of communications networks which individuals choose for differing concerns.

munications hostile to the Council spread most of all and most quickly to those who were active participants in the Council, most but not all of whom, we know, were favorable, too. That is one objection to the conclusions reported. A second objection stems from the inference that since rumors did not spread from the favorable to the unfavorable courts, or vice versa, that communication between groups with different standards is therefore limited. This cannot be conclusively demonstrated since groups with different standards tended also to correspond to different friendship cliques; hence it would be sufficient, therefore, to point out that communications were limited by friendship channels—something we have already been told.

21. Moreno (1953) indicates that mentally retarded individuals seem to choose the same persons for varying activities more than mentally normal individuals do; see pp. 262-264, "Home and Work Groups Compared."

22. Multiple reference groups are discussed in Merton and Kitt (1950), pp. 59-69. Multiple group memberships are considered in Newcomb (1950), Chap. 15, in Hartley (1951), and also in the sociological writings on such things as role conflict, "marginal men," "social self," etc.

Something of a start in this direction is attempted in a later section of this book.[23] There it is demonstrated, on the basis of empirical evidence, that individuals are influenced by quite different kinds of people on different sorts of things. Marketing advice, for example, flows through different networks than fashion advice, and neither of these channels seems to overlap with the channels for political influencing. While the same people may—or may not—be involved in these different spheres of influence, the patterns of communication flow in each case take different shapes. Thus, a first step in describing the patterns of communications flow in a society is to locate individuals in the networks to which they belong, and then to determine which networks are relevant for which kinds of communications.

It is also important to investigate how changes in a situation will influence an individual's choice of network and, similarly, how changes in a situation affect the patterns of communication within a group. A group which suddenly finds itself in a hostile environment, for example, will rapidly solidify its chain of command and often completely shift its patterns of leadership and communication.[24] Studies of the same soldiers in training situations and then later in combat situations,[25] or studies of community structure and leadership in disaster situations illustrate this point very clearly.[26]

However, we are beginning to border on the opening topic of the second major approach to interpersonal communication which we have selected for consideration: the identification

23. Part Two, Section Three.
24. The Festinger and Thibaut (1952) study (discussed above p. 93) on "pressures to uniformity" in a group is obviously relevant here as well. Variation in the pressures to uniformity, that is, may not only be a product of different group "climates" but—perhaps more frequently—a product of the varying situations in which a given group finds itself. Thus, pressures to uniformity may not only be different for different groups, but may also vary, for the very same group, in different situations.
25. Sanford (1952) cites two or three such studies, which reveal the discrepancy between performance grades in the training situation and in combat. We are not dwelling on these matters here because they belong more properly—in terms of our classification—in the second part of this chapter, under the heading of situational factors in leadership.
26. The 1953 meeting of the Society for Applied Anthropology held at the University of Chicago devoted a session to papers on disasters, and the disparity between leadership in disaster and traditional leadership was repeatedly brought out.

of key roles in the flow of communication within a group. The first topic we shall consider, after introducing the idea of a diagnostic approach, is the communications role of a group leader and the part played by situational factors in leadership.

## Strategic Points of Transmission

We call this second approach the diagnostic approach because the essence of it involves the location of *strategic points* in the transmission of communications. We might also have used the word "role" and called this the group role approach, for most of what is diagnosed here pertains to the roles which people play in interaction with their fellows. It is in terms of these roles that it becomes possible to locate the origin, the relay points, and the terminal points—in a word, the strategic points—of intra-group communication.

The human group is never simply an aggregate but a structure involving interlocking roles and dependencies. In more or less stable groups, roles themselves become part and parcel of group norms. Even informal groups that may lack any sense of form or direction soon find themselves with more and less active members, more and less dependent members, more and less powerful members, etc. A peacemaker may develop in the group who functions to settle arguments and disputes; a jokester may be depended upon to relieve tense situations; the initiation of activities may become the province of one or two members; a gossip may spread the group's own news.[27] Practically always—although their functions may vary—there are one or more persons in the group whom the group recognizes as group leaders or influentials.

That a leader can be identified in virtually every group is something we can be quite certain of. "Leader" may not always be the best word, of course; sometimes "influential" or "initiator" or "most popular" might suit the situation better, but let us say "leader" and know that we mean many things by it. Sociometric maps of groups of all kinds consistently show

27. For a discussion of the varieties of roles typical of small, informal groups, see, for example, Benne and Sheats (1948) and Newcomb's (1950) report of a dissertation by H. W. Heyns which deals, in part, with this subject. For a very recent and excellent discussion, see Slater (1955).

individuals who are the center of attraction for others. Group researchers who delineate group boundaries by frequencies of interaction among sets of people can invariably point out those individuals with whom members of the group tend to interact most, or those who initiate most activities, or those from whom approval is most often sought, or those whose actions are most frequently imitated.

It would be well, therefore, to look into the role of group leader or influential insofar as it has bearing on the transmission of influence within the group. The small group leader, we suspect, is the key to an understanding of the process of the interpersonal transmission of influence. The influential we shall talk about first is the leader who has been *nominated* by his fellows as the man most appropriate to the group's particular needs. Recent trends in the study of leadership strongly emphasize that leadership is not so much a trait which some people possess and others do not but rather that it is a response of individuals reacting together to the situation in which they find themselves. We shall show that the idea of nominated leader is closely linked to our earlier discussion of communications networks in varying social *situations*.

There are other ways, however, by which a person may assume a leadership role or at least get a head-start toward nomination. One way is by being strategically situated in the group relative, say, to some desired goal. We shall refer to this kind of leader as a leader by virtue of *social location*. The located leader, then, is a product of the structure of the group's communications network and emerges, it will be seen, as a result of our earlier discussion of the *structural* determinants of patterns of communication.

Then there is a third kind of leader who derives, in a sense, from our discussion of the *climates* of communication. He is the *culturally certified* leader who influences others because he occupies a position in a group—father of the family, for example—which the group's particular culture endows with the "right" to influence.

Altogether, nomination, location and certification are the three diagnostic keys to the strategic points of interpersonal influence which we want to report on throughout almost all of

the remainder of this section. These three correspond, as has
been indicated, to the three approaches to the *patterns* of
interpersonal communication which we have just examined—
structures, climates, and situations. We shall not maintain the
same sequence here, but shall begin this time with the situational—that is, with the nominated leader—and afterwards
consider structural and cultural matters. The situational approach to leadership is a subject which is best introduced, it
so happens, by a brief digression to consider the tradition of
leadership "traits" studies.

(A.) NOMINATION: THE SITUATIONAL ASPECT
OF INFLUENCE TRANSMISSION

The last years have seen a sharp retreat from the "trait"
approach to the study of leadership, mainly as a result of the
wartime stimulus to research in leadership. In a recent discussion of the social science literature on leadership, Sanford
(1952) points out, as do other writers who have reviewed this
literature, that almost no two studies find the same traits characteristic of leaders.[28] Eleven studies reveal emotional stability
as a leadership trait; but five studies find leaders relatively less
stable than their followers; and similar discrepancies show up
over variables such as age, dominance, and many others.
"From all these studies of the leader," Sanford tells us, "we
can conclude with reasonable certainly that: (a) there are
either no general leadership traits, or if they do exist they are
not to be described in any of our familiar psychological or
common sense terms, (b) in a specific situation leaders do
have traits which set them apart from followers but *what*
traits set *what* leaders apart from *what* followers will vary
from situation to situation."[29]

A study by Carter and Nixon (1949) is pertinent. One hun-

28. Sanford (1952). For other critical appraisals of the leadership literature, see Stogdill (1948); Gibb (1947); Gibb (1950) and Jenkins (1947).
29. Sanford also suggests several reasons why those who are interested in
leadership have concentrated so exclusively on the traits of leaders: "In the
first place we have the tools and techniques for dealing with the characteristics of individuals. . . . In the second place we have tended to look at leadership as a function only of the leader rather than of a social relation between
leader and follower. And, in the third place, it would be so handy if we
could isolate leadership traits."

dred high school boys, divided in small groups, were assigned alternately to three different tasks—a clerical task, an intellectual task, and a mechanical task. Each boy, in each task, was rated on the degree to which he assumed a leadership role in the group. It was found that those who assumed leadership in the intellectual situation tended also to do so in the clerical situation, but neither the intellectual leaders nor the clerical leaders rose to leadership in the mechanical situation.

Other studies illustrate, too, the rise of different leadership in response to changed situations, or the nomination of some leader clearly appropriate to a group task. We shall consider some of these research reports during this section, but, at this point, we want only to reiterate the major conclusion that underlies current research in leadership: that there do not appear to be any "born" leaders, nor any infallible leadership traits, but that the situation in which an informal group finds itself will be one of the major determinants of who will be called on to lead.

If we accept here that nominated leaders rise and fall with changing situations, we want to know (1) whether, on a more abstract level, there are any general characteristics which govern the relationship of these situational leaders to their groups and (2) whether there are any general ways in which the flow of influence between leaders and followers can be described.

A number of studies suggest that perhaps the most important relationship between an emergent leader and the group that he leads is the leader's subservience to the norms of his group. That is the point of the study by Merei (1952) reported above which, it will be recalled, found that reintroducing into a group someone known for his past leadership will not result in the old leader's return to power unless he adopts the new "traditions" which were generated during his absence.[30] Other studies, too—in fact, virtually all studies that have departed from the strictly "trait" approach to the study of leadership—support this general line of thought.[31] Where earlier we noted that interpersonal networks of communication tend to be delimited by the interests and values which individuals share,

30. See above, p. 52.
31. For a review of such studies, see Gibb (1950).

now we may say that such shared interests and values are prerequisite for leadership and influentiality in general.

A study by Chowdhry and Newcomb (1952) develops an interesting implication of this idea. These authors studied leadership in four "natural" groups—a religious interest group, a political group, a medical fraternity and a medical sorority. On a quasi-sociometric questionnaire, each member of each group was asked to designate the leading members of the group using the following four criteria: Which three members are most capable of being president? Which would be most worthy delegates to a convention? Which most influences group opinions? Which would you most like to be friendly with? The authors discovered that there were high intercorrelations in this particular case among these four leadership criteria and they decided to use all four to divide the group into (1) leaders (those receiving more than 20 per cent of total choices), (2) nonleaders (less than 20 per cent), and (3) isolates (no choices).

Having made their leadership choices, group members were presented with a series of statements and asked to indicate for each statement whether they agreed or disagreed and where they thought the group as a whole stood on the matter. The statements were of three kinds—one type was relevant to the group's official interest (i.e. religion, politics, medicine), another was not relevant at all to the group's interest, and a third was partly relevant and partly not.

The analysis shows that those who had been chosen as leaders were much more accurate in judging group opinion than either of the other two groups. But this was so only on matters which were relevant to the group's interest—medicine for the medical group, politics for the political group, etc. It seems reasonable to conclude, say the authors, that "leaders of groups like these are chosen, in part at least, because of recognized qualities of 'sensitivity' to other members of the group. . . . Such qualities may or may not be potentially of a general nature . . . if they have the ability to become such all-round good judges, they are not motivated to develop it equally in all directions."[32]

---

32. *Ibid.* This finding must be held as tentative by virtue of the fact that an earlier study, by Hites and Campbell (1950), differs somewhat.

That the leader has a better knowledge of group opinion jibes very well with our earlier finding which indicated that in order to gain leadership one must adopt the norms and "traditions" of the group. This implies that "sensitivity" to relevant group opinions precedes or follows—at any rate, is correlated with—the close conformity to group norms which is characteristic of leadership. (There might be an important lead here, we might note parenthetically, to the methodology of studying the opinions and attitudes of groups without interviewing every single member.)

But do leaders and influential members of informal friendship groups *know* that they are considered leaders by the others? Are they aware, in other words, that they are "leading"? The evidence indicates that they are. A particularly important study relating to this subject is Lippitt, Polansky, Redl and Rosen's (1952) study of what they call "social power." In this study—subtitled "A Field Study of Social Influence in Groups of Children"—boys in several children's summer camps were asked to rank their bunkmates, and themselves, on a set of particular characteristics such as fighting ability, ability in sports, campcrafts, etc., as well as on the general question, "Who is best at getting the others to do what he wants them to do?" The results show high agreement among the members of each bunk about the member with most "power," that is, the one who is best at getting others to do his bidding. The authors report further that an individual's estimate of his own rank will tend to be consistent with the rank which is attributed to him by others. That, of course, is very important for the study of opinion leadership. The leader *knows* that he's a leader. The authors go on to show that nominated leaders are the boys who are best-liked—a consistent finding of small group studies —and also rank highest on group ratings of fighting ability and of campcraft, confirming again that the leader is the best performer of those activities which the group values highly in the prevailing situation.

So far, we have been describing the relationship between nominated leaders and their followers. We have seen that the leaders (1) conform most closely to group norms; (2) are best acquainted with prevailing group opinion on salient matters;

(3) are aware that they have been nominated for leadership; and (4) are best-liked. Now, we would want to see how these nominated leaders *exercise* their leadership, that is, how they influence others. This is precisely what the pioneering study we are now drawing upon proceeds to do, in terms of two observational measures which were employed: *behavioral contagion* (where the influencer is imitated, though he does not attempt to transmit influence); and *direct influence* (where an influence attempt is made manifest, either by ordering, suggesting or requesting).

Behavioral contagion, the authors report, is more likely to take place from the behavior of a member to whom high "power" to influence has been attributed. In other words, the boys tended to imitate those to whom they had attributed influentiality even when no influence-attempt had been exerted. What is more, when influence-attempts were made manifest, those to whom high "power" had been attributed were more successful in their influence-attempts than those who tried to persuade others without the benefit of high "power." These patterns emerge even more sharply when the contaging of each boy was examined relative to the specific individuals whom he had personally named as most influential, and it was found that an individual will follow most closely those others whom he personally considers most influential. Furthermore, we are told, the average member tends to initiate deferential, approval-seeking behavior toward boys with high attributed "power."

Now, another question: What about the *recipient* of high attributed "power"? Does he take advantage of this power-to-influence which the others give him the right to possess? The answer is: not always, but often enough to make it important. The authors report that "the recipient of attributed power will make more frequent attempts to influence the behavior of others . . . (he will also be) more directive in his influence," and as we have seen, "he will be more successful in these attempts."

This study thus provides us with evidence on a whole set of matters that are directly pertinent to our interest in opinion leadership. First of all, we find that members of a group have a high level of agreement among themselves on who possesses how much influence. Secondly, we see that those who rank highest are relatively accurate in the perception of their position.[33] Third, we learn that high "power" members actually exercise the license to influence which is awarded them. Finally, we see that those to whom high "power" is attributed are most successful in their direct influence-attempts, and that they are imitated even when they do not attempt to exert direct influence.

This study is almost a small scale model of the design for research on opinion leadership which is reported in the second part of this book. Like our design, it is based, first, on asking people whom they consider influential and then, on obtaining self-estimates of influentiality. And like our design, it attempts to trace the flow of some actual influence through these mapped sociometric networks. Finally, it attempts, as we do, to characterize the opinion leader on the basis of certain attributes.[34]

Let us cite only one more conclusion from this Lippitt *et al.* study of boys' camps. The authors believe that, "Where group living approaches twenty-four-hour living, attributed power tends to be undifferentiated as to situation and activity. This is to say, the actor's power may have initially derived from pre-eminence in some particular type of activity or characteristic (e.g., fighting, sports, campcraft, disobeying adults, physical size), but fellow members tend to generalize this pre-eminence to the general range of group activities and situations."

The implication is that this generalized kind of "influentiality" will be more characteristic of such groups, than of those groups which are hemmed in by more formal controls, and more varied commitments. Compare, for example, two classics of small group research: the Nortons street corner gang, and

---

33. Compare our evidence for the accuracy of "self-designated" opinion leadership. Part Two, Chapter II.

34. There are, of course, important differences, too. Perhaps we should say that this study is almost an "idealized" version of what a research in the flow of interpersonal influence in a community should be like, providing, of course, that the manageable proportions of such a study could be imposed on the variety of concerns, the multiplicity of affiliations, and the population size of an American city. The following paragraphs, above, cite one such important limitation.

the men of the Bank Wiring Room in the Hawthorne plant of the Western Electric Company.[35] One is a group which is relatively "autonomous" in its environment and which, like the boys' camp groups, governs almost the total lives of its members; the other group is a closely supervised work group in a highly rationalized factory. The leader of the Nortons is "Doc," and "Taylor" is the embryo leader in the Bank Wiring Room of the plant. These two are important figures and it is worth getting to know them.

Take "Doc" of Street Corner Society. How does he influence his group? First of all, Whyte tells us, it is he who makes judgments and acts while the others are still undecided; when he decides, the group, so to speak, has also decided. Others may originate action for him, but if any action is to become group action, Doc is the one who originates it for the rest. The members have a feeling that something is missing when Doc is away, and they wait for him before beginning any activity.[36] Doc is instrumental, too, in molding opinions and attitudes toward politics and neighborhood affairs—in fact, some of his status in the group derives from the respect he has among other gang leaders and local politicians.

The case of the Bank Wiremen seems quite different. The lives of its members can hardly be said to be totally controlled by the group or its norms. Members have only relatively slight control over each other's activities outside the factory, for all of them have a string of other roles and commitments. Even within the factory, where group norms prescribe the patterns of informal activity and, within clearly defined limits, influence productivity as well, it is evident that the formal rules of the factory have by far the largest share in regulating individual behavior.

---

35. Doc and the Nortons are from Whyte (1943) and Taylor and his co-workers are from Roethlisberger and Dickson (1939). Here, we are drawing on Homans' (1950) excellent summary and challenging analysis of both of these minor classics. The name "Taylor" was assigned to the group's leader by Homans; Roethlisberger and Dickson used no names. The word "autonomous," used by Homans, is credited to *The Autonomous Groups Bulletin*, edited by R. Spence and M. Rogers.

36. The dependence of childrens' groups on their peer leader for the initiation and execution of activities is studied by Toki in an interesting set of experiments involving the removal of the leader from the group. Reported in Hartley and Hartley (1952).

As we follow the report of Taylor's emergence as "leader" of the Bank Wiremen it is evident that we have our eye on a man who, like Doc and the children with high attributed "power," meets the conditions of conforming most closely to group norms, of having the respect of superiors outside the group, of being well-liked, etc. But in what sense is he a "leader"? Where in the account do we find out what it is that he is leading or what it is that he is leading toward? We want to know what Taylor actually *does* in this key position, or more directly, how does Taylor's "social power" or influence compare with Doc's?

The hints we have[37] tell us that Taylor was a very well-informed man, always ready for an argument; and when he argued he often won. We are told, too, that Taylor offered a great deal of advice to the other men. This paragraph, cited by Homans, seems to sum up these two elements in Taylor's leadership:

He seldom lost an argument whether it was about baseball, horse racing, movie stars' salaries, the interest rate on postal savings, or the cost of shipping a dozen eggs a hundred miles by express. His superiority was demonstrated not only by the fact that he usually won out in arguments but also by the way in which he advised and cautioned the men. Thus, when Steinhardt said he was thinking of getting a transfer to a subsidiary of the Western Electric Company, Taylor told him he should consider his chances of getting back on his present job in case he didn't get along well on his new job. He told Capek which horses to bet on in the races. When Krupa and some of the others got too boisterous, it was Taylor who warned them to pipe down. If he thought an argument was going too far, as in an argument about religion between Winikowski and Steinhardt, he tried to put a stop to it.[38]

Our guess is that the Bank Wiremen are more typical of informal interpersonal relations in modern society than the Nortons. The informal friendship group, the neighborhood group, the group of men on the job all have in common the fact that they are not primarily organized in one group alone

37. We say "hints" because the study was not concerned specifically with leadership, nor had Taylor emerged as a clear-cut leader by the time the study was concluded.
38. Cited by Homans (1950), p. 70.

or in terms of some goal towards which they must move. Nor
have they any real organization of, or control over, their major
life activities. Thus, the leader's "influencing," in our sense,
may not really be in terms of major life activities at all—though
he will "function" symbolically, or perhaps even actively to
maintain the attitudes that the group has taken vis-a-vis these
activities. His influence, instead, may be in all manner of
"little" things and perhaps occasional "big" things, too, which
concern the group as a whole or individuals within the group.
Much more than Doc, Taylor conforms to our image of the
opinion leader as transmitter of information and influence in
modern society. Doc has too much "power," perhaps.

### (B.) SOCIAL LOCATION: THE STRUCTURAL ASPECT OF INFLUENCE TRANSMISSION

Our discussion of diagnostics has focused almost exclusively
so far on the role of group leader in the flow of influence. And
the kind of group leader we have been talking about is the
man who emerges out of the interaction of individuals relative to a given situation. He is the leader who is *nominated,*
so to speak, for leadership. And leadership in primary groups
means the right and the power to influence.

Nominated leadership, however, is only one of the key
sources of interpersonal influence to which our diagnosis of
strategic points within the group directs attention. Though
they may be less apparent, we can think of at least two others
which are of considerable importance. Here, first of all, we
shall consider the kind of influentiality which seems to come
along with a particular *location* in the *structure* of a group.

But before beginning this discussion, let us note again that
the words we have been using so far—leader, influential, etc.
—often distract attention from the fact that we are interested
not so much in leaders as we are in key communications roles.
That is, we are not interested in leadership or influentiality
*per se* but in those who communicate information and influence. And it may well be that different people, performing
quite different tasks, are involved in this process. Let us illustrate by the case of Doc. We know that Doc's influence extends
over the group in terms of originating activities, sanctioning

some suggestions and disapproving others, giving advice and encouragement, etc. But we are told, too, that not all of Doc's orders are given directly, but that often they are discussed and then funneled to the gang via two lieutenants. This fact leads Homans to observe that it is better to define a leader not as the man who originates interaction for many people at once, but by his key position in the channels of interaction;[39] the leader's is a kind of trigger position for the entire group. From our communications point of view, this important distinction directs us to consider the different kinds of roles which the one label, leader, or influential, or opinion leader subsumes. Thus, opinion leadership may refer to the point of *origin* of a plan or an idea, to the *sanctioning* of the idea, or to the *diffusion* of the idea. An individual qualifies as a key communicator if he fulfills any, or all, of these roles. Here, for example, we are told that Doc often, but not always, originates; that he influences — endorses or rejects — proposals originating from others; that, sometimes, he is the transmitter when the group is all assembled, and that sometimes, he passes an idea down along a chain of command for transmission.

Homans describes Doc's role in these terms: "If Lou, among the Nortons, had an idea about what the gang ought to do, it went to Doc either directly or by way of Angelo or Danny. The chain of interactions might end there: Doc might not take up the idea. But if he did take it up, he would, after consultation with his lieutenants, pass it down the line again, and the gang would act. Or Doc might have an idea of his own and pass it down the same way."[40] At the same time, however, it is not difficult to conceive of other key communication roles in such a group—although they may or may not be part of this particular group. It may be, for example, that one member— more than others—originates plans or ideas and, more than others, persuades Doc of their worth;[41] or it may be that one

39. *Ibid.*, p. 183.
40. *Ibid.*, p. 182.
41. Sociometrists sometimes find that one person who is not especially attractive to the group as a whole seems to have the particular attention of the group leader. This role is called "the power behind the throne." A more exact parallel for the three roles distinguished here may be found in Larsen and De Fleur's (1954) discussion of a study of the diffusion of a message in a community.

member—more than others—takes the role of transmitter or diffusion agent for approved opinions and information.

In most of the groups we have considered so far, it would not be easy to separate the functions of originating, influencing and transmitting. It is probable, as a matter of fact, that the nominated leader in such small groups combines these theoretically distinguishable roles, although we can note such things, for example, as the fact that Taylor in his relatively informal, unstructured group seems to do much more personal transmitting than Doc does in his. But now that we are turning from the communications activity of the *nominated* leader to consider the *located* leader, it is important to note the possible relevance of such distinctions. It may be, for example, that the communications role of someone who is strategically located relative to some group goal or interest more often plays the role of transmitter or originator than influential; and it may be that unless such a person is also nominated by the group for leadership, the approval for what is originated or transmitted may depend on someone else.

The study we shall concentrate on to illustrate social location does not allow for this latter possibility, but it is well to bear it in mind.

The study reports the series of experiments by Bavelas and Leavitt which aims at an analysis of the effects of varying patterns of group organization on communications behavior.[42] Several different structures were employed, each of which was effected by seating five-member experimental groups in such a way that the number of "neighbors" with whom group members could communicate could be varied. Some examples of these different structures are the "chain" pattern which can be visualized as five individuals seated in a straight line so that the two men on the ends have only one neighbor each and the three men in between have two neighbors; the "circle" pattern where everybody has two neighbors; and the "wheel" pattern where each of four men are at four distant corners of a rectangle, and are connected, in spoke-like fashion, with only one man in the center. The structures were controlled by

---

42. Leavitt (1952) has extended Bavelas' original formulation in an excellent set of experiments. For Bavelas' earlier statement, see Bavelas (1951).

partitioning the members into five differently-colored cubicles, each equipped with pencil, matching colored paper, and a communications slot arranged in such a way that contact was possible only along pattern-prescribed routes. This permitted an analysis of the way in which each pattern affected the solution of a standardized problem which involved collecting pieces of information from each man, collating them, and redistributing the resulting solution to all.

In the most rigidly imposed pattern, the "wheel," where one man in the middle serves as the sole connective link, a standardized sequence of communication patterns developed after the first several trials and the group maintained that organization throughout the remainder of the fifteen experimental trials. Furthermore, out of this pattern came the single fastest solution recorded. The organization centered about the man in the middle who gathered all the information and funneled it back again, and when the group was asked—on a post-experiment questionnaire—whether it had a leader and if so, who he was, all who recognized any leader at all unanimously agreed that the middle man was the leader. Asked to describe briefly their image of the organization of the group, more "wheel" members than those of any other pattern perceived their group structure accurately. Asked, however, how they liked their jobs, "wheel" members expressed most dissatisfaction.

Contrast the "wheel" with the "circle." The "circle," where no one position was objectively more strategic than any other, showed no consistency in organizational procedure, and no perception on the part of the members of how the group was organized in space. The "circle" made the most errors of all, too. Only half of those who worked in the "circle" thought that their group had a leader, and even the choosers did not agree among themselves on who the leader was. As for job satisfaction, however, the circle members were most satisfied of all.

To analyze his findings, Leavitt proposes a measure called "centrality," which describes the degree of access a given member has to all others in the group. The man in the middle of the "wheel," for example, clearly has the highest "centrality" measure in that group. Now, in those patterns which were characterized by a relatively even distribution of "centrality" among all members, the influence of members on group affairs tended to be equal, but where high "centrality" was allotted by the structure to only one member then that particular member was most likely to take control. "Centrality," in the latter type of structure, functioned as the major determinant of leadership, for the others recognized their dependence on this key position. The person in the most "central" position expressed most satisfaction with the experimental task; was singled out most often by the others as "leader"; and, in fact, had the crucial role in the solution of the group's experimental problem.

In terms of our own interests, this set of experiments has several interesting implications. It directs us, *first,* to seek out those individuals who, for whatever reason, have greater access to all of the elements involved in a given task or problem; we shall expect such people to be looked up to by those others who are associated with more detailed and dependent aspects of that task or problem. Whether the influence of these overseers extends beyond the specific matter which they oversee is not less important, but quite another question. Here we can note only that in every group we have examined, the leader was better informed than others in the group about relevant matters. And, let us remark in passing, too, that the shadow of the "expert" looms at this point—that is, the person with access to the answers.

*Secondly,* we are reminded by these experiments that *contact* and *mobility* may be important determinants of interpersonal communications roles. We learn from Allport and Postman's (1947) report on a wartime study of rumor conducted by the OWI that "people who participate more in social life were found to be more rumor prone than those who are isolated."[43] The study found that working women, for example, heard and spread more stories than did housewives. Among those rated "socially active," 60 per cent were found to be rumor agents, but among those who led comparatively secluded lives, only 30 per cent. We are directed by this kind of lead to pay at-

---

43. p. 183.

tention to the communications functions of gregarious people and, in fact, Part Two of this book considers the relationship between gregariousness and opinion leadership in greater detail.[44] But the mere frequency of gregariousness is probably less important for influence transmission than the *itinerary* of a gregarious person. It would be interesting to examine those professions which bring their members into contact with a variety of different socially or geographically distinct groups. In another day, the minstrel, for example, used to fit this description, and lately the traveling salesman does.[45] In general, those who move between a group and some relevant part of that group's environment—be it another group or a body of knowledge or anything else—probably play key roles in the communications process.

In sum, these experiments indicate that *strategic social location* seems to lead to a key communications role. Thus, "centrality" tends to be the most significant location judging from the studies we have examined so far. This would seem to be particularly so when the members of a group are interdependent relative to the solution of some problem. Sometimes, however, "peripherality" may be a more significant location in the sense that marginal people are sometimes better situated with reference to a relevant external environment than more central individuals.[46] In any event, an important clue to the

---

44. In Section Three of the second part of this book, gregariousness is one of the dimensions in terms of which opinion leaders are contrasted with non-opinion leaders. In the final section of this chapter, too, where we cite findings which emerge from present-day international communications research, there are some relevant matters: For example, it is reported, that transmitters of news and opinion to the rural areas of the pre-industrial countries which have been studied are people who physically commute between city and village. Thus, bus drivers, for example, are often carriers of news, and a teacher who spends his summers in the big city is viewed as the representative of the outside world. Interesting, too, is the finding that young people in small Near Eastern villages appear to be encroaching somewhat on the traditional opinion leadership of the old by virtue of their frequent trips outside the village, and their consequent contact with the mass media of the city and with city people.

45. This is one of the points where it is well to recall our multidimensional use of the term "opinion leadership" and "leader." Here, for example, it is evident that *transmission* need not be accompanied by *influentiality*.

46. As in minority groups, for example. See our discussion of this point below, p. 117. The international communications studies which will be cited below also focus on peripherality as a key to opinion leadership—at least during the period of changing group interests.

discovery of strategic points of interpersonal communication is tied up with the idea of location within a group structure.

### (c.) CERTIFICATION: CULTURAL ASPECTS
### OF INFLUENCE TRANSMISSION

The final clue we shall offer in the search for key communications roles (and, like location, another of the factors that may also give an individual a head-start toward nomination for group leadership) comes from the idea of cultural differences. We know that cultures ascribe influentiality to certain roles in certain groups. We must look, therefore, into the organization of those relatively more formal groups for which culture—rather than situational patterns of activity or interaction—provide behavioral prescriptions, and single out those roles which are endowed by the culture with "the right to influence." A neat study by Fred Strodtbeck (1951) illustrates very well this idea of *cultural certification*.

Strodtbeck selected a number of married couples representing three different cultural groups and asked each spouse privately to name the single, all-round "best" family each knew and to list the criteria on which the decision was based. After each spouse had indicated a particular family and the relevant criteria, the couples were brought together and asked to reconcile their differences and agree on just one family and one set of criteria. Analyzing these discussions, Strodtbeck found that cultural differences account for which spouse is likely to "win," that is, which is more likely to influence the other to change an announced opinion. Among the Navaho where women are quite independent, and the man comes to live with his wife's family, wives "won" many more decisions than their husbands; among the Mormons, however, where the husband reigns supreme, husbands "won" more times. Among Texas Presbyterian couples—who have an egalitarian norm—as many decisions were "won" by husbands as by wives. Thus, in this substantive sphere at least, whoever has the cultural upper hand is more likely to be influential. Strodtbeck puts it this way: "We were able to predict the balance of decision-winning from our study of the comparative social and cultural organizations from which the sample was drawn."[47]

In our estimation, culture not only ascribes influentiality to certain roles but prescribes the substantive spheres of influence in which that influentiality may be exerted. Thus, while Strodtbeck found equal influence in our culture on the domestic matter which he studied, we know from political studies, for example, that in the arena of politics and public affairs the husband has the upper hand.[48] And it is probably because the culture awards him the upper hand. There simply is no question about which partner is more likely to influence the other's vote and, of course, there is wide agreement that politics is a male sphere of influence. We know too from market research that *children* have considerable influence on certain types of purchases, husbands on others and wives still on others.[49]

All of these studies are of first-rate importance for the study of the flow of influence within interpersonal networks of communication. It is clear now that before setting out to study influence transmission, the subject matter of the influencing must be carefully specified. Then, the situations in which such influence is transmitted and the networks via which it travels must be mapped out. Within these networks, key communications roles—initiators, transmitters and influentials—can be identified and these, in turn, can be related to *nomination,* social *location* and cultural *certification.*

---

47. We might enter a plea of guilty at this point for having underemphasized the best-known primary group of all—the family—in these chapters.

48. Evidence is presented in Lazarsfeld, Berelson and Gaudet (1948).

49. In a paper delivered at the 1953 conference of American Association for Public Opinion Research, Matilda White Riley of Rutgers University discusses this point.

# CHAPTER VII

# The Group and the World Outside:
# Implications for Mass Media Research

Now THAT WE HAVE SEEN SOMETHING of the dynamics of person-to-person communication and influence, we want to return more explicitly to the question of implications. Again—as we did in Chapter IV—we want to look into the relevance of all of this for the study of mass media effectiveness.

Earlier—and this is the opinion leader idea—it was hypothesized that person-to-person transmission may serve as a relay between people who are exposed to mass media influence and others who are not. It was suggested, too, that interpersonal influence may reinforce a mass media campaign. To this point, however, we have been *assuming* that mass media influences make their way, somehow, into interpersonal networks of communication and, thus, we have been speculating about what happens when they get there. For that reason we have examined the patterns, and the strategic points, of communication within the group; and we have been able to specify some of the person-to-person channels of communications flow and some of the people who play key roles in the transmission of influence. All this, of course, has immediate and obvious implications for mass media research and for a better understanding of the processes of effective communication, *provided* that mass communications do, in fact, hook up with these interpersonal networks.

## Communicating to the Group

What evidence have we for the hypothesis that communications are relayed according to a two-step formula? We can muster some impressive empirical evidence to indicate that this is so in several spheres of influence; but the quantity of evidence is still quite modest and the areas explored quite few. In any case that is one of the tasks of the second part of this book.[1] What we shall attempt to do, however, is to try to specify some of the ways in which influences originating outside a group may successfully make their way inside to influence ideas or behavior. Thus, the following pages will attempt to locate evidence which points to the kinds of links that exist between systems of intragroup communication such as those which we have just examined and the world "outside." If we can identify some of these links then the relevance of interpersonal communications for mass media research will appear much more clear.

Consider first the *situational* factor. Part of defining any situation involves the specification of a relevant environment. Minority groups in our society furnish good examples. For some situations, the relevant environment for these groups is the majority group, and thus, minority groups *nominate* ambassadors, so to speak, from among those who are able to relate the group to the majority. At other times and in other situations, the majority may be of little consequence compared, say, with the minority group's own culture, or the "old country"; the desire to relate to this other environment will give rise to quite a different set of relay roles. The characteristics of the kind of leadership which relates minority groups to the majority, in situations where the minority aspires to acceptance by the majority have been discussed by Myrdal in the case of the Negroes, and by Lewin in the case of the Jews.[2] Merton (1949A) makes a related point in his study of the interpersonal communication of news events in a small town. He finds that one kind of influential typically introduces "local" home-town news and quite another kind introduces "cosmopolitan" communications, implying, again, that there are different kinds of transmitters for different sorts of "outside" news.

If we ask which group members are more likely than others to serve as links between the group and some relevant environ-

---

1. See Part Two, Chapter XIV.
2. See Myrdal's (1944) discussion of "accommodating leadership" and Lewin's (1948) essay on "self-hatred."

ment, we shall find that our earlier discussion of structural and cultural factors is suggestive, too. Consider, for example, the kind of communications role which is assigned to an individual who is *located* at a strategic point in the group *structure* relative to some relevant environment. The boss's secretary, for example, may play this kind of role for the office workers; the member who has had social contact with the majority by virtue of his "position" in society may serve in the case of the minority group; the first family with a television set may have a structural head-start for influence transmission in the neighborhood.

Finally, there are those who have particular relay functions by virtue of their *cultural* roles. Adolescents, for example, are notorious for their determination to keep the family abreast of the latest in popular culture. Word of the newest song hit, or the latest movie release may reach the family only because the culture commends particular patterns of adolescent behavior. In a similar way, many of the interests of the members of the family are culturally determined and when news from one of these specialized areas passes to other family members it is thanks to the particular member in charge. The distribution of the sections of the Sunday paper among the family often reflects this division of interest; and when sports, for example, suddenly becomes the concern of all—during the World Series, say—then the sports section reader, father perhaps, may become opinion leader.

These suggestions which can be derived from our earlier discussion of the patterns and processes of communication *within* the group have obvious implications for a discussion of communication *to* the group. Situational, structural, and cultural elements are as important in determining the selection of individuals who will link their peers to some relevant environment, as they are in determining the patterns and the key communicators within the group. Kurt Lewin (1952) had a name for these individuals who link interpersonal communications networks to something "outside": he called them "gatekeepers."[3]

---

3. Pp. 459-462. Thus, Lewin's "gatekeeper" idea is very closely related to our idea of the "opinion leader."

Gatekeeping means controlling a strategic portion of a channel—whether that channel is for the flow of goods, or news, or people—so as to have the power of decision over whether whatever is flowing through the channel will enter the group or not. Lewin's original formulation was in terms of food habits. His problem was whether to recommend that a mass media campaign to change food habits during wartime should be directed at the population as a whole, or whether there might not be strategic elements in the population who, once influenced to change, would also change the habits of others. In the case of food which reaches the family via the grocery, Lewin says, the gatekeeper is the mother, or sometimes the maid, while father would be gatekeeper for family food which is grown in the garden. In other words, Lewin implies, food campaigns—depending on the sphere—may most effectively be directed at one or another of these gatekeepers. And what is true in the case of food, Lewin goes on, holds also "for the traveling of a news item through certain communications channels in a group."[4]

A distinction which was made earlier, in the analysis of transmission within the group, belongs here in our discussion of communicating to the group as well. There the role of *originator* of an idea was distinguished from that of *transmitter* of the idea, and both of these were distinguished from the role of *influential*. The gatekeeper, similarly, may be an originator only—in the sense that he introduces an idea to a group, but he may or may not serve also as a transmitter within the group and may or may not be influential at all. Whether or not gatekeeping leads to influentiality is an important problem, as a matter of fact, and one which is implicit in the following pages.

Let us look now at several of the small number of studies

---

4. *Ibid.*, p. 461. In reality, there are several interrelated problems here. Presuming even that father is gatekeeper for food grown in the garden, that does not mean that his decision about what to grow is made independently of the family. Or, again, if he does make the decision unilaterally it does not mean that the rest of the family will eat what father grows. Of course, that also depends on what else is available to eat, and the kinds of attitudes which prevail relative to "waste," etc. The parallel is that an editor can decide to print one item and not another, but thereby he has not automatically influenced his readers either to read it or believe it. Similarly, Mrs. Smith may make an annual trip to Paris, but her neighbors may not copy her fashions.

which illustrate these points. The studies that will be most directly relevant are those which treat interpersonal relations in terms of some larger context. We shall look into these to see how the small group establishes connections with its context, so to speak. Our plan is as follows: First, we shall report on several studies where the contexts are varied indeed: a factory, a Japanese relocation center in World War II, and Soviet Russia. Then, we will pay particular attention to a new source of information which has recently been reopened via international communications research. Especially interesting for us are sections of several recent studies which bring the opinion leader concept to bear on the flow of news in rural, traditional, Middle Eastern communities just on the verge of social change.

## The Group in an Organizational Context

One theme that runs through recent sociological studies of social control in a stratified community or in a hierarchical institution is that communications directed from the top of an organization downwards will be most effective when they are funneled through the informal leaders of the informal groups which emerge—we now know—on every level of the structure.

In his article on "The Study of the Primary Group," Shils (1951) cites four or five such studies, all of which conclude that the group's normally chosen leaders must mediate between their associates and communications from above if those communications are to be effective at all. Leighton's (1945) report on a wartime relocation center for Japanese in the United States—one of the cases Shils cites—is an excellent example. The study tells of the crescendo of mounting tension among the Japanese-American evacuees as conditions in the camp worsened, and the inability of the United States-appointed Administration to cope adequately with the situation became plain. One of the defects in the organization of the Center to which the study points was the prolonged existence of a Council of residents which was not truly representative of the resident population. And as the Council became the object of more and more mistrust, it became less and less adequate as a medium of information and influence. Leighton cautions

against relying on the assumption that information will somehow "spread": "Because some kinds of information did spread,
there was a tendency for administrators to have an almost
superstitious credence in the 'grapevine' and to assume that
when they said something to one evacuee, they had told all
of them. . . ."[5]

It was not until a real crisis hit the Center that the spontaneous informal primary groups which had grown up around
mutual interests and within residential units sent their leadership forward to be heard. Soon thereafter, through democratic
elections, these representatives were organized into a new
Council and by virtue of their positions of leadership in their
own groups, two-way communications rapidly improved. The
lesson for administration is clear: an administration must realize that it is dealing not only with individuals but with informally organized groups, and take account of the particular
leadership patterns which emerge.

In passing, it is interesting to note that in this Center there
were, in fact, not one, but two patterns of leadership. The
young, American-reared Japanese "emphasized the vigorous
individual who, after popular election, assumes personal responsibility for devising plans and getting things done."[6] Most
of the older people, however, felt that leadership should more
properly be vested in elders and heads of families. Here we see
a cultural difference in the determination of influence: American culture emphasizes nomination from among a variety of
candidates of all sorts; Japanese culture awards leadership, by
certification, to an elder.

That the patterns of interpersonal leadership—whatever they
may be—must be taken into account by anybody who is trying
to bring an integrating influence to bear on a group, from outside, is illustrated by other studies in widely different contexts,
too. William Foote Whyte (1945), for example, has written a
paper dealing with the role of the settlement house in Cornerville, the community context in which he studied the Street
Corner Society of Doc and the Norton gang. The settlement
house, Whyte points out, did not succeed in bringing in the

---

5. Leighton (1945), pp. 331-332.
6. *Ibid.*, p. 293.

Nortons or any other street corner gang because the house was staffed by people who were very unlike the residents of Cornerville in values and behavior, and because they aimed at reaching *individuals* rather than the organized gang as a whole via its leadership.

Russian Communism, it seems, is aware of the importance of these personal lines of contact according to Alex Inkeles' (1952) well-documented book on the Soviet theory and practice of public opinion and communication. Inkeles brings evidence to show that the Russian Communist Party has given careful thought to the power of informal influentials in making official party policy effective. Thus, in the 1930's, Inkeles tells us, the party confronted the problem of putting the job of agitation on a really large scale basis and taking it out of the hands of a small corps of specialists. The model of what such an agitator should be like was then given considerable thought. Inkeles sums up this point as follows:

The successful agitator is, therefore, currently described as the man who knows not only how each person in his shop works, but also how he lives, what his family is like, what his living conditions are, and whether or not he needs advice on one or another personal problem. The agitator is told that "only in the event that the agitator stands in close contact with the people" does he actually win for himself authority and respect. . . .

In every case, the fact of central importance is that the agitator is establishing a relationship of social solidarity with the members of his work group; or, as one man who had been given personal assistance by the agitator is reported to have put it, the agitator had developed the feeling that the shop and the working group in it was a sort of family, with close ties, that each man had certain responsibilities toward it. Reports on the personal experiences of agitators working on collective farms or with the general population, and particularly with housewives, indicate that there too the successful agitator bases his success largely on the same type of personal relationship with his audience.[7]

We are not, of course, developing a theory of successful agitation but of communication—which within certain contexts includes the communication of a set line in a system

---

7. Inkeles (1950), pp. 88-89.

which strictly controls all channels of communication, elimi-
nates all idea-competition and knows the values of repetition,
surveillance and informal opinion leadership.[8]

That administrators must take "gatekeepers" into account,
however, is only one side of this opinion leader story. Another
side—and an equally important one—is that, administration or
no, informal groups *take the initiative* in connecting themselves to those contexts which they consider important via the
mechanisms of group ambassadors, so to speak. Horsfall and
Arensberg (1949) provide evidence for this point in the context of a 28-man production room in a shoe factory.[9] The
production scheme devised by management involved four
teams of seven men each, so organized that the whole structure of both formal and informal relations depended necessarily
on the character of the connections among the groups. For
each group in the room, the other three groups constituted an
important context to which to be related. In these terms, then,
it is quite interesting to see that the analysis of those who were
named as leaders by the others in the room points to a high
degree of *inter-team contact* as one of the major distinguishing
characteristics of the leaders. This same component of leadership is evident too in Street Corner Society where part of the
gang leader's prestige could be attributed to his extragroup
contacts—with politicians, racketeers, and other gangs and
their leaders.

In these examples we see that the gatekeeping role is often
coupled with influentiality within the group—although the two
functions need not necessarily go together. Let us try, however, to examine the conditions under which they are likely
to be so coupled, and then go on to a question that follows
from the observation that it is often the case that they *do*
go together. It is the old question of "which comes first?":
Does a leadership role within the group lead to the role of gatekeeper, or does the ability to relate the group to some important context lead to a position of influence? Undoubtedly, of

---

8. "Monopolization" of the media and "supplementation" by face-to-face
influencing are two of the reasons given by Lazarsfeld and Merton (1949)
for the effectiveness of totalitarian propaganda.

9. See particularly pp. 24-25.

course, there are some situations where one comes first and some situations where the other comes first, and while we don't propose to wrestle with this problem abstractly, we can show some interesting examples of the emergence of influentiality from gatekeeping roles as we turn now to a field from which there is much to learn about the links between groups and the world outside.

## The Traditional Community: Examples from International Communications Research

The new field of research which has developed from the vigorous programs in international communications allows us, among many other things, to return from our preoccupation with modern society to the kind of folk community so often described in the classical sociological writings and in the work of anthropologists. In the 1950's, however, we approach those communities with a new problem: What are the channels through which news of the world flows into the village and what, if any, are the attitudes of the villagers to foreign affairs and the world situation, and how are these attitudes formed?

In an article on the flow of world news into the tiny Greek village of Kalos, we find a discussion of several kinds of communications roles among this almost totally illiterate population.[10] The author describes the town's opinion leader—a teacher, one of the two men in the community who can read—and the process via which he receives a newspaper and conveys that part of its contents which he thinks worth conveying to those in the village who are concerned with the news. These recipients are called "opinion carriers," and it is suggested that they seek news either *per se* (Greek culture emphasizes knowl-

---

10. Stycos (1952). This study and the Lebanese study to which we shall refer below are sections of larger reports on communications patterns in those countries, and are, in turn, parts of a series of studies on international communications in the Near and Middle East recently completed by The Bureau of Applied Social Research, Columbia University. A book reporting the highlights of this series is scheduled for early publication; see Lerner, Berkman and Pevsner (forthcoming). For an overview of the theoretical aspects of this program, see Glock (1953), and for a discussion of various aspects of international communications research see the special issue of the *Public Opinion Quarterly*, vol. 16, no. 4, Winter 1952-53.

edge) or as a means toward achieving prestige among others for whom they, in turn, serve as relayers.

The teacher is the community's only living link with the world outside—both figuratively, in his role as the sole source of information in matters relating to extra-communal affairs, and literally because he makes an annual trip at the end of each school year to the big city. Thus, in our terms the teacher is gatekeeper for the community.

It is pertinent to contrast the role of the teacher as both gatekeeper and influential with the gatekeeping role of the tavern keeper who officially supervises the turning of the dial of the town's only radio. This role is called "information controller," and we are told that such people, usually illiterate and of low social status, are not in the least better informed or more influential. "They are merely people who, by nature of their occupation, are in a strategic position as regards the physical flow of radio communications."

Another recent study of a very unique situation—yet, one which shares many of the attributes of problems in international communications—calls attention to exactly this same kind of institutionalized, semi-formal, but still personalized, communications transmission. This is a study by S. N. Eisenstadt (1952) of the unprecedented mass immigration of Jews coming from a large variety of different cultures to the new state of Israel. The focus of the study is the effect of cultural differences on integration and absorption into the new country.

Discussing communications patterns, Eisenstadt contrasts the highly traditional groups which come from the pre-industrial settings of the Middle Eastern countries with the much less tradition-bound European immigrants to Israel. In the Eastern groups, it is possible to point to the "traditionally defined situations which are specifically constructed as focal points of communication" and which continue to function in Israel much as they did before. Thus, entire communities still assemble to hear the teachings of the traditional leaders at the Sabbath gatherings in the synagogue, the arbitration court meetings, and at the assemblies in traditional schools. Eisenstadt finds that in these groups the major links in the communications process can be located within these traditional settings.

In such groups, we are told, more spontaneous, informal contacts tend to be between peers rather than between leaders and followers and these seem to be very much less effective than the formal occasions as far as the flow of influence is concerned. The contrast with Western groups is especially interesting for its bearing on opinion leader research in modern communities. For in the European groups, Eisenstadt finds, there is a marked increase in informal transmission, different types of opinion leaders for different sorts of topics,[11] and much wider participation by the rank and file in the discussion of important matters.

For us, the most important part of the communications phase of this study is a discussion of the conditions under which groups turn away from one set of opinion leaders and recognize another set. Drawing explicitly on the opinion leader tradition, Eisenstadt suggests that when leaders can no longer effectively relate their groups to a larger social system in such a way that the members understand and are satisfied with their places within that system, new leaders who can fulfill this function are likely to arise. Discussing the Eastern immigrant groups, Eisenstadt attempts to specify the communications requirements which the traditional leadership must fulfill if it is not to lose its influence. These requirements include aiding group members to achieve status in the larger social system which is the group's new context; mediating the values and the demands of the new country; communicating an understanding of the nation's institutions and their workings, and so on. And whenever the traditional leaders cannot or will not fulfill these functions, the study reports, there is a tendency for new leaders—gatekeepers and influentials—to encroach on the traditional leader's role.[12]

---

11. Eisenstadt suggests that two of the types correspond rather closely to the "cosmopolitans" and "locals" in Merton (1949A).

12. Eisenstadt, pp. 52-3, supplies us with an analysis of the explanations offered by those who abandoned their former leaders and rallied round new gatekeepers and influentials. These are the major categories into which the explanations fall:

(1) Growing disillusionment about the traditional leaders' ability to assure them of various amenities and rights accruing to them in the new social system.

(2) Doubts as to the traditional leaders' prestige-positions within the new social system.

The dynamic aspect of this study—and the kinds of conditions which Eisenstadt suggests will result in a change of opinion leadership—is paralleled in a study of "The Radio Audience of Lebanon,"[13] (like the Greek study, part of the International Radio Project of The Bureau of Applied Social Research) and the findings can be dovetailed neatly into the Israeli study. The particular section of this paper which concerns us is the hypothetical reconstruction of the communications process in non-literate, non-radio listening, rural villages of Lebanon. The number of cases on which this section is based is quite small[14] and thus the authors caution the reader on the tentativeness of the findings (although the data obtained from each respondent was considerable and very intensive). But even as hypothesis, the suggestions made here are of extreme interest.

The traditional life of the Lebanese village is being invaded slowly but surely by the world. And the traditional leaders—particularly the elders—are experiencing an inadequacy which limits the range of their influence and, for the first time, makes their leadership dependent on the role of the young. For the young are the new opinion leaders, the study tells us. It is the young who are primarily identified with the introduction of news of the world into the peasant community.

But this new role does not come to the young just because of their youth. First of all, those who become opinion leaders are young people who have obtained some education—but only those educated young people who remain in contact with their families and illiterate neighbors. A second distinguishing characteristic of this new kind of influential is his *mobility;* the "trip to the city" is what makes the difference. And there is evidence in this study that contact with the formal media —which sometimes are available in the village itself, but pri-

---

(3) Disillusionment with the traditional leaders' ability to interpret the new social system and its values to the immigrants.

(4) The feeling that attachment to the traditional leadership blocks their achievement of full status within the new society.

(5) The loss of a feeling of participation in the new social system and of belongingness to it as a result of clinging to the traditional leadership.

13. McPhee and Meyersohn (1951).

14. Although rural, illiterate peasants constitute the numerical majority in the Middle East, this study has so few cases of this type because its sample was weighted heavily in favor of radio listeners and newspaper readers.

marily to the upper classes—is established predominantly as a consequence of trips to the city. Thus, the young people who are educated to read and interpret the news and to understand what the radio is saying when they are somewhat mobile and when they are also in contact with others who cannot read seem to be emerging as the new opinion leaders, the "cosmopolitans," of the peasant villages of the Near East. "Our materials suggest the hypothesis," say the authors, "that as the 'outside world' begins to enter the village, it tends to by-pass the traditional leaders who held positions of influence in the old village."

This stage in social change—as reflected by the processes of opinion leadership—seems to be one step earlier than the stage at which Eisenstadt reports that traditional opinion leaders lose their effectiveness; or, perhaps, it should be seen as the beginnings of a specialization, possibly temporary, in opinion leadership. Thus, the old leaders still control the "local" and the traditional areas of opinion and action, while the new "cosmopolitans" go about relating the village to the outside world.

But there is evidence here, too, that these new opinion leaders are active not only in the circulation of the news, but in the *interpretation* of it as well—and that is a danger sign for traditional leadership, even in its entrenched sphere of local affairs. To illustrate, let us look at one of the many revealing quotations cited here:

I like very much those who read newspapers, because they always have something of great importance to tell. They *understand more than us and their mind is more capable than ours in digesting very difficult news or material read.* They *understand* what the government is doing and what is happening in Damascus or Tripoli. We do not read the newspapers so we must wait for others to *amuse and fascinate us* with what is happening in other villages and towns. A friend of ours *always tells us amazing and strange stories . . .* and he *always says that he read this in the newspaper.*[15]

If, on the other hand, however, the elders receive the "reports" of those who, as they say, "come and go," and if they can keep the role of interpretation and influencing for them-

---

15. McPhee and Meyersohn, *op. cit.* (Italics supplied by original authors.)

selves, their leadership will not be lost. It seems reasonable to suggest the general proposition that if leaders can adjust to new demands and meet the needs of their followers for a feeling of relatedness to newly relevant aspects of the environment, then they may well retain influence even in a very new situation. If they cannot adapt this way, a new set of leaders will arise.[16]

In these last two studies, then, we have seen that when a group experiences the need to relate itself to a newly perceived social context, and if the old leaders cannot function adequately as keepers of the new gates, then new gatekeepers will arise and may soon obtain influence as well. This is one of the answers to our question of "which comes first". Here we have seen that gatekeeping comes first, and then may be followed by influentiality. And when we ask who the new gatekeepers are, we find in the Lebanese case, at least, that they are people whose social *location* permits them to forge the new gate.[17]

---

16. This is the major clue, we think, to an interesting dilemma which emerges when several small group propositions are made to confront each other: There is, first of all, the general principle which we have examined that leadership changes as situations, or group activities, change. Secondly, we are convinced by Homans (1950) that in the normal course of group life, new activities are continuously generated (see, e.g., pp. 108-110). The dilemma: if group activities are constantly being elaborated, and thus situations constantly changed, then it follows that leadership should be a highly unstable phenomenon. Yet, we know intuitively that leadership of stable groups tends to be quite stable.

This somewhat formal logical dilemma leads us to an interesting hypothesis: The reason that leadership does not change each time a group elaborates or changes its patterns of activity is that leaders tend to control the selection of the new activities. Thus, if the gang decides to switch from bowling to some other sport, the leader is more likely than anybody else to influence the new selection—and, of course, he will choose a sport in which he excels. *Only when the leader cannot direct the change will the leader's role be threatened.* Thus, if a boy's gang whose main activity is baseball grows up and finds that its main interest is sex, and if the leader is not quite so good at arranging social parties as he is at setting up baseball matches, then his leadership will begin to give way. Similarly, if the world for whatever reason, begins to make itself felt in the Near Eastern village, and the traditional leader does not know how to relate his village to this new concern, then his leadership, too, will begin to falter.

17. This is a good place perhaps to remark on the innovating role of "isolates," individuals who are disaffected from their communities, individuals rejected by their groups, etc. There is evidence which suggests that such people may be particularly predisposed to serve as transmitters of ideas-from-the-outside into the groups on whose sociometric margins they live. (Whether or not their innovations will be accepted by the group is another matter.) Various technical assistance agencies have found that individuals who are marginal to a community will often leap to assist in the propagation of a

This brings us to the close of our discussion on communication to the group and, indeed, to the close of this final portion of our review of studies that have bearing on the formulation of a modest theory of the flow of influence. In these last few pages, we have dwelt on the role of social location, but also on the roles of certification and nomination, as keys to the part played by people in relaying, reinforcing (and blocking) the messages directed at a group from "the world outside."

## A Summary of Implications

In the four chapters of this section, we have pointed to two ingredients of interpersonal relations which help to explain what there is about an individual's relatedness-to-others that might have bearing on the effectiveness of mass media influence-attempts.

The first ingredient singled out was group norms. It was shown that there is good reason to believe that very often, seemingly private opinions and attitudes are maintained by an individual in conjunction with small numbers of others with whom he is motivated to interact. It follows, therefore, that the success of an attempt to change an individual's opinion or attitude will depend, in some measure, on the resistance to or support for the proposed change which the individual encounters in his group.

The second ingredient singled out was person-to-person transmission. Here it was shown that there are patterned channels of communication between a group and "the world outside," and patterned channels of communication within the group. It follows, therefore, that those individuals who play key roles in these channels will have a major share in determining whether or not it will be circulated and whether or not it will be favorably received. We considered for a moment some of the ways in which these ingredients of interpersonal relations might block an influence-attempt stemming from the mass media and directed at an individual. For example, (1)

---

proposed innovation, thus jeopardizing its acceptance by others. See Public Administration Clearing House (1954). For an extremely pertinent discussion of this matter and of a large number of other matters which concern us here, see Barnett (1953), Part IV (on "dissaffection," pp. 389-401).

the appropriate gatekeeper may not relay it; (2) an influential may not endorse it; (3) it may be perceived as going counter to norms shared with valued others.

To succeed, on the other hand, a proposed change may have to be identified with a valued group norm, or be endorsed as a new group norm; it may have to enlist the support of appropriate influentials and interpersonal transmitters; and it may have to make contact with an appropriate gatekeeper in order to reach the group at all.

This is what we mean when we say that interpersonal relations "intervene" in the mass communications process, and thus that communications research aiming at the study of short-run mass media effects must take systematically into account an individual's relatedness-to-others. The lesson is plain: No longer can mass media research be content with a random sample of disconnected individuals as respondents. Respondents must be studied within the context of the group or groups to which they belong or which they have "in mind"—thus, which may influence them—in their formulation of opinions, attitudes or decisions, and in their rejection or acceptance of mass media in influence-attempts.

It was our interest in opinion leadership which led us to explore the links between small groups and the mass media. This exploration, in turn, now directs our attention to a number of other matters which relate directly or indirectly to some of the assumptions we have made here, some of the assertions we have put forward, as well as to some of the subjects we have intentionally skirted. Looking "toward further research," let us state some of these new interests here:

(1) If mass media influence is dependent on interpersonal relations, we want to know much more about the actual distribution of sociometric connections among individuals. What is the extent of "isolation" in different parts of society, and who are the isolates? Which kinds of people go beyond the neighborhood or off-the-job to seek friendships, and which kinds of people make friends of those who are close by? Are all Americans joiners of clubs, or is this a phenomenon which varies, say, with class? Are interpersonal relations homogeneous as to age, social status, etc.? How important is the family of procrea-

tion as a basis for primary group relations in adult life—and for whom? And so on. Mass media research must inventory the work already done in these areas,[18] and possibly stimulate more extensive investigation.

(2) Similarly, it will be important to determine which kinds of groups "breed" which kinds of norms. In some investigations it will be an individual's work group which is relevant; in others, his family group; in still others, his leisure time group, etc. Different affiliations, in other words, will be relevant for different subjects, and for different kinds of people as well.

(3) We would like also to begin gathering information about the kinds of opinion leaders who emerge for various subject-areas of influence. Once we find the kinds of groups that are anchorage-points ("breeding" places) for different kinds of norms, we shall want to locate the kinds of people within those groups who are the influentials. The second part of this book makes a start in that direction.

(4) Then, too, we must learn which of an individual's opinions are truly individualistic and *not* anchored—that is, generated or maintained—in interpersonal relations. Which kinds of things, in other words, are shared in small groups and which kinds of things vary from person to person? Consider an extreme example: Is choice of cigarette brand typically a completely individualistic phenomenon or is there a greater-than-chance co-incidence of brand choice among interacting individuals?

(5) On the other hand, too, we must not make the mistake of assuming that the *content* of most norms, opinions, attitudes, etc., varies from small group to small group. We must, as a matter of fact, learn to distinguish the role of the small group in *generating* idiosyncratic norms and the role of the small group in *transmitting* and maintaining norms which vary only with larger social categories—social class, for example.

(6) Nor can we overlook the possibility that the degree to

18. For examples of research in this important area, see index items "acquaintance," "association," "neighborhood," etc. in Lynd and Lynd (1928) and Lynd and Lynd (1937); see Warner and Lunt (1941), Dotson (1951), Komarovsky (1946), Goldhamer (1942), Bushee (1945), Smith, Form and Stone (1954), etc. A recent bibliography of such studies in participation is contained in Foskett (1955).

which individuals share opinions and attitudes with others is itself a *cultural* variable—changing from age to age and from culture to culture. This notion is implicit in the suggestions of Riesman (1950), for one, that there has been a change in modern America from an "inner-directed" personality type to an "other-directed" one.[19] The "inner-directed" individual, self-reliant and propelled by a clearly formulated personal goal, would rely less on the approbation of others, and hence on their opinions and tastes, than would the "other-directed" individual whose entire worldly concern, presumably, is with what others think.

The whole moral of these chapters is that knowledge of an individual's interpersonal environment is basic to an understanding of his exposure and reactions to the mass media. Thus, planning for future research on the short-run[20] influencing effects of the mass media must build, first, on the systematic investigation of the everyday processes which influence people and, secondly, on the study of the points of contact between these everyday influences and the mass media. The aim of these chapters has been to spell out some of the implications which arise from a consideration of what is known about one such source of everyday influence: interpersonal relations.

---

19. Of course, the goals even of an "inner-directed" era are not individually determined but products of cultural norms and, therefore, necessarily involve interpersonal transmission and enforcement. Given such goals, however, the institutional means for attaining them prescribe an individualistic striving and a non-concern with changing fashions and opinons, etc.—matters which are of primary concern to the "other-directed" personality.

20. It is perhaps worth reiterating what was said at the very opening: Mass media research has been concerned almost exclusively with the study of only one kind of effect—the effect of short-run attempts ("campaigns") to change opinions and attitudes. The purpose of these chapters was to add to the picture of the processes involved in the transmission and acceptance of such influences. What should not be lost in all of this, however, is the idea that there are other kinds of mass media effects—which have not been much studied—where the impact of the mass media on society may be very much greater. Thus, the mass media surely lend themselves to all kinds of psychological gratifications and social "uses"; they seem to have visible effects on the character of personal "participation" in a variety of cultural and political activities; they have often been credited with being the primary agencies for the transmission of cultural values, etc. These chapters have not been explicitly concerned with these (predominantly long-range) matters. But our prescription—that communications research must take full account of the interpersonal contexts into which the mass media are injected—may hold good, too, for the much needed research on these less apparent, but perhaps more potent, effects of mass communications.

**Part Two**

**THE FLOW OF EVERYDAY INFLUENCE**

**IN A MIDWESTERN COMMUNITY**

CHAPTER I

# Criteria of Influence

HERE WE BEGIN the report of the Decatur study—our attempt to make a start in mapping the flow of influence concerning several everyday matters in a middle-sized American city. Our central problem was to locate key points in the transmission of personal influence. We wanted to single out leaders in the formation of opinion. But popular imagery comprehends many types of leaders, official and unofficial, leaders of small groups and of large nations, organizers, agitators, and clarifiers, specialized leaders and leaders who lead in many life-areas.

Official leaders serve formally organized institutions by virtue of the authority vested in the office they occupy; among them are the presidents of corporations, unions, and governments. Unofficial leaders lead without benefit of authoritative office: here are the Key Men of a work gang, the Sparkplugs of a salesman rally, the Elder Statesmen who sit on park benches talking for the newspapers. Some leaders, club chairmen for example, serve only little groups, all of whose members are in frequent face-to-face contact; others, some radio preachers for example, lead nationwide audiences whose mem-

bers never see one another. Agitators and organizers move men
to join with them in mass movements; clarifiers and verbal
experts vitalize the inert goals and modify the contemplations
of their silent followers. Specialized leaders, such as bridge experts, are confined to some particular sphere; generalized leaders, such as dictators, lead people in a total way in all the
spheres of their lives.

The types of leader in which we are interested in this study
—the ones we call Opinion Leaders—serve informal rather
than formal groups, face-to-face rather than more extensive
groups. They guide opinion and its changes rather than lead
directly in action.

What we shall call opinion leadership, if we may call it
leadership at all, is leadership at its simplest: it is casually
exercised, sometimes unwitting and unbeknown, within the
smallest grouping of friends, family members, and neighbors.
It is not leadership on the high level of a Churchill, nor of a
local politico, nor even of a local social elite. It is at quite the
opposite extreme: it is the almost invisible, certainly incon-
spicuous, form of leadership at the person-to-person level of
ordinary, intimate, informal, everyday contact. Our study is
an attempt to locate and learn something about these everyday
influentials.

We began by interviewing a cross-sectional sample of some
800 women in Decatur, Illinois, a middle-sized city in the Middle West.[1] We inquired into four arenas of everyday decisions:
marketing, fashions, public affairs and movie-going. And for
each arena, we asked our respondents not only about themselves and their own behavior but about other people as well—
people who influence them, and people for whom they are
influential.

Our procedures, the obstacles we encountered, and the mistakes we made will all be unraveled as we go along, together
with whatever results we have to report. But we have to begin
somewhere to tell something about how the study was planned.
Instead of beginning from the beginning, however, let us

---

1. For a discussion of the criteria employed for choosing this city, see
Appendix A.

plunge into one of the four arenas—the arena of public affairs
—and see something of the flow of influence there.

With reference to the formation of judgments and opinions
about public affairs and political life, we asked our respondents about three kinds of other people. We asked them to
name (1) the people whom they believe to be trustworthy
and knowledgeable about matters of public concern; (2) the
people who actually influenced them in some specific change
of opinion in a matter of current concern; and (3) the people
with whom they most often talk over what they hear on the
radio or read in the papers. In addition, from each woman in
the sample we obtained extensive information about herself,
including a self-rating of her own influentiality together with
reports of recent specific occasions on which she claimed to
have influenced others.

In the following three sections of the present chapter, we
shall take up each of these detecting devices in turn and briefly
describe the relations between the people located by each of
them and the women in our sample who named them. We
want to investigate, in other words, the extent to which each
of these three types of designated influentials are influential
in fact, and the extent to which they are actually in close contact with our sample of women. We shall see that these three
ways of going about the study of informal influence form a
rough scale, although the dimensions of this scale remain
somewhat unclear.

From these designated influentials, we shall turn to the self-
rated influential; that is, we shall analyze the adequacy of self-
estimates of opinion leadership. And finally, we shall consider
the meaning, and the usefulness, of each of the four criteria
as bases for different approaches to the study of opinion leadership.

Our discussion in the remaining parts of this chapter, we
should reiterate, will draw examples only from the realm of
politics and public affairs, though later chapters will consider
influentiality in the arenas of marketing, fashions, and movie-
going as well.

## The Generally Influential

From the point of view of the person influenced, the opinion leader type whom we shall sometimes call the "general influential" and sometimes the "expert" is a person in whom one has confidence and whose opinions are held in high regard. In a direct effort to locate our respondents' "general influentials" we asked: "Do you know anyone around here who keeps up with the news and whom you can trust to let you know what is really going on?" Our interviewers were instructed to make sure that the respondent named only persons with whom they actually had some sort of face-to-face contact, not persons whom they knew only because of their prominent position in the public life of the city.

Not every woman interviewed knew someone she thought fitted the description offered in our question; about half, in fact, were unable, or unwilling, to name anyone within their acquaintance whose competence and trustworthiness in public affairs they accepted to let them know "what is really going on." These, we found, were women who had little interest in public affairs and little knowledge about them. Thus, only a third of the women who ranked lowest on knowledge of current affairs, but almost two-thirds of those with highest knowledge knew such a person. Since education, and hence, age, are linked with interest and knowledge, it is the younger, and above all the better educated women who were able to name such a person: only 40 per cent of the older women who did not finish high school, but 64 per cent of the younger ones who were high school graduates named a general influential. Awareness of the generally influential is thus in part self-selective: Many women are simply out of the public affairs market; they are not touched by the currents of personal influence in this sphere.

Now, whenever a respondent indicated that she knew such an "expert," the interviewer obtained that person's name and some information about his or her relation with the respondent. These relationships are as follows: About half of those considered competent and trustworthy on current affairs are people within the respondents' family circles; the remainder are neighbors, friends, or work associates. Among married women, husbands play a larger role than any other relations. Yet, considering the general availability of the husband, it is interesting to find almost as many neighbors as husbands among the married women's listings. Among unmarried women, parents constitute the largest single group of general influentials; these unmarried women are, of course, younger than the others, and their dependence on parents certainly reflects, at least in part, the position of the parents as the most accessible adults. Among the once-married, (separated, divorced, widowed) family relationships are less frequently mentioned than non-family relationships. These women are freer of family ties than either the married or the single; their lower rate of family contact is in large part a reflection of the unavailability of family relations.

But whether women are married, single or separated, they apparently look to men for competence in public matters. Regardless of their family status, two-thirds of the general influentials named by women are men. Most of them are of course members of the respondents' families; in fact, only a third are outside the kinship circle. On the other hand, when a female is named she is more likely to be friend or neighbor than kin. This difference is quite striking. Its most obvious explanation is that face-to-face relationships are differentiated along sex lines according to family status. In other words, outside the family circle, women know more women than men. In addition, there may be a certain reluctance for women to name male friends as more generally trustworthy and competent than their male kin.

## The Specific Influentials

The kinds of influentials we have just described were located by a question concerning the generalized willingness of the respondent to accept influence from someone. If we would carry our study a step closer to actual influences, alleged or real, we must focus upon *specific instances* of contact between people in connection with actual opinion changes. So we asked our sample of women, during the June interview (the first of two interviews), nine questions of opinion on current issues; in August, we asked the same sample of women the same questions again. This second time, our interviewers carried with them the first interview answers, and whenever a respondent proffered a new opinion she was asked a series of specially designed questions in an effort to find out why she had departed from her earlier opinion. In these questions on changes, particular attention was paid to whether or not she had talked to someone about the issue in question, and whether this other person had played some role in bringing about the opinion change.

By thus isolating specific changes of opinion and working back to the influences which allegedly produced them, we tried to locate the specific persons in each instance who had had a part, at least in this one episode, in bringing about a change in opinion. A total of 619 changes in public affairs opinions were detected. Since opinions on more than one specific issue were being studied, more than one change may have been made by one respondent. In fact, women often changed their opinions on more than one issue, although more than three changes per individual was rare.

Not every opinion change involved a personal contact. Fifty-eight per cent (of the *changes*, not the *changers*) were apparently made without involving any remembered personal contact, and were, very often, dependent upon the mass media. But about 40 per cent of the time, in some 260 cases of opinion change, our respondents were able and willing to recall a specific conversation with another person which they alleged played a role in bringing about their change of mind.[2]

Many of these "specific influentials" are inside the family, and this is especially so among the married women, 64 per cent of whose influence relations are intra-familial. Within the family the most important persons for the opinion changes of married women were their husbands; for single women, parents were strongly represented. Among non-family relation-

2. The detection of the personal influence contacts we shall study in this and in the following chapter depend on the "recall" ability of the respondents. Contacts which may possibly have operated on the respondents without their being conscious of them must, of course, be ignored in this discussion. Such matters are more fully discussed below in Section Two.

ships, friends were most important, particularly among the single women. As we began to see in the case of the general influentials, the over-all picture again seems to reflect accessibility, in that most of the male influentials are family members while most of the female influentials are non-family.

## Everyday Contacts

In an effort to get still closer to the most informal, everyday influence contacts, we asked our respondents: "When you hear something on the radio or read something in the newspapers, are you inclined to talk it over with someone before you make up your mind? If so, whom?" Not every woman in the sample indicated that she did talk to someone about the things she read or heard about. About half, in fact, replied that they were not inclined to do so.[3] But from those who indicated that they did often talk things over, we obtained information about their "everyday contacts."

Give-and-take conversation about public affairs is largely carried on within the family circle. Few women, apart from those whose family ties are broken, apparently talk such things over with neighbors or friends. Married women depend mainly on husbands, single women on parents.

## A Comparison and a Tentative Result

It is difficult to compare the characteristics of people named as specific influentials, with those who are thought of as generally influential, for not every woman who named a general

---

3. It was hoped that this question would enable us to get a fair idea of the sorts of person the respondents ordinarily talked with about public matters. But the answers we got are difficult to interpret clearly. The question asks the respondent whether she is inclined to talk to someone "before you make up your mind." The more self-sufficient respondent who said she was not inclined may have felt that she was sufficiently knowledgeable to make up her own mind. Strictly speaking, the question consists of two questions:
1) Are you inclined to talk over things you read or hear?
2) Are you inclined to do so before you make up your mind?
A "yes" answer is fairly unambiguous, but a "no" answer may mean either that the respondent doesn't have enough interest in such things to talk about them, or that, although she might talk about them, she believes she is intelligent enough to make up her own mind without such conversation. The "yes" answers are typical of a certain group of women—those who are sufficiently interested in public affairs to talk about what they read or hear but who are at least slightly uneasy about making up their minds on such matters.

influential reported also that she had recently been influenced by someone in a specific opinion change. A strict comparison can be made only for women who designated influentials of all three types; this restricts us to 136 women who named an everyday consultant, a specific influential and a general influential as well.

Given our data, here is the best comparison we can make between these three types of contact according to family relationships:

**Table 1—Relationships of Respondents and Three Types of Influentials**

| Relationship | Everyday Contacts | Specific Influentials | General Influentials |
|---|---|---|---|
| Non-family | 15% | 34% | 51% |
| Family | 84 | 64 | 48 |
|     Parent | 21 | 17 | 18 |
|     Husband | 53 | 32 | 18 |
|     Other relatives | 10 | 15 | 12 |
| No answer | 1 | 2 | 1 |
| Total (= 100%) | (136) | (136) | (136) |

One principal fact stands out: A large proportion of the people named as generally influential are outside the family circle (51%); the specific influentials are intermediate (34%); the everyday contacts are least likely to be outside the family (15%).

We interpret this to mean, given the character both of the questions and the responses, that these three questions seem to fall into rank order along two different dimensions: from one end, in terms of the *frequency* of the types of contact which they enable us to locate (that is, everyday consultants most, general influentials least); and from the other, in terms of the general *appraisal* of the competence and trustworthiness of the public affairs mentors (that is, general influentials most, everyday consultants least).

Consider the role of husbands: 18 per cent of these women mention their husbands as someone whom they can "trust to let them know what is really going on" (general influentials); 32 per cent report that their husbands influenced them in some particular change of opinion (specific influentials); 53 per cent are inclined to talk over publicly communicated matters with their husbands (everyday contacts). In other words, our respondents carry on most of their everyday public affairs talk with their husbands, but when it comes to reporting a specific influence on a particular opinion, husbands are not as important as non-family contacts, and they are even less important when it comes to naming a generally competent and trustworthy public affairs adviser. Contact, in other words, is not synonymous with influence.

Each of these three questions about "other people" apparently taps a different aspect of the interpersonal environment. At one extreme, the general influentials are people whom these women know and who occupy a special position in their network of contacts; influence from such people is apparently readily accepted. However, it seems reasonable to surmise that these "experts" in public matters would tend also to be at some distance from our respondents, dispersed among friends, neighbors, and work associates—and this would be particularly so because most of the women in our sample can hardly be said to be continually concerned over "what is going on" in the news.

At the other extreme, the everyday consultants are close at hand, but contact with them—it seems safe to assume—is not typically regarded as an influence transaction. Thus, women who name their husbands as everyday contacts do not necessarily regard what their husbands tell them as having influence upon them; rather, they may look upon such talk as conversation between equals—which, in fact, it may be.

In between these two extremes, there are the persons whom our respondents credit with having influenced them in some specific opinion change. Among these there are not so many family relationships as there are among the everyday conversational contacts, but more than there are among the generally influential.

We suppose that each of these three ways of asking about influence is suitable for some purposes. But which would be most useful for actually tracing the usual flow of influence in the arenas of marketing, fashions, movie-going and public affairs? Perhaps the easiest to use are questions regarding general estimations of trustworthiness and competence, but this method has the disadvantage of not giving us information about how frequent the influence from these people upon our respondents may be. Moreover, it encourages respondents to name prestigeful people whom they may know only slightly. It also relies more on memory, with its well known distortive possibilities. On the other hand, if we insist too much on frequency of contact, we may load our findings simply with habitual encounters which, no matter how frequent and accurately remembered, may be less essential in influencing changes of opinion and usage.

Our choice tends toward the middle way. It seems to us that questions concerning recent, recollectable incidents of influence exchange, and the specific influentials involved therein, present the most promising prospect for the study of opinion leadership. It may even be—though this is simply speculative—that actual influence itself derives often from the compromise between higher estimations and easier accessibility. High estimations of someone's competence and trustworthiness make that person more likely to influence, but since such persons are often not accessible, their potential may not fully be realized. The more easily accessible persons in the immediate environment may thus often be able to exert influence simply because they are on hand when the ripe moment for change occurs. If this is the case, the specific influence type of question seems more promising as a criterion for opinion leadership.

## Self-Detected Leaders

We have decided, then, that our analysis will be of the opinion leaders who are indicated by the specific influence questions. But we have not yet completed our discussion of how one goes about the task of physically locating and interviewing such people.

Basically, there are two ways. One way is the approach that has been implicit so far: that is, specific influentials can be located through the testimony of those whom they have influenced. This can be done either by asking the respondents *to describe* the individuals who influenced them (this was the sort of testimony on which we have relied so far), or *to name* them, provide their addresses, and thus enable us to proceed ourselves to obtain the information we require.

But there is another way. Just as members of a sample can be asked whether they have recently been influenced by somebody else in some specific episode, they can also be asked whether they have recently been influential for others. In other words, each respondent can be interviewed about her *own* influentiality; and since it is *specific influence* with which we are concerned, she can also be asked to give names, and dates, and subjects, should she claim to have been influential. The desirability, from an administrative point of view, of thus locating influentials *within* the original sample rather than employing the sample to locate other individuals outside it, is obvious. And, in fact, this is the method we have adopted for most of our analysis.

Here, specifically, is how we went about it: In the first, and again in the second, interview, we asked each woman: "Have you recently been asked your advice about . . . ?" If the answer was "yes," information was collected pertaining to the subject matter of the influence exchange, the advisee's name, the relationship of adviser to advisee, etc. This specific influence question was repeated for each of the arenas of opinion and usage with which we were concerned: marketing, fashions, movie-going, and public affairs. In the second interview, in addition, we asked each woman, with reference to each area: "Compared with other women belonging to your circle of friends, are you more or less likely than any of them to be asked your advice on . . . ?"

From the answers to these questions, we constructed an index which would isolate the influentials in each area of opinion and usage. We would consider a woman an opinion leader, we decided, (1) if she told us twice (that is, both in the June and August interviews) that she had recently been asked for advice in a specific area; or (2) if she told us once (that is, either in June or in August) that her advice had been asked and if she also felt that she was generally "more likely" than her friends to be asked for advice in that area. Thus, by our definition, these two types are opinion leaders; women who answered otherwise are not.

This approach is based then on several "self-detecting" questions. These involve recent, specific, documented, advice-giving incidents, together with the respondent's own self-appraisal of the likelihood, compared with the other women she knows, of her being sought out for advice in each particular topical area.

Granted that this method is most convenient, is it reliable? How do we know that women who say they have been influential have actually communicated this influence successfully? How do we know, even, that the names of the alleged influences or the topic reportedly discussed are not fictitious?

This is a matter which we looked into. We took the names of those who were designated as recipients of influence and went directly to these influencees to see whether they would corroborate the stories which our respondent-influentials had told us. The next chapter will consider the adequacy of that confirmation, and to tell the whole story of the "follow-up" technique, it will start a little further back than the point at which we now stand.

# A Technique of Confirmation

MOST OF OUR INFORMATION on face-to-face influence consists of statements made by the people we interviewed about other people not interviewed. Now, some groups of our respondents, deliberately or unwittingly, might have inflated their position by claiming to have been asked advice more often than was actually the case; or, possibly, in telling us the reasons why they changed their opinions, they may have claimed to have had conversations with prestigeful people which in fact never occurred. So, in order to use this information with assurance, we obviously needed to confirm it in some way.

## The Follow-up Interview

In several of our questions, we asked the women in our sample about an explicit relationship of advice-giving or advice-receiving with another person. The most direct way to check up on the one woman's report is to interview the other person about the transaction, and then compare the two reports. This is more complicated than might at first seem; in order to make clear how we did it, we will use the following four terms:

By a "designation" we will mean that a woman in our sample, the "designator," has referred to a person, the "designatee," with whom she has exchanged advice. The "designatee" may have given advice, in which case she is the "influential," or she may have taken advice, in which case she is the "influencee."

Whether or not we can accept a particular designation depends on whether both parties, designator and designatee, agree with one another about what took place. Since we are most interested in the accuracy of our respondents' accounts,

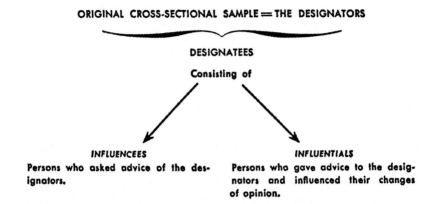

ORIGINAL CROSS-SECTIONAL SAMPLE = THE DESIGNATORS

DESIGNATEES

Consisting of

INFLUENCEES                                      INFLUENTIALS
Persons who asked advice of the des-      Persons who gave advice to the desig-
ignators.                                         nators and influenced their changes
                                                  of opinion.

we want to confirm it by seeing if the designatees agree with
its essential details.

We have of course two kinds of designations: those of persons to whom the respondents claimed to have given advice—
the influencees; and those of persons from whom the respondents claimed to have taken advice—the influentials. Since these
two kinds of designations are in different contexts, the problems of their validation differ.

We came upon the influentials, persons who presumably influenced the respondents, in the course of probing the reasons
for the respondents' changes in opinion or behavior. We asked
each respondent whether she had heard someone "talk about"
the topic in question. Whenever someone said, for example,
that she had recently changed her shade of lipstick, she was
asked whether she had heard someone talking about the new
lipstick before she made the change. What we needed to know
from the designated influential, then, was whether or not the
conversation had taken place, and whether or not she had in
fact given advice on the topic indicated.

In the case of influencees—persons to whom a respondent
claimed to have given advice—the information we had from
the designator was a little more complicated. We asked our
respondents whether or not they had recently been asked their
advice; some of them said yes and upon request gave us the
name of the persons they had allegedly advised. If our respondent told us that her influencee had asked her what was the

best kind of laundry soap to use, what we needed to know was whether or not the woman actually did go to our respondent and ask advice about laundry soap. From the influencees of our respondents we thus needed confirmation not only of the bare fact of communication but also of the communication's content and direction.

Here, then, is the information gotten from the designators:

| About Influentials | About Influencees |
|---|---|
| The names of persons with whom the respondents had talked about the topics on which they had changed. | The names of persons who had asked the respondents for advice. |

And here is the information needed from the designatees in order to confirm a designation:

| From Influentials | From Influencees |
|---|---|
| Whether they had talked to the respondent about the topic as alleged. | Whether they had gone to the respondent for advice as alleged. |

Our requests for the names and addresses of people who had allegedly advised or been advised were planted in appropriate contexts throughout our questionnaire. No special emphasis was given to these requests and unless the respondent asked specifically for the information, she was not informed of the reasons for them. No particularly strong resistance to the furnishing of names and addresses was encountered and in only a few cases were we refused.

A total of 1,549 designations was obtained, although not all of these were subsequently interviewed. Some of the persons designated lived in towns and cities beyond ready interviewing range, others were temporarily out of town, a few refused to be interviewed, etc. All of the troubles which usually plague the researcher trying to fulfill a pre-arranged sampling design, and some which were peculiar to this particular interviewing program, frustrated our attempt to interview all the designatees. In the end, only 634 persons mentioned by the respondents were reached and interviewed.[1]

We call these interviews with designatees "follow-up inter-

---

1. An accounting of the highlights of these interviewing efforts is given in Appendix C. Follow-up interviewing is also elaborated on in this Appendix.

views" because by means of these interviews we can follow the links of influence networks from beginning points in the sample.

In following up *influentials*, the persons whom our respondents said had given them advice, we had available the following information from the interview with the designating respondent: what specific change the respondent had made, the relationship of designatee and respondent—friend, relative, etc. We also knew that the designated influential was someone with whom the respondent had allegedly talked about the topic, and that she claimed that the exchange had had some effect on her opinion or action. Our interviewers were given all this information.

In following up *influences*, we did not know so much; but we did know that the designatee, according to the respondent, had come to her for advice, and we knew the general subject matter of the alleged conversation.

Follow-up interviewing is a delicate job; only our best interviewers were allowed to do it, and then only after considerable training and under close supervision. We never questioned in a point-blank way; we wanted the follow-up to mention the name of the designating person, to have it arise conversationally, in as natural a way as possible. The questionnaire and procedure had to be quite flexible, and considerable latitude had to be allowed the interviewers, who first went through a modified version of the questionnaire administered to the basic sample, in order to set up a straightforward interview situation. Then came the special follow-up questionnaire, beginning with the introduction, made as casually as possible, of the designator's name. If it was established that the two women were acquainted, the interviewer introduced the alleged conversational topic, asking whether the designatee had talked to the designator about it, which one had initiated the conversation, and finally whether the designatee had asked advice of the designator, or vice versa.[2]

2. In addition to the bare fact of confirming whether or not the conversation alleged by the respondent had occurred, other questions were asked, e.g., whether the advice-giving had taken the form of direct suggestion, or whether influence was exerted in a more or less passive way without any active role on the adviser's part; and so on. See Appendix C for details.

## Confirmation of Alleged Contacts

All but three of the 634 designatees interviewed acknowledged knowing the respondent who designated them; these three were probably mistakes on our part having to do with wrong addresses. We went beyond acquaintanceship, however, to the specific conversation described. The designatees were asked: "Do you recall talking with (the respondent who had designated them) about (the designated topic: e.g., nail polish, price control, etc.)?" Some of the advisers or advisees could not recall the specific conversation; others recalled topics different from the designated one; others were simply unable to recall whether the conversation had or had not taken place; and in a few cases, the designatees completely denied having talked to the respondent about the specific topic. But in two-thirds of the cases, confirmation both of the contact and of the conversation was obtained. Moreover, in the remaining one-third, the non-confirmed cases, only a small proportion, 9 per cent, completely denied that the conversation had occurred. If a woman said: "I remember talking to (designating respondent) but it was about furniture, not nail polish," or "I never talked to her about such things," we classified them as complete denials.

In the remaining cases, some 24 per cent, the designatees were unable to recall whether or not the conversation had taken place; they neither denied nor confirmed what the designator had told us. "Mrs. F. (designator) and I always talk about clothes, but I don't remember talking about short skirts with her. Maybe I did, but I just don't remember." An outstanding characteristic of responses in this category was the designatee's general insistence on the possibility that the conversation might well have occurred. The inability to recall the conversation might mean that the conversation was of greater importance to the designating respondent than to the designatee. The conversations may thus have merged into the general stream of everyday conversation for the designatee, but have remained a more salient event for the designator.

There is not any significant difference in the scoreboard of

confirmation between influentials and influencees, although
there is a slight tendency for the influentials to confirm in
higher proportion. Here is the tally:

*Table 2—Follow-up Interviews with Influentials and Influencees*

|  | The Designated Influential | The Designated Influencee |
|---|---|---|
| Confirmed | 69% | 64% |
| Denied | 9 | 10 |
| Could not recall | 22 | 26 |
| Total (= 100%) | (337) | (297) |

Is two-thirds of the confirmed cases high enough to assure
the trustworthiness of the designation technique? There are
no set standards; there are not even other studies with which
the present one might be compared. We might keep in mind,
however, that while direct confirmation was obtained in only
two out of every three of the follow-up interviews, complete
refutation of the designating respondent's claims was found in
only one out of every ten. The remaining cases fall into a sort
of twilight zone, the follow-up neither denying nor confirming
what the designating respondent had told us.

This twilight zone of "can't recall" is greatest in questions
of public affairs (35%), intermediate in fashion opinion (22%),
lowest in marketing (18%). The proportion of denials remains
fairly constant from area to area.

## Acknowledgment of Alleged Roles

So far we have confirmed only the contact and the conversation about some topic of opinion or usage; we have now to
confirm the roles played by each of the conversationalists. We
want to know whether or not the designated influencees acknowledged having asked advice of the respondents who
designated them, and whether or not the designated influentials were aware of and acknowledged their alleged roles. We
also want to gain further insight into the workings of personal
influence in these everyday conversations.

Not one, but several questions in the follow-up interview
were intended to help us evaluate the designatee's view of his

or her role. We thought it important to know whether the respondent or the designatee had initiated the conversation; furthermore, in the case of influencee follow-ups, we wanted to know whether the designatee had asked the respondent for advice or whether the respondent had volunteered her counsel. Our questions varied from one area to another and were modified in the light of daily interviewing experience. Considerable latitude was given the interviewers to depart from the questionnaire in order to fit the interview into as natural a context as possible.

The resulting variation in the material obtained from such interviews meant that we could not evaluate the designatee's view of his or her role simply by classifying answers to specific questions; instead, by inspecting the total contents of each interview, we classified each into one of these four categories:

*I: Role Acknowledged*: Cases in which the role played by the designatee was, by admission, identical with that alleged by the designating respondent. Contains influentials who told the interviewers that they had suggested some change to the designator, and influencees who acknowledged having asked advice of the respondents who designated them.

*II: Role Reversed*: Cases in which designatees claimed that the role they played was exactly the opposite of that alleged by the designating respondent. Contains alleged influentials who claimed to have asked the respondent's advice, and alleged influencees who insisted they had given advice to the respondent, not received it.

*III: Mutual Role*: Cases in which the designatees claimed that neither they nor the designating respondents had taken the initiative in advice-giving, and that as far as influencing was concerned, the relationship was one of peers.

*IV: Not Ascertainable*: This is a residual category, containing interviews whose contents were too meager or too confused to allow a trustworthy classification into any of the above categories.

Only those cases in which both the respondent and the designatee agreed on the occurrence of the conversation and its subject matter were classified in this way.

Here is the result:

**Table 3—Acknowledgment of Role by Designatees (Confirmed cases only)**

| | |
|---|---|
| Role Acknowledged | 77% |
| Role Reversed | 8 |
| Mutual Role | 14 |
| Not Ascertainable | 1 |
| Total (= 100%) | (442) |

In 77 per cent of the cases, the role played by the designatees was acknowledged by them to be the same as was alleged by the respondents who designated them; in only 8 per cent was there a direct clash between the two stories. A larger proportion (14%) fell into the "mutual role" category: from the designatees' points of view, the relationship alleged by the respondent to be a one-way influence appeared to be a transaction in which neither party influenced the other more. We think the proportion of acknowledged roles is quite high. Definite agreement is found in eight out of every ten cases; definite disagreement in less than one out of ten.

There are some differences between designatees according to whether they are influentials or influencees. Here are the role evaluations for these two types of follow-up interviews:

**Table 4—Acknowledgment of Role by Designated Influentials and Influencees (Confirmed cases only)**

| | Influentials | Influencees |
|---|---|---|
| Role Acknowledged | 86% | 82% |
| Role Reversed | 3 | 11 |
| Mutual Role | 10 | 6 |
| Not Ascertainable | 1 | 1 |
| Total (= 100%) | (232) | (144) |

The differences between types of designatees is not very large with respect to acknowledgment of role: 86 per cent of the influentials and 82 per cent of the influencees agreed with the respondents who designated them about the role they played. But there is a somewhat greater difference between the two groups in the "role reversed" and the "mutual role" categories. Only 3 per cent of the influentials, but 11 per cent of the influencees insisted that the designator's statement should have been reversed; and a larger proportion of influentials (10%) than influencees (6%) claimed a peer relationship. These differences are statistically significant. They suggest, among other things, something that we might otherwise have guessed, namely, that advice-giving designators could not always know how serious the designatee was in asking for advice, that is, whether she was simply "making conversation," sounding her out, or seriously seeking guidance. Clues come from some of the influencees who indicated that what may have looked like advice-seeking, in reality had quite a different purpose. "I was curious to know what brand of lipstick she wore," said one, "and I asked her whether she would tell me. I had not the slightest intention of using it, because it wouldn't look nice on me." Another seeming "influencee"—who was operative in the field of public affairs—claimed to use advice-seeking as a screen for getting across her own point of view, and explicitly labelled her practice the "boob technique," telling the interviewer, "I always start off by asking what they think, and then after they get interested I deliver my message."

Such facts as well as the proportions of reversed estimations of roles played, remind us that we are only at the beginning of a technique for ascertaining influences. Yet we must begin somewhere, and the high degree of clear-cut confirmations leads us to believe that we have at least opened up the problem.

## The Extent of Confirmation

Whether or not we can rely on the technique of asking people about their own influentiality depends, ultimately, on the extent to which the persons whom they allegedly advised acknowledge the fact; the designatees must admit having talked about the topic in question to the respondents who designated them and they must admit, moreover, that they took advice from them. Here are the proportions, based on all designated influencees whom we interviewed, who come through, or who don't, in both these tests:

*Table 5—Inventory of Follow-up Interviews with Designated Influencees*

| | | |
|---|---|---|
| Role Acknowledged | 54% | |
| Role Reversed | 7 | |
| Mutual Role | 4 | |
| Not Ascertainable | * | |
| **Total Contacts Confirmed** | | 65% |
| | | |
| Contact Denied | 14% | |
| Can't Recall Contact | 21 | |
| **Total Contacts Not Confirmed** | | 35% |
| | | |
| Total (= 100%) | | (221) |

* Less than one per cent.

We present the total results of our follow-ups in this way because we want to show the overall validity of all influencee designations. Such designations may be invalidated by lack of confirmation, first, with respect to the particular contact which was designated (i.e., that a conversation did not take place concerning the topic indicated) and/or by lack of confirmation of the alleged role played in that conversation. Employing both these tests, 54 per cent of the cases seem to be confirmed. The 54 per cent refers, of course, to the proportion of cases in which all of what was alleged by the designating respondent is explicitly substantiated.

Another way of approaching the problem is to examine the proportion of cases in which there is explicit contradiction of what our respondent-designators said. Such contradictions occur when the designatee denies that the conversation occurred, or if she insists that the topic of the conversation was not as the designator had claimed; 14 per cent of the cases (classified as "denials" in Table 5) were of this sort. Or, the designatee might insist that the role she played was the opposite of what the designator had claimed; contradictions of this kind account for another 7 per cent. Finally, the designatee might say that the actual influence relationship was mutual; cases of this sort amounted to 4 per cent. These three categories together make up 25 per cent of the cases. In other words, in one-fourth of all the cases, the designatees explicitly contradicted what our respondents had told us. The validity of the technique appears to be higher when considered in this way than if we consider the number of explicit affirmations as our standard. Of course, it is all a matter of how strict our standards should be.

The proportion of confirmed conversations decreases as one goes from marketing to fashions to politics, and role acknowledgments decrease in the same way. The difference between marketing and fashions is not very large, but the difference between both of these and public affairs is.

*Table 6—Follow-up Interviews with Designated Influencees in Three Arenas of Influence*

|  | Marketing Influencees | | Fashions Influencees | | Public Affairs Influencees | |
|---|---|---|---|---|---|---|
| Role Acknowledged | 57% | | 56% | | 38% | |
| Role Reversed | 10 | | 6 | | 6 | |
| Mutual Role | 3 | | 4 | | 6 | |
| Not Ascertainable | — | | 1 | | — | |
| Total Confirmed Contacts | | 70% | | 67% | | 50% |
| Contact Denied | 13% | | 12% | | 25% | |
| Can't Recall Contact | 17 | | 22 | | 25 | |
| Total Contacts Not Confirmed | | 30% | | 34% | | 50% |
| Total (= 100%) | | (69) | | (120) | | (32) |

Public affairs designations are apparently the least valid of these three kinds, both for influencee and influential designations. Here is the evidence for influential designations. The same trends apparent in influencee designations are also present here:

*Table 7—Follow-up Interviews with Designated Influentials in Three Arenas of Influence*

|  | Marketing Influentials | | Fashions Influentials | | Public Affairs Influentials | |
|---|---|---|---|---|---|---|
| Role Acknowledged | 71% | | 61% | | 37% | |
| Role Reversed | 2 | | 2 | | 3 | |
| Mutual Role | 3 | | 5 | | 19 | |
| Not Ascertainable | — | | 1 | | — | |
| Total Confirmed Contacts | | 76% | | 69% | | 59% |
| Contact Denied | 7% | | 9% | | 7% | |
| Can't Recall Contact | 17 | | 22 | | 34 | |
| Total Contacts Not Confirmed | | 24% | | 31% | | 41% |
| Total (= 100%) | | (107) | | (162) | | (68) |

There is clearly something particularly characteristic of public affairs that leads to a lower rate of confirmed contact and of role corroboration. One possible explanation is that the more prosaic the relationships and the more they fit into everyday routine, the more valid are the answers. Another is that the poorer showing of public affairs designations may in part be due to the fact that in this arena men play an important role as sources of influence. Men may be unwilling to admit having been influenced by a woman; or they may even fail to acknowledge talking to a woman about public affairs because they do not feel that such conversations with women are serious enough to warrant the status of two-way "discussion."[3] Probably more important then either is the simple fact that politics is a touchier matter about which to question, especially when you are probing for who said what about controversial issues. It is easier to confirm a personal influence for a new brand of peaches than what someone said to you about Communists. Still another reason is that influencing a marketing change may more often take place during a single contact than influencing a change in political attitude. One may be a much more discrete, and therefore recollectable, incident than the other. Such variations obviously need much more study. Yet, we believe that the results of our attempt at confirmation allow us in this exploratory study to use the self-detecting question in isolating "opinion leaders" for description and analysis.

## Conclusion

In the two chapters of this section, we have tried to outline, and to justify, the major themes we want to pursue. Our focus, we have indicated, is upon specific influence incidents, and our heroes, the specific influentials. In general, we shall refer to these specific influence incidents as "decisions" (decisions to change food brands, or fashions, or political opinions, or to go to one movie rather than another); we shall be calling the

---

3. In the study of voting behavior during a presidential campaign, it was found that while wives frequently referred to discussions with their husbands, the latter rarely returned the compliment. The husbands apparently did not feel that they were "discussing" politics with their wives. Rather, they were telling their wives what politics was all about. Lazarsfeld, Berelson, and Gaudet (1948), p. 141.

specific influentials "opinion leaders," and the job that they do, personal contact or personal influence. The section that follows treats "decisions" and particularly, the role that personal influence plays in decision-making. The third section, the final one, then builds explicitly on the present section and attempts to report what "opinion leaders" look like, and how they can be distinguished from those whom they lead.

CHAPTER III

# The Place of Impact Analysis in
# The Study of Influence

WE WANT TO CONTRIBUTE to a picture of how people make up their minds and, as has been suggested in the previous section, our primary interest is in the role of personal influence in specifiable, decision-making episodes. In the present section, we want to set forth a scheme which will permit us to contrast the frequency and the effectiveness of this kind of influence—stemming from "opinion leaders"—with the frequency and effectiveness of influences stemming from the mass media.

Because we have narrowed down our focus to the study of specific, everyday-type decisions, the kind of personal influence which we are examining is quite restricted, too. There is no doubt, for instance, that what our parents told us in early childhood has an everlasting influence on our adult life in terms of the beliefs, prejudices, habits and fears with which we ap-

---

* Peter H. Rossi contributed substantially to the development of this section and to the analysis of the data.

proach every situation. Thus one form of study that might be devised would trace the attitudes of adults back to personal influences which were exercised early in their lives. We, however, take these general attitudes for granted and shall be concerned only with minor variations on this basic theme of opinion and attitude formation, as they are played out over relatively short periods of time. Thus we will not be concerned with why a man has Republican opinions if he has held them for a long time; but if he has changed them quite recently we will be. In the same way, we are interested only in *recent changes* of fashion habits or in recent changes of food brands bought by a housewife. In the movie field, if we learn that a person goes regularly to the movies or that he has a tendency to prefer Western movies to mystery films we will not deal with such information as data. But if a *recent change* has come about, say from Westerns to mystery films, or if a man has had to make a choice between two Westerns, we would be curious to know how this more specific choice was made; and that is where our study comes in.

Restriction to specific choices or to changes which came about recently has been implicit in the previous section of this report where the term "opinion leader" was given to the "specific influential." Suppose that in a town there is a powerful group of liquor dealers which hires people to agitate against the passage of a dry referendum. If the person whom we interview tells us about some friend who has convinced him that prohibition laws never work, it is this friend whom we call an opinion leader, although we are perfectly aware that this friend who influenced our respondent may have himself been influenced by a much more powerful agent. But our study is concerned with face-to-face influences. We hope that as time goes on, more and more links in the general influence chains permeating our society will be studied. As a matter of fact, some beginnings of a more general approach have been indicated already. No reader should confuse the modesty of our present enterprise with a blindness to broader and more complex problems. But those problems will forever be out of reach if we lose patience with very specific investigations such as the present one.

The decision to restrict our study to short-range changes and face-to-face influences, then, is basic. But even within this frame, at least three major approaches have to be distinguished. We shall call them the group, the person, and the incident approach.

To exemplify *the group approach*, we look to a paper by Margaret Mead (1937). She reports that there are three major ways in which primitive tribes make up their minds. The Arapesh have a kind of anarchic way. When some tribal problem comes up, everyone feels that he is entitled to voice an opinion; and the decision he suggests grows out of his mood at the moment of the discussion. The Yatmul tend to react according to specific roles. Sometimes they wait for the head of the family to take the lead in a decision and then all follow. But at other times, the young Yatmul feels that here is an issue which should be decided in terms of the traditional hostility between generations; in the latter case, if the elders of the tribe take one decision the youngsters want to do just the opposite. Finally there is the style which the Balinese tend to follow. According to Margaret Mead, the Balinese do not feel that issues should be met by *ad hoc* opinions. They look for precedents and have their wise men tell them what law and tradition require in such a situation. There might be disagreement on what is expected in a given situation; but there is agreement that the requirements of "the order" should be carried out and that new opinions need not be formed, be they individual decisions, as with the Arapesh, or members of groups acting alike, as with the Yatmul.

Similar studies could be made in the area with which we are concerned here. Much of urban society is made up of circles and cliques within which opinion formation comes about. We know from previous studies, for instance, and from some of the evidence presented above, that in public affairs at least, the husband is usually "telling the wife." We shall say more about this in a later chapter. A similar structure might be found, for instance, around a man who has a local reputation as a great art connoisseur. Or a much more democratic clique might be found among the patrons of a saloon where opinions are more likely to be formed by mutual interaction. On the largest scale, what we call here the group approach would really be the comparative study of governments in different countries. On the smallest scale it would consist in a careful description of various types of opinion-forming groups, how many of them there are, of what kind of people they are composed, how they influence their members, how their collective will is formed and how they fit into the larger social process. This group approach has not been central in our study, though we have considered it in Part One of this volume.

*The person approach* will be exemplified in the section following this one. There, we shall ask ourselves: Who are the people who influence others in face-to-face contact? The question can be understood in a variety of ways and the answer given by numerous methods. The way in which we have proceeded has been so amply discussed that any further comment would be repetitious. The outcome of our inquiry will be characteristically different from that gained by the group approach. We shall not describe types of groups, count their frequencies or assess the way they affect the decisions of their members. Instead, we shall try to show what kind of people are likely to influence others on various subject matters.

In the present section we turn to a third approach, *the incident approach*. The main focus of attention here is neither the group nor the person, but the personal contact itself. We want to know the importance of personal contact as compared with other influences, particularly as compared with the mass media like radio and newspapers. The problem certainly goes far back into history. We could look, for example, at the early days of print, during the Reformation, when for the first time the preacher had to compete with the pamphlet. What problems did this create for the religious propagandists and how were they solved? What was the reaction within various sectors of the population? Nineteenth century France would offer interesting opportunities to compare the influence of the salons with the influence of the then rising newspapers.[1] And, in modern days the role of radio in adult education, as compared to older forms like discussion groups and study circles, would furnish

---

1. For suggestive materials on this subject, see Tarde (1901) and Speier (1950).

another example of competition and interaction between personal influence and media influence.[2]

True to the more microscopic techniques applied in the present study, we have chosen to study not historical episodes, but specific incidents; this is why the term "incident approach" has been proposed for the procedures reported in this section of our study. What we have done is to collect a large number of reports on concrete situations where people made minor decisions. Then we have tried to evaluate, by a standardized kind of interview, the impact of personal contacts as compared with the impact of mass media. This technique of impact analysis now has to be clarified. Here is how we propose to do it:

In the next chapter we shall proceed to discuss our philosophy of *interviewing* and the resulting type of questionnaire. Then we shall turn to the operation of *assessing*: how we decide in each single case what role a personal contact or a specific mass medium played in the course of the decision reported by a respondent. This will bring us to the impact ratings, by means of which all our information can be summarized. At the end of the next chapter (Chapter IV), therefore, we will have the necessary instruments to inspect and interpret our main *statistical results*. This will be done in the chapter following, Chapter V. There the distribution of our impact ratings will be found, together with an interpretation of this first set of findings. But by the end of that chapter, the reader will have many doubts or, at least, many questions, as to the nature of our numerical results. In Chapter VI, therefore, we shall return to consider further the general problems of impact studies. We shall try to clarify several points which were left unmentioned or unsettled in Chapter IV.

Then, in the final chapter of this section we will again turn to data. In a variety of ways we will examine the conditions under which "people," as sources of influences, are more or less effective for each other than are the mass media.

---

2. Lazarsfeld (1941) discusses some of the problems of audience building in educational broadcasting and the compounding of effectiveness that comes from introducing the media into the discussion group setting.

# CHAPTER IV

# Searching for and Assessing
# the Impact of Various Influences

THE GENERAL FORMULATION of the problem we will be concerned with in this chapter is quite simple. We wish to examine the roles played by differing influences on three kinds of everyday decisions. We set about doing this by gathering a representative sample of interviews with people who had made such decisions. Thus, we asked women who had recently changed from one type of household product to another or from one brand of food to the next, what had made them change; we asked women to explain what had made them choose the specific picture they saw at their last movie attendance; and finally, we asked women who had made a recent change in their hairdo, clothes or cosmetics, to tell what brought about this turn in their fashion habits. The interviews were conducted in such a way as to give a maximum chance for influences to be mentioned and compared. Let us elaborate for a moment on the interviewing technique.

## The Art of Asking Why

There are essentially four types of questions which can be asked in such an inquiry. One is a general question, "Why did you make this change?" This would permit each respondent to pick out whatever element in the whole episode she wants to focus upon. If there is much time available, this is usually a good way to start the interview although such initial replies are usually not very valuable for the final analysis.[1] The main

---

1. For a fuller discussion of this point, see Lazarsfeld & Rosenberg (1955), Section V.

difficulty results from the fact that the respondent may not understand at all that we are interested mainly in influences. For instance, in reply to "Why did you make this change?" a woman might tell us at great length about the advantages of her new brand of coffee; but she might never tell us that she had learned it from a household column in a magazine. She might tell us about what had interested her in a certain moving picture, but not that she had read a review of the picture in the newspaper. She would be entitled, of course, to report the experience in the way it appears structured to her. It would be up to us to listen to her first and then use some kind of follow-up question, for example: How did she know about all the advantages of this brand before she ever used it? Then her attention would be turned to channels of information or sources of influence.

In our study, because so many other topics had to be covered, we started right in with such slightly more directed questions. We asked:

How did you *choose* the particular picture that you saw?
How did you happen to *start using* the new brand of food?
How did you *find out* about the new brand?
How did you *come to make* this change to the new fashion?
*Who or what suggested* this change of fashion to you?

It will be seen that all these questions try to suggest that it is appropriate to mention *a source*, the something which attracted your attention to this particular movie or to the new brand or the new fashion you've adopted. The emphasis is on the process of decision: *How* did you choose? What *suggested* the change? Much experimentation is needed to develop good questions of this kind adapted to the specific area of investigation. The wording, moreover, should not favor one channel of influence against another; "How did you *learn?*", for instance, might favor formal media as compared to personal influence; "How did you *hear?*", would obviously favor radio over print. Yet, despite this difficulty, the questions should be worded so that they bring out a maximum of information on channels of influence. Very often, it is advisable to ask several questions. This is necessary to make the respondent go over in his mind the pertinent episodes as carefully as is possible in a short interview. Also, respondents often take questions quite literally; they may mention that an advertisement "helped them" to find out something, although they would not feel, if asked, that they took "advice" from it. They might say yes to "Did you hear someone talk about it?" but they might not volunteer the same episode if they were asked "Who suggested this change?"

As before, we will refer to such questions as *specific influence* questions. They are designed to bring out through the retrospection of the respondents, all the cases in which a personal contact or an advertisement or a story played however minor a role in the whole process which ended with the specific decision under consideration. From these influence questions, two other types have to be distinguished quite clearly. One is the *exposure* question and the other the *assessment* question. Before discussing these, however, a further aspect of impact studies has to be introduced.

## *The Assessment of Impact*

The main purpose of the present study is to assess the impact of personal influence in the performance of a number of personal acts. From the outset, two aspects of our results can be anticipated. For one, they will be of a statistical nature; our results will pertain to groups of decisions, although as we shall see, in order to reach our goal we will have to assess each act individually. Secondly, we shall be satisfied with *relative* results; no efforts will be made to establish absolute findings. We will try to assess the relative impact of personal contact and the mass media like newspapers, radio, etc.; in other words, we shall be making comparisons.[2]

Let us illustrate the complexity of the problem by visualizing a number of cases in which a person decides to go to see a certain picture. Here is Mrs. A who meets Mrs. B at a tea. Mrs. B tells about a fascinating picture she saw yesterday. The description of her enjoyment is so vivid that Mrs. A, who has not previously heard of the picture, decides to leave the party

---

2. This is not inherently necessary as we shall see in Chapter 5. But this restriction makes the present discussion easier and is adequate for our available material.

early and go to this picture herself. Assuming that Mrs. A is honest, and our interviewer skillful, we shall come up with the result that the personal influence of Mrs. B was decisive in Mrs. A's decision to see a certain picture. The reader will easily supply many other cases where there is neither difficulty nor doubt in making a similar statement, although presently we shall see that some further clarification is needed to find out exactly what such statements mean.

Now let us take another case. Mrs. C has finished shopping earlier than she expected. She is downtown and still has a few hours time before the tea party to which she is invited. A movie is indicated to while the time away. She happens to have a newspaper in which the four movies available a few blocks from where she finds herself are listed. One of the pictures features a well-known actor whom she had wanted to see for a long time; this decides her choice. As she reports the decision in an interview, it seems quite clear that no personal influence is involved for there is no mention at all of another person.[3] But for the purpose of our study a second aspect of decision would be called upon: has Mrs. C been influenced by the newspaper? Certainly not in the sense of Mrs. A, whose interest in the movie was "created" by Mrs. B. A review in a newspaper can of course have the same effect of starting a desire or an intention which did not exist before. But in the case of Mrs. C the fondness for the specific actor existed long before her shopping trip. The newspaper merely informed her that the picture was available nearby. So there will probably be agreement between Mrs. C and the interviewer that the newspaper had no impact—especially if upon further questioning it turns out that there were several other means at hand for Mrs. C to find out what was playing in the shopping district. The newspaper, that is, served only an informational role, not an influential one, and it served in a context where other sources of information were equally accessible.

The problem of classification would be more difficult in the case of Mrs. D. She spends her vacation on a lonely ranch "to get away from it all." For weeks she has not read a newspaper

---

3. We shall come back to this "case" in the next chapter.

because there are none around. However, one day a local weekly is brought in by a transient. From it she learns that a school mate of hers is playing in a one-night performance in the local summer theatre. Mrs. D drives 30 miles just to see her old friend. It can be argued that in this case this one newspaper, brought to her attention by extraordinary circumstances, was at least a "contributory" influence in her decision.

No effort will be made for the moment to elaborate on the details of this distinction between main or contributory influences. For the purpose of our present study, we chose the simplest application: We asked the respondents to name the influence they considered the main one in their decisions to buy a certain breakfast food, see a given movie, or change some feature in their makeup. It is interesting that women had no difficulties when they were asked questions of the following kind:

"Summing up now, what do you think was the most important thing in causing you to pick this particular picture?"

"Summing up now, what was the most important in causing you to change to . . . (the new brand)?"

"Summing up now, what do you think was the most important thing in causing you to make this change . . . (in fashion)?"

These questions came at the end of a somewhat more detailed discussion of the whole act of decision. Having been induced to review the situation in their minds in some detail, the respondents' decisions as to the major factor could not be altogether perfunctory.

There are good reasons for choosing this relatively simple procedure. For one, it has been our experience in previous studies that mass media and personal advice are factors which are fairly easily assessed.[4] They come up usually in distinct episodes, and not very complicated psychological processes are involved. (We certainly would not dare to use a similar procedure in assessing, for instance, the role of professional jealousy and competition in the choice of a dissertation topic by a student.) Secondly, we are interested here only in relative impact. The hope was that it would be fairly easy for a

---

4. See Lazarsfeld & Rosenberg (1955), Section V, for selected examples.

respondent to assess at least the *relative* role of each of the various mass media and of personal advice in the minor kind of decisions which we are discussing. (Whether this assumption is true, however, is of rather general interest and should be made the object of special, perhaps experimental studies.) Last, and not least, we were motivated by considerations of expediency; our field force had to be trained locally and we could not put too hard and costly an interviewing task upon them.

But, theoretically speaking, there is no doubt that this assessment of the main factor could have been done in a much more careful way. And even more, there was no necessity to leave it to the respondents themselves to make the assessment. There are many types of studies where such an assessment is better made by the investigator. When we want to assess the weight of bad company in the case study of a juvenile delinquent, or when we want to assess the impact of losing a job on the marital relations of a worker, we certainly would make a much more detailed analysis.[5]

## The Impact Ratings

So far, then, we have two types of questions—the specific influence questions which were described first, and the assessment questions which were just discussed and explained. This permits us to divide our respondents—that is, those of them who reported that their decisions were somehow affected by one of the mass media and/or by personal influence—into two groups: those who said that they were influenced by one or more of the media, or by personal influence, but who did not attribute decisive weight to any one specific influence; and those who assessed a particular influence as the decisive factor. On the basis of these assessments we will be able to distinguish in each case between a *contributory* influence and an *effective* influence. These weights we call impact ratings.

---

5. See, for example, Burt (1938), the Appendix section on "Discerning" in Komarovsky (1940), and the aforementioned Lazarsfeld and Rosenberg (1955). In this connection, a terminological remark might be in place. In previous discussions of this method the word *discerning* has been used for the attribution of the kinds of causal weights which we are discussing here. Now we prefer the word *assessment* because this permits a clearer relationship to certain ideas expressed in MacIver's *Social Causation* (1942).

In addition to the specific influence questions and the assessment questions, however, there is a third type which we call mere exposure questions. During that portion of the interview which attempted to elicit from the respondent his report, then his assessment, of the roles played by various influences in a particular decision, no specific medium was mentioned to him by name. But when the influence questions, and therewith the general description of the episode, were over, respondents were presented with a check list. The questions on this check list were of the following type, varying somewhat according to the subject matter under investigation:

"Did you hear someone talk about it?"
"Did you see someone wearing or using it?"
"Did a salesperson or beauty operator suggest it?"
"Did you pass by the theatre and see that it was on?"
"Did you see it in a preview?"
"Did you hear about it on the radio?"
"Did you read about it in a magazine?"
"Did you read about it in a newspaper?"
"Did you see it in a movie?"

This type of question permits us to focus on a third type of respondent. The women, whom hereafter we will call *exposed,* are the ones who give an affirmative answer to one of the check list questions although they had not mentioned the corresponding medium earlier as influential for them, let alone decisive.

At this point it would be useful to review the situation and establish the way in which we will use our terms. For each respondent we have a series of *assessments.* That is, we have an evaluation of the parts played by personal contacts and by a few mass media in a specific decision. The result of the assessment is a certain measure of effectiveness—an *impact rating—* which is assigned to each influence each time it is mentioned.

We can then take a specific factor like personal contact or newspapers and get the statistical distribution of impact ratings for a whole group. Such a distribution can be described in a variety of ways. We may, for instance, say what proportion of respondents considered this medium as the "most important" one. Or we might say how many were merely exposed to it without giving it any saliency in their report. The study of the impact ratings pertaining to one kind of influence but collected from a whole group of people will be called the *evaluation* of this specific influence. Assessment, therefore, pertains to individual cases while evaluation pertains to a whole group of respondents; both terms, however, pertain to only one specific type of influence at a time, that is, radio, or magazines, or personal contact, and the like.

As has just been mentioned, the statistical distribution of impact ratings can be described in a variety of ways. One especially important yardstick is the *effectiveness index*: we first single out the people who have been exposed to a source of influence and then compute the proportion among them who considered it most important in their decision. We can thus distinguish between mere exposure to a medium and its effectiveness in case of exposure.

This is all we need to keep in mind at the moment. It will be well now to turn to some actual data. This will make it easier to ask ourselves what the most precise meaning of such impact ratings might be. Just one word more, however, about our vocabulary. Except for the terms mentioned, we will not stick to a monotonous glossary. A personal contact or a radio advertisement will indiscriminately be called a factor, an influence, an exposure or a source. We will not make too stuffy a distinction between impact, effectiveness and influence. At the points where precision is needed, the indices which we are using will make clear our meaning. At other points, it will be more helpful to draw on the imagination of the reader, and to that end we shall use a relatively diversified terminology.

CHAPTER V

# Evaluating the Impact of

# Various Influences

OUR MAIN INTEREST lies in the role of personal contacts. But in order to evaluate that role more easily, comparisons are necessary; these are provided by the formal media of mass communication. In the case of small consumer goods, radio and newspaper advertising lend themselves best for comparison; magazines and salespersons, too, are mentioned with some frequency so we shall consider them as well. In the case of movies, it is the magazines and newspapers which come up for comparison with personal influence.

When the fashion items we have investigated are considered, the situation becomes more complex. Outside of personal contacts only magazines play any role at all. But at the same time personal contacts become much more diversified when we discuss fashions, and so it seems advisable to divide these contacts into three types: the influence of salespersons; the personal verbal advice of friends and acquaintances; and finally, the impact of seeing another person's hairdo or dress.

## Marketing: Foods and Household Goods

The type of information to which our procedure leads is well characterized by Chart I. This presents an evaluation of the relative roles of newspapers, radio, magazines, salespersons and informal personal contacts on decisions to change from one food brand to another, one cleansing agent to another, and the like.

**Chart I—Assessment Results for Marketing Shifts[1]**

(Total Number of Brand Shifters 386 = 100%)

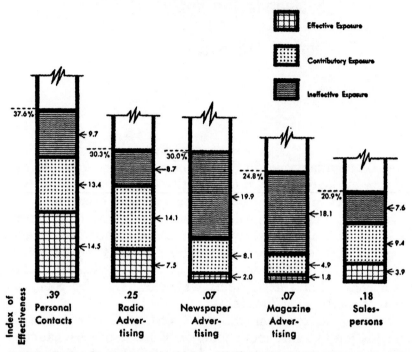

Index of Effectiveness

| .39 | .25 | .07 | .07 | .18 |
|-----|-----|-----|-----|-----|
| Personal Contacts | Radio Advertising | Newspaper Advertising | Magazine Advertising | Sales-persons |

NOTE: The first bar, for example, reads as follows: 37.6% of all those who made a recent change in a brand or product reported some manner of exposure to personal contacts. This percentage (appearing at the upper left of the bar) may be broken down as follows (reading now from the bottom up): 14.5% of the shifters were "effectively exposed" to personal contacts; 13.4% experienced "contributory exposure" to personal contacts; and 9.7% were "ineffectively exposed" to personal contacts. The difference between 37.6% and 100% (62.4%) represents those brand shifters who were not exposed to personal contacts at all.

The second bar then means that 30.3% of all brand or product shifters reported some manner of exposure to radio advertising, of which 7.5% was "effective exposure," etc. *Note that each bar is based on the same total*—that is, the 386 people who reported some recent change in a brand or product.

That the "exposure" totals of all the bars add to more than 100% results from the fact that respondents reported more than one source of influence in connection with their shifts of brand or product.

---

## 1. TYPES OF MARKETING SHIFTS MADE

| | |
|---|---|
| Small food items | 49% |
| Soaps and cleansing agents | 37 |
| Household goods (pots, irons, etc.) | 11 |
| Miscellaneous | 3 |
| Total (= 100%) | (386) |

Two questions were employed to elicit reports of these changes. Respondents were asked first of all, "During the last month or so have you bought any new brand or product that you don't usually buy? (I don't mean something you had to buy because it was the only one available.)" If this question was answered in the negative, respondents were asked, "On which of these have

Each bar is devoted to a particular type of influence, and the four categories within the bar can now be easily explained as a result of our preceding discussion. "Effective Exposure" refers to people who mention a given influence, claiming that it played a specific role (like having taught them something or directed them toward something), and stating further that this source was the most important factor in their decision. "Contributory Exposure" pertains to those cases in which only the first two factors are involved. People mention the exposure and attribute to the source some specific role; but they do not call it the most important one. "Ineffective Exposure" occurs with those people who just mention that they talked with someone or that they heard a radio advertisement for the product they bought etc., but they do not acknowledge that the source played any role in their decision. Still, these cases are obviously different from those in which the respondent denies having had any contact at all with the given source. Such cases are not reported in Chart I, but are easily inferred from the total provided on the left hand side of each bar which includes all three groups; that is to say, the difference between this "total exposure" and 100 per cent gives the number of persons who do not report any contact whatsoever with the source in question. The base figure for all five bars is the same; in each case, 100 per cent equals all the people who reported some recent marketing change.

And now that we can read the chart, let us look at the results. The most prominent item in the chart is the fact that the greatest concentration of "effective exposure" is to be found among those exposed to personal contacts. When this is coupled with the fact that brand and product shifters report a larger total exposure to personal contacts than to any one of the mass media, the role of personal contacts looms even larger.

Exposure to radio advertising is next in importance to personal contacts. While total exposure to radio does not exceed exposure to newspapers, comparing the effectiveness of the two media with regard to shifts in small consumer goods indicates

you tried a new brand most recently? Breakfast cereals? Coffee? Soap flakes or chips?" Respondents who replied to the first question affirmatively were not asked the second question.

that radio is the medium more often reported as having been an "effective" or a "contributory" influence.

Magazines follow newspapers in reports of overall exposure, but "effective exposure" to magazines is no greater than to newspapers.

Salespersons were also named to some extent. And while overall exposure to this specialized sort of personal contact was less than exposure to the several mass media, the relative effectiveness of this exposure is almost as high as that of radio. Undoubtedly in this "supermarket" era, the role of the foodstore clerk as *salesman* is rapidly changing, yet when he *is* consulted—that is when there is "exposure"—he still has some influence.

Since the total amount of exposure to these sources of influence varies, we must be concerned with relative effectiveness —since what appears as the greater effectiveness of a given medium may reflect nothing more than that medium's greater coverage. We need a relative measure which holds coverage constant, as it were, and allows us to compare the relative effectiveness of the different media regardless of the amount of exposure to each. Such an index of effectiveness might simply be the ratio of effective exposure to a particular medium to total exposure to that medium; this index is given under each bar of Chart I.

In regard to marketing, then, the impact of informal personal advice is greater than the impact of mass media advertising, and this is true in the two respects we have examined. First, our respondents report more exposure to personal advice than to advertisements; and, second, among those exposed to each source, "most important influence" is more often attributed to people than to formal advertisements. There was good reason to expect such a result. In a previous study of voting, the impression was gained that we are much more influenced in our voting decision by other people than by formal party propaganda, like radio speeches and pamphlets.[2] But in this previous study no quantitative measurement was taken to back up such a statement. Here, for the field of marketing, a limited first step has been taken toward developing such a

---

2. Lazarsfeld, Berelson, and Gaudet (1948), Chapter 16.

measurement. And "personal influence" emerges with the
strength which the qualitative aproach had led us to expect.

**Chart II—Assessment Results for Motion Picture Selections**
(Total Number of Movie-Goers 584 = 100%)

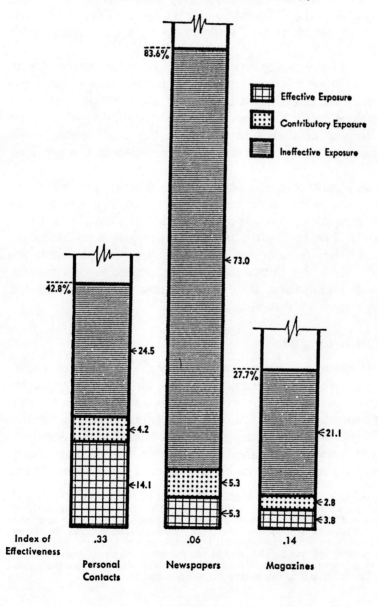

Effective Exposure

Contributory Exposure

Ineffective Exposure

83.6%

73.0

42.8%

24.5

4.2

14.1

5.3

5.3

27.7%

21.1

2.8

3.8

Index of
Effectiveness  .33   .06   .14

Personal  Newspapers  Magazines
Contacts

## Selection of a Motion Picture

Now let us turn to the movies. What influences did our
respondents mention when they reported how they made up
their minds to see the last movie they attended? What weight
did they give to the different elements? The results are reported
in Chart II, which is best understood by a comparison with
Chart I.

The role of the newspaper is especially conspicuous in Chart
II and this is certainly not surprising in the light of common
experience. Almost everyone consults a newspaper for some
detail before going to a movie, but no special weight is given
to the impact of such information in the final decision. We
have discussed some variations on this theme in the previous
chapter.

Personal contact again has considerably greater effectiveness than any of the other media. The total amount of exposure
to other people's opinions is about as high in Chart II as it was
in Chart I. But in regard to movies, our graph undoubtedly
underrates the frequency of discussion preceding a movie attendance. And the importance of the magazine needs some
important qualification. Both of these points will be taken up
at some length in subsequent chapters.[3]

## Fashion Changes

For marketing decisions, we compared the roles of radio,
newspapers and magazines with that of personal contacts;
for movie decisions, the media discussed were magazines
and newspapers. When it comes to fashion changes, of the
three formal media, only magazines are mentioned frequently
enough to warrant any statistical treatment. On the other hand,
personal influence must now be presented in three forms. There

---

3. See below, pp. 214-5 and Section Three, Chaps. XIII and XIV. Handel
(1950) tells an intriguing story of the way in which motion picture distribu-
tors reckon with the potent role of personal influence: if the movie is a bad
one, the pattern of distribution aims for rapid saturation, that is, many
theatres show the picture simultaneously; if the movie is good, distribution
slows to a creeping pace. The saturation pattern minimizes the impact of
word-of-mouth and maximizes the impact of advertising; the creeping pattern, on the other hand, capitalizes on word-of-mouth.

is first the commercialized position of the salesperson. There are two reasons why salespeople appear more often in this area than in the two others discussed before. For one, there is

*Chart III—Assessment Results for Fashion Changes*[4]
(Total Number of Fashion Changers 502 = 100%)

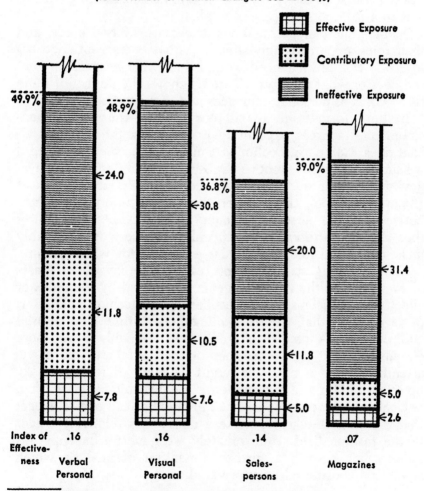

4. The 502 fashion changes are distributed as follows:

TYPES OF FASHION CHANGES MADE

| | |
|---|---|
| Hairdo style | 32% |
| Make-up technique or cosmetic | 38 |
| Clothing style | 29 |
| Total ( = 100% ) | (502) |

the beauty operator who is a professional disseminator of opinions on personal grooming without a parallel in the food or movie field. In addition, the salesperson at the perfume counter or in the dress shop seems to play a greater role in the purchases she induces than the clerk in the grocery store. (In the course of the typical movie attendance, nothing equivalent to a salesperson appears at all.)

Non-commercial personal influences are of two kinds, and their roles are surprisingly similar. As has been mentioned before, one can be influenced by a person either because of what she does or what she says. Chart III shows the impact of these three types of personal influences and of magazines.

In both forms, and by all our indices, the private non-commercial sources have more impact than the commercialized ones. Comparing columns 1 and 2 with columns 3 and 4 we find that both "effective exposure" and index of effectiveness are greater in the first two columns. As far as index of effectiveness goes, the salesperson takes an intermediary role between private personal influences and magazines. The figures thus tend to corroborate the speculations one would probably make about the role of the salesperson in this whole picture.

Chart III suggests a final observation. The low effectiveness of every one of the relevant media (measured by the index of effectiveness) seems to be peculiar to the fashion field. It is quite possible that we are dealing here with a kind of trial and error situation. Fashion changes probably have more ego-involvement for women than do food purchases and movie attendances. As a result, it might be more difficult to make up one's mind; more information is sought which is more often neglected than really acted on. This should lead one to expect that the time it takes to make a decision is relatively longer in the fashion field. Unfortunately we have no data on this matter, but here is a further dimension of analysis which should be considered in future studies.

## Summary and Interpretation

The three charts discussed in this chapter are based on figures which for many reasons indicate only general trends. It is important, therefore, to summarize the findings in a form which is more qualitative and sets a minimum of reliance on the actual numerical values of the statistical counts. The best way seems to be to distinguish just two kinds of exposure to a particular influence; in an arbitrary way we will call exposure of one-third or more (of all changers in a given area) high (H) while a total exposure of less than that will be called low (L). In the same way we will consider an index of effectiveness high (H) if it is .20 or larger; and we will talk of low (L) effectiveness if the index is less than .20. We thus can classify all our influences into four groups. HH will indicate that the exposure occurs frequently, and if it occurs, plays a considerable role in the reported decision. LL indicates those cases where a certain factor did not play much of a role either in terms of frequency of occurrence or in terms of actual impact. That leaves two other obvious groups where either one—total exposure or index of effectiveness—is high, but not the other. It is then possible to summarize the content of all three charts in the following way:.

EXPOSURE

|  |  | High | Low |
|---|---|---|---|
| EFFECTIVENESS | High | Marketing: Personal contact<br>Movies: Personal contact | Marketing: Radio |
|  | Low | Fashion: All four factors<br>Movies: Newspapers | Marketing: Newspapers,<br>Magazines, Salespersons<br>Movies: Mazagines* |

* This entry will be qualified in a subsequent chapter in this section.

The dominant role of personal contact now comes out fairly clearly. In two areas (marketing and movies) it is above the average on both frequency of exposure and effectiveness. In the fashion area, it is high in regard to exposure and, as we remember, relatively more frequent than any other factor; but its index of effectiveness is not pronounced. This is the only exception to the general conclusion that the impact of personal contact is greater than that of any other sources investigated in this study. Now the question of how such a result can be interpreted presents itself.

Any analysis has to start with certain ideas which are accepted, if only qualifiedly, for the purpose at hand. In the present case, we will be well served by distinguishing four major ways in which people can be induced or activated or carried forward toward a certain goal. The first way is by *force*. A football kicked towards a goal or a child put to bed by his mother are examples. A physicist or a physiologist could analyze this process in much greater detail. It is one basic type of direction-giving, but obviously it does not appear in the areas we have studied.

The second type might be called *immediate attraction*. A moth attracted by a candle or a man drawn irresistibly toward a woman are the more poetic type of examples. But here also belong the rat eager to eat the cheese it sees before it, or the child confronted with candy. As a matter of fact, we can include here cases where the object desired is not immediately present but where the memory of previous experiences induces a man to look for it; the hungry person going to the icebox for some food would be a case in point. Immediate attraction is applicable to our material at one point: the woman who is impressed by the sight of another woman's hairdo and decides to imitate it. But otherwise this second type does not play a major role in our analysis either. For the psychologist, however, this immediate attraction is by no means taken for granted but becomes an object of complicated analysis.

The third type we shall call *indirect or represented attraction*. An apple may not be at hand, but if it is described to us in glowing terms, we might go out and look for it. A *communication* which makes an object desirable to us or brings a desirable object vividly to mind can play a decisive role in channeling our activities. The communication can be by word of mouth, by print as well as by picture. This type of influence obviously covers many of the cases included in our study. There are certain borderline cases for which it would not be easy to say whether they belong in Type 2 or 3. A dog might have been conditioned to look for food at the ring of a bell;

is this direct or mediated attraction? In the type of material we are dealing with in this study such borderline cases are not likely to appear, however.

Finally, we have a type of activation which might be called *control*. All the cases in this group have one thing in common —a command is carried out largely irrespective of its content; the essential element is the *source* of the directive. Quite a number of variations can occur here: the execution of an order received under hypnosis; obedience under terror; compliance with the wishes of a beloved person; following some advice because of pervasive confidence in the adviser; traditional obedience of the child towards his parents; etc. In general it is not difficult to distinguish between Type 3 and 4. In Type 3 we do something because of what a source is communicating to us; in Type 4 we do it for the sake of the source itself. There are many logical and psychological problems one can raise concerning this distinction, but for the purpose of a rough orientation the reader should have no difficulty in accepting this fourth type as something he can identify fairly easily in his own experience.

Employing these distinctions, we now may say that our use of the term "influence," up to this point, has implied situations of indirect attraction and of control. When a magazine describes a new dress so appealingly that a woman feels she simply must have it; or if the boss advises us to see a picture and we do so because we would be embarrassed if he asked us next morning whether we'd seen it—then the term *influence* is in order. But now we know that we are really dealing with two types of influence. With this in mind, the following interpretation can be made on the basis of commonsense experience. Formal media will influence mainly by representation or by indirect attraction, that is, *by what they tell*. People, however, can influence both this way and by *control*. People can induce each other to a variety of activities as a result of their interpersonal relations and thus their influence goes far beyond the content of their communications.

This is probably the most important reason why we have found the impact of personal contact to be greater than the impact of formal media. There are undoubtedly exceptions.

Some people might have so much confidence in their favorite magazine that they would buy some goods advertised there without entering into sales argumentation. Or we might find an occasional television listener who has a crush on an announcer and is ready to follow all his commands. Or, as we shall suggest much later, opinion leaders may accept influences stemming from the media more often than will non-leaders.[5] Occasionally, therefore, the influence of a formal medium might fall into Type 4. But by and large, it is fair to say that persons have *two* major avenues of influence while formal mass media, like radio and print, have only one. Now from this preliminary presentation of our findings, let us go into more detail about how they were obtained.

---

5. Below, Section Three, Chap. XIV.

# CHAPTER VI

# The Role and Sequence of

# Various Influences

IMPACT STUDIES serve the purpose of evaluation. They are indicated when we want to know whether a certain propaganda campaign is successful, whether a certain institution needs change, and the like. Of course, impact studies are not the only means to this end: Experiments or repeated surveys are often more to the point. As a matter of fact, there are students who think that the present approach is quite out of order, because "people don't know why they act the way they do." But this objection is based on a misunderstanding and, in part too, on self-deception.

First, as we have just seen, there are many areas where people *do* know why they act. The task of the research man is to single out legitimate from hopeless applications of impact analysis; the claim here is not that the impact approach can always be used, but that it is sometimes adequate for evaluating the role of certain factors.

The self-deception comes in when social scientists allow themselves to feel that the best of all methods is "just around the corner." In medicine, for example, a rigorous experimental design can be used with considerable ease to test whether a drug really relieves headaches. In matters of social relations and administrative activities, similar work is logically possible but very expensive, and, in practice often hopelessly involved. Realistically speaking, since there simply is no easy way "just around the corner," why not make use of whatever avenues of information are available? A man cannot tell us what makes his headache disappear, and an animal cannot tell why it took the left turn on a road. But a man does experience, and can describe, the way in which many influences are exercised upon him, how some of his plans are carried into action, and sometimes even how his plans have developed or changed. To what extent such knowledge is scientifically useful should not be decided in advance; it will only become clear after systematic efforts have been made to collect and analyze retrospective reports on the kinds of actions discussed in this section.

Such progress, furthermore, will be possible only if a very clear awareness prevails as to the logical and operational nature of impact studies. Authors as a rule have either dogmatically rejected the analysis of "reasons" or they have carried them out in a naïve and unreflective way. This chapter and the next will discuss briefly some of the assumptions implied and the decisions required even in a simple impact study such as the present one. We are motivated to attempt this partly out of a felt need for clarification and partly with the hope that further work along such lines may thus be encouraged. The following pages will also explain why we consider the results of this section primarily a basis for a set of general leads rather than an explicit report of quantitative results from which detailed inferences can be drawn. As we now summarize the main steps of an impact analysis, it will become clear how many pitfalls our first effort failed to avoid. Without a careful discussion of our findings on the impact of personal influences among the women of Decatur, we could not have reached even the modest degree of clarification on methods now available. Certainly the insight we now have shows how badly this clarification was lacking in the field stage of our enterprise.

## The Five Main Elements
## of an Impact Analysis

We shall briefly sketch the considerations which have to be kept in mind in carrying out such a study, and indicate at what points more or less serious difficulties develop.

For this purpose, five steps can be clearly distinguished:
1. Developing an accounting scheme.
2. Distinguishing between different classes of cases and

the selection of those appropriate for the study.

3. Devising adequate interviewing procedures to get the necessary information.

4. Assessing impact for each of the factors decided upon in the accounting scheme.

5. Executing a statistical analysis and interpretation.

Steps 3 and 4 have been partly covered in the second chapter of this section but we shall make some additional remarks in subsequent pages. The present chapter is devoted to a discussion of Step 1 and the following chapter to Steps 2, 3, 4 and 5.

## The Accounting Scheme

The present study should be grouped with studies into the "causes" of crime and accidents, the "reasons" for suicide and voting, etc. In all such researches, a final act is traced back to some earlier point and the "causes" or "reasons" or "determining factors" are singled out. From the beginning there is a necessary arbitrariness in such efforts. A woman commits a crime or she chooses to buy a certain brand of coffee; in both cases, her whole preceding life has in a way contributed to this final event. If she had not been born so many years ago, or if she had not taken a certain turn in the street last week, or if the weather had been different that morning, the final act might not have come about at all. In this sense, the general question *why* doesn't really make sense. It has to be translated into a series of more specific questions aimed at discovering whether a specific set of factors did or did not play an important role. What factors we will need to study will be determined partly by the purpose of the study and partly by the general nature of the area under investigation.

Suppose we were to investigate why people migrate from one part of the country to the other. At the very least, we would want to know what were the disadvantages of the old place and what was attractive about the new one. If in this same study we were especially interested in evaluating the propaganda of a Chamber of Commerce, we would also pay attention to the ways in which people learned about the new place and not only what features of it attracted them there. Again, suppose our study were to put more stress on the psychological side. Then we might divide the "push" into at least two parts: the negative features of the old place which acted as pressures toward migration; and the "trigger event" which finally made the situation unbearable.

The set of factors which we finally decide to include in our inquiry is called the accounting scheme. These factors form, so to speak, a primitive model by which we compare all the specific cases to be investigated. It is as if we were saying something like this: In order for a man to move there has to be a "push" away from the old place and a "pull" towards the new place; in each case, therefore, we have to get at least one push and one pull to have a minimum of necessary information. The accounting scheme, then, would consist of two elements. Or we might say that for each person migration comes about only if there is (1) a push, (2) a trigger event which "activates" the push, (3) a pull and (4) a channel by which the attraction of the pull is brought to bear. Then the accounting scheme would have four elements and the interviews would be considerably more complex.

Now purchases of inexpensive items are as a rule fairly simple actions and do not require an elaborate accounting scheme. Still, a number of appropriate schemes are easily thought of, even if the purpose is only to assess the role of a few influences like personal contacts or advertising. We might be interested, for instance, in the following kinds of questions: Which types of influences are most likely to arouse people's *interest;* to which source do they turn most for *information;* which is most likely to induce final *action?* In such a case an accounting scheme providing at least these three elements would be required: (1) Influences which start an action, (2) sources to which the actor turns during indecision, and (3) clinching factors. But whatever the degree of refinement desired, our point here is that in any impact study there is inherent an accounting scheme which must be made explicit; this requires a preliminary decision which states what causal factors and what steps in the causal process are to be investigated.

Although our present study did not require a very elaborate scheme, the idea of an accounting scheme has been discussed in some detail because it is a basic feature of any impact study. Essentially, our accounting scheme consisted of the following elements. We assumed that a decision to go to the movies or to buy a certain brand of food is made in at least two steps. In the first step interest in or desire for the act is created and in the second step the matter is "clinched" and the act is actually performed. This two-step nature of our accounting scheme comes out in two ways: (1) Our questions sometimes distinguished between "learning about something" and "making up one's mind," and (2) we included in all our interviews, questions about the sequences of exposure.[1] Thus, for each of the areas we studied—marketing, fashions, movies and public affairs—the "changers" were asked the following question: "You mentioned the various things that brought it (new food brand, new fashion, movie) to your attention; will you tell me which of them brought it to your attention first . . . second . . . third . . . fourth . . . ?"

We shall now leave the general discussion of accounting schemes and turn to the findings provided by the application of our own, primitive scheme to these items in our questionnaire.

## *The Number and Order of Influences*

Let us look at movie decisions first. One-third of our respondents were exposed to only one influence; two-thirds had heard or read about the movie they attended from several sources. Here is the full tabulation:

**Table 8—Multiple Exposure to Sources of Influence About Movies**

| | | |
|---|---:|---:|
| Exposed to one source only | | 36% |
| Exposed to more than one source | | 64% |
| Including: | | |
| Exposed to two sources only | 32 | |
| Exposed to three sources | 20 | |
| Exposed to four or more sources | 12 | |
| Total (= 100%) | | (584) |

1. As a matter of fact, the tables given in the previous section do not really distinguish between the two steps; all the influences are lumped together there. We shall, however, distinguish below between positions in the temporal sequence of influence.

We asked those who reported exposure to more than one influence about the sequence in which they were exposed. If a woman told us she had read in a magazine about the movie she attended and had also heard a friend talking about it, we asked which had come first. It was often difficult for respondents to recall the sequence: 14 per cent, in fact, were entirely unable to do so, and it is likely that those who did recall, experienced difficulty.[2]

Our first problem is descriptive: What are the sequences of the different influences? And do each of the several media have characteristic positions in this sequence? For the moment, impact ratings will not be used; below, however, we shall try to see whether influences which come first in a series are likely to be more or less effective than influences which come later.

Because we are dealing here with exposure only, our base figures are large. We are able, therefore, to include in our count media which appeared less frequently, something which we could not do in Chapter V where we reported on impact ratings. Let us take our main example from the realm of moviegoing where we can add books, previews and theater marquees to the factors previously discussed. The types of exposure questions used in the field were exemplified in Chapter IV.

---

2. The ability to report the sequence of exposure is not a simple function of the number of exposures recalled, as might be supposed.

NUMBER OF EXPOSURES RECALLED

|  | 2 Exposures | 3 Exposures | 4 or More Exposures |
|---|---|---|---|
| % unable to report sequence | 18% | 8% | 16% |
| Total ( = 100% ) | (318) | (146) | (57) |

The highest rate of recall-failure occurs among those exposed to only two sources, the least amount occurs among those exposed to three sources. But, recall-failure among those exposed to four sources is almost as great as among those who were exposed to only two sources! A possible, but rather elaborate, explanation is that there are two opposing tendencies at work. The *number* of exposures recalled may be, at least partly, a function of general recall ability. The more exposures recalled the greater the likelihood that recall ability is high, and hence that the *order* of these influences will be remembered. This tendency might account for the decrease in recall-failure between those who recall two and those who recall three sources. Opposing this tendency there is an increasing difficulty in recalling the order of exposure as the number of exposures is increased, *regardless of general recall ability.* This last tendency might account for the differences between the 3 and 4 exposures groups. Admittedly, the explanation is somewhat tenuous; but it has the merit of being easily tested, and therefore, perhaps, warrants being stated.

Reflections on the different roles played by the various media suggest a characteristic temporal order. We would expect newspapers, for example, to play a "fact-feeding" role, presenting to the movie-goer a list of alternative pictures she might see or announcing where a movie she may be looking for is being shown. Newspapers, then, should probably appear somewhat later in the sequence than other sources. Then we would surmise that the typical role of personal contacts would be that of arousing a favorable predisposition towards attendance at a particular movie; and if that is so, personal contact should precede newspapers. Magazines might be expected to appear often as the first in a series of influences, because magazine pieces about a picture usually appear quite some time before the picture itself is offered in a particular city. And finally books, upon which motion pictures are based, should also appear early in the temporal order of exposure.

These expectations are largely borne out by our calculations. Here are the frequencies with which each influence appears in each of three temporal positions:

**Table 9—Positions in the Sequence of Movie Influences[3]**

|  | Personal Contact | Theater Marquee | Previews | Newspapers | Magazines | Books |
|---|---|---|---|---|---|---|
| First | 44% | 12% | 48% | 22% | 52% | 64% |
| Second | 37 | 29 | 29 | 51 | 26 | 3 |
| Third or later | 19 | 59 | 23 | 27 | 22 | 33 |
| Total (= 100%) | (190) | (61) | (114) | (295) | (139) | (36) |

Let us begin by comparing personal contacts and books. Both come early, especially books. But even at this stage, each probably plays a different role. After a picture is out, some person is likely to *tell* us about it; but a book may be read

3. The percentages indicate the frequencies with which the influences indicated in the column headings appear in the time sequences indicated by the row stubs. The totals of each column are the number of times each source was mentioned in connection with at least one other source.

Note that Table 9 does not take into account the differing tendencies of each source to be associated with other sources. For example, it may be that newspapers occur more frequently in combination with two other sources while personal contacts tend to be coupled only with a single additional source. If that were the case, then the apparently greater tendency of newspapers (compared with personal contacts) to appear in third position might be spurious.

long before the picture appears and be *remembered* on this occasion. Personal influences are more evenly divided between the three positions—they can "initiate," "inform," and "clinch." Books also have a tendency to appear relatively often in a late position; but they are almost never mentioned in second place. An interesting conjecture is suggested: Some people read or reread books because they know that the story is on the screen; only if they like the book do they go to the showing. It is well known that the sale of a book increases when it is shown on the screen. This is usually considered an *effect* of movie attendance but Table 9 seems to indicate that increased reading also *precedes* attendance.

Magazines have a distribution somewhere between books and personal contacts, but seem more similar to people than to books in their influence role. A story may be serialized in a magazine and so play the same preparatory role played by books. But more often magazines also tell *about* a film and its actors, editorially as well as in advertisements. Unfortunately, we cannot separate these functions in our material.

Previews are not very different from personal influences either, and in one respect this is surprising. It seemed reasonable to expect that the preview would occur mostly at the beginning of a sequence, as the first signal of the coming event. But in one out of four cases previews come late and obviously serve to reinforce other things one has learned about earlier; probably this is the case mostly with rather frequent movie customers.

Newspapers are likely to be used as a source of information to settle details about an attendance already decided upon. One might expect newspaper exposure most often to be in a terminal position. This, however, is not the case; most frequently it is in second place. This seems to indicate that quite a bit of debating goes on up to the end, with the newspaper employed as a kind of guide to what is available while other sources are looked to for a final decision. In many cases, also, a scrutiny of the newspaper may not have turned up a desirable picture and therefore other sources of information or advice are sought out. It is exposure to theater marquees which becomes increasingly frequent as we go from first to third place in the influence sequence. Many decisions as to which movie to see are probably finally set by what appears on the theater marquee. Their function perhaps is to clinch the cumulative effects of other influences; or, many people may be marquee shoppers, some postponing their choice until they look at the marquees of several theaters.

A similar analysis was carried out in the fashion field. Because it does not yield any basically new ideas we shall not report the findings. In regard to marketing, however, no such analysis seemed worthwhile. The decisions are made within a very short span of time and this plan for the distinction of sequences would not have been very helpful.

## Position and Impact

How is the sequence of influences related to impact? It might be that respondents experience the final, clinching influence as the most effective one. It could also be the other way around: the first exposure, perhaps, is experienced as the most important one. And, of course, we may find no relationship at all between the position of an influence in a time sequence and the weight with which it is experienced. Chart IV shows quite clear-cut findings. The exposure occurring first is likely to be reported as the most influential one. There are many individual exceptions but the statistical trend is quite strong. And this is not only true for our movie data; in our analysis of fashion changes the same result is apparent: the first exposure was most often considered most important.[4]

It is worthwhile speculating on this finding for a moment because it might have a variety of explanations. The most likely one is as follows. In connection with some influence, a person makes up her mind that she will attend a certain movie

---

4. In Chart IV only those people are included who report an exposure to a factor under investigation. They are the ones who in each bar add up to 100%. In the previous charts we had a final category, "unexposed." which by the nature of the present problem does not appear in Chart IV. The question could also be raised as to whether it is justified to combine all the respondents in one chart irrespective of how many exposures they report. In a larger sample it might be worthwhile to give results analogous to Chart IV separately for people who report one, two, three and more exposures respectively. This might lead to some further refinements but would not change the major interrelationship discussed in the following pages.

**Chart IV—Impact of Media in Varying Positions in the Sequence of Movie Influences**

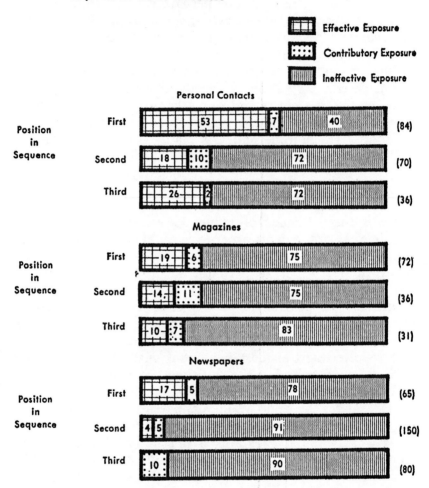

Effective Exposure

Contributory Exposure

Ineffective Exposure

Personal Contacts

Position in Sequence

First (84): 53 | 7 | 40
Second (70): 18 | 10 | 72
Third (36): 26 | 2 | 72

Magazines

Position in Sequence

First (72): 19 | 6 | 75
Second (36): 14 | 11 | 75
Third (31): 10 | 7 | 83

Newspapers

Position in Sequence

First (65): 17 | 5 | 78
Second (150): 4 | 5 | 91
Third (80): 10 | 90

NOTE: Each bar in the above chart adds to 100% and 100% equals the total number of people who reported exposure to a given influence in a given position. The first bar, for example, reads as follows: 53% of all movie-goers who named personal contact as the initial influence in their decisions were assessed as having been "effectively exposed"; 7% experienced "contributory exposure" to personal contact when it was the initial influence; and 40% were "ineffectively exposed."

or that she will change her type of hairdo. After such a decision is made she is more alert to other exposures: she looks at more ads and talks with more people. But she uses these further exposures mainly for confirmation or for elaboration of details. In these cases, then, we would expect that exposures which are ineffective are claimed to have happened most frequently in sequence positions *following* the most effective one.

But this is obviously not the only way it could have happened. Some women shop around for advice, look at a lot of ads and only after considerable hesitation make up their minds. In Chart IV these women are represented in the third bar in each block. They report that an exposure has happened in the third position, or later, but they call it the most influential one.

In this respect, however, the sources differ markedly. Personal contacts can almost be called bimodal: they are more likely to be given top impact rating either in first or in last sequential position. In the middle of a sequence they are experienced as less important (see second bar in group one). The newspapers, on the other hand, are effective only in first position: the later they come the less important their role (see the rapid decline of the cross-hatched sector in the last block of bars).

Obviously we have done no more than highlight the problem; we have not solved it by any means. The relation between impact and time sequence seems to us of considerable importance. Only detailed case studies or, still better, repeated interviews with the same people while they are considering a decision, will give further insights into these problems. In any case, to handle more information a more detailed accounting scheme will be needed. In Chart IV we have only two pieces of information available: position in the sequence and a kind of average impact rating for the whole process of a decision. Then, we have tried to infer, by speculation, *what kind of role* the various sources might have played. But it must be emphasized that this information could have been obtained *directly* by more systematic interviewing along the lines discussed earlier in this chapter. There are many complex actions where a more refined analysis would be indispensable; for the present purpose, our very much more elementary procedure has perhaps shed some further light on the important and diversified functions of personal contacts.

# CHAPTER VII

# Some Further
# Technical Problems

AT THE BEGINNING of the preceding chapter we outlined the five main steps of an impact study. The first one, the accounting scheme, has now been discussed. The second step is closely related to the first.

## *The Pre-Classification of Cases*

Among our movie cases there is a woman who, for years, has gone to the same movie theater every Tuesday night regardless of what was being presented. Obviously, it would make little sense to ask her why she decided to see the specific picture she saw the last time she went. Such addicted patrons might be asked how their habit developed—though it would not be an easy task to find out, and if there were many such cases, they might have to be treated as a special group. On the other hand, those who do make actual choices among alternatives certainly can be studied in terms of their last decision. Thus, a pre-classification of such different cases would direct us to construct different accounting schemes, different interviewing techniques and different procedures of analysis for the two groups; or, as a result of pre-classification, we might decide not to study particular parts of a sample at all.

Let us examine some of the implications of pre-classification for our study—that is, for movie-going, fashions and marketing. If we are studying decisions involving voluntary change, we are directed first to consider "supply." That is, we need to know the extent to which objects to *change to* are available, the extent to which change is a requirement of the situation, as well as the extent to which options to change are actually taken advantage of. It is in the nature of the distribution of movies, for example, that once or twice a week the supply is changed. Therefore, excepting the special cases mentioned above, we can be pretty sure that each movie attendance involves a new decision. We would not be in the same situation, however, if we were to interview people about the brand of cigarettes they smoke. A smoker who has just shifted brands, a smoker who has used the same brand for many years, and one who randomly picks any brand at hand, represent three very different types: the three cannot be interviewed in the same way nor can they be made members of the same statistical class. In other words, if the structure of the "supply" does not itself guarantee that most people have made a recent decision, different types of cases must be anticipated and distinguished in the research design. One way is to ask people whether they happened to make a recent change. This is what we did in the fashion field. We asked: "Have you recently changed anything about your hairdo, type of clothing, cosmetics, make-up or made any other change to something more fashionable?"[1] Five hundred and two women (over half of our June sample) acknowledged having made such changes.

In the case of movie-going we studied the reasons for every motion picture selection reported—with the exception of those of the several addicted movie-goers in our sample. In the case of fashions we studied only changes—those which were reported to us on the basis of the retrospective question.

With regard to marketing for foods and household goods we also concentrated on changes, but these changes were, from our point of view, of several types. Some changes were forced upon the respondent by the mere unavailability of the desired brand at the time of purchase; in other cases, the purchase was made by someone else within the family; in still other cases, the respondents were not the regular purchasers of food supplies for the household. Only those changes which

---

1. If the respondent mentioned more than one change, only the first one mentioned was followed up in the assessment interview. The 502 changes, then, correspond to 502 individual respondents and each change represents one respondent.

reflect a free choice between several brands can be studied by the assessment technique. When there was no choice open to the respondent, or when she did not personally make the choice, no influence, in our sense, could have been at work.[2]

The last example shows very clearly that in the course of an impact study it may be necessary to refine the definition of some aspect of the investigation. Thus, we began loosely by wanting to study changes in marketing behavior. We ended up by studying only those changes in which a voluntary, personal decision of the respondents was involved; all other cases were discarded. In other situations, however, we might have acted differently. Take, for instance, a study of residential mobility. In such a study, it is quite likely that we would distinguish two main classes of respondents in a pre-classification: those who moved of their own free will and those who had to move for a variety of reasons—because their old apartment house was torn down, because their landlord needed the apartment for himself, and so on. But while we would analyze the two groups separately, we would probably not discard the second group (as we do here in the case of marketing). In the first group we would be interested in what drove them away, what they disliked about the old place and how they chose a new one. Among the second group—those who were forced to move—the "pushes" away from the old house would be of no psychological interest. But the "pulls" toward the new house are still as worthy of investigation among the forced movers as among the voluntary movers. The main point is to realize that the pre-classification of cases is often an essential part of a systematic impact study, because different accounting schemes have to be applied to different groups of cases.

---

2. In marketing, furthermore, we collected not only the respondent's own retrospective account of some recent change in her marketing behavior, but also instances of "objective" change, as well. Thus in our June interview each woman was asked what coffee and cereals she then had on her pantry shelf and in August—when all respondents were reinterviewed—the same question was repeated. In this way, objectively, a total of 439 brand changes were found of which 142 were of coffee and 297 of breakfast cereal; 29 per cent of these were later classified as "non voluntary" changes—changes made because no other brand was available, etc. Assessment data for these "panel" changes are not reported in the text. In general, they are comparable to the "recall" data reported here (for which we have a larger number of cases) though some differences between the two types of data are touched on at the end of Chapter X below.

## Pitfalls in Interviewing

We have made comments in Chapter IV on appropriate interviewing techniques; and, as we have noted, some previous
writings on the "art of asking why" are available. This is not
the place to repeat these observations. Suffice it to say that
the questionnaire and the field work were designed so that the
information collected would best serve the purpose at hand.
If a respondent did not mention an influence but reported a
situation in which an influence was likely to have been exercised, follow-up questions were used to clarify the matter. It
was not left to the respondent to interpret our questions in
any way he pleased; efforts were made to ferret out his tacit
assumptions and to bring about a reasonable amount of understanding between interviewer and respondent as to what the
purpose of the inquiry was. Provisions were made to help a
willing respondent to remember the details of the episode
which she reported; hesitant and embarrassed respondents
were reassured that it was not a disgrace to be influenced by
someone else and that the information was to be used for scientific purposes. Wherever possible the concrete structure of
a person's experience was taken into consideration: She could
start her story at the point which seemed to her most salient
even if it was not pertinent to our problem. The interviewer
tried to lead the respondents along pathways which would
seem "natural" to them.

Still there is no doubt that we missed a considerable amount
of information due to a variety of mistakes and misfortunes.
Four types of difficulties can be distinguished in our study:

(1) *The "Fit" of the Questionnaire:* It can happen that
the whole structure of a questionnaire is wrong because it does
not fit the social or psychological structure of the action under
investigation. It is the purpose of pretests to avoid such accidents, but often the trouble is spotted only in the course of
the final analysis.

To illustrate, we know now that the following reaction
among respondents occurred quite a few times. When people
were asked whether they talked with someone about a moving

picture they would very often say no. In the course of the interview, it became clear, however, that they went to the movie with a companion and had, in fact, discussed the right choice with him or her. Many people seem to make a distinction between the person who accompanies them to the movie and "other people." If you buy some object, everyone you talk with about the purchase is "another person"; but if you go to the movies, your companion is part of your own act and not another person. People, therefore, quite consistently said they did not talk about a movie with anyone even when they later indicated that they had had long discussions with their own companion.

Chart II in Chapter V, therefore, probably gives a blurred picture. Undoubtedly, more respondents than that chart indicates were influenced by personal contacts, if we use this term in its inclusive meaning. This is the type of difficulty which would have been avoided had we developed a better accounting scheme. In a previous example we mentioned that a more thorough accounting scheme might distinguish between initiating influences and clinching influences. Now it turns out —at least when movies are the subject of study—that our scheme should have distinguished between two types of personal influence: "Inner" ones pertaining to the primary group which attended the movie jointly, and "outer" ones pertaining to all other people.

(2) *The Wording of Specific Questions:* Sometimes it is the wording of a specific question which causes trouble. It will be remembered that at the end of our question series we asked:

". . . what was the most important thing in causing you to . . . ?"

This question was preceded by many others, all of which put continuous emphasis on influences like personal contacts, advertisements, reading and so on. It was assumed that by then the minds of all respondents would be set so as to interpret the question to mean: "Which of these influences we have been talking about was the most important one?" But many people did not react in this way. When it came to this point in the interview they "broke out": There are numerous examples where the respondents somehow abandoned the entire focus on influences

and mentioned a movie actor or the special flavor of a brand
of coffee as the most important thing. In other words, they discussed *attributes* of the selected object rather than channels
through which these attributes became effective—as we had
meant they should. It might be added that even now considerable pretesting would be necessary to get the appropriate question wording. But there is probably no generally current term
which would easily cover such meanings as channel, source,
influence. A term less vague than "thing" but less specific than
those just mentioned will have to be found.

(3) *Respondent Misunderstandings:* A third group of errors
is connected with bad interviewing. Even if a question is worded
correctly, the respondents often misunderstand it. The movie
questions, for instance, were so introduced that the topic was
quite clearly the choice of a specific picture. And yet quite a
number of people thought they were being interviewed about
why they went to a movie at all on that particular day. Really
well-trained interviewers would catch such a misunderstanding.
They would accept the respondent's answer and then follow
up with a question of this kind: "Oh, I see, and having been
tired the way you were 'what was your main reason for choosing picture X the evening you went?'" The last part of the
question is the one which was printed in the questionnaire.
Sometimes, part of the information lost through such slips in
the field is recovered automatically in the course of the interview. In this case, for example, the respondents were asked
later how they had learned about the picture and similar questions, thus providing another opportunity to get at the kind of
specific influences in which we were interested. But still the
statistical results suffer in an obvious way from such insufficient
training of the interviewers.

(4) *The Limits of Impact Studies:* The fourth source of
errors points to the general limits which exist for impact studies
of the present kind. There are certain intrinsic difficulties in
obtaining appropriate answers from people. In about one case
out of fifteen, people would say that they just could not remember at all where they had heard or from what source they had
gotten a piece of information which they remembered was important in their decision. It should be remembered that in this

respect the three topics we are discussing here are probably relatively easy to investigate. Suppose a question of the following kind were to be asked: "Since our last interview you changed your mind as to whether the local police chief is doing a good job; on what do you base your new opinion; where did you get the information?" If at this time the performance of the local official was a topic of heated discussion, it would require considerable skill to sort out some of the major factors which determined this change of mind. It is obviously possible to imagine still other changes coming about slowly and in almost imperceptible steps where one should not even think of doing the kind of impact study exemplified in this section. What for our topic became a minor source of statistical difficulty would for other topics be a major argument in favor of a different kind of research design.

One final remark is of interest with regard to the sequence of questions in such an interview. From a logical point of view the order should be as follows: "Have you talked with anyone at all?" "Has it contributed in some minor way to your decision?" "Was this personal contact a major factor?" But from a psychological point of view such an order of interviewing would very likely be all wrong. If we started by asking people explicitly whether they talked with someone or read about the matter, this could very well affect their subsequent judgment as to the impact of various other factors. Then, those media or influences which might have played some role but which were not provided for specifically in the interview might not be reported by the respondent. Psychologically, therefore, it is necessary to ask the questions essentially in reverse order: "What was the most important factor?" "What other things contributed?" "Have you talked with anyone at all?"

But this contradiction between the best logical and the best psychological sequence can easily lead to statistical difficulties A person might have answered the first question—in the psychological sequence—by reporting that a talk with Mrs. X very strongly influenced her. Then a minute later we ask her whether she has talked with anyone about the matter. Many respondents would consider it silly to reiterate that they talked with Mrs. X. They interpret the later question as if it read: "Have you talked

with anyone else?" As a result we often find cases of the following kind: A person cites a radio advertisement as the main
influence; but to the question, "Have you heard about this
product over the radio?" she answers no. This leads to seeming statistical contradictions which must be taken care of by
proper editing of the returns. In our material, for instance,
our procedure is exemplified by the following rule: if a
person mentioned a factor as influential, we assumed automatically that she also was exposed to it irrespective of whether
such exposure was explicitly mentioned by the respondent
or not.

We do not pretend that our few remarks have exhausted all
the problems of interviewing which come up in this kind of
impact study. But it is hoped that the reader will get a general
idea of the kind of considerations which have to enter into all
phases of such research.

## The Problem of Assessment

Impact ratings assign weights to various factors according
to their causal role in a decision process. Even if these factors
are only weighed relative to each other it is very complicated
to discuss the logic behind such a procedure beyond what was
attempted in Chapter IV. Here we can only highlight the
nature of some of these difficulties once more.

Behind all these assessments always lurks the main question:
Would the respondent have attended the movies, or changed
her hair style, or bought a new food brand had this influence
not been exercised upon her? The answer will always depend
on a variety of additional considerations: How likely is it that
other influences in the same direction would have taken the
place of the one under consideration? How determined was
the respondent to take this action? To what extent was the
whole situation such that something was sure to create her
determination? Obviously, we never have enough information
to make such judgments with very great confidence. It is here
that the statistical element enters in a very important way. We
certainly make many mistakes in each single case. Sometimes
we overrate and sometimes we underrate the impact of a specific factor. But we hope that for a larger number of cases those

mistakes cancel out each other. When we say that people are influenced more by other people than by any other source, we assume that our result is statistically correct even if many of our individual assessments are unjustified. It is, therefore, very important to distinguish always between the *assessment* in a single case and the statistical *evaluations* which derive from the accumulation of many such individual assessments. Charts I, II and III, in Chapter V, were typical examples of such impact statistics. To what extent it is justified to assume the statistical cancellation of errors is again a matter too complicated to discuss here. It is quite obvious that our confidence is justified to different degrees, according to the substantive material with which we are dealing.

How can we ever prove whether our impact statistics lead to correct results? Here again the distinction between individual and statistical findings is crucial. In an individual case we probably can never prove the assessment of an impact. We can only make it more or less plausible by the nature of our argument and the background information introduced. But the statistical results seem to permit a kind of verification. It would not be too difficult to make an experiment of the following kind: We can expose one group of people to advertisements for some commercial product and keep another group unexposed. Suppose, then, that the group of people to whom advertising was directed buy the product in larger numbers; the difference might be, say, 10 per cent. Let us now interview the people who were exposed to advertising and have bought the product. If 10 per cent tell us that they bought the product because of the advertisement, then we may conclude that our assessment procedure is correct.

Some data reported in the literature come near this kind of verification. It has been shown in one study, for instance, that the more crowded people are in fact, the more likely they are to give over-crowding as a reason for moving to another place.[3] Or, again, the farther away people live from a department store the more likely they are to give distance as a reason for not buying there. A British criminologist, Cyril Burt, has compared

3. Rossi (1955). This and subsequent examples are also discussed in Lazarsfeld and Rosenberg (1955), Section V.

in detail two sets of data of the following kind: on the one hand he analyzed individual cases of juvenile delinquents to assess the role of poverty in the commission of a crime; concomitantly, he studied statistically how much greater the crime rate was in poor as compared with well-to-do groups. The reasonable agreement between the two types of analysis gave him confidence in his assessment procedure. But such comparative studies are still very rare and it would be highly desirable that more of them be carried out. In the present study it was not possible to introduce such costly kinds of verification of our impact statistics.

There is one final question which has to be raised. Does it ever make sense to talk of the impact of a source? Isn't it always the *argument* of the adviser or the advertisement which is transmitted by a source which influences the respondent? This is undoubtedly true. Our language is somewhat elliptic here. When we find that, in general, personal advice has more impact than advertising and other information in formal media, we mean the combination of both the source and its content. Suppose we find with the help of our evaluation that one medium has a greater impact than another. This can be the result of a number of differences between the two sources. It could be, for instance, that they are both equally effective if they reach people, but the one has a much greater *coverage* than the other. Or it could mean that the two have the same coverage but one has a greater *impact*, uses much more convincing arguments or has some other way of affecting the audience it reaches more successfully. Perhaps the whole matter can be put into a kind of formula: impact equals coverage times effectiveness.

We thus study channels and their content as we find them in a specific situation. This is characteristic for any evaluation study. We do not raise the question: What *could* the various media do if used at their best? Such investigations have been carried out before. In two previous publications we have tried to investigate the specific properties of reading versus listening[4] and of the nature of personal influence.[5] Such investigations, however, serve a different purpose and require techniques different from the ones employed in the present study.

4. Lazarsfeld (1940), Chap. 5.
5. Lazarsfeld, Berelson and Gaudet (1948), Chap. 14.

# CHAPTER VIII

# Variations
# in Impact

OUR IMPACT RATINGS were reported for the entire sample of
Decatur respondents. But one might expect that varying conditions would make quite a difference within the sample, that
is, people may be more or less susceptible to influences depending on the situations in which they find themselves and people
of different characteristics might also differ in the type of
sources by which they are affected. This leads us to the last of
the five steps outlined at the beginning of Chapter VI: statistical analysis.

Our graphs were merely descriptions of an actual situation.
If, for instance, at the time of the study more advertisements
had been on the air, the impact figures for radio would undoubtedly have been higher. There are, so to speak, no generalizations which can be derived from such information. In order
to find results of broader validity, additional information has
to be introduced. And there are two directions in which we can
proceed. We can take into consideration the attitudes and characteristics of the respondents included in our study; and we can
study the impact of the media in relation to each other rather
than in isolation. We shall restrict ourselves, here, mainly to the
first kind of elaboration.

## The Role of Dissatisfaction

In the course of our interviews, we asked questions which
were meant to illuminate the psychological context in which the
decision was made. We speculated that among other things we
would encounter two kinds of changes: those which were made

because of dissatisfaction with a previous state of affairs, and those which were made more in an experimental trial-and-error context—change for change's sake. To spot these two types of change, we asked women who had made a marketing change in a brand or product the following question:

"When you made the change, were you dissatisfied with the product you used before, or did you just want to make a change?"

A corresponding question was asked of women who reported a change in a fashion habit. According to their answers, respondents were divided into *satisfied* and *dissatisfied* changers. The term "dissatisfaction," it should be kept in mind, refers to the attitude prior to the change and not to the reaction after the change.

It is important to understand clearly the nature of such attitude or disposition questions in the course of an impact study. It is not implied that a woman changed simply because she was dissatisfied. Many women might be dissatisfied with something without changing, just as many women might be fairly well satisfied and still change.

It should also be clear that we can distinguish here between effective and ineffective "exposure" to a mood or an attitude just as we distinguished between effective and ineffective exposure when we discussed outside influences. Thus, we might be "exposed" to a variety of moods but act upon only one of them. An illustration of this can be found in a study of residential mobility where dissatisfaction is analyzed in a systematic way—in the way we concentrate in this study on outside influences, for example.[5] A careful distinction is made between, say, mere dissatisfaction with noise in the house and the kind of dissatisfaction with noise which impels the tenant to look for another place. This sort of distinction between effective exposure and mere exposure to noise can, of course, be presented in the same form as our charts in Chapter V. But in our present context we shall not distinguish between different forms of exposure to dissatisfaction. That is, we shall talk about exposure irrespective of effect as far as dissatisfaction goes. We want to know whether the impact of personal contact and formal media

5. Rossi (1955).

is different for women who report themselves as having been satisfied than it is for those who say they were dissatisfied prior to their decision making. This is what we shall mean by the distinction between satisfied and dissatisfied respondents.

To give a first synopsis of our results let us concentrate on the effectiveness index. Compare the effectiveness of our main sources as it was reported by satisfied and dissatisfied respondents for changes in fashion habits, for example.

**Table 10—The Impact of Various Influences on Fashion Changes Among Satisfied and Dissatisfied Women[1]**

| Source | INDEX OF EFFECTIVENESS[2] | |
| --- | --- | --- |
| | Satisfied Respondents | Dissatisfied Respondents |
| Verbal personal contact | .09 | .20 |
| Visual personal contact | .13 | .18 |
| Salesperson | .08 | .13 |
| Magazine | .04 | .08 |

The table shows that the effectiveness of a source—any source—is greater among dissatisfied people. And what is true in the case of fashions is true for the other areas as well. A dissatisfied person, if reached by advice or some other kind of information, is more likely to act upon it. It should be stressed that this is not as obvious a result as it might seem to be. It could very well be that a dissatisfied person is more cautious; he may look around more for help and guidance but be less readily influenced. He may be inclined to hear more and varied opinions and to think through consequences more carefully. He may want to avoid being dissatisfied all over again.

Such a situation would reverse the relation between the effectiveness indices as lined up in Table 10. Actually, of course, our findings are certainly the result of a large variety of patterns which should be investigated in more detail. The present findings are only the net results of a considerable number of possible variations.

1. In regard to fashion changes, just about half of the women reported changes without dissatisfaction with the previous habit, while half were dissatisfied before they had made the change. In the marketing study, less than one-third of the women changed from a brand with which they were satisfied; more than two-thirds reported dissatisfaction with the brand they had been using prior to the change.
2. This Index is explained in Chapter V, p. 178.

Table 10 tells what proportion of the reported exposure to each medium was experienced as effective in the decision to be made. But we can also raise the question whether the two groups of respondents showed different *amounts of exposure* to media according to their state of satisfaction. Here the results are different for the two areas investigated. In marketing, the dissatisfied women reported more exposure to both personal contacts and radio advertising. Dissatisfaction, then, does seem to have had two consequences: such women were more aware of available sources and more susceptible to their advice and influence. In the fashion field, we did not find differences in total exposure between the two types of women. Only the *effectiveness of exposure*, but not exposure itself, was greater for dissatisfied women. It would not be too difficult to speculate about this difference. In the fashion field, perhaps, women may be always on the alert, while as regards consumer goods, dissatisfaction may be required to sharpen their awareness. But before going into further interpretation, it would be better to wait and see whether future studies corroborate the difference which, after all, is based on rather small figures. So is Table 10, of course, but at least there all the statistical differences between dissatisfied and satisfied women are consistently in the same direction.

## Another Situational Difference

Another dispositional factor was investigated, one rather similar to the dissatisfaction just discussed. In the case of movies we asked:

"Did you go to see a particular picture or just to go to the movies?"

The reason for inserting this question is obvious. A person who goes to the movies just to relax or to while the time away is likely to show a different influence pattern than the one who goes for the sake of a specific picture. Accordingly, employing this question, we distinguish between discriminating and non-discriminating movie-goers. The distinction here pertains only to the specific movie visit investigated. But we know from other parts of our study that people who at any one time are more discriminating in their selection of a picture are, at other times too, more likely to be among the more discriminating.

It is not surprising that discriminating movie-goers report more total *exposure* to the different media of influence. After all, if you care about what movie you see, you will be more likely to explore the possibilities you have. Table 11 shows that this is the case.

**Table 11—How Various Sources Affect Discriminating and Non-Discriminating Movie-Goers[3]**

|  | RESPONDENT | |
|---|---|---|
| Source and Measure | Discriminating | Non-Discriminating |
| **Personal Contacts** | | |
| Total exposure | 50% | 37% |
| Index of effectiveness | .36 | .27 |
| **Newspapers** | | |
| Total exposure | 86% | 75% |
| Index of effectiveness | .06 | .07 |
| **Magazines** | | |
| Total exposure | 31% | 17% |
| Index of effectiveness | .14 | .10 |

With regard to personal contacts and to magazines, relative *effectiveness* is greater with discriminating movie-goers, too. Only newspapers do not show a difference. Now, we already know that for our sample as a whole, total exposure to newspapers is greatest but *effective* exposure to newspapers is smallest.[4] Here we see that more of the discriminating movie-goers look for information in the newspapers than do non-discriminating people but both groups remain equally uninfluenced by the mere factual information they receive.

The findings of Tables 10 and 11 can be combined into a more general formulation. People who are dissatisfied with something they have been doing so far and people who are interested in a specific moving picture are probably special

3. "Discriminating movie-goers" are defined as respondents who said that they usually go to the movies to see "a particular picture." "Non-discriminating movie-goers" are persons who said they go primarily "just to go to the movies."

4. See Chart II, p. 179.

cases of a more general attitude: They are on the lookout for a solution to a problem; either they want to find something better than they have used before or they want to find something in which they have a particular interest. Such people have a specific mental set. They scan their environment with a specific goal in mind. People in such a state of mind are more often subject to persuasion by outside influences, be they personal contacts or formal media. And while our data are very scanty indeed they do at least point to an additional qualification. Not only are "people on the lookout" more open to persuasion; personal contact seems to be an especially effective source of persuasion under such circumstances. Tables 10 and 11 both show that the difference in effectiveness of personal contact for dissatisfied and discriminating people, as compared with satisfied and non-discriminating ones, is greater than that of any of the formal media.

## Differentials in the Impact of Personal Influence

We might add here one additional set of findings, though we shall not be able to generalize from them in the way that the introduction of attitudes and the general characteristics of the respondent permitted us to. But there are hints nonetheless as to results which can be obtained by more refined applications of the present approach. All through this section we have been talking about the influence of "personal contacts" or mass media. But, of course, personal contacts can be of various kinds—the advice of a family member might play more or less of a role than the advice of a stranger. In the previous section of this report we discussed a very characteristic example. In matters of public affairs, a married woman talks more with her husband than with other people, but she respects his knowledge less; thus, the extent of his actual influence is a compromise between these two tendencies. From the analysis of impact ratings, three more findings can be added which amplify the role of personal contacts. As far as the women in our sample go:

1. Family members, and especially children, have a greater impact

on their small food purchases than people outside the family.[5]

2. People who are considered experts in any area influence our respondents in that area more than the average run of advisers.

3. The more specific the suggestion which a personal contact makes, the more likely it is that his or her advice will be followed.

## The Role of Specificity

Not only personal influence, but each of the other media of influence can also be subdivided according to degree of specificity on a given subject.

For example, magazines vary in their concern with motion pictures. Some devote their entire content to the world of Hollywood; others treat the topic only peripherally or not at all. We want to compare different kinds of magazines and their different treatments of movies to see how their effectiveness on movie choices differ.

When one of our respondents told us she had read something in a magazine about the movie she attended, we asked her to name the magazine. We classified all these magazines into three broad categories: "movie magazines," devoted exclusively to motion pictures; "women's magazines," dealing primarily with womanly topics for women as an audience; and "general magazines," a left-over category containing all other periodicals.

Now, 41 per cent of the magazines mentioned were "movie magazines"; 32 per cent were "general magazines"; 14 per cent were "women's magazines"; and 13 per cent we either

---

5. In all of our discussion of marketing influences in this chapter we have excluded "husbands" and "children" from the category of personal contacts despite the fact that our data indicate that they play an important role. Our decision to exclude such intra-household contacts stems from our desire to distinguish clearly between "requests" and "influences." When a husband says to his wife, "Please buy Coffee A," that is a "request" for which the woman of the house merely acts as purchasing agent, so to speak. Clearly this is something different than "influence," which takes the form of suggestions, advice, testimonials, etc., and which also go on within the household. Our examination of the intra-family data revealed that "requests" were reported to our interviewers more frequently than "influences"; we therefore decided to exclude intra-family data entirely in this section. By doing this, we have obviously understated the role of "personal influence"—that is, the frequency and effectiveness of personal contacts—in the marketing arena. (In Chapter X, below, we shall note that husbands and children seem to be most active in two particular marketing domains: coffees and cereals.)

could not classify or were not told. Here is an assessment of the effectiveness of these types of magazines:

*Table 12—Magazine Types and Effectiveness in Motion Picture Selections*[6]

|  | TYPE OF MAGAZINE | | |
|  | Movie | General | Women's |
|---|---|---|---|
| Effective Exposures | 16% | 12% | 9% |
| Contributory Exposures | 7 | 17 | 13 |
| Ineffective Exposures | 77 | 71 | 78 |
| Index of Effectiveness | .20 | .17 | .11 |
| Total (= 100%) | (68) | (52) | (23) |

Movie magazines are most effective (16 per cent); general magazines are next, with 12 per cent effective exposures; and women's magazines come last, with 9 per cent. Their effectiveness thus seems to parallel the content emphasis of the three types, for movie magazines certainly devote the greatest proportion of space to the movies, general magazines are probably next, and women's magazines last.

A little more than half (55 per cent) of the respondents in mentioning particular magazines referred to movie reviews or articles about movies; 25 per cent referred to advertisements, and 20 per cent were unable to recall what content they had read. Reviews and articles are more effective than advertisements: 15 per cent of them are effective; and another 16 per cent are contributory. Of advertisements, 12 per cent are effective, only another 2 per cent contributory.

## Some Concluding Questions

This is about as far as our data permit us to go. And the result shows the role impact studies can play in future research. Let us speculate for a moment on what further questions we might raise. People who are in agreement with their environment could be contrasted with people in a minority position; which of the two would be more susceptible to persuasion by advice or propaganda? What would we find if we were to compare the susceptibility of people who have had a variety of

6. Note that this table is based only upon magazine exposures. The totals in each column are the number of exposures to each kind of magazine mentioned.

experiences in a particular area with people who have followed a pretty uniform line of behavior until now; are there personality differences—are there certain personal traits which make some people more vulnerable to influences than others? This version of the question gives us the occasion to comment on a negative result of our study. We can ask whether people with low education are more susceptible to influence irrespective of the specific decision to be made; whether personal contact has greater impact for older people and mass media for the younger generation. Obviously, the answer to such questions would require a large number of studies in order to eliminate the peculiarities of the few specific kinds of decision areas we have studied here; but from our present material, with one exception, no consistent findings can be reported. The exception is part of our analysis of opinion leadership where, to a limited extent, we are able to compare the exposure of leaders and non-leaders to various sources of influence.[7]

We thus have three types of statistical qualifications of impact ratings. The role of a source can be different according to various dispositions and attitudes which develop in the course of the action under investigation; for this we saw some clear-cut examples when we analyzed the roles of dissatisfaction and discrimination. The sources themselves can be further specified; thus, we indicated how different personal contacts and different magazines can vary in their impact ratings. Finally, the impact of various sources might be different for different types of people; for this our study did not provide any consistent data. In order to complete the range of possible qualifications a fourth type of analysis has to be mentioned even though our study does not provide a concrete example of it.

Let us first speculate on the matter in more general terms. Suppose we are studying drug addiction and focus our attention on two elements of a reasonable accounting scheme. For each case, we shall want to know (1) how a youngster happened to use a drug the first time, and (2) what kind of gratification he received from the drug that kept him at it. We

---

7. See below, Chap. XIV, on "The Two-Step Flow of Communication."

would thus distinguish between factors accounting for initiation and factors accounting for continuation. Some youngsters will undoubtedly start using the drug just because they want to be one of the gang. A similar type of reason will also appear in the tabulation of reasons for continuation. It is not clear, however, from the beginning, whether the case histories of boys who respond to this social element in the initiation episode will also show similar determinants in their continuation phase. Some youngsters are undoubtedly so susceptible to their environment that social factors will play a decisive role in both phases. But as a general rule it may be the other way around. Youngsters who in their initiation fall so easily under the spell of other youngsters might have especially "weak resistance." Therefore, later on, they may not be able to break the habit even if the social influences have in the meantime disappeared. In other words, we cannot tell in advance whether there will be a positive or a negative or no interrelationship between what we might loosely call reasons for initiation and reasons for continuation. A similar question could be raised in other contexts, too. For instance, people who leave their old home for one set of reasons may pick their new home on quite a different basis without regard to their original reasons at all. The statistical relationship between these pushes and pulls is a matter of empirical investigation. It can neither be guessed in advance, nor can it be derived from the careful study of a few detailed cases.

And as soon as we become aware of the possibility that there are different phases or stages of decision (push and pull; initiation and continuation) we are also led to ask whether there may not be a difference in the degree to which various media are operative and effective at various stages of decision. The pattern for this kind of analysis is already suggested in Chapter VI in our examination of varying positions in the sequence of influence. We have reason to suspect—to give one example—that such an analysis would reveal that advertising plays a more effective role in maintaining and reinforcing decisions, once made, than in initiating them.[8] In the present re-

---

8. More recent work of the Bureau of Applied Social Research, Columbia University, continuing in the tradition of "reason analysis" outlined in this

port, we cannot present detailed information of this kind because our accounting scheme is too simple. But our point is that a more elaborate accounting scheme would permit such analysis and, alternatively, if we had had no accounting scheme at all, it would have been quite impossible to present even the primitive story we have tried to tell so far.

section, lends credence to this possibility. See, for example, Ennis (1954), and Katz and Menzel (1954), unpublished studies concerned, respectively, with decisions regarding beverage habits and decisions of physicians with respect to the adoption of new drugs.

CHAPTER IX

# On Describing the Flow of Influence

THE KINDS OF INFLUENCES, and the types of influentials, in which we are interested were described in Section One. There we tried to make clear that our concern is with specific incidents of informal interpersonal influencing, in everyday situations, in the arenas of marketing, fashions, public affairs and movie-going. The frequency of this kind of influence, and its effectiveness in these four arenas, was then contrasted, in Section Two, with the frequency and the effectiveness of influences stemming from the mass media. Here, in Section Three, attention will be focused on the distinguishing characteristics of the individuals who are transmitters of such influences—the "opinion leaders."

In much of our discussion we will be dealing, it will be recalled, with "self-detected" opinion leaders. These are the women who told us that they had recently been asked their advice relative to some specific matter of marketing, fashions,

---

* Leo Srole and David B. Gleicher contributed substantially to the formulation of this section and to the analysis of the data.

public affairs or movie-going. Some of the merits and some of the shortcomings, as well as the degree of reliability, of this method of locating opinion leaders have already been discussed. The pages which follow, therefore, begin immediately with the question, "Who are these opinion leaders and who are the people whom they influence?"

If we were concerned with more formal social structures—a factory, say, or a hospital—the task might be easier; that is, we probably could portray opinion leaders and describe the flow of influence in terms of the comparatively well defined statuses associated with those particular settings. Thus, we might find that union officers were typically the ones to whom the other workers looked for advice; or, perhaps ,that the skilled workers would be opinion leaders for the unskilled; or, in the setting of the hospitals, that innovations in medical practice are transmitted from specialists to general practicitioners.[1]

Our setting, however, is not so clearly delimited. First of all, the structure with which we are dealing is not very sharply defined. We call it a community, and typically the units with which we deal are the small, relatively informal networks which go to make up a community: families, friendship groups, neighbors. The second difficulty is that unlike the factory or the hospital which would provide us with convenient labels for each of the individuals involved (interne, nurse, specialist, general practitioner), the members of our units—with the exception of the members of the family—cannot easily be differentiated. Therefore, it is much more difficult to describe the flow of influence: Do the women who are influential for their neighbors look any different from the women whom they influence? Is there any label by means of which we can easily distinguish influential friends from non-influential ones?

## Three Relevant Dimensions

Those are the problems we attempt to confront in this chapter. Broadly speaking, we have decided to employ three factors in terms of which the members of our sample may be

---

1. A pilot study on the flow of scientific information in the medical profession has been carried out by Katz and Menzel (1954) and is presently being continued on a larger scale.

differentiated, and thus which may serve us as frameworks in terms of which the flow of interpersonal influence can be described. These three factors are: position in the "life-cycle"; position on the community's social and economic ladder; and gregariousness, or the extent of social contacts.

(1) *The Life-Cycle*: How old a woman is, whether she is married on not, and if she is married, how many children she has and how old they are—these are bases for differentiating among the members of our sample. We shall call the various phases of family life and child rearing the "life-cycle," expecting that these phases will not only help us in assigning labels to the people in our sample, but will also be associated with differing rates of opinion leadership on different sorts of subjects. In other words, we anticipate that holding a position in one phase of the life-cycle rather than another will incline a woman to some interests rather than others and will make her more or less likely to be an opinion leader in the several influence arenas which we shall consider.

Our plan will be to consider the distribution of the members of our sample in the several different life-cycle phases to see whether opinion leaders tend to congregate in one or another phase or whether they are more or less evenly distributed Then, we shall ask whether there seems to be any patterned direction of flow through the life-cycle: Do older women influence younger women—and on which matters? Do women with larger families tend to play an opinion leader role for small family wives—and on which matters?

(2) *Social and Economic Status*: Position on the ladder of social and economic status is another factor that may be helpful in describing opinion leaders and the flow of influence. Traditionally, high status has been regarded as the almost exclusive determinant of influence in the community. It has been assumed, in other words, that influence flows down the status ladder by virtue either of the "power" of those above, or the motivated emulation of those above by those below. In general, it seems, most hypotheses about the flow of influence have focused on some such idea of a vertical flow. Yet, even if influences can be shown generally to begin at the top of the status ladder and then to filter down, that does not mean,

necessarily, that each person on every rung is *personally* influenced by someone higher up. It is at least as plausible to assume, if influence does proceed downward, that it is transmitted across status lines only at a few key points—between status ambassadors, so to speak—while the majority of influence acts of the kind with which we are concerned go on among persons of like status.[2]

In any event, we are proposing here to make room for a hypothesis of *horizontal influence* to stand alongside the hypothesis of vertical influence. And, just as with the life-cycle, we shall examine two types of evidence relating to these hypotheses: First, for each of the four arenas of our inquiry, we shall determine whether influentials tend to be concentrated on the higher status levels, or whether they tend to be fairly evenly distributed among all status levels. If we find a relatively even distribution, for example, we shall have some reason for assuming that the flow of influence is largely horizontal, that is, that those on each status level look to their own corps of leaders. If, on the other hand, we find a disproportionate concentration of opinion leaders in one, but not another, status grouping, we shall begin to suspect that influence may flow from this group to the others.

But we possess a second type of evidence, too, which has more direct bearing (though, unfortunately, as will be indicated below, the data cannot be treated as more than "suggestive"). For a portion of our sample, it will be recalled, we have gathered information about both influential and influencee. By examining this information, we shall be able to specify both the "who" and the "whom" of an influence exchange. If we find that typically the influential is of higher status than the influencee, we shall conclude that even in the everyday influence situations with which we are dealing, the flow of influence is predominantly vertical. Should we find, however, that influence moves more frequently between status equals than between individuals of different status, we shall

2. It is also possible that many kinds of influence do not flow *down* the status ladder at all, but rather stay within the confines of each status level without ever invading other spheres. Similarly, it is probable that influence also flows *up* from lower to upper strata—consider jazz, for example.

conclude that the hypothesis of horizontal influence more nearly fits the facts.

(3) *Gregariousness*: The third factor which we shall employ to describe opinion leaders is gregariousness, or extent of contact with other people. Whatever other characteristic opinion leaders may turn out to have, they must, it seems to us, have access to other people. We shall study the extent to which this factor of gregariousness gives women a head-start toward opinion leadership. In part, of course, the extent of a woman's gregariousness will be determined by the amount of free time she commands, and free time, in turn, is a function of such things as life-cycle position (unmarried girl vs. woman with three young children) and social status (rich woman with household help vs. poor woman). Therefore, to assess the part played by gregariousness in making for opinion leadership we shall have to make certain to compare women of a given life-cycle or status position only with other women like themselves.

## The Distribution of the Sample in the Three Dimensions

First, then, we must find indices for each of the three factors we have just introduced. Ultimately, we want to see how effective each is for locating concentrations of opinion leaders and for tracing the flow of influence in marketing, fashions, public affairs and movie-going. Here is the thinking that went into the construction of our indices:

(1) *Life-Cycle Types*: In order to describe our respondents in terms of their positions in the life-cycle, we must develop types which take into account the major turning-points in a woman's typical life progression: from girlhood, through marriage, to motherhood, and older matronhood.

The single woman, or "girl," represents the initial position in the female life-progression. Generally her major concern is with the next step—marriage—and many of her activities and interests are oriented to this next step. Her position in the family structure is typically that of the near-adult dependent, though she may also have a job and contribute wages or salary to the household income. She is rarely responsible for household affairs and decisions, however, and her range of activities and concerns reflects this freedom. Our sample includes 101 single women, of whom 80 per cent are under 35 years of age. Those single women who are older than 35 years are usually outside the marriage market and probably differ from the younger single women in their several activities and interests. Since we want to sort out a type that is fairly homogeneous, we shall omit from the category of "girls" those who are above 35 years of age.

Unlike the girls, who constitute a fairly clear-cut type, wives as a group include women of 15 as well as of 80 years of age, childless wives as well as mothers of six children, mothers with infant children and mothers whose children are grown. These variations reflect differences in age and in the extent of motherhood responsibilities. What we must do is to subdivide the wives into types that are more or less homogeneous with respect to these variables.

First, we shall divide the wives in our sample into two basic age groups—younger wives and older wives—using age 45 as a dividing line. This gives us a division which corresponds roughly to the biological turning point with its attendant shifts in feminine interests and activities, and at the same time, clearly sorts out the women in our sample according to the ages of their children. Thus, 80 per cent of the children of the young wives (under 45) are less than 15 years of age; 91 per cent of the children of the older wives (over 45) are older than 15.

The older wives—that is, the married women over 45 years of age—we shall identify as "matrons." But we must subclassify the women under 45 once more in order to arrive at relatively clear-cut categories.

This second sub-division we shall make according to family size, using two or more children as the mark of the large family unit and thus, one child, or none, as the definition of the small family unit. We select this point because the average number of children for the younger wives lies between one and two children. Ideally, we should have liked to separate the childless wives from the mothers, but their number is small—only 55 out of the 350 younger wives (under 45) are childless.

With this final division of married women under 45 years of age into "large family wives" and "small family wives," we have mapped out four basic positions in the feminine life-cycle. The proportion of our sample which fits into each position is as follows:

**Table 13—Distribution of Life-Cycle Types in the Sample**

| | |
|---|---|
| GIRLS: <br> (Single women under 35 years of age) | 12% |
| SMALL FAMILY WIVES: <br> (Married women, under 45, with one or no children) | 26 |
| LARGE FAMILY WIVES <br> (Married women, under 45, with two or more children) | 25 |
| MATRONS: <br> (Married women, over 45, most of whose children are over 15 years of age) | 37 |
| Total (= 100%) | (693) |

This classification locates our respondents in one type of social structure—the family—defined by the life-cycle factors of age, marriage and motherhood. These positions we think will have something to do with a woman's interests and activities in the various areas of marketing, fashion, public affairs and movie-going; and, consequently, with the likelihood of playing an opinion leadership role in these arenas.

But, regardless of a woman's position in the family, the family itself has a position which may be related to this woman's power to influence others or to her chances at opinion leadership. This position has to do with the structure of social and economic status.

(2) *Social and Economic Status*: That significant differences in thought and action are exhibited by people with differential access to the economic and social opportunities of society is a well-documented fact, but whether the status structure should be viewed as composed of three or four or six strata is not

agreed upon.[3] The purpose which a classification is to serve
should be the major determinant of the degree of refinement
which is required, and here we want only the crudest measure
of status differences. So we shall adopt a broad division into
high, middle and low status. The utility of this classification
can of course be judged only with reference to what it can
teach.

To divide our respondents into these three roughly-defined
status groups, we have selected two factors—rent and education—and combined them into an index of social and economic status. This was done by taking each factor and locating
a dividing point at which half the sample fell on one side and
half on the other. For education, a high school diploma proved
to be the dividing point—that is, about half the people in our
sample had completed high school or more, the other half had
some high school or less. In the case of rent, the dividing point
was $40 per month.[4] Let us assume that both items are of
roughly equal importance for our status index, taking the presence of both high education and high rent as an indication of
high status; the absence of both, as an indication of low status;
and the presence of one or the other, but not both, as an indication of a middle status position. Using these categories, our
sample divides into 35 per cent which can be classified low
status (low education, low rent), 37 per cent middle status
(low education, high rent or high education, low rent), and
the remaining 28 per cent high status (high education, high
rent). About one third of the sample falls into each status
category.

(3) *Gregariousness*: Position in the life-cycle, and on the
status ladder, may or may not be useful in locating opinion
leaders in all of the four topical areas with which we are con-

3. Ideally, perhaps, social status should be considered apart from economic
status; that is, there are research findings to indicate that it is often useful to
distinguish between, say, income and prestige. For a discussion of this matter
from the vantage point of market research, see Smith (1952) which draws
on the Warner (1949) researches. Unfortunately, we have not been able
to treat these two aspects of stratification separately in these pages.
4. Home owners were asked, "What would be the rent (for this house) if
you were renting?" Their replies were treated in the same way as those
provided by respondents actually paying rent. It will be recalled here that
these data were collected in 1945.

cerned. It may turn out, that is to say, that opinion leadership in a given arena is concentrated among women in a given life-cycle position but that status position makes no difference at all; and, for another arena, it may be just the opposite. The notion of social contacts, however, as an ingredient in opinion leadership seems basic to any discussion. Almost by definition —for the idea of leader implies followers—it would be reasonable to postulate that persons who influence the opinions and habits of others are more likely to have a broader range of social contacts than non-opinion leaders.

To test this assertion, we shall construct a simple index of "gregariousness"—that is, a measure of the extent of a woman's social contacts. In our questionnaire, we asked: 1) "How many people are there with whom you are friendly and talk with fairly often who are not and never have been your neighbor?" and 2) "What organizations, clubs or discussion groups do you belong to?" The first question calls for an answer in terms of active friendships. It provides a measure of the magnitude of the individual's sphere of intimate, informal relationships beyond the immediate environs of the household. The second question covers social participation in more or less public associations. Both questions, presumably, reflect the degree of opportunity to participate in the person-to-person process of influence. Since it is this aspect, primarily, in which we are interested, we shall use both types of social relations in our measure.

In order to combine the two into one scale, we shall reduce each to a high-low dichotomy. The median number of friends named by the women in our sample is seven; therefore, we use this figure as a norm for grouping women into two classes: the 43 per cent with fewer than seven friends (the "low-friend" group), and the 57 per cent with seven or more friends (the "high-friend" group). Then we divide the entire sample again into another high-low classification using membership in one or more clubs as an index of high organizational activity: 41 per cent of the sample falls into this high category; 59 per cent falls into the low. When both indices are applied simultaneously, our sample divides as follows:

**Table 14—Distribution of the Sample According to Social Activity**

|  |  | Number of Friendships | |
|---|---|---|---|
|  |  | High | Low |
| Number of | High | 27% | 14% |
| Organizations | Low | 31% | 28% |

Thus, we rate 27 per cent of the women in our sample highly active in friendships and in club-oriented social activity while 28 per cent rate low in both these aspects of social life. Standing mid-way between these two extremes are the 45 per cent (14% plus 31%) whose social activities predominate in only one of the two dimensions. Since we are interested in a general factor of gregariousness rather than in the character of social contacts, let us combine these two mid-groups and assign them a medium gregariousness score. In our sample then, 27 per cent score high, 45 per cent score medium, and 28 per cent score low in gregariousness.

## The Life-Cycle and Social Status as Determinants of Gregariousness

Since we intend to describe opinion leadership in terms of life-cycle, social status and gregariousness, we must first examine what relationships these three major variables may have to each other. We want to know whether each is "independent" or whether it is somehow related to the other two.

Obviously, we should expect to find no relationship between status and life-cycle since neither income nor education can appreciably alter the girlhood-marriage-motherhood phases of the life-cycle; therefore, we should find that the proportion of women in each life-cycle type should be the same on all three status levels. With a slight exception, that is what we find. The exception is among women of low status where we find slightly fewer single women (8% compared with 13% and 14% on the other two status levels) and slightly more matrons (41% compared with 34% and 37%). This probably reflects the fact that younger women are, on the average, getting more education than their elders and therefore, because our definition of social status is based partly on education, fewer younger women appear on the low status level. But, in all, the difference is minute: Income and education do not appreciably modify the proportion of women on each step of the life-cycle.

But when we relate life-cycle, or social status, to gregariousness, there are interesting and important findings to report. The relationship between status and gregariousness is clearcut: The higher a woman's status the greater the range of her social activity:

Table 15—Distribution of Gregariousness Scores on Different Status Levels

| Gregariousness Score | STATUS LEVEL | | |
|---|---|---|---|
| | High | Middle | Low |
| High | 39% | 28% | 15% |
| Medium | 44 | 47 | 46 |
| Low | 17 | 25 | 39 |
| Total (= 100%) | (196) | (253) | (243) |

Women on the high status level are considerably more likely than are those of low status to be very active socially; women of middle status are in between. Moreover, the pattern of relationship is such that the proportion of women who have medium gregariousness scores is about the same in all three status groups, while the variations occur in terms of the extreme scores of high and low.

We shall discuss the implications of this relationship more fully below. Here we want merely to note that this table illustrates what was referred to earlier as the different degrees of opportunity, and the differing styles of life, associated with different status positions. Should we find, later, that high status and high gregariousness are related to opinion leadership, we can anticipate that one tie-up between status and leadership will be provided by this link between status and gregariousness.

Just as status is a determinant of opportunity for gregariousness, we should expect to find that position in the life-cycle, too, modifies the extent of a woman's social activity. Primarily, we presume, the degree to which family responsibilities tie women to their households will be the major factor involved. If that is so, it follows that we should find the "girls" to be most gregarious of all. Proceeding with this line of reasoning,

matrons would be next most gregarious, small family wives
should follow them, and large family wives should be least
gregarious of all. Table 16, however, indicates that our expectations are not quite fulfilled:

**Table 16—Distribution of Gregariousness Scores Among the Life-Cycle Types**

|  | | LIFE-CYCLE TYPES | | |
|---|---|---|---|---|
| Gregariousness Score | Girls | Small Family Wife | Large Family Wife | Matron |
| High | 21% | 19% | 23% | 34% |
| Medium | 56 | 48 | 48 | 40 |
| Low | 23 | 33 | 29 | 26 |
| Total (= 100%) | (80) | (176) | (170) | (257) |

Only the matrons—women whose families no longer demand
undivided attention—are significantly distinguished by their
high gregariousness. Thirty-four per cent of the matrons compared with about 20 per cent of each of the other groups are
highly gregarious. That, for the matrons, is more or less what
we expected. But what happened to the girls?

Checking over our data, it becomes clear that for the girls
the two components of our gregariousness index have to be
examined singly. It turns out that the single woman, although
most likely to score highly on number of friendships, is not
very often a particularly active member of clubs or organizations. This may reflect the fact that, as husband-seekers, girls
prefer to expend their social time and energies on informal
contacts, rather than on formal and (generally) female organizational affiliations. Considering that our index is based on
both friendships and memberships it becomes clear why single
women congregate on the medium gregariousness level but
not on the high.

Overall, the variations of social activity among the life-cycle
types are not very great. Should we find later that social activity is related to opinion leadership we can be fairly certain
that the extent of social activity is about equally distributed
among the four life-cycle types.

Nevertheless, there is one important relationship between
the life-cycle and gregariousness which does not emerge clearly
until status position is "controlled." To demonstrate this, let

us examine the extent of gregariousness of each of the life-cycle types on different status levels. And to simplify the matter, we will divide our sample simply into high and low status groups:

*Chart V—Distribution of Gregariousness Scores According to Status Level and Life-Cycle Type*

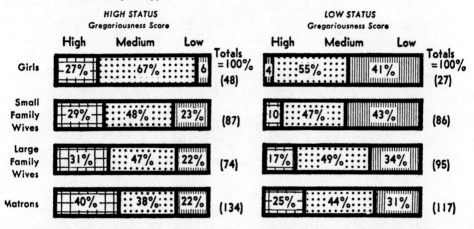

What we are concerned with is most apparent among the girls: It is the disparity between the distribution of low gregariousness scores among upper status girls as compared with girls of lower status. On the upper level, almost none of the girls (6%) are socially inactive as measured by the gregariousness index, while on the lower status level, over 40 per cent rank as inactive. That means that 4 out of every 10 lower status girls have fewer than the average number of friends and do not belong to any organization. The explanation, presumably, has to do with the lower status girl's early assumption of obligations which restrict her social activity. Perhaps she helps in the household, or has to go to work. But whatever she does, she is likely to be quite different from her age peers of high status, almost none of whom rank among the least gregarious.

Somewhat the same phenomenon is also evident among the small family wives. The percentage of small family wives of lower status who score low on the gregariousness index, is twice that of the small family wives of upper status. The difference diminishes among the large family wives and matrons.

Looked at in terms of the life-cycle progression within each status level, the same story can be seen from a somewhat different angle: On the high status level, the small family wives are four times as likely as girls of the same status to have low gregariousness scores, indicating the sharp break in the extent of the social life of the comparatively well-to-do young woman when she finds a husband. Not so for the young woman of low status, however. As a single woman, she is comparatively ungregarious to begin with, and she stays that way as a small family wife. Later in life, however, her gregariousness increases more rapidly than does that of her life-cycle peer of higher status.

Now, we should have a fairly clear idea of the relationship between life-cycle type and gregariousness:

1. On both status levels, high gregariousness increases with the life-cycle progression.

2. The girls, on both status levels, are least likely to score high, and most likely to score medium, on the gregariousness index. This, as we noted earlier, reflects the fact that young single women concentrate their social energies on the informal friendship type of associations and are relatively inactive in the organizational sphere.

3. Lower status women of each life-cycle type are more likely to score low on gregariousness than upper status women, but this is strikingly so among the girls and also quite marked among the small family wives.

4. Upper status women are particularly likely to join the ranks of the least gregarious in the transition from girlhood to marriage; beginning with the small family wives, the rate of low gregariousness remains constant. Among the low status women, there is no corresponding swell in the ranks of the low gregariousness level.

Thus, controlling status levels helps us better to understand the relationship between life-cycle types and gregariousness.

The relevance of the three factors we have examined for opinion leadership probably lies in their power, singly and in combination, to determine a woman's interest in certain life-areas, as well as to increase or reduce her opportunities to translate such interests into actual influentiality. Our task in the several chapters that follow is to employ these three dimensions to sketch the profiles of opinion leaders in marketing, fashions, public affairs and movie-going and to describe the flow of influence from these leaders to those who follow them.

# CHAPTER X

# Marketing Leaders

By DEFINITION, opinion leadership is everyday and casual. If this is true for opinion leadership in general, it holds particularly for the arena of marketing, since, for most women, marketing for household goods is virtually a continuous routine. Yet, despite the habitual character of this feminine occupation—or perhaps because of it—changes in the buying patterns of individuals, and in the market as a whole, are constantly taking place. About half of the women in our sample reported that they had recently made some change from a product or brand to which they were accustomed to something new. The fact that one third of these changes involved personal influences indicates that there is also considerable traffic in marketing advice. Women consult each other for opinions about new products, about the quality of different brands, about shopping economies and the like, and it is this kind of give-and-take which we have attempted to study.

First of all, we want to see if the three factors we have outlined—life-cycle, social status and gregariousness—will help us to describe the characteristics of opinion leaders—the "specific" influentials—in this arena of marketing.[1] We propose to try to locate concentrations of marketing leaders in the population by comparing the incidence of marketing leadership among women with different life-cycle positions, differing social sta-

---

1. Specific influentials—what we here call opinion leaders—are discussed and defined in Chapter I, pp. 146-8. In the realm of marketing, they are (a) those women who indicated, on both interviews, that they had recently been asked their advice on some matter relative to the purchase of food or household products, and (b) those who said, on only one interview, that their advice had been asked, but who also considered themselves "more likely" than others to be consulted for marketing advice.

tuses and varying degrees of gregariousness. Our initial step will be to compare the proportions of opinion leaders who congregate on each of the three steps of the status ladder to see whether one status level, more than the others, tends to produce greater numbers of marketing leaders.

## Marketing Leadership and Social Status: A Horizontal Flow Pattern

If the flow of everyday influence is a vertical process, as has often been suggested, then proportionately more opinion leaders should be found among women of higher status. Though there is little reason to expect that higher status women are more skilled in marketing than other women, the hypothesis of vertical influence would suggest that it is the prestige of the higher status woman which would make her more attractive as an advice-giver than women, equally endowed, but of lower status. Let us look, now, to see what the relationship between status level and marketing leadership actually is:

**Chart VI—Marketing Leaders Are Found In Almost Equal Numbers on All Three Status Levels**

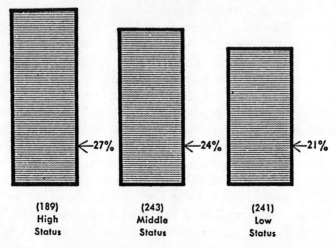

|  |  |  |
|---|---|---|
| ←27% | ←24% | ←21% |
| (189) | (243) | (241) |
| High | Middle | Low |
| Status | Status | Status |

NOTE: Numbers in parentheses under each bar represent the total number of cases on which the percentage of opinion leadership is based. Thus, 27 per cent of the 189 high status women in our sample are marketing leaders. This procedure is used in all subsequent charts.

Chart VI shows that holding a higher status position in-creases a woman's chances for marketing leadership very little. Women of the highest status are only a trifle more likely than those of the lowest status to be marketing leaders. Given the universality of activity in the arena of marketing, it seems reasonable to infer, therefore, that each status level has its own corps of opinion leaders. This might mean either that traffic in marketing advice is conducted without regard to status differences (so that marketing leaders of low status would be just as likely to influence high status women as high status leaders would be likely to influence women of low status) or it might mean that women of each status level typi-cally turn to marketing leaders of their own status level for advice.

Of these two possibilities, it is more reasonable to expect that marketing influence is confined within the boundaries of each of the several social strata than that it is a random ex-change conducted without regard to status differences. Seek-ing out a woman of like status for advice means seeking out a woman with similar budgetary problems and limitations. That is one major reason why we may expect that traffic in mar-keting advice is a status-bound activity. Secondly, since stores and shopping centers are likely to cater somewhat more to women of one status than another—by design or because of location or the like—women are more likely to encounter status peers during the course of their marketing activities than to encounter status unequals. Therefore, at a time when advice may be most needed, the woman standing nearby is likely to be of similar status. In short, we are suggesting that marketing leaders share the same social status as their "followers."

We have evidence that bears directly on this question of who influences whom. From Chapter II it will be recalled that "follow-up" interviews were conducted with individuals who were designated by our initial respondents as having been in-fluential for them in recent decisions. In the case of marketing, we were able to complete follow-up interviews with only about half of the people who had been so designated.[2] Incor-

---

2. 168 names were elicited, in connection with 386 specific changes of a product or a brand about which our respondents volunteered information.

rect addresses, sickness, refusals, and the like, plus the limitations of time and money (we did not go out of town or to the suburbs, for example), conspired to impede the follow-up procedure.[3] Therefore, the story we shall tell here—and subsequent analysis based on such "follow-up" material—cannot be treated as more than suggestive.

Having sounded our warning, however, let us proceed to examine these data. We want to know (1) whether women go more to influentials of their own or of different status level for marketing advice, and (2) when status lines *are* crossed in the seeking of marketing advice, whether there is any discernible direction which describes the flow of influence. Here we treat only adviser-advisee pairs who are not within the same family unit:

**Table 17—The Flow of Marketing Influence Among Status Levels[4]**

| Her Marketing | INFLUENCEE'S STATUS IS | | | |
| Leader's Status Is | Low | Middle | High | Totals |
|---|---|---|---|---|
| Low | 4 | 7 | 2 | 13 |
| Middle | 6 | 21 | 3 | 30 |
| High | — | 4 | 19 | 23 |
| Totals | 10 | 32 | 24 | 66 |

Of these 168, we attempted to obtain interviews with the 130 or so who were not members of the same household and succeeded in 76 cases. Appendix C considers the problem of "mortality" in the follow-up interviews.

A second set of influentials derives from the "panel" investigation, where a pantry check was made by the interviewer in two successive visits to see whether the same brands of coffee and breakfast cereal were on the respondents' shelves both times. From this "panel" procedure, 102 names were obtained in connection with 297 purposive changes (reported in footnote 2, p. 200) of whom only 31 were interviewed. These two groups of "follow-ups" (76 plus 31) total 107 people, which is the number upon which our statements on "confirmation" in marketing, in Chapter 2, are based. Here, we are basing our analysis on the 76 adviser cases because in some ways—as we shall show below—it is worth keeping the two groups of advisers separate.

3. In addition to our uncertainty concerning the extent to which the "follow-up" interviews are "representative" of those influentials we could not reach, it should also be noted here that our analysis above is based on all influential-influencee pairs for whom we have "follow-up" data regardless of whether these were "confirmed" exchanges or not. The small number of cases available compels us to handle the matter this way, though the picture would not change substantially if we used only those relationships which were confirmed. Another source of possible unreliability in these "follow-up" data is discussed in Appendix C on designation. Altogether, we must proceed with great caution here.

4. This measure of social status is not the same one we introduced earlier; it is a measure based on interview ratings in four socio-economic categories

If we compare the social status level of each respondent with that of the opinion leader she names, we find that influencees turn to influentials of their own status level much more often than they turn to those of other statuses; two-thirds of the 66 influence pairs in Table 17 share the same social status.[5] In other words, influence exchange in marketing appears to go on between pairs of women of like status.

When the direction of flow is analyzed—that is, when we examine those cases where influence *does* cross status lines and ask whether the flow tends to move up or down the status structure—we find that there is no discernible direction; in other words, when influence traffic in the arena of marketing goes on among women of unlike status, it is just as likely to move from lower status to higher as vice versa.[6] Furthermore, where there is a difference in status between the two members of a marketing influence exchange, the difference tends to be only one status step; only rarely does advice-giving cross from the highest to the lowest status (just 2 cases out of a possible 22 in Table 17).

Earlier, we found that marketing leaders appear to be spread, status-wise, evenly throughout the community. Now, combining that fact with our present finding that interpersonal influencing tends to take place between people of like status, we obtain a fairly clear picture of the role of social status in the determination of marketing leadership and in the flow of marketing advice. That is to say, marketing leaders can be

---

A, B, C, D. This table considers A and B "high" status, C "middle" and D "low." For a discussion of this measure, see Appendix D; it is substituted here because the "follow-up" interviews did not contain information on one of the components of our earlier index. A number of studies have shown, however, that there is a high degree of comparability among various measures of socio-economic status.

5. The diagonal in Table 17—reading from upper left to lower right—represents pairs of like social status. The three figures on the diagonal add to 44 (4 plus 21 plus 19) which is two-thirds of 66, the total number of pairs. The pairs that fall outside the diagonal represent influence from an influential of one social status level to an influencee on another. In the text our discussion is limited to a straightforward discussion of these flow tables; in Appendix C, however, we consider the way in which more sophisticated statistical analysis of such tables might be approached. In the Appendix, we also discuss the shortcomings of our flow data in general.

6. That is, 10 advisees go to higher status advisers while 12 go to advisers of lower status. Appendix C concludes with a discussion of how such tables are most fruitfully analyzed.

found in roughly equal proportions on each status level and
women of their own levels tend to seek them out for advice.
Only perhaps in the case of the lowest status women (where
we have but 10 cases) does there seem to be any substantial
proportion of advice-seeking at all from status unequals.

## Life-Cycle Position and Marketing Leadership: "The Large Family Wives"

We have seen that position on the status ladder plays no part
in determining concentrations of opinion leaders in the arena
of marketing. Let us turn to the second ladder on which the
women of our sample are arrayed—the ladder of the life-
cycle—to see whether marketing leaders tend to congregate
on any one of the life-cycle steps more than on the others.
Our expectation is that the life-cycle will have much more
to do with determining a woman's chances for marketing leadership than did social status. For example, it occurs to us immediately that unmarried girls should be both less interested
in marketing affairs and less experienced in their conduct than
married women; therefore, there should be little reason for
older women to consult the marketing advice of girls, or for
that matter, for girls to consult each other. We shall expect,
therefore, that the life-cycle type we call "girls" should have
relatively few marketing leaders among its ranks. Among the
married women, however, it is not so clear which of the three
life-cycle types—small family wives, large family wives or
matrons—will produce the largest proportion of opinion leadership. If the *current* responsibilities of marketing for a family
with young children are paramount in determining opinion
leadership, then we shall find that the matrons are low in
marketing leadership and the wives—particularly the large
family wives who have the greater responsibilities—are high
in such leadership. If, on the other hand, *years* of marketing
experience and expertise are the more important qualifications,
then the matrons should have the best chances for marketing
leadership. Chart VII tells us which of these two speculations
is the more accurate:

**Chart VII—The Large Family Wives Are the Marketing Leaders**

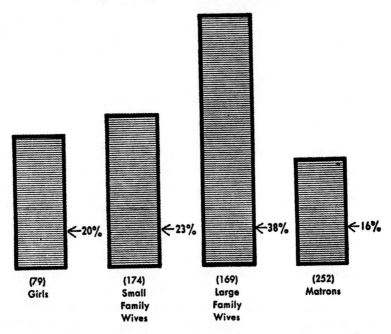

The answer is that it is the more intensive phase of household management, associated with the life-cycle type of the large family wife, which leads to marketing leadership: on the average, such women are almost twice as likely as those of any other life-cycle type to be marketing leaders. Among the other life-cycle types we find little variation with respect to chances for leadership. The matron, with her years of experience in managing households, is no more likely to be a leader than the unmarried girl or small family wife.

This concentration of opinion leaders among large family wives is strong evidence that what counts, at least in marketing leadership, is the intensive, everyday "experiencing" of marketing problems characteristic of the woman with a large, growing family. "Experiencing," we might say, seems more important for marketing leadership than "experience"—the symbol of the matron and her years. Thus, leadership predominates in that area of the life-cycle where current interest and participation are, presumably, at a peak.

But now that we have found that the concentration of marketing leadership is among the large family wives we must ask another question: Do the large family wives really influence the majority of other women or does their influence tend to be directed only to other women like themselves? It is possible to argue both ways. On one hand, it may be that the large family wives, generally, are most concerned with the arena of marketing and therefore generate a greater proportion of marketing leaders to turn to themselves for advice. On the other hand, however, it is just as reasonable to suggest that marketing activities are so widespread that advice-seeking in this arena is distributed almost evenly throughout the population. If that is the case, then the concentration of marketing leaders among the large family wives can mean only that women of all life-cycle types come calling on the large family wives for their advice.

Which one of these alternatives is correct is a question we cannot answer directly. Unfortunately, we do not have adequate data on this point either from the advisers' characterizations of the women to whom they gave advice or from the follow-up interviews. From these sources we have data only on the ages of both of the members of the influence pair, but not on the other factors which go into the construction of our life-cycle index. Circumstantially, from these data on age, it would appear that the latter alternative is the more plausible —that is, that the large family wives serve women of the other life-cycle types as well. Consider the follow-up data, for women who went to a non-family member for advice:

**Table 18—The Flow of Marketing Influence Among Age Groups Outside the Family**

| Her Marketing Leader's Age Is | ADVISEE'S AGE IS | | | |
|---|---|---|---|---|
| | 15-24 | 25-44 | 45+ | Totals |
| 15-24 | 3 | 3 | 4 | 10 |
| 25-44 | 10 | 17 | 9 | 36 |
| 45+ | 2 | 9 | 18 | 29 |
| Totals | 15 | 29 | 31 | 75 |

About 50 per cent of the advice-seekers sought out age peers for marketing information. The other half went for advice to

women who were older or younger than themselves. Among
this group of women, the 25-44 age group seemed to be the
most frequent target: 10 of the 12 girls who consulted an older
woman went to this group, and 9 of the 13 matrons who consulted a younger woman did likewise. When these "wives,"
themselves, sought advice outside their ranks, they tended
to consult the older group somewhat more than the younger.
Furthermore, a greater proportion of the youngest women consulted their seniors than the oldest group consulted their
juniors. Thus, the overall flow of influence is somewhat more
from old to young than vice versa and the most prominent
group of influentials are the "wives." Clearly, our information
is very inadequate; in addition to life-cycle data, and a representative sample—both of which we lack—there is much
more that we would need to know before we would be prepared to make conclusive statements about influence flow.
Yet, it must be acknowledged, we think, that taken together
these findings lend weight to the fruitfulness of this follow-up
approach.

## Gregariousness and Marketing Leadership

We know now the phase of the life-cycle that best char-
acterizes the marketing leader, and something of the patterns
of influence flow between women of different ages and different
social status levels. Now let us consider the third of the factors which we believed might aid us in our attempt to describe
the characteristics of opinion leaders—the factor of gregariousness. Are those women who have recently served as advisers
in marketing matters more socially active than those who have
not?

The answer is yes. Highly gregarious women—those who
have a large number of friends and belong to several organizations—are two and one-half times more likely to be marketing
leaders than women of lowest gregariousness. The greater the
extent of a woman's social contacts, the greater her chances for
marketing leadership. This, of course, is as we expected. To
act in any position of leadership, a woman must have at least
some contact with potential followers, and the more she has

such contacts—other things being equal—the greater should be her opportunity for leadership. The greater gregariousness of the marketing leaders confirms our expectation.

Gregariousness, then, is a characteristic of the marketing leader. And the relationship between gregariousness and marketing leadership holds true for women of each life-cycle type. Whether she is a girl, a matron, a small or large family wife, the highly gregarious woman has a better chance to be a marketing leader than other women on the same life-cycle step.[7] But it should not be thought that gregariousness alone

**Chart VIII—The More Gregarious Women Are More Likely to be Marketing Leaders**

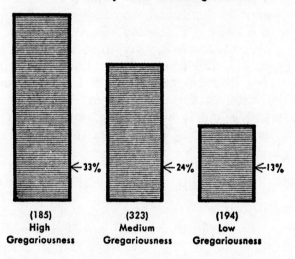

|   |   |   |
|---|---|---|
| ←33% | ←24% | ←13% |
| (185) | (323) | (194) |
| High | Medium | Low |
| Gregariousness | Gregariousness | Gregariousness |

makes for marketing leadership. In fact, the single most important head-start toward opinion leadership in this arena can be secured simply by occupying the position of large family wife. For among this life-cycle type, even the least gregarious women have a better than average chance of being marketing leaders.[8] But among these women as well as among those with lesser

7. We shall present tabulations only at major points. Such statements, however, are based on tabulations, of course.

8. We shall occasionally use the notion of "average" chance for leadership by which we mean the simple ratio of number of leaders to total sample. "Better than average chance," therefore, refers to any group where the ratio of leaders exceeds the average in the sample as a whole.

chances for marketing leadership—that is, within the limits determined by the different life-cycle positions—a woman with greater gregariousness has a better chance for this kind of leadership than her life-cycle peer of lesser gregariousness.

Taken together, life-cycle and gregariousness tell the marketing leadership story. As a matter of fact, even the slight differences in the incidence of opinion leadership on the different status levels which we observed earlier[9] may be attributed directly to the increased opportunity for gregariousness on the high status levels. That is, if we compare women of different status positions who have equal degrees of gregariousness we find that the lower status woman is just as likely to be a marketing leader as the higher status woman. In other words, once gregariousness is controlled, the independent effect of status level on chances for marketing leadership almost completely disappears, so that we may say, in effect, that whatever differences appear to derive from status position are, in reality, by-products of the different opportunities for gregariousness available to the different social status positions. In fact, the low status woman, if she is highly gregarious, is four times more likely to be a marketing leader than the non-gregarious woman of high status.

## The Extent of Marketing Influence Within the Family

Either implicitly or explicitly (as with our "follow-up" data) we have been talking so far only about that portion of the flow of influence in marketing that goes on *outside* the family. But, obviously, before we close this chapter we must stop to consider the extent to which personal influence in this very domestic realm originates within the home and within the circle of relatives.

In analyzing the flow of influence within the household, it is important to separate "requests" from "influences." When a husband says to his wife, "Let's try Coffee X for breakfast tomorrow," that is a request; it is something different, obviously, from declarations such as "I certainly enjoyed that coffee Mrs.

---

9. Above, Chart VI, p. 235.

Jones served last night," or "I see by the paper that they're
having a sale on Coffee X today." Sometimes, of course, even
these latter statements may be intended, or interpreted, as requests, but that, in general, they are something other than influences should be manifest: In the case of influences, the
decision-making power is solely in the hands of the wife—
though she may take account of advice, testimonials, etc. from
other family members, just as she may give heed to friends,
neighbors, and others; in the case of requests, however, the
decision-maker is, in effect, the one who makes the request
(husband, or child, or other household member) and unless
the wife dissents, she acts merely as a purchasing agent to
carry the request into action. Our interest, of course, is in influence rather than requests, and since a large proportion of marketing communication within the family takes the form of
requests we have excluded intra-household communication
completely from our analysis to this point.

Examination of the data, moreover, indicates that the flow
of influence in marketing is very largely an extra-family affair.
Relatives who do not reside in the household play a substantial
part—second only to friends and neighbors—indicating that the
family circle of adult female kin is a relevant network of influence in the marketing arena. At family gatherings, it appears,
the women get together to talk things over and to discuss the
daily problems of running a home. But within the household
itself, there is little influencing and even requests appear to be
quite limited—except when certain particular products are involved. Thus we had occasion to analyze coffees and cereals
apart from other products and found that husbands and children were particularly active in decisions concerning these
products. The interpretation that suggests itself, of course—one
which has received much attention in marketing research—is
that coffee and cereal are the culturally certified domains of
husband and child, respectively, in the American domestic
economy.[11]

11. Our respondents, it will be recalled, provided us with the names of
marketing leaders in response to two separate questions. We have, first of all,
influentials whose names came up in connection with the product or brand
changes which were reported to us when we asked, "During the last month or
so, have you bought any new product or brand that you don't usually buy?"
A second list of influentials derives from our second (August) interview with

## *The Flow of Marketing Influence:*
## *A Summary*

To sum up, we have learned that the intensity of involvement in the business of marketing, as shaped by life-cycle position, inclined a woman toward marketing leadership; thus, the large family wives are the most frequent source of marketing leaders. We found, too, that the greater the range of a woman's social contacts, and hence the better her balance of family and non-family demands, the greater is her chance to translate marketing dispositions into an actual opinion leader role.

Status position, we saw, played no role in the determination of marketing leader concentrations. Instead, marketing leaders appeared in consistent proportions on each status level. Nevertheless, social status positions constituted fairly clear-cut boundaries for the flow of influence. Both advisee and opinion leader tended to share the same status position.

We have noted that women of a given social status tend to approach others like themselves for advice; in the case of age, we had the impression that there was something of a downward flow of influence from old to young. And, for products of all kinds, friends and neighbors were named influentials most often, with adult female kin ranking next.

---

respondents when interviewers checked on all brands of coffee and breakfast cereal then in use which had not been in use at the time of the June interview. We refer to the changes that were volunteered by respondents as "Recall Changes," and the changes which were objectively determined at the time of the second interview as "Panel Changes." Since the Panel Changes were exclusively breakfast cereals and coffees, while the Recall Changes covered a much wider range of household goods—see footnote 1, Chapter V, p. 176—the greater influence of husbands and children in the Panel data as compared with their negligible role in the Recall data suggests the interpretation submitted in the text.

It is also possible, however, that part of the difference noted here may be a product of the two different questionnaire-situations. In the one case, where women were asked to *recall* a recent change and then report how they found out about the new product involved in the change, it may be that respondents were more selective in their memories and reported a change which was significant for them and which perhaps involved a significant influential. In the *panel* questions, however, where the fact that a woman had recently made a change was objectively determined, the role of children and husbands may have become more prominent by virtue of the fact that the respondent was forced to recall this particular change.

For a discussion of methodological problems in assessing the relative influence of various family members on marketing decisions see Ferber (1955).

# CHAPTER XI

# Fashion Leaders

MORE THAN IN MARKETING, fashion is an arena of constant change. In fact, the essence of being "in fashion" is the making of right changes at the right time. About two-thirds of the women in our sample told us they had recently made some fashion change—in clothing, or cosmetics, or the like, and most of them said that personal influences had in some way entered into the making of their decisions. Here as before, our problem is to locate the opinion leaders—the leaders of change—in this arena.[1]

Where are the fashion leaders concentrated? Do they emerge throughout the life-cycle or do they congregate in a particular life-cycle position? Are they high up on the status ladder or are they represented equally on every status level? Are they more gregarious than the non-leaders or is gregariousness not a major factor here? Answering these questions, we shall learn not only about some of the distinguishing characteristics of the fashion leader, but also something about participation in the fashion market as well.

## The Girls: Life-Cycle Position and Fashion Leadership

Let us begin here with life-cycle position—the factor that proved most discriminating in the case of the marketing leader. The general accent on youth and youthfulness among men and women in America leads us to expect that fashion leadership

---

1. As before, leaders are here defined as (a) those women who indicated on both interviews that they had recently been asked their advice on some matter—in this case, a matter relative to clothes, cosmetics, etc., and (b) those who said, on only one interview, that their advice had been asked, but who considered themselves "more likely" than others to be consulted for fashion advice.

might be more typical of girls than of matrons. These young women are single; many of them are on the market for dates and marriage, and fashion is of obvious advantage in these markets. But, even if fashion is a concern to most women, it is more likely to have a greater sway among the girls than among the mothers of children since girls may well have fewer interests competing for their time, energy and finances. According to this view, marriage, as the realization of one goal of fashion participation, would be associated with a decrease in fashion activities and leadership; motherhood, as a competing interest and activity, would also be accompanied by a further decrease in such fashion leadership; and matronhood, which for most women involves a withdrawal from youth-oriented fashion competitiveness, should be associated with least fashion advice giving. And, in fact, the life-cycle typology which represents these major stages is strongly related to fashion leadership. Here are the figures:

Chart IX—Fashion Leadership Declines With Each Step In the Life Cycle

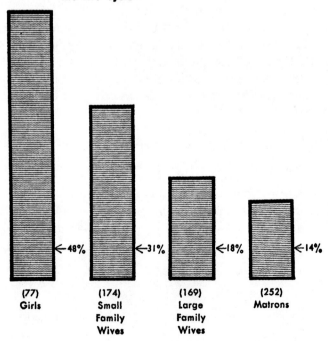

←48%          ←31%          ←18%          ←14%

(77)          (174)         (169)         (252)
Girls         Small         Large         Matrons
              Family        Family
              Wives         Wives

Each successive life-cycle position is associated with a declining leadership rate: among the girls, almost five out of ten, but among the matrons, only one in ten, is a fashion opinion leader. This direct relationship between fashion leadership and the life cycle emphasizes the cumulative effects of age, marriage, and motherhood on a woman's chances for leadership in this area.

In the case of marketing, we had no measure of interest or involvement. Perhaps it is even reasonable to make the assumption that there is a near universality of involvement—at least among married women—in the daily problems of selecting food for the family table. In any event, we did not emphasize the possibility that those life-cycle types which produced fewer leaders were not concerned with or interested in marketing. In the arena of fashions, however, we cannot assume universality of interest or involvement. Intuitively, one feels that there must be sharp variations not only in fashion leadership but also in advice-seeking, and in fashion interest generally, among the life-cycle types.

## Does Interest Determine Leadership?

In our interviews, we asked three questions which may serve as an index of fashion interest. We asked (1) "Do you feel it is very important, moderately important, or not important at all to be in style?"; (2) "Have you recently changed anything about your hairdo, type of clothes, cosmetics, make-up or any other change to something more fashionable?"; and (3) "How many new dresses have you bought or made since the beginning of last summer?" (twelve months earlier). Answers to these three questions are indicative, we think, of a woman's attitude toward the importance of being in fashion. What is more, these questions are intentionally phrased in such a way that the income factor is not of appreciable significance. A change to a new perfume costing fifty cents or to a shorter skirt priced at a few dollars is just as much a fashion change as the shift to a $50 perfume or to an expensive, new Paris creation. Here is the way replies to the three questions are distributed:

**Table 19—Replies to Three Questions Indicating Interest in Fashion**

| | |
|---|---|
| (1) Important to be in style? | |
|     Very important | 37% |
|     Moderately important | 55 |
|     Not important | 8 |
| (2) Made a recent Fashion change? | |
|     Yes | 56% |
|     No | 44 |
| (3) How many new dresses bought or made? | |
|     7 or more | 29% |
|     5-6 | 27 |
|     3-4 | 25 |
|     1-2 | 13 |
|     None | 6 |
| Totals (= 100%) | (711) |

We combined answers to these three questions into a scale simply by ranking women according to whether their answers, in each case, indicated "high" or "low" fashion interest and then by counting the total number of "high" answers.[2] A woman who ranked "high" on two or three of the questions was considered to have an overall "high interest" in fashion. Given this measure of interest, now we can ask whether or not a woman's life-cycle position is associated with the degree of her expressed interest in fashion.

**Table 20—Interest in Fashion Declines With the Life-Cycle**

| Life-Cycle Type | Per Cent with High Interest | Total (= 100%) |
|---|---|---|
| Girls | 80% | (77) |
| Small Family Wives | 59% | (173) |
| Large Family Wives | 56% | (169) |
| Matrons | 34% | (252) |

2. On the first question (importance of being in style), women who answered "very important" were ranked "high"; an affirmative answer to the second question (recent change) ranked "high"; and a report of 5 or more new dresses on the third question ranked "high." An overall rank of two or more "high" answers was considered "high interest," as follows:

| | | Per cent of Cases |
|---|---|---|
| 3 } "high | | 18% |
| 2 } interest" | | 33 |
| 1 | | 30 |
| 0 | | 19 |
| Total (= 100%) | | (711) |

Clearly, fashion interest is highly correlated with the life-cycle. It is at its peak among young, single women (the girls); it decreases by one-third among married women under 45 regardless of the size of their families; and it falls sharply among married women over 45 (the matrons). We can say that high fashion interest is a majority characteristic among women under 45 and a minority characteristic of women 45 and over.

This distribution of fashion interest along the life-cycle generally parallels the distribution of fashion leadership. It directs us to ask whether leadership may not simply be a by-product of interest—that is, perhaps the more interested a woman is in fashions, the more likely she is to be a fashion leader. That there is a strong relationship between fashion interest and leadership is evident in Table 21.

**Table 21—Interested Women Are More Likely To Be Fashion Leaders**

| Interest Scores | Per cent who are Fashion Leaders | Total (== 100%) |
|---|---|---|
| 3 (high) | 49% | (129) |
| 2 | 28% | (235) |
| 1 | 13% | (212) |
| 0 (low) | 4% | (135) |

Proportionately, there are twelve times as many fashion leaders among the highly interested women as there are among women who are completely uninterested in fashion. At the upper extreme of interest, close to half of the respondents are opinion leaders in fashion matters; at the lower extreme only 4 per cent are fashion leaders.

This strong relationship between interest and leadership forces us to reopen the question of the relationship between fashion leadership and the life-cycle. We must ask, in other words, whether the varying concentrations of leadership which we observed above (Chart IX) is something more than simply a reflection of the different concentrations of interest among the different types of women. Thus, it may be that a woman's chances for fashion leadership are determined exclusively by the degree of her fashion interest and that life-cycle type enters the picture only by virtue of the differing amounts of interest characteristic of the several different life-cycle positions. If this is the case, then a comparison of women of differing life-cycle types who have an equivalent amount of interest should reveal an equal incidence of opinion leadership; thus, matrons, for example, should emerge as fashion leaders as often as girls, provided only that they express an equal amount of fashion interest.

**Table 22—Fashion Leadership Still Varies With the Life-Cycle Even When Interest In Fashion Is Controlled**

| | | PER CENT WHO ARE FASHION LEADERS | | |
|---|---|---|---|---|
| Interest[3] | Girls | Small Family Wives | Large Family Wives | Matrons |
| High | 55% (62) | 46% (102) | 20% (95) | 27% (84) |
| Low | 20% (15) | 10% (71) | 16% (75) | 7% (168) |

Table 22 does not bear out our conjecture at all. That is, life-cycle variations in leadership do not disappear by any means when women of differing life-cycle positions, but equally high interest, are compared.[4]

Somehow, then, we must account for why a girl with high fashion interest is so much more likely to be asked her advice than a matron with equivalently high interest. In other words, we must ask what there is about being a single, unmarried woman with a high interest in fashion that provides so much more opportunity for fashion leadership than that provided a married woman over 45 whose interest in fashion is just as great. Or, again, why are small family wives with high fashion interest so much more likely to be fashion leaders than equally interested large family wives?

## *The Flow of Influence: Two Approaches*

The clue to the answer, we think, comes with remembering that any influence exchange, any act of advice-giving, takes

3. High interest consists of 2 or 3 "high" replies; low interest is 1 or 0 "high" replies. See footnote 2, above.
4. The irregular results on the low interest level together with the relatively small differences suggest the hypothesis that position in the life-cycle cannot appreciably affect a woman's leadership chances if she herself is *not personally interested*. It appears, in other words, that the effect of life-cycle position as a predisposing factor for leadership is maximized on the level of high fashion interest and almost, but not quite, obliterated on the low interest level.

two people. Thus, a matron who is highly interested in fashions may be eager and "ready" to give advice, but she must have somebody to give it to. Now, who is that going to be? Other matrons? Very few of them, we saw, are interested in fashions. Younger women? Their fashion problems are likely to be quite different than hers. Here, then, we have a situation where an individual's predisposition to lead in a given realm is not "activated" because there are no followers available to her.

Not so with the girls, of course. Among the girls, the traffic in fashion advice must be very heavy. Judging from the extensive interest in this realm that almost all the girls profess, we have reason to believe that the "demand" for fashion leadership among groups of girls is very lively. Thus, the chances that a girl with high interest will be consulted by another girl seems particularly great. This presumes, of course, that girls are leaders and followers for each other. But even if we assume that fashion advice-giving often crosses life-cycle lines, there is still considerably more reason to believe that it is the old who come for advice to the young rather than vice versa. This should be the case, first of all, because the American fashion market is so manifestly geared to youth; thus, the girls are surely the *avant garde* of fashion change. And there is a second reason, too, which is worth considering: Imagine a woman looking for some fashion advice and suppose that she does not quite know whom to ask. Now, although she does not personally know a fashion consultant, she may very well know (as we do from Table 20) that almost 8 out of every 10 girls are highly interested in fashions and that the same is true for only one-half of the wives and one-third of the matrons. Where would she go? Clearly, to the girls. Presuming that some such knowledge about the concentration of fashion interest is widespread in the community, it stands to reason that an interested woman—and hence, someone at least theoretically capable of giving advice—can be located much more readily among the girls than among older women. The maxim, of course, is to look where you know there's a concentration of what you're looking for.

Among the large and the small family wives, the story is not so neat. Both types of women have almost equal interest in fashion but while the small family wives have almost as many leaders as the highly interested girls, the large family wives have as few as the uninterested matrons. The explanation in this case seems also to have something to do with the accessibility of advice-seekers. While we have no evidence on this point, our guess is that small family wives may have more rapidly changing fashion trends to keep up with, and at the same time, fewer everyday problems of other sorts to engage their attention. That there is such a large concentration of marketing leaders among the large family wives is some evidence for this point, but, of course, our whole interpretation must be put to the test of future research.

In any event, as we have been noting throughout our explanation, we are making the assumption—and only the "follow-up" data will permit us to test it—that fashion influencing tends to take place most of all among women of similar life-cycle position. Thus, when we explained that the concentration of high fashion interest among the girls generates many advice-seekers which, in turn, generates many advice-givers, we made it clear that we were assuming that girls tend to influence other girls. In other words, fashion give-and-take tends to be carried on, we think, primarily among life-cycle peers.

All this, of course, presumes that these life-cycle categories we have created—girls, matrons, etc.—are, in a sense, real-life "groups" in that girls really associate with other girls, matrons with matrons, etc. If we proceed with this presumption that this, in fact, is the case, we can suggest an approach to tracing the flow of influence which we have not considered so far. Let us examine this new approach before turning again to the "follow-up" data with which we have already become familiar —the limitations of which we have also noted—in the previous chapter.

### (1) THE "EXPORT" INDEX

The new approach is readily explained. It proposes that the rate of opinion leadership in any group will be determined by two social forces. The first force is the level of interest—the "saliency"—of a given topic for the members of the group. High "saliency" would lead, of course, to much intra-group advice-seeking and leadership with reference to that particular topic. The second force is the "attractiveness" of the group as an advice-giving source for members of other groups. Thus, the proportion of opinion leaders in a group may be said to have two components reflecting (1) the degree of interchange on a given topic carried on by members of the group among themselves and (2) the extent of their interaction with members of other groups with reference to this area.

Now what we want to know is how much of the opinion leadership which emerges in a given group serves members of the same group and how much of it is "exported" to other groups. This is the problem which we seek to answer directly with our follow-up data and, more indirectly, with the data at hand. For if the rate of opinion leadership in a group is the resultant of "saliency" plus "attractiveness," since we have measures for both leadership rate and "saliency" we ought to be able to deduce "attractiveness"—the extent to which others come calling on a given group for advice.

Consider the fashion realm. The measure of fashion interest with which we have been dealing may be taken as a measure of the "saliency" of fashions for any group. What we can do, then, is to examine the extent to which the opinion leader rate for each group parallels or deviates from the "saliency" rate and we will take the extent of this variation as a measure of the group's "attractiveness." For example, if in a given group the proportion of women who are fashion leaders compared with women who are highly interested exceeds the average value of this proportion for our total population, we may infer that the leaders of this group satisfy not only their own group's leadership needs but are attractive as sources of influence to members of other groups as well. In other words, we would conclude that the "excess" of leadership (over that which a given measure of "saliency" would "require") is "exported."

To carry out this idea, we must first compute a ratio of fashion leadership to fashion interest for the sample as a whole. Altogether, 155 of 672 respondents concerning whom we have sufficient information are fashion leaders, and 345 of the 672 are highly interested. The ratio 155:345 is .45, meaning that

for every two highly interested women, taking the sample as
a whole, there is slightly less than one fashion leader. Now, if
we divide our sample once again into groups, we shall expect
to find that some groups maintain this "average" ratio—that is,
they will have about two highly interested women for every
one fashion leader—while other groups exceed the average or
fall behind it. Where a group maintains the "average" ratio,
we shall infer that its leader supply is just about equal to its
internal demand for leadership based on the "saliency" of the
topic for the group. Where a group exceeds the "average"
ratio—that is, where the leadership rate is relatively larger than
the rate of interest—we shall infer that this group not only supplies its own leadership needs, but is approached by other
groups for leadership as well. Where the leadership rate falls
behind the interest rate, we shall infer that the group has not
enough leadership even for itself and presumably, therefore,
turns to others.

To make things easy, we can compute an index where the
"average" ratio—.45 in this case—is equal to "one." Then, for
each group, we can compute the ratio of leaders to highly interested people, and, translating the resultant ratio into our
index, we shall find that some groups exceed "one," and some
groups fall behind. Let us try this for the four life-cycle groups
in the realm of fashion:

**Table 23—Fashion Leadership Is "Exported" by the Girls**

| | Ratio of Fashion Leadership to Fashion "Saliency" (The "average" ratio for the entire sample == 1.00) |
|---|---|
| Girls | 1.33 |
| Small Family Wives | 1.18 |
| Large Family Wives | .71 |
| Matrons | .93 |

The girls exceed the "average" ratio most of all; the large
family wives fall far behind; while the small family wives and
the matrons hover near the "average." In accordance with the
interpretation we have been suggesting, these results would
seem to mean that the small family wives and the matrons have
just enough leadership in their own ranks to satisfy the amount
of interest present in their groups. The large family wives, for

their part, seem for some reason to have less than the quota of leaders their interest would appear to require.[5] The girls, on the other hand, have an overabundance of leaders, from which we propose to infer that the girls satisfy not only their own demand for fashion advice but also provide leadership for others. The girls, in other words, meet the demand for fashion advice in their own internal market and "export" advice as well.

## (2) THE FOLLOW-UP STORY

Now that we have examined this new way of looking at things, let us return to the more familiar follow-up data to seek further corroboration for our story. If our appraisal of the situation is correct we should find that (1) fashion influencing tends to take place most of all among life-cycle peers, and (2) in those fashion exchanges that do take place between women of different ages, that the younger women are more often influentials than influencees. Let us, therefore, look at these flow-of-influence data remembering that they deal not with life-cycle as such but with age, and that they cannot, for reasons already mentioned, be treated as more than "suggestive."

Of the follow-up interviews that were completed, 33 were with fashion leaders who were named by some member of their own families, and 125 were with non-family influentials. Let us consider the handful of intra-family influence incidents first:

**Table 24—The Flow of Fashion Influence Among Age Groups Within the Family**

| Her Fashion Leader's Age Is | INFLUENCEE'S AGE IS | | | |
|---|---|---|---|---|
| | 15-24 | 25-44 | 45+ | Totals |
| 15-24 | 4 | 4 | 6 | 14 |
| 25-44 | 5 | 9 | – | 14 |
| 45+ | 2 | 1 | 2 | 5 |
| Totals | 11 | 14 | 8 | 33 |

Within the family—if we can make any statement at all from the few cases in Table 24—less than half of all influential-influencee pairs are of the same age. (We shall see, below, that this figure is larger for extra-family influences.) And when

---

5. This suggests that in the realm of fashions the large family wives may be a less self-contained "group" than the others.

family members of different ages do exchange influence, the
influence tends to flow somewhat more from young to old than
from old to young; this is as we expected. This is particularly
clear for the women over 45 whom we may assume have grown
children; three-fourths of these (6 of 8 cases) are influenced
by women aged 15-24.

**Table 25—The Flow of Fashion Influence Among Age Groups Outside the Family**

|  | INFLUENCEE'S AGE IS | | | |
| --- | --- | --- | --- | --- |
| Her Fashion Leader's Age Is | 15-24 | 25-44 | 45+ | Totals |
| 15-24 | 27 | 12 | 2 | 41 |
| 25-44 | 13 | 32 | 9 | 54 |
| 45+ | 2 | 14 | 14 | 30 |
| Totals | 42 | 58 | 25 | 125 |

But Table 25—reporting on the flow of influence outside the
household—does not corroborate our expectations. It is true
that we find greater age homogeneity here between influential
and influencee—about six of every ten influence pairs are age
peers—but among the women who did cross age lines in quest
of fashion advice, the direction of influence was no more from
young to old than it was from old to young. Thus, while we
may say that age peers are the predominant source of influence, we do not find confirmation for our expectation that
younger people would be more likely to be influential for their
elders than vice versa.

It is not immediately clear why these follow-up data do not
support the "export" data of Table 23. Except for the slight
intra-family trend reported in Table 24, then, we are left with
the suggestion of the "export" data that fashion influence travels
from young to old but with no direct confirmation from the
interviews with influential-influencee pairs themselves.

It is interesting, finally, to observe what a small part men
play in everyday fashion advice-giving. Of the many hundreds
of women who credited some recent fashion decision they had
made at least partly to the advice of some other individual,
only 13 named men, and of these, 11 were husbands. Men are
spectators rather than direct participants in the changing world
of fashions; such influence as they do have is the indirect and

passive influence of members of the audience. They do not often make so bold as to give direct advice.

## Gregariousness and Fashion Leadership

Along with the life-cycle, a second factor that proved discriminating in the case of marketing leadership was the gregariousness index. This relationship also holds true for opinion leadership in the arena of fashion:

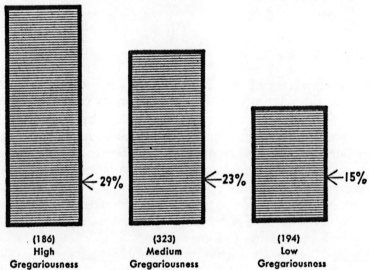

**Chart X—Fashion Leadership Increases With Increasing Gregariousness**

←29%    ←23%    ←15%

(186)            (323)            (194)
High             Medium           Low
Gregariousness   Gregariousness   Gregariousness

The rate of fashion leadership is twice as great among the highly gregarious as among those who score low on gregariousness. The woman with many social contacts is most likely to be a fashion leader, if only because of her greater opportunities to lead. But in the field of fashion there is another reason why more highly gregarious women should more frequently emerge as fashion leaders. The reason is that gregariousness itself is not merely an index of the volume of contacts a woman has, but an indication, also, of the character of her interests. The highly gregarious woman, we think, is likely to be sensitive to the impression she makes on others. She is concerned with interaction and integration among varying groups and indi-

viduals, and one of the ways she expresses this is by being in
style. This would mean that, compared to the socially isolate,
gregarious women have a greater opportunity to be asked for
fashion advice not only because they are more accessible to
advice-seekers, but also because they are under a kind of pressure to be more concerned with and active in the fashion market. If this is the case in fact, we should expect it to be reflected
on our fashion-interest index:

**Table 26—Gregarious Women Are Somewhat More Interested In Fashion**

| Gregariousness Score | Per cent with High Interest | Total (= 100%) |
|---|---|---|
| High | 56% | (178) |
| Medium | 54% | (323) |
| Low | 43% | (174) |

Table 26 bears out our contention to some extent only; surprisingly, the relationship is by no means as strong as we had
anticipated. Fashion interest is stimulated by gregarious activity, we may conclude—but not very much. Apparently, apart
from her personal involvement in fashion, the social demand
made on the highly gregarious woman to be *au courant* makes
for the increased likelihood of her being a fashion influential.
In other words, even if she is not very interested, the gregarious
woman, by virtue of her gregariousness is somewhat more
likely to be asked for fashion advice.[6]

Again, then, we see that the psychological factor of high
personal interest does not by itself create opinion leadership.
Leadership involves also the social context in which the woman
with high interest moves. In connection with the life-cycle, it
will be recalled, we found that highly interested girls were
quite likely to become fashion leaders, but that equally interested matrons were not; in the present instance, where interest
is almost equally divided among the three gregariousness
levels, we find that the highly gregarious woman is quite likely
to become a fashion leader while the ungregarious woman is
not. Thus, as we suggested in connection with the earlier observation, there would seem to be a contextual factor operative

---

6. Even among women with low fashion interest, 17% of the highly gregarious, but only 5% of the ungregarious, are opinion leaders.

here, too: It is not enough for a woman to be highly interested; to be a leader she must have contact with other people who (1) are seeking leadership and (2) who recognize her qualities as appropriate for the kind of leadership desired. It is important, so to speak, to be in the right context at the right time.

That gregarious women provide influence for others more often than they accept influence in return can be surmised from the measure of "export" leadership which was introduced earlier in this chapter. Here, again, we can take the "average" ratio of leadership-to-interest for the sample as a whole, make it equal to "one," and then see how each of the three "groups" of differing gregariousness compares with the "average."[7]

**Table 27—Fashion Leadership Is "Exported" by the Highly Gregarious**

|  | Ratio of Fashion Leadership to Fashion "Saliency" (The "average" ratio for the entire sample — 1.00) |
|---|---|
| High Gregariousness | 1.24 |
| Medium Gregariousness | 1.02 |
| Low Gregariousness | .81 |

The women with low gregariousness have less than enough leadership to satisfy the degree of interest in fashion which prevails in their midst while the middle group corresponds almost exactly to the "average" in its leadership-interest ratio. Only the women with high gregariousness have an "excess" of leadership which, according to our interpretation, means that this group is "attractive" for other groups in this realm of fashion and thus, in addition to satisfying its own internal demand for fashion give-and-take, "exports" some advice as well.

Now that we have seen the relevance of life-cycle position and of gregariousness for fashion leadership, it might be interesting to consider the combined effects of these two factors on a woman's chances for leadership. What difference does it make for fashion leadership if, for example, a girl is low in gregariousness and a matron is high? Our expectation is that

---

7. The ratio for the sample as a whole is .42. The very slight difference from the .45 ratio reported for the sample as whole in the case of life-cycle results from the slight variation in total number of cases for whom we have information in the two instances.

gregariousness will be most important as a stimulus to fashion leadership for women whose life-cycle types provide least opportunity, or inclination, for fashion participation and leadership, that is, for the large family wives and for the matrons. These are the women whose household-anchored life-cycle positions impose objective restrictions on the extent and intensity of their participation in the fashion-market—restrictions of time, energy and money and restrictions on "social location" relative to others who are interested. When such a woman is highly gregarious, however—that is, if her extra-household interests are sufficiently strong and the opportunity to pursue them sufficiently great—we expect that she, unlike her less gregarious life-cycle peers, will be active in the fashion market and will have a better chance, too, for opinion leadership.

By the same token, gregariousness scores are not very likely, we would expect, to make very much difference in the chances that a girl has for fashion leadership. For while gregariousness may be a major stimulus to the fashion activity of family-anchored and older women, the universal urge among girls toward fashion participation may perhaps be intensified by increased gregariousness but certainly not completely dependent on it. Small family wives, too, compared with the large family wives, are likely to be more active in fashions and more inclined toward leadership even when they are not highly gregarious. In other words, we are suggesting that among the girls, whose natural inclination to fashions is greatest, being a fashion leader should depend least of all on being highly gregarious, while for each subsequent life cycle type, this condition for fashion leadership should become increasingly important.

To test this hypothesis we have only to sub-classify women in each of the four life-cycle types, according to their gregariousness—this gives us twelve groups of women—and then see how fashion leadership varies among them.

In the following table, those groups of women who have a better than average chance[8] to be fashion leaders are identified

---

8. As was explained earlier, we mean by "a better than average" chance for leadership that the ratio of leaders to non-leaders in a given group exceeds the ratio of leaders to non-leaders in the sample as a whole.

by an "x." The pattern of these crosses indicates clearly that with the progression of the life-cycle, a high degree of gregariousness becomes a more important condition for a woman's chances for leadership in fashion.

**Table 28—Better-Than-Average Chances for Fashion Leadership According to Life-Cycle Type and Gregariousness**

|  | LIFE-CYCLE TYPE | | | |
|---|---|---|---|---|
| Gregariousness Score | Girls | Small Family Wives | Large Family Wives | Matrons |
| High | x | x | x | x |
| Medium | x | x | | |
| Low | x | | | |

All girls, whatever their gregariousness, small family wives only if they are at least moderately gregarious, and large family wives and matrons only if they are highly gregarious, have a better than average chance to be leaders in fashion. For older and/or family-anchored women, then, a high degree of gregariousness is a necessary condition for a good chance at fashion leadership. The quantity and quality of social contact expressed in a high degree of gregariousness seems to act as the equivalent of youth and its accompanying freedom from family responsibilities, in stimulating participation in fashion and fashion leadership.

## Social Status and Fashion Leadership

So far, then, we have seen that the two factors which are paramount in pointing to concentrations of marketing leaders —life-cycle and gregariousness—are also proving to be major keys for an understanding of fashion leadership, despite the considerable differences between the two arenas. Now, we shall turn to the third factor—that of social status—to see whether it plays any role in determining who shall be the fashion leaders.

When most people speak of fashion leaders, they mean the glamorous women who first display the expensive fashions. However true this may be, we are interested in another type of fashion leader: the woman who is influential face to face. In such relations, we may be sure, the fashion leader is not necessarily the most glamorous woman, but rather a woman known personally to the advice-seeker, a woman to whom she can feel free to turn for advice. Thus, the two women, the adviser and the one advised, are not likely to be separated from each other by a wide gap in their social standing. They are, rather, more likely to move in generally similar social circles. Moreover, we suggested earlier, that in looking for advice, women are likely to turn to those who face problems like their own and this fact would reinforce the likelihood that the advice-seeker would seek out fashion leaders within her own status level. Following this view, we should find that fashion leaders exist on all social strata, and that influence rarely crosses status lines.

Even so, one can argue that there still remains some reason to believe that status-linked factors do produce differences in the incidence of fashion leadership. Women on the low- or middle-status levels may not emulate cafe society directly, but they may express their desire for social mobility by consulting the taste of women just a little above them in status but still within their own social orbit or its outskirts. If this is the case, and if our data are sensitive enough on this point, we should find that fashion leadership is not equally distributed but that the higher status levels have the greater proportions. Furthermore, even if leadership does not tend to cross status lines, it may be that a greater concern with fashion, and a greater participation in fashionable activities is characteristic of the higher statuses. Similarly, there may be differential value attached to being in style on the several status levels. Should any or all of these be the case, we will find increasing proportions of fashion leaders on each succeeding status level. If, however, fashion interest is relatively evenly distributed among the status levels, and if women predominantly tend to look to others like themselves for advice, we shall find equal proportions of fashion leaders on each status level. Chart XI should have an answer for us:

**Chart XI—Only the Low Status Group Has Fewer Fashion Leaders**

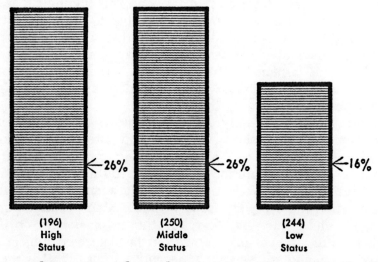

| (196) | (250) | (244) |
|-------|-------|-------|
| High | Middle | Low |
| Status | Status | Status |

According to our data, there are as many fashion leaders on the middle status level as on the high, but somewhat fewer on the low status level; the difference between the lowest level and the two higher levels is 10 per cent. In other words, the differences in fashion leadership among the status levels are not very great, and their peculiar distribution leaves us in doubt about the proper interpretation to invoke. If from the difference between the low and middle status we decide there is an increase in the rate of leadership with an increase in status, we are forced to pose the question: Why is there no comparable difference between the middle and the high levels? But even this question demands interpretation: We may ask either why there are so few leaders on the high level—where we most expect them—or, alternatively, why there are so many on the middle level. Let us look into this matter more closely. Perhaps we can find our clue, again, by examining the distribution of interest in fashion on these three levels.

**Table 29—Interest In Fashion Increases With Each Step Up the Status Ladder**

| Social Status Level | Per cent with High Interest | Total (= 100%) |
|---------------------|------------------------------|----------------|
| High | 61% | (191) |
| Middle | 53% | (253) |
| Low | 42% | (237) |

Each higher status level contains a somewhat greater proportion of women interested in fashion. This finding suggests to us that our attention should be directed to the high status group rather than the middle one. In other words, the interesting problem does not seem to be why there are so many middle status fashion leaders but why, given their greater interest, there are not more fashion leaders among the high status group.

There seems to be only one way to answer this question: The women of high status, with all their interest in fashion, *simply talk about it less*. We can think of two reasons why this might be so. First of all, for such women, fashion may be only one item on a relatively more elaborate agenda of informal conversation and everyday activity. Public affairs, charity work, women's clubs, etc.—in short, all the involvements of the higher status woman—may crowd out fashions as a subject of conversation and advice-giving. Secondly, it may be that there is even some deliberate unconcern with fashion talk among women of this status level. Although there is great fashion interest among such women, perhaps it is not considered good gamesmanship to ask for advice, or good taste to proffer it.

While we have no data to test this interpretation adequately, it is interesting, perhaps, to point out that this type of interpretation is the same one we have employed at several previous points. Immediately above, it will be recalled, we suggested that the lower incidence of fashion leaders in the ranks of older women, women with large families and women with low gregariousness—even when these women have high fashion interest—may be explained by the fact that they are not so likely to come into contact with others who are interested and, thus, who are seeking advice. In the same way, we are suggesting now that it is a similar contextual factor which explains the lower proportion of fashion leadership on the high status level. Here, however, this contextual factor is not a generally low level of interest but rather, we think, a general avoidance of fashions as a subject for discussion.

Our "export" measure, in effect, summarizes some of what we have been saying:

**Table 30—Only Middle Status Women "Export" Fashion Leadership**
**(but even they don't "export" very much)**

|  | Ratio of Fashion Leadership to Fashion "Saliency" (The "average" ratio for the entire sample = 1.00) |
|---|---|
| High Status | 1.00 |
| Middle Status | 1.14 |
| Low Status | .88 |

Table 30 indicates that the leaders among women of high status are just enough to satisfy the extent of fashion interest among those women. The low status level, on the other hand, would seem to have a slight predominance of interest over leadership indicating that, to some extent, they must seek out others' leadership to satisfy the extent of their concern with fashions. Only the middle status group has a predominance of leadership over interest. To a slight extent, then, we may say that the middle status women are attractive enough for others —presumably women of lower status—to "export" some amount of leadership, although the major conclusion of this table would seem to be that fashion leadership within each stratum seems relatively self-contained.

We have been assuming, of course, that women discuss fashions with others like themselves. But the "follow-up" data will bear this out.

**Table 31—The Flow of Fashion Influence Among Status Levels**
**Outside the Family[9]**

| Her Fashion Leader's Status Is | INFLUENCEE'S STATUS IS | | | |
|---|---|---|---|---|
|  | Low | Middle | High | Totals |
| Low | 5 | 7 | 3 | 15 |
| Middle | 17 | 47 | 11 | 75 |
| High | 2 | 13 | 17 | 32 |
| Totals | 24 | 67 | 31 | 122 |

Fifty-seven per cent of all influence transactions outside the family went on between women of equal social status. Only the low status women went outside their class to any appre-

9. We are again employing here the measure of social status (A,B,C,D) attributed by our interviewers to influential and influencee.

ciable extent. Furthermore, when influence did cross status lines, it did not travel very far: almost invariably it was an exchange between women of immediately adjacent status levels. This, of course, means that the middle status level is called on somewhat more and thus the table shows—comparing the "totals" this time—that the middle status group is the only one with more influentials (75) than influencees (67). Although this difference is hardly dramatic, the findings of this table are directly in line with what Table 30 had led us to anticipate.

## The Joint Role of Status Level and Gregariousness

So far, we have seen that status plays some part—although not a very important one—in determining the incidence of opinion leadership; we saw that there were somewhat larger numbers of fashion leaders on the high and middle status levels as compared with the lower. Now, before we leave the subject of status, we must ask ourselves whether perhaps variations in the extent of gregariousness may not account for this difference. It will be recalled that this was the case in marketing; that is, the emergence of a greater proportion of marketing leaders on the upper status levels was shown to be a mere reflection of the greater opportunity for gregariousness available to upper-status women. Is this the case, too, in fashions?

**Table 32—Status Level and Gregariousness Are Equally Important as Determinants of Fashion Leadership**

|                      | PER CENT WHO ARE FASHION LEADERS | | |
|----------------------|-------------|---------------|------------|
| Gregariousness Score | High Status | Middle Status | Low Status |
| High                 | 22%         | 36%           | 24%        |
| Medium               | 31%         | 24%           | 17%        |
| Low                  | 21%         | 17%           | 11%        |

While Table 32 does tell us something more about the relationship between social status and fashion leadership when gregariousness is held constant, it tells us something unexpected, too, which is of primary importance. The reader will recall the main point of Chart XI, that the highest status level

—which has the highest fashion interest—shows no more fashion
leadership than the middle status level and in Table 30 and 31
we have just seen that the upper status level does not "export"
at all. Table 32 provides us with another clue to the interpretation of these relationships; the table indicates that it is *among
the most gregarious women* on the high status level that the
drop in fashion leadership takes place. This is in marked contrast to the other two levels where the women with highest
gregariousness have the greatest opportunities for leadership.
That the glamorous women of highest status and highest gregariousness fall behind in fashion leadership seems to lend
weight to the suggestion we ventured earlier: These are the
women who do not talk much about fashion. Perhaps, as we
suggested earlier, it is because the range of their interests is
broader and fashion is only one of many concerns; perhaps it
is because it is somehow not "smart" to talk about fashion and
to give and take fashion advice. At any rate, the very women
whom popular imagery would point to as the most likely fashion leaders fall behind other groups in this respect.

Other than this one group which is high in both status and
gregariousness there are two noticeable trends in Table 32:
(1) as status level increases so does the proportion of opinion
leaders; (2) as gregariousness increases so does the proportion
of opinion leaders. In sum, this table clarifies very much. It
tells us, first of all, about the major exception we pointed out
above. And, secondly, we learn that, for all other groups, gregariousness as well as social status each contribute modestly,
and independently, to the incidence of fashion leadership.

## The Flow of Fashion Influence:
## A Summary

To sum up, we may say that—just as in marketing—fashion
leadership is dependent most of all on life-cycle type; the difference in the proportion of fashion leaders among the several
life-cycle positions is especially sharp. But whereas in marketing, leadership was concentrated among the large family wives,
in fashions the girls are the key influentials.

In marketing, only gregariousness has a share along with

life-cycle in determining the incidence of opinion leadership. In fashion, however, social status must also be taken into account—although its role is uneven. High gregariousness and high status conspire to produce an actual drop in anticipated leadership, and this goes some distance, we think, in closing in on an adequate interpretation for our observation that the highest status level revealed no more leadership than the middle level. The lowest status level, on the other hand, yielded fewer leaders than the others and with the one important exception noted above it would appear that even when gregariousness is controlled, social status has some part in making for concentra tions of fashion leaders.

Again, as in marketing, we find a fairly high degree of similarity of age and social status as between influential and influencee. When fashion influence does cross age lines, however, it is not at all clear that it travels from young to old as we had expected. While our "export" index would seem to support this expectation, and follow-up interviewing with influentials *within* the family support it, too, the extra-household influence pairs who were followed-up do not. When influence traveled across status lines, it stemmed somewhat more from women of middle status than from others and when it was exchanged between gregariousness levels, it was somewhat more likely to emanate from women of highest gregariousness.

# CHAPTER XII

# Public Affairs Leaders

IN PUBLIC AFFAIRS, much more than in marketing or fashion, women are free to decide whether or not they will participate or even take an interest. Without endangering their self-respect or the respect of others, women can, to a greater extent than men, get through life without participating in, or having opinions about, public affairs. Much more often than men, women express ignorance about current national and local events and issues; they talk less about these matters, and, when asked directly about their interest in politics and specific political events, they claim less interest than men.[1]

We have chosen the sector of information and opinion, rather than that of direct political or civic activity, as the context in which to study the feminine public affairs leader. The women we shall call opinion leaders in public affairs are those who told us that they had recently been asked their advice concerning some social or political issue current in the news.[2] As we define her, in other words, the feminine public affairs leader is the woman who knows what is going on, the woman to whom other women turn for public affairs informa-

1. For evidence from the 1940 election study, see Lazarsfeld, Berelson and Gaudet (1948), pp. 48-9. The 1948 election study, Berelson, Lazarsfeld and McPhee (1954) elaborate further, pp. 25, 28.

2. Specifically: Respondents were asked for their opinions on a variety of domestic and international problems then current in the news, e.g., on Truman's foreign policy, on demobilization policy for the army, etc. They were asked whether they had recently changed their opinions about these or any similar matters, or whether they felt more strongly about any of them than they had in the past. Finally, they were asked, "Have you recently been asked your advice on any such topics?" As before those women who (a) indicated on both interviews that they had recently been asked their advice, and (b) those who said, on only one interview, that their advice had been asked but who considered themselves "more likely" than others to be consulted are here defined as public affairs leaders.

tion and opinion. As we shall see, this type of opinion leader is relatively rare.

## Social Status
## and Public Affairs Leadership

If we ask ourselves, first, what factors are most likely to be related to feminine participation in the arena of public affairs —or, in other words, which social circles are the most likely habitats of public affairs leaders—three factors present themselves for immediate consideration. Each of them is related, at least in part, to some aspect of our definition of social status.

First of all, there is education. From cumulative research in mass communication habits, we know that the better-educated people are the ones who read more books and magazines and listen more frequently to radio programs and forums which deal with the world of current affairs. Furthermore, the interests which are stimulated by a better education, and the perspectives which are gained, surely operate to encourage the better-educated woman to participate more in political affairs. Now, our definition of social status includes educational level,[3] so we shall expect to find that the higher a woman's status, the greater is both her interest in public affairs and the likelihood that she will be a public affairs leader.

But education alone is probably not enough to sustain participation in public affairs activity. Education must be accompanied by social reinforcement, and the most basic kind of reinforcement is motivated interaction with other people who, themselves, are active in the market of political ideas and information. Social climate, then, is the second factor which we consider important. The woman whose status position places her in contact with people who are politically interested and active—the politician, lawyer, teacher, and such—is often expected to know something about the issues, events and people involved in public affairs. Women so placed are more likely than others to feel the pressure for at least minimal participation in this arena of information and opinion.

---

3. That is, educational level is a component of the main index of social status which we are employing.

The third of the three factors which we expect to be related to a woman's chances for public affairs leadership is the leisure available to her for the pursuit of extra-household interests. It is clear that women of higher status are favored in this respect, one index of this being the fact that such women have a substantially greater amount of social contact, that is, they are very much more gregarious than the women of lower status.[4] This means also, that to the extent that these social contacts expose her to the intellectual currents of her community, the woman of high status has a greater chance of being stimulated to participation in the traffic of public affairs ideas and opinion.

With respect to the three social and economic factors cited, it follows that more public affairs leaders should come from the high-status level than elsewhere. And it is, in fact, on this level that we do find the greatest proportion of public affairs leadership. Chart XII tells the story:

**Chart XII—Public Affairs Leadership Increases With Each Step Up the Status Ladder**

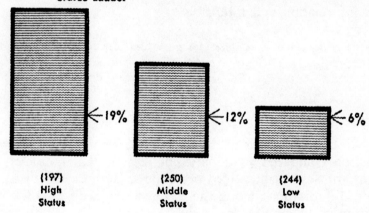

First of all, let it be noted, the proportion of public affairs leaders in the sample as a whole is very small. Of the four subject-areas we are investigating, there is least opinion leadership of all in the area of public affairs. That is, the number of

4. The relationship between status and gregariousness is presented in Table 16, p. 230.

women who are advice-givers in marketing, fashions or movie-going far exceeds the number who are influential in public affairs.

Secondly—and this is the major point—Chart XII reveals that the woman of high status has relatively the greatest chance to be a public affairs opinion leader. Women of the high status level are three times more likely to be public affairs leaders than women of low status. In the arena of marketing and fashions, status level is of very minor importance; but it is quite important, as we expected, for leadership in the arena of public affairs.

It follows, of course, that these high-status women should also be the people most interested in public affairs. We asked the women in our sample about several items which were then current in domestic and foreign affairs and from their responses constructed an index of public affairs information.[5] We assume that the women who score high on this index—those who were correctly informed about then-current events—are those who are also most interested in public affairs. Table 33 indicates the relationship between status level and public affairs information and interest:

**Table 33—Information Level Increases With Each Step Up the Status Ladder**

| Social Status Level | Per cent with High Information | Total (= 100%) |
|---|---|---|
| High | 72% | (197) |
| Middle | 52% | (253) |
| Low | 28% | (246) |

Almost three-fourths of the high-status women are very well informed compared with only one-half of the middle-status group and less than a third of the low. Because the distribution of information among the three status levels parallels the distribution of opinion leadership, we are led to ask again, as we did in the fashion arena, whether it might not simply be that the more informed people are the opinion leaders and

---

5. The items used in this index were questions about the then recent British elections and about a proposed Central Highway plan which was important at the time. Correct answers to both items was considered "high" information; wrong answers to both was considered "low"; and one correct item was considered "middle."

thus, that status is related to public affairs leadership only insofar as it brings with it differing concentrations of informed people. If this is so, we should find that equally interested people, regardless of their status level, should have roughly the same chances for opinion leadership. Table 34 shows again that this is not the case:

**Table 34—Public Affairs Leadership Still Varies According to Social Status Even When Information Level Is Controlled**

PER CENT WHO ARE PUBLIC AFFAIRS LEADERS

| Information Level | High Status | | Middle Status | | Low Status | |
|---|---|---|---|---|---|---|
| High | 21% | (141) | 15% | (127) | 10% | (69) |
| Medium | 16% | (45) | 11% | (79) | 8% | (77) |
| Low | — | (11) | 2% | (40) | 1% | (97) |

The highly informed woman of high social status is twice as likely to emerge as a public affairs leader as the equally informed woman of low status. This finding, in varying degree, persists on the other information levels, as well. Despite equal levels of information and interest, more leaders still emerge from the high-status category. It is evident, therefore, that subjective interest, or advanced knowledge, in the arena of public affairs—as in the other arenas—cannot operate independently to generate opinion leadership. Along with information and interest, there must be some objective "enabling" factor which makes it possible to translate subjective predispositions into the actual give-and-take of participation and leadership. In the case of public affairs, this enabling factor is social status which affords the social climate, and the leisure time, and the contextual "demand" for leadership and for participation.

## Sex, Social Status and the Flow of Influence

In public affairs, we did not follow-up as many respondents' designations as we did in the other arenas (and what's more, as Chapter II demonstrates, the extent of confirmation by designatees was lowest in this arena).[6] We have decided therefore

6. We were not able, that is, to follow-up as large a proportion of the designations of *specific influentials* in public affairs incidents as we were

to report here not our scanty follow-up data but instead the influencee's own characterization of her opinion leader. It will be recalled that we asked each respondent, when she reported having been influenced by someone, to name and describe the individual to whom she attributed influence. This method has the advantage of providing relatively complete coverage of influentials but at the same time it has the disadvantage of forcing us to rely on the testimony of an influencee about the person who influenced her. Moreover, some respondents were unable to provide us with certain types of information about their influentials, particularly concerning the occupation of the chief breadwinner of the influential's family—which we used as a substitute index of social status.[7]

Unlike marketing and fashions, the public affairs arena is one in which men play an important role in influencing opinions and attitudes. Almost two-thirds of the persons named by the respondents as having influenced their opinion changes were men.[8] Equally interesting is that two-thirds of those men were members of the respondents' immediate families,[9] while about 80 per cent of the women who were named as influential were non-family members.

For married women, the important male influentials are their husbands, while for single women, fathers play the important role in opinion changes. Female opinion leaders, on the other hand, are mainly friends and neighbors of the respondents. Few of them are members of the respondent's own family.

---

in the other areas. Partly this is because we decided to wage an all-out campaign to follow-up the individuals named in response to the *general influence* question, "Do you know anyone around here who keeps up with the news and whom you can trust to let you know what is really going on?" The distinction between specific and general influentials is discussed in Chapter I above. Data from the follow-up study of general influentials is reported below in this chapter.

7. Since we could not readily ask one woman to tell us the rent or income level of another, we substituted questions about occupation. As an index of social and economic status, occupation is known to be roughly interchangeable with the other indices. The drawback here, then, is not the adequacy of the index, but rather the unknown reliability of the respondents' testimony.

8. Altogether, personal influences were involved in about 40% of opinion changes.

9. This includes, as Table 35 shows, only husbands and parents; "other relatives" do not belong to the respondent's immediate (nuclear) family.

**Table 35—Sex and Relationship of Influencees and Their Public Affairs Leaders**

| | INFLUENCEE IS | | | |
| | Married | | Single | |
| | HER OPINION LEADER IS | | HER OPINION LEADER IS | |
| | Male | Female | Male | Female |
| Friend, neighbor, co-worker, etc. | 16% | 75% | 25% | 87% |
| Parent | 5 | 8 | 59 | 12 |
| Husband | 66 | — | — | — |
| Other relative | 15 | 27 | 16 | — |
| 100% = | (116) | (62) | (24) | (16) |

It is clear from this information that if we distinguish between influence that is exchanged among family members and the non-family influence exchanges, that we shall also have crudely distinguished between the influence flow from male and female opinion leaders respectively. Employing this distinction, let us examine the social status relationship between influential-influencee pairs, looking first outside the family, or in other words, at the social status of our respondents vis-a-vis their non-family (mostly female) opinion leaders, remembering however that the real locus of public affairs influence for our female respondents is within the household unit. Because influencees often failed to supply us with information about the occupation of their influentials' "breadwinners," we are, unfortunately, left with extremely few cases:

**Table 36—The Flow of Public Affairs Influence Among Social Status Levels Outside the Family**

| Her Opinion Leader's Breadwinner's Occupation Is | INFLUENCEE'S BREADWINNER'S OCCUPATION IS | | | |
| | Wage Earner | White Collar | Business and Professional | Totals |
| Wage Earner | 9 | 2 | 4 | 15 |
| White Collar | 3 | 1 | 1 | 5 |
| Business and Professional | 5 | 5 | 7 | 17 |
| Totals | 17 | 8 | 12 | 37 |

Comparing the flow of extra-family influence in public affairs with the arenas of marketing and fashions we can say that there seems to be a greater amount of cross-status exchanging in public affairs. Table 36 shows us that 46 per cent of the influential-influencee pairs in this arena are of the same status while the comparable figures in marketing and fashions are 66 per cent and 57 per cent respectively. If one can make any statement at all concerning so few cases, it appears from the table that extra-family advice-seeking in the realm of public affairs tends to be directed toward individuals of upper status; 5 of the 7 white collar people who leave their own orbit for public affairs advice seek out business and professional people, while the wage earners—though apparently more solidary than the white collar people—also ascend the occupational ladder. It also seem that, often, professional people cross status lines as well.

Although the proportion of influencing that goes on outside the family is minimal, the hint we have here that it goes on among people of diverse status is particularly interesting especially when compared with the relatively insignificant degree of cross-status traffic in the case of marketing and fashions. If these highly tentative findings could be substantiated with a very much larger number of cases, it might be in order to suggest that in this one arena, upper-status people become accessible to people lower down in status. Activities such as electioneering, health and community welfare campaigns, civic and political concerns, and the like immediately come to mind as examples of how such cross-status contact might take place. Furthermore, the sparse numbers who are interested in public affairs among lower status groups make upper status people natural targets of inquiry, and in this arena, at least, there is reason to suspect that there are gratifications both for lower class advisees and upper class advisers. The former have "borrowed prestige" from their advisers; the latter have done a civic good deed.

Of the intra-family influence transactions, a far greater proportion, of course, involve persons on the same status level. Almost eight out of every ten intra-family influence incidents were between members of the same social status. Of course, this is in accord with common sense. Since the largest proportion of the respondents were influenced by their husbands and fathers and since their breadwinners' occupations are the measures of their own social status, it would be very surprising had we found a large status differential between influential and influencee. The fact that there is any discrepancy at all can be explained by the fact that our classification of "within the family" includes a variety of relatives, many of whom did not live in the same household and thus did not necessarily share the social positions of their relatives, our respondents. When influence did pass between relatives of differing social status, again it showed some tendency to travel from an influential of higher status to an influencee of lower status.

As in the other arenas, the flow-of-influence data which have just been cited derive from our study of the exchange of *specific influence*—that is, from situations where a specific piece of advice passed from one individual to another. It will be re-called—from Section I above—that we also have data concerning the *generally influential,* so called because their names came up not in connection with a specific influence exchange but rather in response to the question, "Do you know anyone around here who keeps up with the news and whom you can trust to let you know what is really going on?" In general, we have elected to report only the specific influence data, but in the realm of public affairs—because something very special was tried here—we want to report on the general influential as well. We often refer to them as the "experts." To tell this story, we shall have to digress somewhat to explain the procedures that were employed.

## The Experts in Public Affairs

We began, of course, with our original sample, asking the women to name some person who is generally influential for them, that is, somebody—an "expert"—"who keeps up with the news and whom you can trust to let you know what is really going on." Then, as in all of our follow-up procedure reported so far, we went to the people who were thus named as influ-ential and interviewed them. But, this time, we did not stop there. Instead, we asked these influentials to designate, in turn, people whom they considered generally influential, and we interviewed these people, too. And, once again, we asked this second group of experts to give us the names of their experts, and we went to that group, too. Altogether, we made three jumps: from our original sample to the experts they designated (Jump 1); from this first influential group to those whom they named (Jump 2); and from the second group of influentials to those who are influential for them (Jump 3).

From our original sample, we obtained 368 names; that is, about half of the women in the sample named somebody whom they considered generally influential or expert, and about half did not—could not—name anybody. As is always the case when we use the follow-up procedure, we were not able to contact for interview all the people named—though in this case extra special effort was made. Thus, of the initial 368 influentials we looked for, we were able to locate and interview 322. These 322 influentials, in turn, told us of 216 people whom they considered generally influential; thus, two-thirds of this first expert group named an expert's expert, and one-third named no one. We succeeded in interviewing 214 of the 216 experts' experts, four-fifths of whom, in turn, furnished us with 164 more names that is, experts' experts' experts. We interviewed 107 members of this final group. In this all-out effort, we managed to find and to interview four out of every five persons who were pointed out as generally influential. And what's more, there seems to be no appreciable difference between the characteristics of the experts whom we were able to locate and interview and what we know (from those who designated them) of the characteristics of those whom we did not interview.[10]

Ostensibly it might seem as if the respondent who knows a well-informed individual whom he can trust to let him know "what is really going on" is relatively passive in opinion for-

10.

| | Persons Named as Experts | Persons Interviewed |
|---|---|---|
| Male | 74% | 72% |
| Under 45 | 35% | 29% |
| Business & Prof. | 47% | 44% |
| White Collar | 26% | 28% |
| Wage Earner | 27% | 28% |
| Total ( = 100%) | (748) | (643) |

mation, content to be swayed by somebody else in making judgments on public affairs. But this is not the case at all. If we use our measure of self-appraisal of leadership ("Compared with other women belonging to your circle of friends, are you more or less likely than any of them to be asked for your advice on what one should think about social or political affairs?") or our indicator of opinion leadership in specific influence incidents ("Have you recently been asked your views about international, national, or community affairs or news events?"), we find—as Table 37 shows—that those women in our original sample who are able to furnish the name of a general influential are more likely, than those who cannot, to be actively influential for others:

**Table 37—Those Who Name a Public Affairs Expert Are More Likely To Be Influential Themselves**

|  | Names Expert | Does Not |
|---|---|---|
| Considers self more *likely* than peers to be asked for public affairs advice | 27% | 17% |
| Has recently been asked advice on public affairs | 22% | 10% |
| Total (= 100%) | (368) | (347) |

These data are only for our original sample. As we take each of our three jumps, moreover, we find that the relationship between knowing an informed and trusted person and being an opinion leader oneself becomes even sharper. We saw this earlier when we found that only about half of the original sample were able to furnish us with names of persons who were generally influential, but that two-thirds of the first group of designated influentials and four-fifths of the second group were able to name individuals who were influential for them. This difference between the original sample and the expert groups, and between each expert group and the next higher one, is also revealed in the responses to the questions on self-appraisal of influentiality in specific influence incidents. This, of course, is also an important confirmation of our follow-up technique:

**Table 38—The Expert Follow-ups Acknowledge Their Influentiality**

|  | Original Sample | Expert Group I | Expert Group II | Expert Group III |
|---|---|---|---|---|
| Considers self *more likely* than peers to be asked for public affairs advice | 22% | 62% | 67% | 69% |
| Has recently been asked advice on public affairs | 16% | 46% | 57% | 57% |
| Total (= 100%) | (718) | (322) | (214) | (107) |

In sum, the further out we move, (1) the more the follow-up groups say that they know others who are generally influential, and (2) the more they confirm their own influentiality.

We can also compare the level of public affairs knowledge of the follow-ups with the original sample and of each follow-up jump with the next. Using the same information index introduced earlier in this chapter,—and comparing men and women —separately—we find the expert groups far better informed than the original sample, and each successive expert group better informed than those who named them. The differences are especially marked among the women, and less so among the men.[11]

If we continue this comparison of our original sample with the follow-up groups, and the follow-up groups with each other, we shall find other interesting things, too. For example, we saw above that opinion leaders in this realm—that is, the *specific* influentials—are much more likely to be men than women; almost two-thirds of the women in our sample who designated a public affairs leader in connection with a specific influence incident named a man. Here, too, in the case of the generally influential, we find that most of the women in our original

---

11. These same general statements hold true, as well, when these groups are compared on an "index of formulated opinions." We asked ten questions about matters then current in the news and our interest was not in the substance of opinions held but rather in whether or not our respondents held any opinions at all on these matters. And, again, we find that there is a great difference among the women in the original sample and the women in the follow-up groups; and when education is held constant, the differences between the cross-section and the expert groups, and between one expert group and the next still persist. Among the men, however (there are no men, of course, in our original sample) the differences between membership in the first expert group and in the second or third is negligible once education is held constant; men are much more likely than women to have formulated opinions on public affairs regardless of their status in the influence hierarchy.

sample name a male expert but women in the follow-ups name
fewer men and more women.

Table 39—Women In the Follow-ups Name More Women as Experts

| Her Expert Is | RESPONDENTS (WOMEN ONLY) | | |
|---|---|---|---|
| | Original Sample | Expert Group I | Expert Group II |
| Male | 67% | 52% | 48% |
| Female | 33 | 48 | 52 |
| Total (= 100%) | (368) | (75) | (38) |

Comparing the choices of the women in each of the three
groups we find that more than two-thirds of the original sample
name male experts (Jump 1), but that the women of each
succeeding expert group name a greater proportion of female
experts. (The men in the expert groups choose only men, however.)[12] Thus, although the flow of influence in public affairs
is clearly from men to women, nevertheless, on the upper range
of the influence hierarchy, women tend more often to name
other women as well-informed and trustworthy.[13]

## The Experts and the Flow of Influence

Having now clarified the special meaning of generalized influentials, or experts, we want to study them further in terms
of social stratification. Each of the three major criteria of
social and economic status that are available indicates that
the persons designated as generally influential are higher-up
on the status ladder than the people who named them, and
that each successive group of experts stands higher than its
predecessor: this is true of income, of the intuitive rating of
socio-economic status employed by our interviewers, and of
occupations. Consider the distribution of occupations, for
example:

---

12. About 95% of the men in both Jumps 2 and 3 (no men, of course,
were in the original sample) name male experts.
13. In a study of the League of Women Voters, March (1954) demonstrates that the more politically active women rely less on their husbands' advice than less active women. Our data seem to support this finding.

**Table 40—The Follow-ups Have Much Higher Occupational Standing**[14]

|  | Original Sample | Expert Group I | Expert Group II | Expert Group III |
|---|---|---|---|---|
| Business and Professional | 9% | 24% | 33% | 33% |
| High White Collar | 21 | 27 | 39 | 47 |
| Low White Collar | 19 | 14 | 10 | 10 |
| Wage Worker | 51 | 35 | 18 | 10 |
| Total (= 100%) | (793) | (219) | (189) | (99) |

Recalling that the original sample is representative of the population of the community, we can learn from Table 40 the extent to which people who are considered by others as experts are representative of the population from which they are drawn. Clearly, in comparison with the incidence of wage earners in the population (51%), the representation of wage earners among the experts is low, and declines with the jump to each succeeding expert group. Professional and business people, and people in upper white collar jobs are more heavily represented in the corps of influentials. That is the basic thing the table teaches us and, of course, it strongly supports our earlier finding concerning specific influentials, namely, that concentrations of public affairs opinion leaders are to be found in the upper status categories.

But let us look more carefully at the actual patterns of who designated whom; this can be done by examining Table 41. Respondents are divided in the table according to occupation and according to whether they are original respondents, experts named by original respondents (Expert Group I) or experts' experts (Expert Group II). Each column in the table, then, reports the occupations of the experts named by each successive group.

Almost always the largest proportion of designations goes to the occupational group to which the respondent herself (himself) belongs. This is sharply the case for seven of the nine columns in Table 41. The only exception are the wage earners of Expert Groups I and II. But even they, when they go out of their own class to designate experts, point to the middle and

---

14. Where influencee or expert is not the household breadwinner, the breadwinner's occupation is recorded.

**Table 41—The Flow of Expert Influence in Public Affairs Among Occupational Levels**

| | RESPONDENT'S OCCUPATION IS | | | | | | | | |
| | BUSINESS AND PROFESSIONAL | | | WHITE COLLAR | | | WAGE EARNER | | |
| Expert's Occupation Is | Orig- inal Sample | Expert Group 1 | Expert Group 2 | Orig- inal Sample | Expert Group 1 | Expert Group 2 | Orig- inal Sample | Expert Group 1 | Expert Group 2 |
|---|---|---|---|---|---|---|---|---|---|
| Business and Professional | 71% | 49% | 60% | 23% | 33% | 32% | 10% | 19% | 22% |
| White Collar | 23 | 44 | 28 | 57 | 59 | 64 | 31 | 46 | 44 |
| Wage Earner | 6 | 7 | 12 | 20 | 9 | 4 | 59 | 35 | 33 |
| Total (= 100%) | (31) | (53) | (25) | (103) | (82) | (56) | (105) | (59) | (18) |

not to the top group in our classification. To put it in still different terms: As we read Table 41 from left to right we see that the average occupational status of the designated expert declines sharply and without exception as the status of the respondent-designator declines.

The preceding statement analyzes the overall occupational relations between respondents and generalized influentials. Some additional observations can be made, however, if we focus on differences from one follow-up step to the next. Among business and professional people the terminal experts (that is, the experts designated by Expert Group II) are more catholic in their designations; their choices are spread more widely than are those of the preceding groups. Probably they are the top leaders who have their "ear to the ground" and begin to consider barbers and gas station attendants as valuable sources of information. The same thing is true for the terminal designatees among the wage earners. This is probably the reverse of the coin just minted: These are the barbers and gas station attendants who have contact with middle and upper class people; as a matter of fact, their designations are the most evenly spread in the whole of Table 41 (compare the last column with all the others).

The middle class group shows a trend different from the other two classes. As we go up what seems to be the ladder of prestige in their own class, that is, from the initial respondents to each succeeding set of experts there is a tendency to consider one's own peers, more and more, as the best people to turn to for advice.[15] This parochialism of the middle class has often been commented upon by observers of the American scene. To what extent our data contribute to such interpretation has to be left to the judgment of specialists in this kind of analysis.

We can thus describe the flow of general influence in the arena of public affairs as follows. People are most likely to choose their experts mainly from within their own social group. But as we move up the ladder of prestige to each succeeding expert group, we find a tendency toward vertical influence—an increasing probability that persons from higher strata will be designated as general influentials. This finding, however, requires two qualifications. First, it must be remembered that we are talking here about broad public issues, not about elections; thus our findings do not contradict other studies which show that, when it comes to voting, the general experts of the upper strata do not seem to influence the actual vote of the citizens in lower occupational groups. Secondly, we are talking here about people who have a general *reputation* for expertise with our respondents and these need not be those who are most influential for them in everyday face-to-face contacts. As we have already begun our report on these more specific, and direct, influentials, a comparison of the two sets of findings is an obvious next step.

In the specific influence data—to point to an important parallel, first of all—we noted that the flow of extra-family influence in this realm seems to take a somewhat downward direction. And, in general, that is the case here, as well.[16]

---

15. Although only a small number of cases remain, an interesting and possibly important observation can be made if the middle group—the white collar stratum—is split according to income level into high and low groups (managerial employees, salaried professionals would be high; clerks would be low): The low white collar group is much less solidary than the high, naming a smaller proportion of its own than even the wage earners. Its out-group choices tend to be rather evenly distributed on the first jump but to center very heavily on the upper white collar group in succeeding jumps. Furthermore, it is the high group rather than the low which is the focus for the out-group choices of both business and professional and wage earner groups; in other words, wage earners skip over the low white collars and name the highs as experts much more often. The high group, it should also be noted, is the best educated group, being somewhat better educated than the average of the business and free professional group.

16. The main discrepancy between the two tables is the white collar

There are major differences to be recorded, too, however. In the case of specific influence, we found that influencees typically named influentials—opinion leaders—within their own families; the flow of general influence, we know, is much more an extra-family affair.[17] Furthermore, in the case of specific influence, we found that when outside-the-family influencing does take place, both influencee and influential are both likely to be female (contrasted with the man-to-woman influence flow within the family); in the realm of general influence, however, men were named as influentials much more often than women regardless of whether they were inside or outside the family group. These differences, of course, reflect the different character of the two questions that were asked: in the case of specific influence, a recent incident of advice-taking was recalled; in the case of general influence it is more a matter of merely being acquainted with someone within one's orbit who is, presumably, approachable, informed and trustworthy.

But now let us leave these general influence data and return once more to our continuing concern with specific influence incidents and to our specific influentials, the opinion leaders.

## Gregariousness and Public Affairs Leadership

In our discussion, at the outset, of the links between status position and public affairs leadership, it was suggested that one reason for the association of high status position with a high leadership rate was the implicit relationship between status level and the degree of gregariousness permitted by a greater quantity of leisure time. That gregariousness is significantly

group. Because of the tiny number of extra-family influence incidents, Table 36 includes only 8 white collar people. But the white collar group in the case of specific influence was the least solidary of all in advice-seeking, and furthermore was less sought out by wage earners than the business and professional group and less sought out by business and professionals than wage earners. This is in sharp contrast to the general influence story, though taking account of the preceding footnote, it would appear that the discrepancy is only with the *high* white collar group among the experts. The *low* white collar experts, in fact, seem to resemble the specific influentials quite a lot, though the number of cases available hardly makes extended speculation worthwhile.

17. This point is documented, it will be recalled, in Chapter I, above.

related to public affairs leadership can be seen from the following chart:

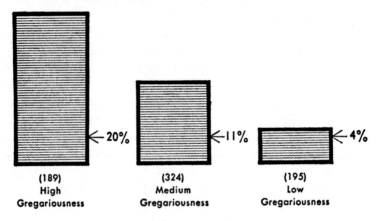

**Chart XIII—Public Affairs Leadership Increases With Increasing Gregariousness**

The gregarious women number in their ranks, proportionately, five times as many public affairs leaders as do the women who are not gregarious; the relationship, in fact, is more marked in this area of public affairs than in any other area we have examined. The non-gregarious woman rarely is an opinion leader in public affairs.

If we examine the relationship between gregariousness and public affairs information and interest we find, exactly as we did in the case of social status (Table 33, p. 274), that the women who are more gregarious are also considerably more likely to be well-informed and therefore, presumably, more interested, in matters concerning public affairs. But, if level of information is held constant, and then if equally well-informed women with different degrees of gregariousness are contrasted, we find, once more, that level of information alone is not enough to account for the incidence of opinion leadership. That is, the more gregarious women are still more likely to be public affairs leaders than equally (or even better) informed women of lesser gregariousness.[18]

18. Holding level of information constant, here is the percentage of public affairs leaders on each level of gregariousness:

Now, in our discussion of marketing, we reported that this same sort of link between gregariousness and opinion leadership explained away the link we had observed between status level and leadership. In other words, it turned out that higher status was associated with increased leadership primarily by virtue of the greater opportunity for gregariousness which it provided. Among women with equal gregariousness, the chances for marketing leadership were roughly similar on every status level.[19] So we must ask, therefore, whether this may not also be the case for public affairs leadership:

**Table 42—Status Level and Gregariousness Are Both Related to Public Affairs Leadership**

| Gregariousness Score | PER CENT PUBLIC AFFAIRS LEADERS | | |
|---|---|---|---|
| | High Status | Middle Status | Low Status |
| High | 25% | 17% | 13% |
| Middle | 17% | 12% | 5% |
| Low | 3% | 6% | 3% |

Controlling gregariousness does not completely account for the variations in the proportion of public affairs leaders on each status level. Status and gregariousness are, in fact, independently related to public affairs leadership; holding one factor constant, leadership is found to vary with the other. Of the two factors, however, gregariousness is the more important. Thus, even if a woman is of low status, if she is highly gregarious she has a better-than-average chance of being a public affairs leader.[20] But, for the non-gregarious woman, status level makes no difference; she is rarely a leader, whatever her status.[21]

| Information | PER CENT PUBLIC AFFAIRS LEADERS | | |
|---|---|---|---|
| | High Greg. | Medium Greg. | Low Greg. |
| High | 25% (118) | 14% (155) | 7% (73) |
| Middle | 18% ( 52) | 12% ( 97) | 3% (59) |
| Low | — ( 19) | 1% ( 72) | 2% (63) |

19. Pp. 242-4 above.
20. For the sample as a whole, 12% are opinion leaders in this area.
21. For the area of fashions, it will be recalled, gregariousness and status also varied independently, but the two factors were equally strong throughout. Thus, on the level of low gregariousness, the high status woman was more likely to be a fashion leader than the middle status woman, and the middle status woman was more likely than the low status woman. Here, low-gregarious women have no chance at all for leadership in public affairs.

## Life-Cycle Position and
## Public Affairs Leadership

To round out our picture of leadership in this arena we have
to consider the third of our key variables, the life-cycle, to see
whether there is any variation in the incidence of opinion
leadership among women of different ages and different stages
of family responsibility.

It is a common assumption that the domestic functions of
women—care of the household and the rearing of children—
successfully compete with public affairs interests and activity,
relegating them to subordinate status. According to this view,
"first things come first," and women whose domestic functions
are greatest, probably would be least motivated to participation in this area. In terms of their primary concerns, the world
of public affairs would not seem to be particularly relevant
for such women. And even if it were, extensive household
responsibilities might strictly limit a woman's participation.
According to another view, the feminine role in our society is
rapidly changing and these changes are expressed particularly among the young. Holders of this view cite, for example, the vastly extended coeducational system, which trains
women as well as men for the full and equal assumption of
responsibility and which stimulates their interest in this realm
of ideas. Of course, it is predominantly the young who have
had such training. These latter views, then, lead us to expect
younger women to be the ones most interested and active in
the area of public affairs.

Despite this plausible expectation, we must also note that
younger people—both men and women—have been reported
in many studies to be less interested in politics, less well-
informed and much less frequent participants than older people.
If public affairs advice-giving reflects this general finding of
political studies we should expect the girls to be less active as
opinion leaders and the older women to be more active.

Chart XIV reveals that life-cycle differences are related,
though only weakly, to public affairs leadership. Of the four
areas we are investigating, public affairs leadership is least

related to variations in the life-cycle. The slight differences that do exist, however, are worth commenting on. It appears that public affairs leadership declines steadily, though very undramatically, with advancing age. The largest proportion of opinion leaders is among the girls; the smallest proportion among the matrons.

The direction of declining leadership—however slight the absolute figures—contrasts with studies of political participation which indicate that, in the United States, interest and participation in politics increase with increasing age. This contrast seems to suggest that opinion leadership in public affairs may be something qualitatively different from political participation. Thus it may be that the approach of these feminine

**Chart XIV—Public Affairs Leadership Decreases Somewhat With Each Step in the Life-Cycle**

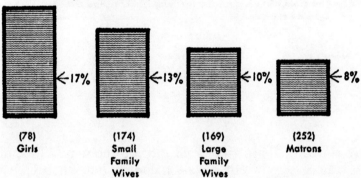

public affairs leaders is fundamentally a-political, treating current events as "news," and community issues in terms of "good" and "bad" rather than as part of the realm of political partisanship. Or it may be that at this stage of the life-cycle, girls talk more about public affairs because they move in the world of men on a more equal level and therefore, must maintain their competence in such matters without translating their concern into political participation. Or, it may be that younger women are not really more concerned with public affairs at all—just as they are not much concerned with participation— but that other people *think they are* by virtue of their more recent, and more extensive education; therefore, others may seek them out for information and advice.

## Age and the Flow of Influence

Nevertheless, although there are proportionately a few more leaders in public affairs among the girls, our data on the flow of influence indicate that when influence travels between people of different ages—whether inside or outside the family—there is a marked downward tendency: public affairs influence flows from older influentials to young influencees. In other words, though the girls as a group may talk among themselves more than other women do, the younger opinion leader is not likely to be influential for someone older than herself. This is clear from an examination of the influential-influencee pairs who are not members of the same family:

**Table 43—The Flow of Public Affairs Influence Among Age Groups Outside the Family**

|  |  | INFLUENCEE'S AGE IS |  |  |
|---|---|---|---|---|
| Her Opinion Leader's Age Is | 15-24 | 25-44 | 45+ | Totals |
| 15-24 | 14 | 2 | 1 | 17 |
| 25-44 | 6 | 19 | 6 | 31 |
| 45+ | 1 | 12 | 20 | 33 |
| Totals | 21 | 33 | 27 | 81 |

Two-thirds of those who went outside the family for public affairs advice sought out a contemporary, but when influence did cross over from one age category to another, there was a greater tendency for it to flow from old to young than vice versa.

Within the family, the picture is the same except that here there is evident an even sharper downward flow of influence.

**Table 44—The Flow of Public Affairs Influence Among Age Groups Within the Family**

|  |  | INFLUENCEE'S AGE IS |  |  |
|---|---|---|---|---|
| Her Opinion Leader's Age Is | 15-24 | 25-44 | 45+ | Totals |
| 15-24 | 3 | 6 | 2 | 11 |
| 25-44 | 15 | 43 | 9 | 67 |
| 45+ | 15 | 14 | 30 | 59 |
| Totals | 33 | 63 | 41 | 137 |

Indeed, within the family, young women are very likely to consult only their elders; thus, of the 33 women between 15 and 24 years of age who credited a change to a family member, only 3 were influenced by age peers. Among older women, much more influencing went on between age peers than was the case for the girls. But from the table as a whole, it is obvious that the channels of intra-family influencing flow from older influentials to younger influencees. And, of course, this is not at all surprising since we know that the family's opinion leaders are very largely the husbands and the fathers.

It is evident then that the flow of influence in this arena of public affairs is characterized by a downward tendency. Outside the family there are many more exchanges among contemporaries than there are inside the family; but both outside and inside, when public affairs influence crosses the boundaries of age, it tends to go from older to younger.

## The Joint Role of Status Level and Life-Cycle

Earlier we had been considering the relationship between life-cycle and the incidence of public affairs leadership. We observed that life-cycle position made some difference, but not very much, in the proportion of public affairs leadership. Before concluding this chapter, we should like to investigate one more idea which occurs to us in this connection—namely, that life-cycle position may be more sharply related to public affairs leadership on the lower status levels than on the higher.

Let us speculate for a moment about why this might be. First of all, it is clear that the restrictive effects of family responsibilities are less for women of high status than for women of low status. The high status woman has more conveniences, more household help, and the like. Furthermore, as we have already indicated, high status women are exposed throughout their life-cycle to booster or supplementary stimuli to public affairs participation by the action of their environment: their contact with people "in the know"; the fact that on the high status level, prestige attaches to the woman with knowledge in the world of public affairs, and so on. Women of lower status by and large lack these supplementary stimuli to participate in public affairs, where such participation, at best, is marginal to most women's activities. They would be most likely to lose whatever interest or concern they might once have had in this area of information and opinion. And, if supplementary stimuli are important to a woman's chances for leadership in public affairs, then, with the passage of time, women of low status should become increasingly less likely to be public affairs leaders, whereas, on the high status level, this "drop-off" might be expected to be much less marked. In other words, we suspect that the decline in female public affairs leadership with advancing age and increased family responsibility should be more pronounced among low status women than among high.

**Table 45—High Status Confers Opportunities for Leadership Which Are Available on the Low Status Level Only to the Young**

| Status Level | PER CENT WHO ARE PUBLIC AFFAIRS LEADERS | | | |
|---|---|---|---|---|
|  | Girls | Small Family Wives | Large Family Wives | Matrons |
| High | 24% | 15% | 21% | 17% |
| Middle | 12% | 19% | 5% | 8% |
| Low | 15% | 5% | 6% | 3% |

The data of Table 45 are much as we expected. On the high status level, life-cycle type makes relatively little difference to chances for public affairs leadership. Thus, the girls are little more likely than the large family wives to be public affairs leaders. On the other levels, however, a woman's chances for leadership do depend on her life-cycle type somewhat more. Among women of middle status, only the girls and small family wives have an average chance or better of being a public affairs leader and, among those on the low status level, the girls alone have that chance.[22]

## The Flow of Influence in Public Affairs: A Summary

The typical public affairs leader, then, is quite different from opinion leaders in the arenas of marketing or fashions. Life-cycle type, which was so important in both those areas, makes

---

22. For the sample as a whole, 12% are leaders in this area.

only a little difference here in the incidence of opinion leadership except on the low status level. On the other hand, social status—which was only remotely related to marketing leadership and somewhat deviously to leadership in fashions—plays a very much more important role in public affairs leadership. Better educated, wealthier women—that is, women of higher status, no matter what their life-cycle position—seem to move in a climate which promotes greater participation in public affairs. The flow of influence, too, seems to move more often from higher to lower status people than vice versa. Much of the explanation for the greater incidence of public affairs leaders among higher status women is that they are also relatively more free from household responsibility. And although the effect of status can still be seen even when gregariousness is held constant, gregariousness, it must be noted, is the stronger of the two factors and seems to be the major key to leadership in public affairs.

# CHAPTER XIII

# Movie Leaders

APPROXIMATELY 60 PER CENT of our respondents said that they go to the movies once a month or more; 40 per cent go less often than once a month or do not go at all. In view of this fact, we have decided to confine our analysis of the flow of influence about movies only to those who may be considered active participants in the movie arena—that is, to those who go to the movies at least once a month.

From previous research, we know that there is a strong relationship between movie-going and age.[1] Our data confirm this: it is the young people who go to the movies:

**Table 46—Young People Constitute the Major Element in the Movie Market**

| Frequency of Attendance | Under 25 | 25-34 | 35-44 | 45 and over |
|---|---|---|---|---|
| Once a Week or More | 68% | 49% | 34% | 19% |
| One to Three Times per Month | 20 | 31 | 35 | 27 |
| Less than Once a Month | 7 | 14 | 26 | 37 |
| Never | 5 | 6 | 5 | 17 |
| Total (= 100%) | (141) | (157) | (148) | (271) |

While 88 per cent of the youngest age group goes to the movies once a month or more, Table 46 reveals that each succeeding age group shows a marked decline, so that by the time women reach the age of 45, more than half of them go to the movies less often than once a month.

## *"Youth Culture": Movie Leadership and the Life-Cycle*

Judging from this distribution of participation in the movie arena, we shall certainly expect to find that the concentration

---

1. See, for example, Lazarsfeld and Kendall (1948) and Handel (1950).

of opinion leadership is among the girls. But our curiosity extends further. We do not know, for example, how marriage and motherhood affect a woman's chances for movie leadership, if they do at all. Let us look, then, at the relationship between the life-cycle and movie leadership.

**Chart XV—The Concentration of Movie Leadership Is Among the Girls**

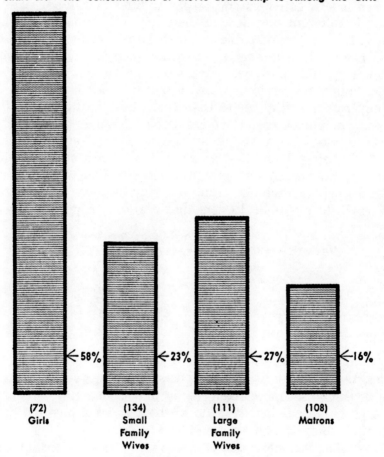

|  |  |  |  |
|---|---|---|---|
| ←58% | ←23% | ←27% | ←16% |
| (72) Girls | (134) Small Family Wives | (111) Large Family Wives | (108) Matrons |

Overwhelmingly, even more than in the fashion arena, the movie leaders can be found among the girls—the young, single women with fewest family responsibilities. Well over half of the girls say that they have recently been asked their opinions about current movie fare.[2] Of course, it is not age alone that makes the difference. The difference between the movie leadership rates of the girls and the wives is so very sharp (58% to 23%) and the difference among the three types of married women so very small (23%, 27%, 16%) that it is evident that the fact of being married or single is as important as age in being a predisposing factor in movie leadership. Obviously, the pattern of social activities and responsibilities in the one case is entirely different than it is in the other. The unmarried girl is not only younger than the small or large family wife; she is also freer. The difference between the girls and the wives, then, is the difference between a woman relatively unburdened with family responsibility, and a mother with a full load of family responsibility; more than that, it is the difference between an unmarried girl and the role of movie-going in her social affairs, and a young woman who has "settled down."

While being young and unmarried is associated both with more frequent movie-going and more frequent leadership chances, within each age group the very frequent movie-goers are more likely to be leaders than those who go less often.

**Table 47—The More Frequent Movie-Goers Among Both Young and Old Are More Likely To Be Movie Leaders**

|  | UNDER 25 | | 25 AND OVER | |
|---|---|---|---|---|
|  | Frequent Goers | Occasional Goers | Frequent Goers | Occasional Goers |
| Leaders | 55% | 32% | 28% | 13% |
| Non-Leaders | 45 | 68 | 72 | 87 |
| Total (= 100% | (87) | (28) | (165) | (157) |

Among the women under 25 years of age, the table indicates, those who are frequent goers (once a week or more) are considerably more likely to be movie leaders than those who go only occasionally (one to three times a month); and the same thing is true for the older age group.

Now that we know something about the relationship between the life-cycle and movie leadership, we should ask—as

2. As in the other arenas movie leaders are (a) those women who told us twice that they had recently been asked their advice about what picture to see, and (b) those women who reported only one incident of advice-giving but who considered themselves "more likely" than others to be sought out for advice about movies.

we have done in the previous sections—about the flow of influence within and between age groups. We shall expect, as in the other areas, to find considerable homogeneity of age between influential and influencee. But at the same time—in view of the striking concentration of movie leadership among the girls—we shall expect, too, that in addition to influence exchanges among age peers, there is a flow from young to old. Rather than enter into that discussion at this point, however, we should like first to introduce a finding which complicates our analysis of the movie arena in a very interesting way and has important bearing, too, on the character of the flow of movie influence. That finding can be most clearly perceived by considering the relationship between movie leadership and our index of gregariousness.

## Movie Leadership and Gregariousness: A Special Case

In every other arena we have examined so far, we have found gregariousness to be an attribute of the opinion leader. As a matter of fact, it is reasonable to posit that some greater-than-average degree of contact with other people is a requirement for any kind of informal leadership. Yet, we find that in the case of movie leadership, there is virtually no relationship between the incidence of leadership and our index of gregariousness.

In other words, we are forced to explain why leadership in the fields of marketing, fashions and public affairs is so much more highly related to our measure of gregariousness than leadership in the arena of movie-going. And we think we have an answer.

In fact, we have three answers. One answer should be apparent from the relationship which we reported in Chapter IX between the life-cycle and gregariousness.[3] There we found, it will be recalled, that the girls—by virtue of their relatively low level of organizational affiliation but relatively large number of friends—tended to fall into our category of "medium gregariousness." And since we have observed that the ranks of

---

3. P. 230 above.

movie leadership are filled to an overwhelming degree with girls, it is easy to understand why the movie leaders tend to be concentrated somewhat more among women of medium gregariousness than among women of high and low gregariousness.

A second factor which undoubtedly plays a part in explaining why women of high gregariousness are not more likely to be leaders in this arena is that women of high gregariousness

**Chart XVI—Movie Leadership Does Not Parallel Gregariousness**

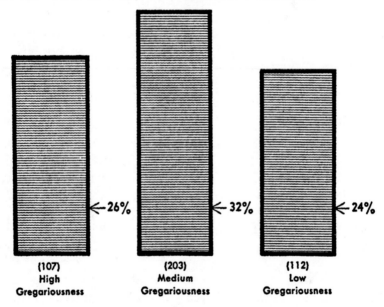

|            | (107)<br>High<br>Gregariousness | (203)<br>Medium<br>Gregariousness | (112)<br>Low<br>Gregariousness |
|------------|------|------|------|
|            | ←26% | ←32% | ←24% |

—those who have many organizational contacts and a large number of personal friends—may have reason to be less interested in the movies than women whose social lives are less full.

But there is a third answer, too, one which is very important for an understanding of what goes on in this sphere of influence. For even if we explain that the women of highest gregariousness are less interested in movies, and that the girls are concentrated in the medium gregariousness level, we still must understand how it is that the proportion of leaders even among the least gregarious women—the women with fewest friends and fewest organizational contacts—is virtually as high as it is among the much more gregarious women. And the answer, we think, is that the act of movie-going itself is a gregarious activity, although one which our index of gregariousness cannot measure. Here is our explanation:

Upon examining the context for decision-making in the movie arena—that is, the conditions under which people decide to go to one movie rather than another—we find that virtually no one of our respondents goes to the movies alone.[4] Unlike public affairs, or more strictly speaking, the holding of opinions on public affairs, movie-going is an activity which is shared in a direct way with other people. Almost nine out of ten of our respondents stated that they had attended their last motion picture exhibition accompanied by someone else. This shared movie-going is almost unanimous among women under 25, and it is almost so among older women as well. There is no significant difference in shared attendance between married and unmarried women, nor is there any between movie leaders and non-leaders.

Since movie-going is so strongly characterized by its group nature, it seems highly reasonable to suppose that it is within the movie-attending groups themselves that most of the give-and-take about movies and the movie world goes on. The movie leader finds her following immediately at hand among her movie-going companions; to lead, she does not require the audience of many friendships and organizational affiliations which are characteristic of the more gregarious leaders in the other areas. In the realm of the movies, there are no isolates; if you find a movie-goer, the chances are you have found a movie-going group. The act of movie-going, therefore, is more properly studied as a product of group decision rather than of individual decision; and in such decisions, presumably, our movie leaders should have the upper hand.[5] But the point here

---

4. This is reported also by Handel (1950), who cites a study which indicates that 86% of women and 70% of men were accompanied by another person the last time they went to the movies. The typical attendance unit consists of two people. See pp. 113-115.

5. The marketing arena is the only one of the other three arenas we are considering which can be characterized by some degree of shared decisions. We have treated this possibility only very briefly in our chapter on marketing leaders, but see, for example, Riley (1953) for the suggestion that joint decisions of mother and child govern choice of breakfast cereals.

is that movie leaders are "gregarious" in the very special sense that movie-going itself is a gregarious enterprise.

## Shared Movie-Going and the Flow of Influence

If we are correct, it should follow that the flow of influence in this realm is concentrated in these movie-going groups. But, since we did not anticipate this problem sufficiently in advance we can only hint at the possibility that this is the case.[6] Evidence that might lend circumstantial weight to our argument is that there is a similarity between the kind of people women report as influential in their movie decisions and those whom they say (in answer to another question) are their steady movie companions. Compare the movie companions and the movie leaders[7] named by married and single women, for example:

**Table 48—Movie-Going Companions and Movie Leaders Seem To Be Somewhat the Same Sort of People**

|  | SINGLE WOMEN | | MARRIED WOMEN | |
|---|---|---|---|---|
|  | Their Companions | Their Leaders | Their Companions | Their Leaders |
| Non-Family (friends, neighbors, others) | 67% | 76% | 15% | 40% |
| Family (parents, husbands, children, others) | 33 | 23 | 85 | 60 |
| Total (= 100%) | (66) | (35) | (316) | (132) |

It is quite clear from Table 48 that the single women, the girls, name as their movie-going companions, and as their movie leaders, individuals who are not members of their families; the wives, on the other hand, seek the advice as well as

---

6. Had we planned for this possibility and asked explicitly about the joint movie-going decision, we would have obtained many more affirmative replies. As it is, most people, we think, simply did not associate our question, "Did you hear someone talk about it?" with the everyday give-and-take which they carry on with movie-going companions. This matter is discussed above, in Section II, pp. 201-2.

7. When women answered that they "heard someone talk about it," they were asked to name this influential and state their relationship to her. These are the people we are here calling "their leaders."

the companionship of their kin. Closer scrutiny of the details of the table reveals that both groups, but particularly the wives, seek non-family advice in somewhat greater proportion than non-family companions. This disparity is probably a reflection of the fact that the family is more readily available and, for the wives, more socially acceptable as a movie-going group. Although one might prefer to be escorted by a non-family companion, either the unavailability of other people or the demands of family loyalties and obligations objectively restrict this possibility. In this connection, it is very interesting to note that even among women of equivalent age and marital status, leaders are more likely than non-leaders to go to the movies with non-family companions.

**Table 49—Leaders Go to the Movies With Non-Family Members More Often than Do Non-Leaders**

|  | PER CENT WHO GO WITH NON-FAMILY MEMBERS | |
|  | Leaders | Non-Leaders |
| Under 25 | 53% (57) | 38% (58) |
| 25 or Older | 31% (66) | 15% (249) |
| Unmarried | 70% (42) | 52% (30) |
| Married | 26% (78) | 12% (275) |

One way to explain this phenomenon might be as follows: The women who go to the movies in the company of non-family members would be more likely to remember having been asked advice than those who go with family members; in the family situation, that is, it would be more usual for advice to have been a give-and-take affair and not to recall it when interviewed. If this is the case, then Table 49 is not of great moment. It simply means that the non-family moviegoers are more likely to recall influence exchanges, and therefore are more likely to designate themselves as movie leaders.

Another explanation is possible, however: It may be that going to the movies with non-family members has something special about it which is more directly connected with movie leadership. Specifically, our guess is that attending with the family may be a somewhat more ritualistic activity—and, therefore, one involving less careful choosing—than attending with non-family companions. The husband-wife attendance unit, say, or the child-parent unit may tend more toward seeing whatever film is playing in the local theater on their usual day of attendance, while non-family units may be less ritualistic.

As a matter of fact, we have some evidence which tends to support this speculation. All the movie-goers were asked: "When are you most likely to go to a movie?" with several possibilities provided for, among them "When there are pictures which especially interest you." Our expectation is that the leaders—who go more often with non-family attendance units than with the family units—would indicate this motive more strongly than the non-leaders, and this is indeed the case:

**Table 50—Movie Leaders Are More Likely To Go to the Movies When There Is a Film Which Especially Interests**

| | PER CENT WHO GO WHEN THE PICTURE SOUNDS INTERESTING | | | |
| | FREQUENT GOERS | | OCCASIONAL GOERS | |
| | Under 25 | 25 & Older | Under 25 | 25 & Older |
|---|---|---|---|---|
| Leaders | 70% (48) | 76% (46) | 89% (9) | 71% (20) |
| Non-Leaders | 56% (39) | 57% (112) | 58% (19) | 73% (137) |

Among both frequent and occasional goers in the younger groups, and among the older, more frequent goers, leaders are much more likely than non-leaders to go when the picture sounds interesting. Conversely, only 19 per cent of the leaders as compared with 27 per cent of the non-leaders report that they go when they have "a free evening."

There is further evidence of interest in the particular picture itself. In the first interview these women were asked, regarding the last movie they had seen: "Did you go primarily just to go to a movie, to see a certain picture, or for both reasons?" Again we find that more of the leaders were interested in the picture itself:

**Table 51—Leaders Make Particular Choices More Than Non-Leaders**

| | PER CENT WHO WENT TO SEE A CERTAIN PICTURE | | | |
| | FREQUENT GOERS | | OCCASIONAL GOERS | |
| | Under 25 | 25 & Older | Under 25 | 25 & Older |
|---|---|---|---|---|
| Leaders | 57% (48) | 63% (46) | 78% (9) | 81% (20) |
| Non-Leaders | 54% (39) | 57% (112) | 26% (19) | 68% (137) |

Although the difference is relatively small between those leaders and non-leaders who are young and go frequently, the differences are larger in the other categories and are consistent throughout.

Compared with non-leaders, then, movie leaders are more likely to pick out a particular picture to see; this is true "usually," as well as for the most recent movie attended. This finding probably means two things: First of all, it suggests that the companions of the movie leaders may be less particular than their leaders; secondly, it lends weight to our suggestion that movie-going groups composed of non-family members may, as groups, be more choosy than groups made up of family members. In any event, this is an interesting matter for further investigation.

Despite these important considerations, however, we must not allow ourselves to lose sight of the fundamental point which was established earlier. This was the finding that, *in general*, the norm for married women is to seek both the companionship and leadership of members of their families, while the norm for the girls is to share these things with their friends.

## Age and the Flow of Influence

This basic difference in the movie habits of the young, unmarried girl and the older, married woman has important implications for the flow of influence among the several age groups in the arena of movie-going. It will be recalled that our discussion of this topic was intentionally postponed, so that the social setting of movie-going could be presented first. Our contention has been that the kind of advice-giving which is reflected in movie leadership and in our data on the flow of influence probably takes place within the framework of these movie-going groups. Just as we saw that a woman's movie leaders and her companions seem to be the same kinds of people, now we will see that advice-giving is most likely to flow among people of more or less the same age:

*Table 52—The Flow of Movie Influence Among Age Groups*[8]

| Her Movie Leader's Age Is | INFLUENCEE'S AGE IS | | | |
|---|---|---|---|---|
|  | 15-24 | 25-44 | 45+ | Totals |
| 15-24 | 30 | 9 | 4 | 43 |
| 25-44 | 11 | 36 | 6 | 53 |
| 45+ | 2 | 8 | 11 | 21 |
| Totals | 43 | 53 | 21 | 117 |

Our respondents report having influenced people of pretty much the same ages as themselves. Thus 70 per cent (30 out of 43) of the 15-24 age group were influenced by age-peers and the same hold true for 68 per cent (36 out of 53) of the 25-44 age group and 52 per cent (11 out of 21) of the women over 45. In sum, putting together what we have learned so far, girls are most likely to have been influenced by age peers and older women by other adults; the girls, of course, were influenced by friends, and older, married women primarily by age-peers within the family.

## The Role of the Movie Expert

The picture we get from the reports in Table 52 of the actual incidents of influence seems to indicate a sharp demarcation between the "youth culture" and the world of adults as far as movie influence, attendance and decisions are concerned. But if, as has been suggested, the kind of movie leader we have described thus far is typically part of a movie-going group (whose companions, when she is young, are age-peers and when she is older are adult family members) and if the influence flow we have described takes place within such groups, then it may be that we have not yet told the entire story of the flow of movie influence. For it may be that a different type of influence transaction typically takes place *outside* these groups.

One way of getting at such an influence flow, if it exists, is by means of another of the questions we asked our respondents: "Do you know anybody around here who usually knows some-

---

8. This table is based on respondents' designations of influencees. Hence, the leaders are sample members and those whom they advised are not.

thing about the movies and can tell what's a good picture to see?"⁹ About 40% of our respondents said they did know such a person. Predominantly, these respondents were people who go more frequently to the movies and who were more likely to say that the last time they went to the movies, they went "to see a certain picture" rather than "just to go to the movies."

In any event, our interest here is in whether the relationships between these movie "experts"—the "general influentials"— and their advisees are any different from those of the specific influentials and their influencees which we have seen up to now. If, as we suspect, the specific influentials are part of the movie-going group which they lead but that these "experts" are not, perhaps we shall be able to round out our picture of the flow of movie influence. Let us duplicate the table we just examined, substituting the "expert" for the specific influential.

Table 53—The Flow of Expert Advice About Movies Among Age Groups

| Her Movie Expert Is | RESPONDENT'S AGE IS | | | |
|---|---|---|---|---|
| | 15-24 | 25-44 | 45+ | Totals |
| 15-24 | 24 | 27 | 12 | 63 |
| 25-44 | 5 | 42 | 17 | 64 |
| 45+ | 5 | 9 | 9 | 23 |
| Totals | 34 | 78 | 38 | 150 |

The table indicates, quite clearly, that there is a major difference between the two types of opinion leadership. While the movie "experts" of the youngest group are still people like themselves, the older groups have substituted younger women as experts in far greater proportion than they name such people as specific influentials. This can best be seen by comparing the row and the column of "totals." Whereas 23 per cent of all respondents are below 25 years of age, 42 per cent of the experts they designate belong in this age group.

An examination of the relationships between these respondents and their movie experts reveals that the category of children seems to make the major difference. For women 35 years of age or over, children—that is, their own children—account for almost a third of the experts they designate.

---

9. This question was asked in each of the other areas as well, but we have not reported it except here and in the case of public affairs.

If this "general influential" question is a good indication, then, it appears that both younger and older women seek out movie experts among the young, although the final decision may often be modified by primary influentials in the movie-going groups who are more likely to be in the same age bracket as their groups.

## Social Status and Movie Leadership

Of the three factors which we are employing to locate and describe opinion leaders—life-cycle, social status and gregariousness—only the life-cycle is relevant in the realm of movie-going. Our measure of gregariousness, we have seen, is not associated with movie leadership and, now we may add, neither is our index of social status. This, of course, is what might have been expected. There was no reason to suppose, say, that girls of any given status level would produce fewer movie leaders than girls of any other level, and the same holds true for wives and matrons. On each status level, approximately one person in four is a movie leader, and of the four arenas of leadership with which we are concerned in this study, status level is least relevant to that of movie leadership.

## The Flow of Influence About Movies:
## A Summary

In sum, it is evident that movie-going is a main theme of American youth culture and that the influentials in this realm arise from the ranks of the young and carefree. What's more, within every life-cycle bracket, the leader is the more frequent movie-goer, more particular about what she sees and more exogamous in the choice of her movie companions.

Movie-going, we have seen, is not a solitary activity; people go to the movies in groups. The flow of influence in this realm, we think, takes place largely within these movie-going groups which are usually made up of age peers. But when it comes to consulting a movie "expert," people of all ages turn to the girls.

# CHAPTER XIV

# The Two-Step Flow of Communication

IDEALLY, WE SHOULD HAVE LIKED to trace out all of the interpersonal networks in the community to see how they link up with each other; instead, we have had to content ourselves with a cross section of influential-influencee relationships. Nevertheless, even if we had been able to present a complete "map" of the flow of influence from person to person as we began to do when we examined the flow of general (expert) influence in public affairs, we should not have exhausted our subject, because influencing in modern society stems not only from other people nearby, but also from the mass media.

As a matter of fact, one of the specific hypotheses with which this study set out is the hypothesis of "the two-step flow of communication." Formulated first in *The People's Choice*, the hypothesis suggests that "ideas often flow *from* radio and print *to* the opinion leaders and *from* them to the less active sections of the population."[1] But since this formulation, and the evidence to substantiate it, were based only upon one kind of opinion leader—people who were influential for others during the course of an election campaign—we do not yet know whether the hypothesis is applicable to opinion leadership in other realms as well. In this chapter, then, we want to compare the media behavior of opinion leaders and non-leaders to see whether the leaders tend to be the more exposed, and the more responsive group when it comes to influence stemming from the mass media. In general, we shall find that the hypothesis is substantiated in each of the arenas of influence with which

---

1. Lazarsfeld, Berelson and Gaudet (1948), p. 151. It is important to distinguish between the flow of *influence* and of *information*. The roles of media and interpersonal sources in the spread of a news event is considered, for example, in Bogart (1950), Larsen and Hill (1954). See Whyte (1954) for an example, paralleling our own, of the role of word-of-mouth in the flow of consumer *influence* together with suggestions concerning linkages with mass media.

we are concerned. In addition, at the close of the chapter, we shall try to refine and further specify our understanding of the workings of this interesting phenomenon by introducing one further aspect of the "relay" role which opinion leaders play.

## Opinion Leadership and Exposure to the Mass Media

The kind of information it takes to be an opinion leader in marketing is quite different, of course, from the kind required for influentiality, say, in public affairs. We shall not expect, therefore, that opinion leaders in each of the different realms will consistently outdo the non-leaders in exposure to every single medium of mass communication. Yet, on the other hand, considering the vast span of interest encompassed by such broad categories as "magazines" or "radio," we should not be surprised either if opinion leaders, no matter what their spheres of influence, do actually exceed non-opinion leaders in mass media exposure in general. We shall find, in varying instances, that both generalizations are true. For a first example, let us look at the data on magazine readership, comparing the extent of readership of each of the brands of opinion leaders with those who are not influential at all.[2]

It is plain from the table that influentials of every type read a larger number of magazines than those who are not influential. Thus, the non-leader group includes in its ranks many fewer readers of five or more magazines; and this is true, too, the table shows, when education is taken into account.[3] In other words, then, opinion leaders in each arena—whether it be marketing, fashions, politics or movie-going—tend to have

---

2. To simplify the presentation of Table 54, we present the data for each leader group separately and then for the group which is not influential at all in any area (the "non-leaders"). In an area-by-area comparison, the readership of the non-leaders would increase slightly because the non-leaders in any given area would also include women who are leaders in other areas. Nevertheless, the leader-non-leader difference persists very clearly in each area. It should be noted, too, that the leadership groups presented in this table are not mutually exclusive, that is, a woman will reappear in every area in which she is a leader; only the non-leader group is exclusive. The extent to which our sample actually contains women who are leaders in more than one area is a problem which is considered in the following chapter.

3. "High education" begins with high school graduates; "low education" includes all who have less than a complete high school education.

**Table 54—Opinion Leaders Read More Magazines than Non-Leaders**

|  | | LOW EDUCATION | | | |
|---|---|---|---|---|---|
| Number of Magazines | Marketing Leaders | Fashion Leaders | Public Affairs Leaders | Movie Leaders | Non-Leaders |
| 5 or more | 41% | 58% | 60% | 58% | 30% |
| less than 5 | 59 | 42 | 40 | 42 | 70 |
| 100% = | (91) | (79) | (30) | (64) | (270) |
|  | | HIGH EDUCATION | | | |
|  | Marketing Leaders | Fashion Leaders | Public Affairs Leaders | Movie Leaders | Non-Leaders |
| 5 or more | 65% | 69% | 63% | 71% | 53% |
| less than 5 | 35 | 31 | 37 | 29 | 47 |
| 100% = | (75) | (80) | (50) | (58) | (146) |

greater contact than non-leaders with the features and advertisements in America's magazines.

When we turn from magazines to other media, we find that, as a rule, the same phenomenon holds true; that is, opinion leaders exceed non-leaders in exposure. But at the same time, these other media begin to reveal some idiosyncrasies of the different leader types as well. Consider book reading, for example:

**Table 55—Opinion Leaders Read More Books than Non-Leaders**

|  | | LOW EDUCATION | | | |
|---|---|---|---|---|---|
| Number of Books per Month | Marketing Leaders | Fashion Leaders | Public Affairs Leaders | Movie Leaders | Non-Leaders |
| 1 or more | 25% | 47% | 38% | 38% | 20% |
| less than 1 | 75 | 53 | 62 | 62 | 80 |
| 100% = | (81) | (76) | (29) | (61) | (270) |
|  | | HIGH EDUCATION | | | |
|  | Marketing Leaders | Fashion Leaders | Public Affairs Leaders | Movie Leaders | Non-Leaders |
| 1 or more | 39% | 42% | 57% | 51% | 34% |
| less than 1 | 61 | 58 | 43 | 49 | 66 |
| 100% = | (74) | (79) | (49) | (55) | (146) |

Again, on both levels of education, all the leaders are more likely to read at least one book per month than are the non-leaders. Again, too, this is true on both high and low levels of education. Notice, however, that on both educational levels the marketing leaders exceed the non-leaders by only very

little, while each of the other leader types seems to be more
clearly differentiated. This, of course, is as we might have expected; intuitively at least, one would not say that the "requirements" for marketing leadership include the reading of a
greater number of books, whereas a case could be made for the
relationship between reading books and leadership in the other
three areas.

Leaders tend to exceed non-leaders in number of hours of
radio listening, too, although the differences are quite small
and not always consistent. The movie leaders of both educational levels seem to be particularly attentive to radio, together with the lower-educated marketing and fashion leaders.
However, the well-educated leaders in the latter two realms,
plus the political leaders on both educational levels, do not
exceed the non-leaders in time spent listening to the radio.[4]
The political leaders, furthermore, are the only group which
does not exceed the non-leaders in movie-going; all other leaders do.[5]

In sum, it can safely be stated that the opinion leaders in
every realm tend to be more highly exposed to the mass media
than are the non-leaders. But while we have begun to talk
about these variations, that is, about the different media habits
of one kind of leader as compared with another, we have
not yet talked explicitly about the relationship between such
variations and the different *content* of the several media.

## Opinion Leadership and the Content
## of Mass Communications

Within each of the media, of course, there is a world of variation. The name "radio" includes both the soap opera and the
Metropolitan Opera; the category "magazines" has an almost
incredible range; and the same is true for all of the other
media. So far, we have seen only that opinion leaders are, as
a rule, more exposed to the media *in general* than non-leaders.
But we also have begun to see that the marketing leader or the
movie leader may be more or less exposed to a given medium

---

4. The study was completed before the general introduction of television.
5. These tables are not shown here.

than the fashion leader, say, or the public affairs leader. Our intention now is to inquire more specifically into the kinds of media content with which different sorts of leaders are more likely to be in touch.

One of the first studies of opinion leadership—in fact, it was a study of what we are now calling public affairs leadership—discovered that it was important to distinguish between two kinds of public affairs leaders in a community: those who are influential in local affairs, and those who exert influence concerning national and international affairs.[6] It was found that the "cosmopolitans"—those who were concerned particularly with news of the world outside their community—typically had access to news media which originated outside and brought them such news, while the "locals"—the experts on township affairs—were local in their communications habits, too. In the present study, we cannot distinguish between "local" and "cosmopolitan" leaders within the one realm we call political affairs, but we can compare the media habits of our several leader types, this time to see which is more "local" and which is more "cosmopolitan" in its readership of news. In other words, while we shall not distinguish between two types of public affairs leaders as the earlier study did, we shall compare the leaders in each of our four arenas to see how they differ from each other on this matter of "cosmopolitan" and "local" news orientation.

To make this comparison, we have combined the answers to two questions relating to newspaper and magazine readership.[7] Those who said that they read newspapers which were published out of town as well as news or news analysis in the national magazines were classed as "cosmopolitans"; those who maintained neither of these contacts with the world outside (but who did have access to local papers) were labeled "locals"; and those who qualified either on out-of-town news-

---

6. Merton (1949B).
7. Respondents were asked in the June interview, first, whether they read any Decatur newspapers and then "Do you read any out-of-town papers?" and they were asked to name which ones. In the August interview, respondents were asked the following question: "Do you try to read fairly regularly articles in magazines which discuss news events in greater detail?" Answers to these two questions form the basis for the "local-cosmopolitan" index.

papers or on magazine news were labeled "intermediate." Here we shall compare the proportion of "cosmopolitans" among each of the leader types as well as between the leaders and non-leaders in each arena, thus modifying somewhat the procedure in the last few tables above:

**Table 56—The "Cosmopolitans" Among the Opinion Leaders Are In Fashions and Public Affairs**

PER CENT WHO READ BOTH OUT-OF-TOWN NEWSPAPERS AND NEWS IN NATIONAL MAGAZINES

|  | Marketing | | Fashion | | Public Affairs | | Movie | |
|---|---|---|---|---|---|---|---|---|
|  | Leaders | Non-Leaders | Leaders | Non-Leaders | Leaders | Non-Leaders | Leaders | Non-Leaders |
| Low Ed'n | 27% | 20% | 39% | 17% | 50% | 20% | 25% | 24% |
| 100% = | (88) | (324) | (79) | (330) | (30) | (381) | (64) | (159) |
| High Ed'n | 48% | 43% | 53% | 41% | 55% | 41% | 45% | 47% |
| 100% = | (77) | (219) | (81) | (218) | (51) | (247) | (58) | (148) |

First, let us read along the top line. Among these low educated groups, it is quite evident that the movie leaders do not exceed non-movie leaders in "cosmopolitan" exposure, and that the marketing leaders are only slightly more oriented to the outside world than the non-marketing leaders. The arenas of fashions and of public affairs, however, show striking differences. In these two realms, the leaders far exceed the non-leaders in "cosmopolitan" communications exposure. Smaller differences, but essentially the same story, hold true also for the well educated groups. Again, the movie and marketing leaders are indistinguishable from non-leaders, while the leaders in fashions and public affairs markedly exceed the non-leaders.

The explanation for these differences seems apparent to us: Neither the movie leaders nor the marketing leaders have much "need" for out-of-town papers or magazine news in order to exert their particular brand of influence; as a matter of fact, there is no reason to suppose that these groups should be more interested in news in general than are the non-leaders. Obviously, however, the metropolitan press means much more for influentials in political affairs and in fashions. The advertisements and the features of the metropolitan press and the news in the national magazines provide a channel for these small-city residents to keep up with "big city" fashions and world-wide news, and this information, in turn, bolsters their respective types of influentiality.

Another illustration of the relationship between media content and the readership choice of varying types of leaders is provided by the magazines. Earlier, we observed that leaders of all four types tended to read a larger number of magazines than their followers. But we did not look there to see which magazines which leaders tend to read. Comparing the magazines read by fashion leaders and non-leaders, for example, we find that on both levels of education, the leaders are more likely to read a fashion magazine. Thus on the low education level, 9 per cent of the fashion leaders but only 2 per cent of the non-leaders read one or more fashion magazines while among upper educated women, 30 per cent of the leaders compared with 15 per cent of the non-leaders report fashion magazine readership. In the same way, it can be shown that public affairs leaders exceed non-leaders in their readership of one or another of the national news weeklies; 22 per cent of the former, compared with 14 per cent of the latter do so. This finding becomes even more convincing when it is pointed out that in no realm other than public affairs is opinion leadership associated at all with news magazine readership.[8]

Continuing along the same line, let us look at the arena of movie-going. As Table 57 indicates, movie magazine readership clearly distinguishes between movie leaders and non-leaders.

On both levels of education, movie leaders are more likely than non-leaders to read movie magazines. They are also more likely to purchase these magazines themselves than are the

---

8. Interesting, too, are the data from the "general influence" question. Here we can compare women of the original sample with the public affairs experts they named, and men of the first expert group with the men they named as generally influential, and so on. (For details of these "jumps," see Chapter XII.) Here is the comparison:

| | WOMEN | | MEN | |
|---|---|---|---|---|
| *Reads* | Original Sample | Expert Group I | Expert Group I | Expert Group II |
| News magazine | 34% | 41% | 57% | 69% |
| Total ( = 100%) | (718) | (122) | (201) | (162) |

non-leaders; in other words, the movie leaders don't rely as much as the non-leaders on borrowing, or on second-hand copies, or on beauty parlor reading. They are more likely to go out and buy a copy directly.[9] Again, an examination of each of the other types of leaders—in fashions, marketing and public affairs—reveals that none of these particularly exceeds the corresponding non-leaders in readership of movie magazines. And so it appears evident that the specialized interests which are associated with leadership in one area rather than another go hand in hand with some kinds of media content and not with others.

**Table 57—More Movie Leaders Read Movie Magazines**

| Reads Movie Magazines | LOW EDUCATION | | HIGH EDUCATION | |
|---|---|---|---|---|
| | Movie Leaders | Non-Movie Leaders | Movie Leaders | Non-Movie Leaders |
| Yes | 56% | 34% | 50% | 42% |
| No | 44 | 66 | 50 | 58 |
| Total (= 100%) | (66) | (157) | (58) | (151) |

## Opinion Leadership and Mass Media Effect

So far we have seen that the opinion leaders tend to be both more generally exposed to the mass media, and more specifically exposed to the content most closely associated with their leadership. Presumably this increased exposure then becomes a component—witting or unwitting—of the influence which such influentials transmit to others. As a result of these findings, the idea of the "two-step flow of communication" gains credence.

That is as far as the idea of the "two-step flow" takes us. Yet it would seem worthwhile to proceed one step further, to see whether opinion leaders actually make more "use" of their greater media exposure in their own decisions. We want to see whether opinion leaders are not only more *exposed* to the

---

9. Among the low educated, 74% of the leaders and 52% of the non-leaders personally purchase movie magazines; among the well educated, it is 52% to 48%.

media—which is all that the two-step flow hypothesis claims—but, compared with non-leaders, whether they are relatively more *affected* by them as well.

Actually, there is no need to expect that this will necessarily be true. Take marketing, for example. We have seen that marketing leaders are exposed to the media generally somewhat more than non-leaders. The advice they pass on to others may incorporate this greater exposure; yet, there is little reason to expect that their own decisions will be based, much more than others, on the content of the media which we have studied. It would seem much more reasonable to assume that marketing leaders, like non-leaders, will also base their decisions primarily on personal contacts with others—with other marketing leaders, perhaps—and "use" the media only in a supplementary way.

In fashions, on the other hand, or in public affairs, there would be more reason to expect the leaders to be relatively more influenced by the media in their own decisions. In these arenas, unlike marketing, the relevant "environment" with which the opinion leader must bring his group into contact is much less immediate and much more dependent on the media for transmission. Thus, the media carry the fashion word from the big city, and politics—at least cosmopolitan politics—also comes from the world "outside." And opinion leaders, presumably, are looked to for precisely such information.

Let us consider this possibility in the case of fashions. Specifically, we can assess the relevant influences that went into the making of the opinion leaders' decisions and compare them with those factors which were influential for non-leaders. Thus, Table 58 is a comparison of those fashion leaders and non-leaders who, upon reporting some recent change in their clothes, hairdo, make-up style, etc., were asked: "Who or what suggested this change to you?" For each level of education, the table reports the percentage of all influences named which were personal influences and the percentage which were mass media influences:

*Table 58—Fashion Leaders Are Influenced More by Mass Media and
Less by Other People Than Are Non-Leaders*[10]

|  | PER CENT OF ALL INFLUENCES MENTIONED (RECENT CHANGERS ONLY) | | | |
|  | LOW EDUCATION | | HIGH EDUCATION | |
| "Who or What Suggested Change?" | Fashion Leaders | Non-Fashion Leaders | Fashion Leaders | Non-Fashion Leaders |
| Heard or Saw Somebody | 40% | 56% | 37% | 47% |
| Mass Media | 42 | 31 | 42 | 33 |
| Other | 18 | 13 | 21 | 20 |
| Total Influences (= 100%) | (164) | (308) | (135) | (250) |

On each level of education, Table 58 clearly indicates that
fashion leaders who recently made some change were more influenced in their decisions by the mass media, and less by
other people, than recent changers among the non-leaders.
Although not very large, the differences in the table are consistent throughout.[11]

As we expected, the data for marketing and also for movie-
going are inconclusive; that is, the several channels of influence impinge on the leaders in much the same way as they do
upon the non-leaders. Contrary to our expectations, however,
the public affairs leaders do not behave like the fashion leaders
either. If anything, these leaders are more likely than non-
leaders to report personal influence as the more significant
component of their recent opinion changes. In other words,
although each of the leader types is more exposed to the media
than non-leaders—and, presumably, therefore more likely to
incorporate media content into the influences they pass on—
nevertheless when it comes to crediting the media with impact
on personal decisions, only the fashion leaders significantly exceed the non-leaders in this.

It is interesting to ask why the public affairs leader, whom
we expected to make more use of her greater media exposure
in her personal decisions, tends to rely less, not more, on the

---

10. This table is based only on those who reported a recent fashion change
(in clothes, hairdo, makeup, etc.). The base figures under each column represent the total number of *influences* mentioned by each group in connection
with their fashion decisions.
11. Controlling level of interest—that is, comparing equally interested
leaders and non-leaders on each level of education—the differences still persist as markedly as when education alone is controlled.

media than non-leaders. It may be, perhaps, that our sample contains a disproportionately large number of "local" rather than "cosmopolitan" leaders, and that the latter—if our data permitted us to examine them separately—would in fact show greater media impact in their decisions. Or, it may be that the effect of the media in public affairs would be more clearly visible if we traced the networks of interpersonal influence further back; in other words, we might find that the next step —that is, the opinion leaders of the opinion leaders—are the ones who form opinions in more direct response to the media. Or, it might be that we would have to go back several steps before we found the link between the interpersonal networks of public affairs opinion and disproportionate mass media effect. Compared with the realm of fashions at any rate, one is led to suspect that the chain of interpersonal influence is longer in the realm of public affairs and that "inside dope" as well as influencing in specific influence episodes is much more a person-to-person affair. In any event, the different combinations of media and personal influence which go into the several opinion leader roles we have examined, seem to corroborate much that, to date, has been merely speculative as well as pointing to new lines of research on the flow of influence.

There is one final point that deserves mention. We have just learned that movie leaders are not necessarily more likely than non-leaders to attribute influentiality to the mass media; in fact, we did not expect them to. But we have been limiting our discussion in moves, as in the other realms, to "decisions" —in this case, decisions concerning which movie to see. We have been asking, in other words, where leaders and non-leaders in this realm get their ideas about what movies to see but we have not yet asked, apart from such decisions, what people get from the movies themselves. This, of course, is a full-scale investigation in its own right but we should like to introduce only one set of findings from our data which is relevant to the concern of this chapter: Movie leaders say that movies are helpful in their daily lives. Stated otherwise, movie leaders "get more out" of the movies than non-leaders.

For example, we asked, "Have you ever happened to get any

ideas about what clothes to wear or how to fix your hair from the movies you see?" Leaders, both young and old and with high and low education, answered affirmatively more than matched groups of non-leaders. Similarly, we asked, "Do the movies help you to deal better with the problems in your own everyday life?" and again the leaders answered "yes" more often than non-leaders. And the same pattern reveals itself in answer to, "Do you think the movies make you more contented or less contented with your own life?"

In sum, there is need to inquire not only into the media exposure patterns of opinion leaders and the extent to which their own opinions and decisions are shaped by the media, but also into the different kinds of "uses" to which the media are put by leaders in each realm, as compared with non-leaders.[12]

12. For another example of the "uses" approach, though not a comparison of leaders and non-leaders, see the Addendum to Appendix D, "On Gregariousness, Anxiety, and an Index of Popular Fiction."

CHAPTER **XV**

# A Summary of Influences
# and Influentials

EXCEPT IN THE PREVIOUS CHAPTER, where we were interested in the relationship between opinion leaders and the mass media, we have been concerned almost exclusively with the flow of influence from person to person. We have brought up again and again two basic sorts of questions:

First of all we have been asking, "What are the social characteristics of opinion leaders in each influence arena?" To answer this question we have introduced measures of life-cycle types, of social status and of gregariousness in terms of which we have attempted to describe the "typical" leader in marketing, fashions, public affairs and movie-going. More accurately, we have been trying to locate *concentrations* of leaders—trying, that is, to find out which groups in the population harbor disproportionately large numbers of certain types of opinion leaders.

As part of this effort we have been investigating the extent to which *subjective interest* in a given subject area is sufficiently important to be a "determinant" of opinion leadership. We dwelt on this problem particularly in the realms of fashions and public affairs. Whenever we found that concentrations of opinion leaders emerged from the same social settings as did concentrations of interest, we asked whether a woman's personal interest was enough to make her an opinion leader or—despite her interest—whether such factors as her social status, or life-cycle position or gregariousness persisted nevertheless as determinants of opinion leadership.

And secondly we have been asking about the *flow of in-*

*fluence*—that is, about the ways in which advice-seekers are related to their opinion leaders. We have proposed two ways of looking at this—and pointed out the inadequacies of each. In the realm of fashions, first of all, we introduced the notion of an "export" index to measure, inferentially, the extent to which opinion leaders serve their own groups compared with the extent to which they influence members of other social groupings. Our second and more direct approach consisted of a tentative analysis, in each area, of influential-influencee pairs in terms of the age and the social status of each, in order to gain some insight into the "direction" which different kinds of influences take in their paths through these two societal hierarchies. Similarly, we have indicated influential-influencee pairs where both members are part of the same family, and where they are not. And, finally, in the sphere of public affairs, we extended our study from the isolated influential-influencee dyad to a three-link chain of influence in which we included the respondents of our original sample, their influentials, their influentials' influentials and their influentials' influentials' influentials. And with all that, we have hardly begun.

In this chapter, we shall summarize our findings with respect to these questions and, in addition, we shall raise—and attempt to answer—one further question which has not yet been touched on at all. That is the question of whether a leader who is influential in one arena is also likely to turn up as a leader in a second arena. In other words, to what extent is there overlapping opinion leadership in these four subject areas?

## *The Social Location of Opinion Leader Concentrations*

From the outset, we assumed that social status, life-cycle and a measure of gregariousness might be meaningfully related to opinion leadership. Each provides categories in terms of which opinion leaders can be located and labeled. Our aim in this was not so much to say, for example, that opinion leaders in the realm of fashion are girls, but that among the girls, there is a concentration of opinion leadership. The former statement tends to be ambiguous—it might mean that most girls are fashion leaders, or that most fashion leaders are girls, or that girls are fashion leaders for all other women. While each of these possibilities may be empirically true, nevertheless, given our data and their limitations, the careful and correct statement is the second one: In the life-cycle position called "girls" (unmarried women under 35 years of age), there is to be found a greater concentration of opinion leaders than among women of any other life-cycle type.

Now what we found, of course, is that different kinds of leaders tend to congregate in differing proportions in each phase of the life-cycle, on each step of the social status ladder and among groups with varying degrees of gregariousness. In other words, different arenas of influence call different assortments of these three factors into play. Fashion leadership, for example, is strongly related to life-cycle type and gregariousness and somewhat less to social status, while leadership in public affairs is related primarily to social status and to gregariousness but to a much lesser extent to the life-cycle, and so on. In the following paragraphs, we shall review the relative importance of each of these three factors for the four subject areas of influence transmission.

To do this, we need some measure which will indicate which of the factors is relevant for which areas and how important each is relative to the others. That is to say, we must devise some measure which will tell us how much it matters for a woman's chance at leadership in one of the arenas to have one or another status position, one or another life-cycle type, and one or another degree of gregariousness. Also, we want to know the extent to which each of the three factors is important for all four arenas of influence. The measure which we shall use, and refer to as the "index of importance" meets these conditions.[1]

The following table presents our findings. Reading *across* the rows, the table reports on the relative importance of each of the three factors for each of the four arenas. It indicates,

---

1. This measure was devised by Prof. F. Mosteller of the Department of Social Relations, Harvard University, and a mathematical account of its workings can be found in Appendix D.

for example, whether life-cycle is a more important determinant of fashion leadership than of marketing leadership. Reading *down* the columns, the table permits a comparison, for each arena, of the relative importance of each of the three factors. It shows, for instance, whether gregariousness or social status is the more important factor for fashion leadership.

**Table 59—The "Index of Importance" of Life-Cycle Type, Status and Gregariousness for Various Areas of Opinion Leadership**

|  | Marketing | Fashion | Public Affairs | Movie-Going |
|---|---|---|---|---|
| Life-Cycle | .203 | .267 | .089 | .326 |
| Gregariousness | .176 | .126 | .184 | .080 |
| Social Status | .055 | .113 | .161 | .040 |

NOTE: An index value of 0 would indicate that a given factor (e.g. life-cycle) is totally irrelevant for opinion leadership in a given area; an index value of 1 would indicate that opinion leadership in the area is completely accounted for by the given factor. Index values should be treated comparatively, however, rather than absolutely. For details, see Appendix D.

For three of the four topical areas, life-cycle is the most important key to opinion leadership. For movie-going, it is the only relevant factor. For public affairs, it is least important, but even there it is not irrelevant.

Gregariousness, somewhat less than life-cycle, is important to three of the areas. It is the most significant factor in public affairs leadership, quite important for marketing, and considerably less important than life-cycle position for fashion leadership.[2] Only for movies, because movie-going itself is an odd sort of gregarious activity (though outside the province of our gregariousness index) does our measure of the extent of friendships and social contacts prove nearly inapplicable.

Status, clearly, is the least important of the three factors—and that is a finding of major interest. In marketing and movie-going, its role is negligible; in fashion, it is somewhat more important but relative to the other factors, its over-all effects are small. Only in public affairs is status a major key to the concentration of opinion leadership.

That underlines an hypothesis with which we began.[3] Our expectation was that any group which participates in a given

---

2. The lower level of importance of gregariousness for fashions is in part due to the fact that the girls, who are likely to be the fashion leaders, are also likely to be moderately, but not highly, gregarious.

3. Above, p. 222.

area can also be expected to produce opinion leaders who exert influence over others in matters related to that area. Popular imagery has equated opinion leadership with high status, assuming that the process of influence is a *vertical* process exclusively, moving downward from high status or high prestige levels. Now, confronted with an actual study of everyday influence, it is evident that that image of the flow of influence is not the whole story. Any image of the process of interpersonal influence must now be revised to include *horizontal* opinion leadership, that is, leadership which emerges on each rung of the socio-economic ladder, and all through the community. The picture that emerges from our study, to this point, is one of concentrations of opinion leaders who can be located in varying densities in each of the different life-cycle types, in almost equal densities on every status level, and generally among the more gregarious people in those groups.

The variations within this pattern require much more study (as we have indicated throughout) but the picture, basically, is quite clear. For as Table 59 shows, with the exception of the arena of public affairs, higher status does not automatically confer a greater proportion of opinion leadership in the kind of face-to-face influence situations with which we are concerned. The "power" of the opinion leader in marketing, fashions and movie-going which finds expression in informal persuasion and friendly influence, probably does not derive from wealth or high position but from casual, everyday contact with peers.

## Subjective Interest as a Leadership Determinant

The kind of influentiality which we have been discussing probably does not require any outstanding ability or any great leadership talent. As a matter of fact, it is reasonable to suspect that a person who becomes sufficiently interested in any one of these areas and/or an active participant in it will be turned to for advice by others. This would suggest that interest in a given arena might be enough to make for opinion leadership. At several points in the course of analyzing our findings, this hypothesis seemed to gain strength. Both in the arenas of fashions and of public affairs, it will be recalled, we found that leaders were, in fact, more interested than non-leaders,[4] and furthermore, that greater concentrations of leaders appeared at almost exactly the same points where we found concentrations of high interest. Thus, for example, when we found that fashion leaders congregated among the girls we found also that the girls were most interested; when we found that the incidence of public affairs leadership was high among upper status people, we also found that upper status people were better informed about public affairs; and so on. In each of these cases, we asked ourselves this question: Might it be that the leaders are simply the more interested people and that these other factors—life-cycle and the like—are related to leadership only because they are also related to interest?

Consistently we found that that was not the case. By "controlling" interest—that is, by comparing people of different status levels, or different life-cycle types or different degrees of gregariousness *but equal amounts of interest*—we were able to show that "objective" determinants did not disappear when the "subjective" factor of interest was considered. Thus, when girls, say, who had high fashion interest were compared with women of equal fashion interest but different life-cycle type, the girls still produced a considerably higher proportion of opinion leadership than the others. This means that a woman's objective position—in the life-cycle, or on the status ladder, or with reference to quantity of social contacts—has a lot to do with whether or not she will be an opinion leader—even when she has a high level of interest.

It does not mean that opinion leadership is unrelated to interest; as a matter of fact, the two are very strongly related, although not in the specific sense that interest directly *bestows* opinion leadership. The relationship is much more complicated. First of all, we must repeat, there is a greater interest among leaders than among non-leaders. But, secondly—and this is the important part—it appears that this greater interest results in leadership primarily when one associates with others who also are interested.

---

4. In public affairs, we used "information" as a measure of interest.

For example, in our discussion of fashions we suggested that the reason highly interested girls were so much more likely to be fashion leaders than matrons who were just as interested, is that the girls are much more likely to meet people who want advice than the matrons. We suggested that the matron's predisposition to leadership—by virtue of her high interest—was not activated, because there were so few other matrons who sought her advice. This, of course, implies two things: First, that matrons associate with other matrons (and girls with other girls), and secondly, that influence exchanges in the arena of fashions takes place among life-cycle peers. Our flow-of-influence data seem to corroborate these assumptions: people tend to be influenced concerning fashions by people very much like themselves.

Leadership, then, is not simply a matter of being more interested than others; it is a matter of being interested when others are interested, too. Thus, the higher rate of fashion interest among the girls surely gives rise to opinion leadership, and opinion leaders, in turn, will then be somewhat more interested, and possibly more "qualified" in some other way as well, than those whom they influence. In sum, it seems reasonable to infer that the flow of influence is not so much directed from highly interested people to people who are not interested at all, but from interested people to people of equal, or perhaps very slightly lower, interest.[5] Shared interest, in short, appears to be a channel through which communications flow.[6]

## *The Flow of Influence: A Review*

We investigated the flow of influence—the second problem

5. This is a basic point for future research on opinion leadership. It cautions against making the tacit assumption that leaders who are "cosmopolitan," or "highly interested," or "very gregarious," etc. are going to be influential for others who are very much less cosmopolitan, much less interested, or much less gregarious than themselves. At least in the everyday kinds of influence with which we are concerned, it is much more warranted to assume that opinion leaders influence women of their own groups—women who are very much like themselves. Thus, it is important, first, to locate the kinds of groups in which influence transactions take place, and, secondly, to determine in what ways opinion leaders differ from the close associates whom they influence.

6. This idea is considered above, in Part I, Chapter 6, where reference is made to Allport and Postman (1947), to Festinger, Schachter and Back (1950) etc.

to which we gave systematic attention—in two separate ways. One way was by means of an "export" index which we constructed as follows: Let us assume, we said, that women tend to be in contact most of all with life-cycle and social status peers. Let us assume, too, that each life-cycle and status group has first call on its own opinion leaders—that is, girls influence other girls "before" they turn to older women. Proceeding with these assumptions in mind, we entered the arena of fashion, computed the ratio of fashion leadership to fashion interest for the sample as a whole, and proposed this as the "average" ratio of leadership-to-interest.

Against this "average" ratio, we matched the leadership-to-interest ratio of each life-cycle and social status group, suggesting that the extent to which the ratio for any group deviated from the "average" ratio would reflect the extent to which the proportion of leaders exceeded or fell short of the amount of interest present in that particular group. Where we found that leadership exceeded the interest level of the group we interpreted this to mean that the leadership demands of the group had been fulfilled and that the "excess" of leadership was "exported" to other, less self-sufficient, groups. Our formula, in short, is that opinion leadership is made up of internal demand (measured by the saliency of a group's interest in a given subject) plus external demand (reflecting the group's attractiveness to other groups as a source of influence).

Our findings in the realm of fashions indicate that among the several life-cycle types the girls do most "exporting," while the large family wives have less than enough leadership to satisfy even their internal level of interest. Among social status groups, there was almost no "exporting" at all, though if any one group may be said to exceed the others it is the middle status group; neither high nor low status groups have more leaders than the prevailing amount of interest would seem to demand.

But our primary emphasis in studying the flow of influence was the problem of who influences whom—where "who" and "whom" were specific individuals with attributes of age, sex, social status, and specifiable relations—family, friends, co-workers—to each other. We warned repeatedly that for a variety of reasons these findings must be treated as suggestive rather than conclusive. In the following paragraphs we shall summarize the modest conclusions that seem warranted from our very cautious, but adventuresome, excursion into "survey sociometry."

Let us consider first the flow of influence among age groups, distinguishing—as we have done above—between influence exchanges transacted by two members of the same family, and extra-family influence transactions. Within the family, the first thing to note is the age disparity between influential and influencee. Compared with extra-family influence pairs who are much more likely to be age peers, intra-family influencing tends to take place between members of different ages. This is to be expected, of course: the immediate family, at any rate, is made up of individuals of different ages. In the realm of fashions, intra-family influence flows somewhat more from young to old than from old to young; in public affairs, of course, it is the reverse and even more sharply so. In public affairs, moreover, it was clearly a case of men influencing their women. In marketing, we distinguished two types of intra-family influence-flow. As far as general marketing matters are concerned, that is, when a whole range of household products are inquired about, we find that intra-family influencing tends to go on between kinfolk who are age peers, more or less, but who are not members of the same household. However, when products such as coffee and cereal, which are culturally certified to the domain of particular household members, are inquired about, it appears that husbands and children exert a substantial share of influence. In the realm of movie-going, if our interpretation is correct, intra-family influencing tends to take place between age-peers (largely between husband and wife we expect) since the young people tend to look outside the family for their movie companions and for their movie advice. When an "expert" is sought out, however, everybody turns to the girls—and presumably this happens both within the family as well as outside.

As far as the flow of influence between age groups outside the family is concerned, the following would seem to be the case: In marketing, there is most crossing of age lines and in fashions there is quite a bit. But where in marketing, there is a discernible flow from older to younger women, in fashions it is difficult to find any pattern (though a flow from young to old is implicit in the "export" data and is evident, too, *within* the family). In the arenas of public affairs and movie-going, there is evidence of much greater age homogeneity between influential and influencee. The flow across age lines is from old to young in public affairs while in movie-going, as we have noted, there is only weak evidence of upward flow when specific movie decisions are investigated, but this becomes very evident in the flow of "expert" movie advice.

Turning now to the flow of influence between status groups, we shall consider only extra-family influencing since influentials and influencees of the same family are so likely to share the same social status. While influence transactions in marketing revealed least age homogeneity, they reveal more status homogeneity than do the other three arenas. Almost 7 out of every 10 influence incidents which were followed-up revealed a marketing pair of the same social status. This was somewhat less the case in the fashion realm where 6 out of every 10 shared the same social status and much less so in the arena of public affairs (where only 46% of the extra-family influence pairs were peers). When influence did cross status lines, we could find no discernible direction in marketing—that is, it did not seem that there was any more advice-giving coming down the status ladder than going up. In the arena of fashions, we found evidence of a slight downward flow, predominantly from women of middle status to women of lower status. In the realm of public affairs (though extra-family influencing in specific incidents is least important in this realm), we found a more marked downward flow. And when public affairs "experts" were sought out (these were more likely to be outside the family), they were even more frequently of higher status than the specific influentials; what's more, each "expert" group tended to name new "experts" of still higher status.

## Opinion Leader Profiles

Combined with our data on the concentration of opinion leaders, these flow data suggest the following:

*The marketing leaders* are married women with comparatively large families. They tend to be high on the gregariousness scale, but they do not congregate on any particular social status level, being spread fairly evenly through all status levels. The flow of influence in this arena tends—as it does in every arena—to remain within the boundaries of each status level, but when it does cross status lines, there is no indication that the direction of flow is any more from high to low than it is from low to high. As far as the flow between age levels is concerned, the evidence indicates that, at least among adults, older people influence their juniors more often than the young influence them. Only in the case of very specific products which fall within the domain of husband or child is immediate-family influencing prominent at all.

*Fashion leaders* are concentrated among young women, and among young women of high gregariousness. Status level plays some part, too, in giving women a head start for leadership in this arena, but it is not a major factor. There is some indication that fashion influence travels down the status ladder to a modest extent and there is very slight evidence for an upward flow between age groups. The overall picture in the case of fashion is of women influencing other women very much like themselves, with particularly heavy traffic within the group of younger, gregarious women who do not belong to the lowest status level. Whereas, judging from our data, marketing influences pass between family members only on very specific matters, intra-family fashion influences seem to be more usual; but male influentials are virtually absent from both arenas.

The one arena where status level assumes considerable importance is that of *public affairs,* where high status women are much more likely to be influential than women of other statuses. Furthermore, there is evidence implying that the flow of influence in this arena crosses status boundaries, travelling from upper status people to people beneath them in status. Similarly, there is an equally strong indication that when influence crosses age lines, older people influence people younger than themselves—despite the fact that there is a slightly higher proportion of public affairs leadership among younger women. As in the other areas, gregariousness plays a role in public affairs leadership, too. Most marked in this sphere is the dominant role of husbands and of male parents.

In the arena of *movie-going*, the concentration of leadership is among the girls, just as it is in the case of fashion. The flow data indicate that this influence has a decided tendency to move from younger women who are "experts" to older ones. The inherently social character of movie-going makes our gregariousness index inapplicable to this arena; and social status, too, plays no role at all.

## Multiple-Area Leadership

To this point we have been speaking of marketing leaders, fashion leaders, and so on, but before we conclude this section we will want to ask a broader question: Is there a *general leader* type? That is, does a woman's inclination to leadership stem from some constellation of personality or social characteristics such that she has a relatively high potential for leadership in any area of life? In short, when we speak about leaders in various areas, are we speaking about the same people all the time?

In exaggerated form, the assumptions which underlie the hypothesis of a general leader type are the following: 1) Certain traits or attributes are generally required for leadership. 2) In any group and in any situation, those people who embody these leadership traits to the greatest extent will emerge as leaders. If these assumptions are valid, then the following should be true: Those people who are found to be leaders in any one area should be more likely than others to be leaders in other areas, because being leaders in any one area means that they should have, in significant measure, those traits or characteristics required for leadership in other areas. We are not at all convinced of this, but let us see. The following table contains the proportions of women who are leaders in three areas, in various paired combinations, in only one area, and in none.[7]

---

7. We shall deal only with marketing, fashion and public affairs; leadership in movie-going, as we have reported above, involves a special subsample so that the difficulties of including it in the following discussion are greater than the benefits to be gained.

**Table 60—Distribution in the Total Sample of Multiple, Single and Non-Leaders**

| Leadership In | Per Cent | |
|---|---|---|
| **Three Areas** | | 3.1% |
| **Two Areas** | | |
| Fashion and Marketing | 5.1 | |
| Fashion and Public Affairs | 2.4 | |
| Marketing and Public Affairs | 2.8 | |
| | | 10.3 |
| **One Area** | | |
| Fashion | 12.0 | |
| Marketing | 12.4 | |
| Public Affairs | 3.0 | |
| | | 27.4 |
| **Non-Leaders** | | 59.2 |
| (Total (= 100%) | | (704) |

In all, 41 per cent of the women in our sample are opinion leaders in at least one arena; of these, almost two-thirds are leaders in only one area, one-fourth are leaders in two areas, and less than one-tenth lead opinion in all three areas. In these gross terms, it would seem that overlapping opinion leadership is infrequent. But the inference that leadership in these areas is mutually independent cannot be made without reference to some norm. In other words, although the frequency of over-lapping leadership appears small, it may nevertheless be statistically significant.

Using a simple statistical procedure, we can test the extent to which overlapping leadership in our sample is greater than the overlap we would expect as a result of chance.[8] In the following table, we shall compute the hypothetical frequency of overlap we should expect to result from chance and along-side it we shall compare the actual overlap in leadership as it exists in each of the three pairs of activities, as well as the over-

---

8. The chance probability of the joint occurrence of two events is the product of the probability of their separate occurrences, so by multiplying the proportion of leaders in two or more areas we will be able to say what degree of overlapping leadership would be produced by chance alone. For example, if 10 per cent of all women are leaders in one area, and 20 per cent are leaders in another, and if leadership in these two areas is mutually independent—that is, if chance alone produced whatever overlap is observed —then the proportion of all women who are leaders in both areas should be 2 per cent (.10 times .20).

lap for all three activities. If the actual frequencies are significantly greater than the hypothetical ones, then we will be correct in concluding that there seems to be a generalized leadership factor at work; if they are not significantly greater, we can assume that chance alone is operative and thus, that the evidence will not support the hypothesis that a leader in one area is more likely to emerge as a leader in another area as well.

**Table 61—Comparison of Frequencies of Overlap in Leadership With Hypothetical Frequencies to Be Expected from Chance Alone**

|  | Actual | Hypothetical |
|---|---|---|
| Leaders in Three Areas | 3.1% | .6% |
| Fashion and Marketing | 5.1 | 5.3 |
| Fashion and Public Affairs | 2.4 | 2.6 |
| Marketing and Public Affairs | 2.8 | 2.7 |
| Total (= 100%) | (704) | (704) |

In all cases of leadership in two areas there is no significant difference between the observed and hypothetical proportions. The fact that a woman is a leader in one area has no bearing on the likelihood that she will be a leader in another. Only for those women who are leaders in three areas does the picture change. The observed proportion of such leaders is 5 times greater than one would expect by chance alone. Thus, only among leaders in three areas is there any possibility of finding confirmation in our data for the hypothesis of a generalized leadership type. But the leaders in three areas are so very few that we cannot base any real conclusions on this result, for there is always the possibility that there is something of a generalized factor of exaggeration rather than a generalized leadership factor in operation here. Whether these 3 per cent are general leaders, in fact, or are among the relatively small proportion of spuriously self-designated leaders cannot be ascertained from our data. By and large, however, the hypothesis of a generalized leader receives little support in this study. There is no overlap in any of the pairs of activities. Each arena, it seems, has a corps of leaders of its own.

APPENDIX A

# Choice

# of the City

THE APPROXIMATE SIZE of the city in which to locate the study was determined by the number of interviews financially feasible. That is, it was desired to maintain a ratio of not less than one interview to every twenty homes, and with a sample of 800 this ratio indicated that a city of around 60,000 population should be used. It was further decided that the city should be located in the Middle West because that part of the country is least characterized by sectional pecularities. The problem then is to select the most "typical" town (or the few most typical towns) from cities in the Middle West with a population of around 60,000. We shall first describe the procedure used in studying the cities and we shall then evaluate the results.

## 1. Procedure Used in Selecting Cities

1. We first listed all the cities in seven Middle Western states (Ohio, Michigan, Indiana, Illinois, Wisconsin, Iowa, Kansas) with a population from 50,000-80,000. We included all those towns which covered this population range either within the city limits or in their metropolitan areas. In all, this gave us twenty-eight cities.

2. From this group we eliminated all the suburban or near-suburban towns, i.e., all those dominated by a large city.

3. We were then left with eighteen cities, which constituted the group for final study. For each of them, we collected data on some thirty-six social indices selected because of their relevance to the problem under study. The broad clusters of social characteristics included in the analysis and the specific indices used are listed below, together with their sources:

## COMPOSITION OF THE POPULATION

Sex: Percentage of females, of the total population (1940 census).
Age: Percentage of persons over 21, of the total population (1940 census).
Nativity: Percentage of native-born whites, of the total population (1940 census).

## ECONOMIC STATUS

Standard of Living: Per capita index derived from three factors—ownership of cars and of telephones and income tax returns (*Urban Markets and Retail Sales*, 1938).
Buying Income: Per capita income as a ratio of the national figure (*Sales Management*, May 1943).
Retail Sales: Estimated percentage of national retail sales for 1942 (*Sales Management*, May 1943).
Occupation: Percentage of the population, 14 and over, employed in professional, semi-professional, and proprietary occupations (1940 census).

## COMMERCIAL STRUCTURE

Manufacturing Establishments: Number of establishments, per thousand population, reporting products valued at $5,000 or more (1939 census of manufacturers).
Retail Establishments: Number of establishments, per thousand population, engaged in selling merchandise for personal or household consumption or utilization and rendering service incidental to the sale of goods (1939 census of manufacturers).
Service Establishments: Number of establishments, per thousand population, whose primary activity is selling services (1939 census of manufacturers).

## COMMUNICATIONS BEHAVIOR

Magazine Reading: Circulation of each of the following magazines, and the average of all, per thousand population: *True Story, True Romance, Photoplay, Life, Liberty, Collier's, Saturday Evening Post, Ladies' Home Journal, Woman's Home Companion, Good Housekeeping, McCall's* (private sources).
Radio Homes: Percentage of dwelling units with a radio of all occupied dwelling units (1940 census).
Education: Percentage of the population, 25 years and over, with some high school education or more (1940 census).

## GENERAL QUALITY (MISCELLANEOUS)

G-Score: General "goodness" index, a composite score derived from a total of 37 items (E. L. Thorndike, *Your City*, 1939).
Stability: Percentage of owner-occupied dwellings of all occupied dwelling units (1940 census).

Political Participation: Percentage of political registration in 1942 of population 21 and over (1940 census).

4. For each of these indices an average was computed for the eighteen towns as a group. This average for each index was then taken as 100 and the ranking of each of the eighteen cities was computed on that basis. This allows us to measure not only the deviation of the town from the average for the total group, but also the direction of the deviation for each of our social characteristics. The indices were figured on the basis of the "upper" level for each characteristic; for example, a score of 110 for education means that the town is *over* the average in amount of formal schooling, and a score of 90 means that the town is *under* the average.

5. Averages were then figured for each *cluster* of characteristics in order to gauge the representativeness of the towns in each broad group of social indices. For example, a town might fall below the average in economic status but rank above it in communication behavior. No weighting was used in computing this average; it represents simply the mean of the indices within the group.

6. Finally, a grand average of all the indices was computed on the basis of the averages for the different clusters of characteristics. This grand average is the distilled, overall score of representativeness for these towns. Again we assumed equal importance for each cluster of characteristics; we did not weight any of them above any other.

7. In order to secure information on an important criterion of the towns—the diversity or concentration of the residents in various occupation groupings—we computed another set of statistical data. This set was not summated with the other data because it was not completely parallel. We first computed, for each town, the percentages which each of the following occupational groupings is of the total labor force:

> Extractive and Construction
> Manufacturing
> Transportation, Communication, and other Public Utilities
> Wholesale Trade
> Retail Trade
> Business, Personal, and Domestic Service
> Professional and related services
> Government Service

We then computed the average of each occupational grouping for the eighteen towns as a group, and with this average as 100, figured the indices for each town separately for each occupational grouping. This gave us the amount and the direction of the deviation for each town on each set of occupations. The simple averaging of these index figures would not be appropriate because a town high in one occupation and low in another might average 100 although actually it does not have a diversified occupational distribution. Instead, we must add up the total *deviations* of each town regardless of the direction of the deviation. Thus, a town which scored 76 in, say, manufacturing would receive the same amount of deviation as a town which scored 124. After these deviations were summated for each town, we again constructed an index based upon 100 for the average deviation for the eighteen towns as a group. But this index of deviations should not be read in the same way as the previous indices used in the study. In this case, a score of 100 still represents the average amount of diversity-versus-concentration for these towns. However, a lower score here represents a town with greater diversity in its occupational distribution. The lower the score, the more diversified the occupational structure of the town; the higher the score the greater the concentration of the occupational structure.

8. In addition to all this statistical material, we collected brief descriptions of the towns as well as summary classifications of type of town. This last classification is the result of an elaborate statistical analysis of American towns done by another research office. On the basis of their analysis, they have classified towns into these categories: institutional, marketing, industrial, and balanced. Fortunately, we were able to gain access to these important classifications.

## 2. Evaluation of the Results

On the basis of all this material, then, what town (or towns) is most representative? The best way to get the answer to this question is to proceed by *eliminating* towns instead of selecting them. The following eliminations are indicated:

1. *The four Iowa towns* (Cedar Rapids, Waterloo, Sioux City, Davenport): Although these towns have good economic and educational ratings, they are all unsatisfactorily low in magazine reading. In addition, Cedar Rapids and Sioux City are rated as marketing towns for the surrounding rural area.

2. *The state capitols* (Topeka, Lansing, Madison, Springfield, Ill.): The first three of these rank too high in education and general "goodness" and they score too high in magazine reading. Because they contain the bureaucracy of the state governments, all four rank as institutional towns. (In addition, Madison and Lansing contain state institutions of higher learning.) Spring-

field (Ill.) is the least undesirable of these towns, but in addition to the peculiarities attaching to a state capitol it also has a somewhat larger population than we wanted.
3. *"The low towns"* (Hamilton, Bay City, Kenosha, Racine): These four towns rank too low in economic status, in education, and in magazine reading.
4. *Kalamazoo:* This town ranks too high in most characteristics, especially in general "goodness" and in magazine reading.
5. *Pontiac:* Although this town ranks very close to the average on many social characteristics, it is too heavily industrialized and is a one-industry town (automobiles). In addition, it tends to be dominated by Detroit which is only 25 miles away.
6. *Muncie:* Although this town also ranks very close to the average, it is also a one-industry town and, furthermore, it was decided that we ought not to select "Middletown" for this study.

This left us with three towns for final consideration: Decatur, Illinois; Terre Haute, Indiana; Springfield, Ohio. Here is the way their characteristics are revealed in our indices.

| | Economic Status Ave. | Magazine Reading Ave. | Education | Communication Behavior Ave. | G-Score | Grand Average | Occupational Diversity (low score best) | Type of Town |
|---|---|---|---|---|---|---|---|---|
| Decatur, Ill. | 94 | 99 | 102 | 103 | 92 | 99 | 39 | Institutional |
| Terre Haute, Ind. | 106 | 102 | 118 | 97 | 96 | 102 | 91 | Balanced |
| Springfield, Ohio | 88 | 92 | 105 | 95 | 95 | 97 | 71 | Industrial |

We chose Decatur.

## 3. Selection of Sample

Within Decatur, the sample to be interviewed was drawn according to usual probability methods and nothing special need be said about it. Within each household, women residents (not domestic help) age 16 and over were interviewed alternating on successive interviews between older and younger women whenever more than two women occupied the same household.

# A Guide
# to the Questionnaire

THE QUESTIONNAIRE CONSISTED of two basic parts: Wave I administered in June, 1945; Wave II administered in August, 1945. In both cases, the respondents were the same (minus the "mortality" common to such "panel studies"). In addition, there were a variety of special follow-up questionnaires for the purpose of interviewing the several types of influentials and influencees designated by our panel respondents. Rather than merely reproduce the questionnaire here, it would seem most useful to classify the different questions so that the reader can clearly relate them to the different parts of the main body of the text. This classification, in addition, will include some of the additional parts of the questionnaire which were not utilized for the present report; as was mentioned in the Introduction, the scope of the Decatur Study went well beyond the specific groups of data which were selected for inclusion in the text.[1] Bearing in mind that the special follow-up questions and procedure will be discussed in Appendix C, the following grouping exhausts the total content of the basic (panel) questionnaire schedules addressed to the cross-sectional sample of women in Decatur, Illinois:[2]

1. Questions intended to ascertain whether certain decisions took place.

2. Questions intended to trace the role of certain influences in these decisions.

3. More general questions as to the people the respondent considers as potential influentials or experts.

---

1. Tabulations for many of these unreported items are on file at the Bureau of Applied Social Research, Columbia University. The complete text of the questionnaire is available, too, at the Bureau.

2. We shall employ roman numerals I and II to refer to the first (June) and second (August) waves of the questionnaire. Thus, I,8,9 means Wave I, questions 8 and 9.

4. Questions regarding reading and listening habits.

5. Questions intended to assess the respondent's own opinion-leadership position.

6. Questions intended to clarify the respondent's place in terms of the main indicators used, to wit, social status, gregariousness and position in the life cycle.

7. Questions eliciting the respondent's general attitude toward a variety of specific substantive matters under investigation.

8. Questions which served purposes extraneous to the present study.

## 1. Factual Decision Questions

Two different types of questions were used to elicit reports concerning decisions according to whether they were asked in the first or second interview. The first time we had to rely on the respondent's retrospective report as to whether a change or a recent decision had been made. In regard to small consumer items the questions read as follows (I, 8, 9):

8. During the last month or so, have you bought any new product or brand that you don't usually buy? (I don't mean something you had to buy because it was the only one available.) Yes........ No........
   (If No, ask Question 9:)
9. On which of these have you tried a new brand most recently?
   a. breakfast cereals ............      b. soap flakes or chips  ............
   c. coffee            ............      d. None of these         ............

In regard to fashion these were the questions (I, 16, 17):

16. Have you recently changed anything about your hairdo, type of clothing, cosmetics, make-up, or made any other *change to something more fashionable?* Yes........ No........
   (If No, get any comments. If Yes, ask Question 17:)
17. What sort of change did you make?

As to movies, our starting point was to ask the respondent to tell us the name of the last movie that she saw. On public affairs topics, the situation was somewhat complicated because there was no simple way to identify what we had in mind. We therefore asked a number of typical poll questions which will be reported in a later section. After the respondent had given her opinion we then asked her whether on any of these matters she had recently changed her mind. The wording was as follows (I, 44, 45, 46):

44. Have you recently changed your opinion about any important social or political issue? . . . like what to do in Europe, how the government

should handle any problem at home, or anything like that? Yes........ No........
(If No, ask Question 45. If Yes, go to Question 46:)

45. Do you feel more strongly now about any of the political questions we just spoke of than you have in the past? Yes........ No........
(If Yes, ask Question 46:)

46. On what topic:
    From: .....................................................................................................
    To: .........................................................................................................

Whatever specific example the respondent gave was then followed up by the "reason for change" sequence which will be reviewed in the section that follows.

It is obvious, however, that respondents can not easily remember offhand what changes of opinion they undergo on matters which are often not important to them. Therefore, another technique was added in the second interview. The opinion questions of Wave I were repeated and the interviewer knew what answers the respondent had given the first time. If the answer was different the second time this was considered a change and made the object of further questioning. A similar additional technique was used in regard to the three small consumer items. In the first interview each respondent was asked what brand of breakfast cereal, soap flakes, and coffee she had on her shelves. In the second interview the identical questions were repeated. Wherever the brand on hand was now different the "reason for change" sequence (that is, the Impact Analysis questions reported just below) set in.

In the course of the present report it is always indicated which group of data were used for analysis and interpretation. As our findings are used mainly for the purpose of exemplifying the general idea of the study we have not included any special discussion as to the differences which occur when different reporting techniques are used. Some of our observations will be used in connection with a general report on panel techniques which is now under preparation.

## 2. *The Impact Analysis*

The questions in this group were amply discussed in the text (Part Two, Section II). Just for the sake of an overview we are reproducing here the whole sequence which was used for the small consumer items (II, Sheet B; I, 13, 14):

(IF SUBSTITUTION IS MADE, ASK 1:)

1. (a) When we spoke to you in June, you were using (insert old brand).

Now you are using (insert new brand). Why did you stop using (insert old brand)?

.........................................................................................

(b) How did you happen to start using (insert new brand)?

.........................................................................................

(IF ANOTHER BRAND IS ADDED, ASK 2:)

2. When we spoke to you in June, you were not using (insert new brand). How did you happen to start using (insert new brand)?

.........................................................................................

(ASK THE FOLLOWING AFTER EITHER 1 OR 2:)

3. (a) Did you buy the new brand yourself? Yes........ No........
   (If Yes, ask b:)
   (b) Did you ask especially for (insert new brand)? Yes........ No........
   (If No, ask c:)
   (c) Who did?............................................................................
   Did you tell them to get that brand? Yes........ No........
   (If No, discontinue these panel questions and go back to questionnaire.)

4. Was it the only one available? Yes........ No........ Don't know........
   (If Yes, discontinue panel questions and go back to questionnaire.)

5. Had you ever used (the new brand) before? Yes........ No........
   (If Yes, ask:) Could you tell me why it was not on your shelf in June?

.........................................................................................

6. Before you started to use (the new brand) were you satisfied or dissatisfied with any of the other brand(s) you were using? Satisfied........ Dissatisfied........

7. Before you started to use (the new brand) were other members of your family satisfied or dissatisfied with any of the other brand(s) you were using? Satisfied........ Dissatisfied........
   (If Yes) Who was dissatisfied? ..................................................

8. Before you made the change, what about (the new brand) attracted you?

.........................................................................................

9. (a) Did any other members of your family say anything good about (the new brand) before you started to use it? Yes........ No........
   (If Yes, ask b:)
   (b) Who? .........................................................................

10. How did you find out about (the new brand)?

.........................................................................................

11. Did you hear someone talk about it? Yes........ No........
    (If Yes, ask:)
    (a) Do you know them personally (1)..........., know who they are (2) .........., don't know them (3)...........?
    (If 3, go to 12. If 1 or 2, ask b, c, d, e.)
    (b) How did you happen to know them? (Get relation to respondent.)

.........................................................................................

    (c) Were they or were they not using it before you did? Were........ Were not........
    (d) Do they usually have good ideas on what to buy? Yes ....... No........
    (e) Occupation of breadwinner ................................. (f) Age...............
    (g) Who? ................................. Address ................................

12. Did you hear about it on the radio? Yes........ No........
    What program? ...............................................................

13. Did you see it in the newspaper? Yes........ No........

Which?.............................................. What?.......................................

14. Did any storekeeper happen to suggest it to you? Yes....... No.......
    (If Yes, ask:) Did he suggest only this brand or did he also suggest others?
    Suggest only this brand..................................................................
    Suggest others also:......................................................................
    What store?......................... Address...................................
    Storekeeper's name ....................................................................
15. Did someone else in the store suggest it? Yes....... No.......
    (If Yes) Do you know them personally (1)..........., Know who they are (2)..........., Don't know them (3)...........?
    (If 1 or 2)
    How did you happen to know them? (relation:)...............................
    Were they or were they not using it before you did?
    Were....... Were not.......
    Who?................................. Address...................................
16. Did you see it in a magazine? Yes....... No.......
    Who?................................. What?...................................
17. Did you see it in a movie? Yes....... No ...... Which?...............................
18. Other................................................(Specify)

13. You mentioned the various things that drew it to your attention. Will you tell me which of them brought it to your attention first...........? second...........? third...........? fourth...........?
14. Summing it up now—what do you think was most important in causing you to change brands or to buy this product?...............................

The questions in the other areas were very much the same, although at specific points additional questions were indicated. In the fashion field, for instance, we knew from pretests that a change might be preceded by considerable hesitation. Therefore the following question was added there (I, 21B):

21B. Have you considered such a change before? Yes....... No.......
     (If Yes, ask:) Why did you not change then, but only change now?
     ...............................................................................................

In the movie field certain types of discussions had to be distinguished, and therefore the following three questions were included (I, 24.2, 27; II, 3):

24.2 Do you go to the movies regularly on any particular day of the week?
     Yes ...... No.......
27. Did you go primarily just to go to a movie...........? to see a certain picture ...........? for both reasons...........
 3. The last time you saw a picture, did you go (a) primarily because somebody you went with—a friend or family member—wanted to go, or (b) primarily because you yourself wanted to?
    (a) Somebody else ...... (b) Yourself ...... (Both....... Don't know.......)
    (If "somebody else" ask:) Who (relation)?

## 3. Sources of Potential Influence

In most areas we asked people questions like the following ones (II, 13.2, 35):

13.2 Do you know anybody around here who usually knows something about the movies, and can tell what's a good picture to see? Yes........ No........
(If Yes, ask:)
(a) How do you happen to know them?
(b) Age...................... (c) Sex......................
(d) Occupation of breadwinner?.................................................................
................................................................................................
(e) Name.................................................... (f) Address................................
35. Do you know anyone around here who keeps up with the news and whom you can trust to let you know what is really going on? Yes........ No........
(If Yes, ask:)
(a) How do you happen to know them (relation)?............................
(b) Age...................... (c) Sex......................
(d) Occupation of breadwinner?.................................................................
(e) Name.................................................................................
(f) Address............................................................................................

The reader will remember from the text (Part Two, Section 1) that there is often considerable difference between the people from whom a respondent actually obtains advice in a specific episode and the people whom he feels are generally competent to give such advice. These latter are those whom we call in the text (Part Two, Sections I and III) "general influentials," "potential influentials," or "experts."

## 4. Communication Behavior

For a variety of reasons both waves of the questionnaire contained a large number of questions regarding the respondents' listening and reading habits. A good part of this material was used in other contexts.[3] A selected number of findings are reported in Part Two, Section III of the text. It doesn't seem worth-while to repeat all the questions here since many were of the conventional and well known audience survey type. A few of the questions were somewhat more specific and deserve mention for possible later reference (I, 54; II, 62, 65, 67, 68; II, 5, 6, 7):

54. Do you try to listen fairly regularly to any discussions of public issues on the air, like a forum or a debate? Yes........ No........
(If Yes) Which?.................................................................................

---

3. See, for example, Lazarsfeld (1948), Handel (1950), Lazarsfeld (1947).

62. Do you try to read fairly regularly biographies of prominent people in magazines? Yes....... No.......

65. Do you try to read fairly regularly articles in magazines which discuss news events in more detail? Yes........ No........

67. Now that the European war is over, do you listen to news more or less than you did before V-E Day? More........ Less........ About the same........

68. How about newspapers? Do you *read* more or less news since the European war is over? More........ Less........ About the same........

5. Within the last three months or so, have you seen any of these short films where they try to teach you something—documentary movies or "fact films" as they are called? Yes........ No........
   {If Yes, ask:}
   (a) What was it?.............................................................................
   (b) Where did you see it?—in a regular movie theater........, or somewhere else........?

6. Do you ever read any movie magazine? Yes........ No........
   (If Yes, ask:)
   (a) Which?.....................................................................................
   (b) Where do you get them?
   ...................................................................................................

7. Have you recently read about movies or movie stars in any other type of magazine? Yes....... No........
   (If Yes) Which?..............................................................................

## 5. Self-Designated Opinion Leadership

One of the main sections of our report makes an effort to characterize the opinion leader. As the reader knows by now, an opinion leader, for the purpose of this part of our discussion, was spotted by self-designation on the basis of two questions. The wording of these questions was practically identical for the various areas. We quote as an example the questions pertaining to movies (I, 32; II, 13.1):

32. (a) Have you recently been asked your advice about what pictures to see? Yes....... No.......
    (If No, skip to "Social Opinions." If Yes, ask rest under 32:)
    (b) Which picture? .....................................................................
    (c) By whom?.................................... Address ...........................
    (d) How do you happen to know them? (Get relation to respondent):
13.1. Have you recently been asked your advice about what picture to see? Yes....... No.......
    (If Yes, ask:)
    (a) How do you happen to know them (relation to respondent)?
    ...................................................................................................
    (b) Age.................... (c) Sex....................
    (d) Occupation of breadwinner?..............................................

It will be seen that in each of the two interviews we tried to get different information on the people who turn to our respondents

for advice. (This was the starting point for the follow-up interviews with advisees. The questions developed for this special follow-
up part of the study will be discussed in the next Appendix section.)
In addition to two concrete incidents of advice-giving we asked
the respondent to evaluate her relative influence in each of the four
areas of our investigation in more general terms (II, 15):

15. Compared with other women belonging to your circle of friends—are you
    *more or less likely* than any of them to be asked for your advice on—
    (a) what clothes or hair-do's are attractive and stylish?More........ Less........
    (b) what brands and products are good? More........ Less........
    (c) what movies are good to see? More........ Less........
    (d) what one should think about social or political opinions?
        More........ Less........

These questions were combined to form an index of opinion leadership in each arena of influence. (See, for example, footnote 1, page
234.) The reader should also remember that this set of ratings was
in a number of cases checked with the person who presumably
asked for advice (Part Two, Chapter 2).

## 6. Correlates of Opinion Leadership

A respondent's position in the life cycle was determined by her
age, her marital status and the number of children who still lived
with her. Gregariousness was derived from an analysis of the following questions (I, 62; II, 21, 57, 59, 61):[4]

62. What organizations, clubs, or discussion groups do you belong to—where
    current events are discussed, books read, or speakers heard or where
    people just get together and talk?.....................................................................
21. Please think for a moment of the people whom you see and talk with—
    your family and neighbors, relatives and friends. How many people are
    there with whom you are friendly and talk with fairly often who are—
    (a) living in your immediate household?...........
    (b) relatives and in-laws not living in your household?...........
    (c) How many of your present neighbors do you talk with fairly
        often? ...........
    (d) Ex-neighbors: people who used to be your neighbors but now liv-
        ing elsewhere?...........
    (e) People you work with whom you talk with fairly often?........
    (f) last, friends who *are not* and *never have been* your neighbors; just
        friends with whom you talk fairly often?
57. Do you like to meet new people, go to social gatherings, and generally
    get around a lot or not? Do........ Do not........

---

4. Following a "latent structure" analysis two of these questions were
selected to form an index of gregariousness. See the discussion below in Appendix D, and in Part Two, Chapter 9.

59. Do you ever attend any social affairs in the afternoon? Yes........ No........
   (If Yes) What sort?.................................................................................
61. Do you like to visit over the telephone? Yes........ No........

Similarly, we included a variety of questions on socio-economic status from which we ultimately selected two to compose our index of socio-economic status (I, 64, 65; II, 75, 76, 77):[5]

64. a. *Economic Level* (*Interviewer's Appraisal*)
       A ............
       B ............
       C ............
       D ............
    b. Do you have a telephone? Yes........ No........
65. *Education*

| | | | |
|---|---|---|---|
| No School | ............ | Some college | ............ |
| Some grade school | ............ | College grad | ............ |
| Grammar school grad | ............ | Trade school | ............ |
| Some high school | ............ | "Business" school | ............ |
| High school grad | ............ | Other (specify) | ............ |

75. How many women living in this household (over 16 years of age) are employed (a) full time................? part time................?
76. Which of these numbers is closest to your present rent? (If own home, ask: What would be your rent paid if you were renting?
   (See Rent Card. Circle the number:)
   1   2   3   4   5   6   7   8   9   10   11   12
77. Which of these numbers most nearly represents your total family income—from all sources?
   (See Income Card. Circle the number:)
   1   2   3   4   5   6   7   8   9   10   11   12

## 7. Other Attitude Questions

The following questions tapped the attitudes of our respondents which seemed relevant to the area under scrutiny. Feelings toward fashion were gauged in the following way (II, 37, 40, 41, 43):

37. Do you feel it is very important........, moderately important........, not important at all........ to be in style?
40. Do you think that women in general dress more for men or more for other women?
   More for men........ More for other women........
41. Do you feel on the whole that you are better dressed, or not so well dressed as other women in Decatur?
   ........better dressed ........dressed about the same ........not so well dressed
   ........never thought about it or don't pay attention
43. In general, do you think of yourself in appearance as more on the attractive side or more on the unattractive side? attractive........ unattractive........
   Don't know and No answer:........

---

5. See below, Appendix D, and Part Two, Chapter 9.

In regard to movies, we were interested in two points. First, what was the respondent's general motivation in attending? (II, 3, 4):

3. The last time you saw a picture, did you go (a) primarily because somebody you went with—a friend or family member—wanted to go, or (b) primarily because you yourself wanted to?
   (a) Somebody else........ (b) Yourself........ (Both........ Don't know........)
   (If "somebody else" ask:) Who (relation)?.....................................................
4. When are you most likely to go to a movie?—when you
   ........(a) feel tired or depressed?
   ........(b) just happen to have a free evening?
   ........(c) when there is a picture which especially interests you?
   ........(d) when someone else asks you to go?
   ..........(e) Other (specify) ................................................................................

Secondly, we wanted to know how the respondent assessed in a general way the impact which movies had upon her (II, 10, 11, 12):

10. Have you ever happened to get any ideas on what kind of clothes to wear or how to fix your hair from the movies you see? Yes........ No........
    (If Yes, ask:)
    (a) What idea?........................... (b) From what actress?...........................
    (c) In what movie?...........................
11. Do the movies help you to deal better with the problems in your own everyday life? Yes........ No........
    (If Yes, ask:) What sort of problems do they help you with?.....................
12. (a) Do you think the movies make you more contented or less contented with your own life?
    More contented........ Less contented........ Neither........
    (b) In what way? ................................................................................

The questions on public issues were quite numerous and some of them pertained to local issues. We are reproducing here, however, only those questions which were repeated on both waves of the interview (I, 33 through 43):

33. Should German men be required to spend two or three years helping rebuild cities in Europe, outside Germany, which they have destroyed?
    Yes........ No........ Don't know........ Haven't thought about it........
34. Do you think President Truman is handling international problems:
    Very well........ Fairly well........ Rather poorly........?
    Have to wait and see........ Haven't thought about it........ Don't know........
35. Do you think President Truman is more for labor or more for business?
    More for labor ........ More for business........ About equally........
    Haven't thought about it........ Don't know.... ....Have to wait and see........
36. Do you think it is worthwhile to continue the war with Japan until she is broken into bits, or do you think we should consider a reasonable peace offer by Japan which would end the war now?
    Continue ........ Accept offer........ Don't know........
    Haven't thought about it........

37. Do you think the way they are now releasing veterans from the army is fair?
Yes........ No........ Don't know........ Haven't thought about it........

38. Do you think the Jewish people in the United States have too much influence, not enough influence, or about the amount of influence they should have?
Too much........ Not enough........ About the amount they should have........
Haven't thought about it........ Don't know........

39. Do you worry about how the postwar situation will affect you and your family?
Great deal........ Just somewhat........ Not very much........ Not at all........?
Haven't thought about it........

40. Who do you think can do the best job straightening out here in the U.S. after the war: business leaders, the government in Washington, labor leaders, all three together?
Business leaders........ Government in Washington........ Labor leaders........
All three together........ Haven't thought about it........ Don't know........

41. (a) Do you think that today any young man with thrift, ability and ambition, has the opportunity to rise in the world, own his own home, and earn $5000 a year?
Yes........ No........ Don't know........
(b) Could he do it in Decatur? Yes........ No........ Don't know........

42. Do you think that the U.S. and Russia will be able to get along together?
Yes........ No........ Haven't thought about it........ Don't know........

43. If they (U.S. and Russia) don't get along, whose fault do you think it will be? United States........ Russia........ Other........

Because of the central role which personal contacts play in our inquiry we asked a number of general questions on this (II, 14, 16 through 21):

14. When you hear something on the radio or read something in the newspaper, are you inclined to talk it over with somebody before you make up your mind? Yes........ No........
(If Yes, ask:)
(a) Who (relation)? ............................................................
(b) Sex.............. (c) Age.............. (d) Occupation of breadwinner?
....................................................

16. When you are talking about some topic with a woman (or girl) friend of yours, of about your age, and your viewpoints are different, does it usually happen that—
........(a) you get her to accept your view,
........(b) each continues to hold their own view,
........(c) you give in even though you're not convinced,
........(d) you come around to her view?
........(e) Other (specific) ....................................................

17. What kind of issue or topic did you have in mind in answering Question 16?

18. (If married) When you are talking about some issue with your husband and your viewpoints are different, does it usually happen that—
........(a) you get him to accept your view,
........(b) each continues to hold their own view,
........(c) you give in even though you're not convinced,

........(d) you come around to his view?

........(e) Other (specific) ...................................................................................

19. What kind of issue or topic did you have in mind in answering Question 18? ...................................................................................................

20. Would you say that you met your best friend in Decatur (a) because she happened to be your neighbor, or (b) did you meet her in some other way? (a) As neighbor.... ....(b) In some other way........
(If b, ask:) How did you meet?...............................................................

21. Please think for a moment of the people whom you see and talk with— your family and neighbors, relatives and friends. How many people are there with whom you are friendly and talk with fairly often who are—
(a) living in your immediate household?........
(b) relatives and in-laws not living in your household?........
(c) How many of your present neighbors do you talk with fairly often?........
(d) Ex-neighbors: people who used to be your neighbors but now living elsewhere?........
(e) People you work with whom you talk with fairly often?........
(f) Last, friends who *are not* and *never have been* your neighbors; just friends with whom you talk fairly often?........

Finally, we had a number of questions in which we tried to characterize the respondent in somewhat more subtle psychological terms (II, 55, 56, 58, 60):[6]

55. (a) In general, do you think you worry more or less as compared with other people?
........More ........Less ........About the same
........Haven't thought about it.
(b) What are the things you worry most about?...................................
56. (a) Are you ever blue or depressed about things in your life?
Yes........ No........
(If Yes)
(b) What sort of things usually?...................................................
(c) What do you find is a good thing to do when you feel that way?
...................................................................................................
58. (a) If you could live your life all over again, would you want to live it differently? Yes........ No........
(If Yes)
(b) What things would you have different?.......................................
60. Over the last ten or fifteen years, do you feel that your family has been doing better......., about the same......., or not doing so well.......?
Why? (In what way?)...............................................................

# 8. *Extraneous Questions*

Two groups of questions were included because participants in the study wanted to use this occasion to get information on points

---

6. For a discussion of the relationship between these "mood" questions and mass media behavior, see the final section of Appendix D, below.

of special interest. Because the problem of postwar economy was very much discussed at that time, a number of questions were asked regarding the plans the respondent had for postwar purchases of durable consumer goods. The director of field work for the study was especially interested in occupational mobility. As a result, our questionnaires include about twelve items on the occupational history of the respondent's father, the respondent (or her husband), and regarding the occupational plans she had for her children.

# On Follow-up Interviewing
# and Analysis

THE PREVIOUS APPENDIX SECTION reported on the basic "panel" questionnaire which was administered to a cross-section of respondents in Decatur. In this Appendix, we should like to report on the special problems attendant on the "follow-up" aspects of the study. We shall begin by reporting on the evolution of the follow-up questionnaire. Here, in excerpts from a memorandum written by one of the overseers of field work for the study, there will become evident the sense of exploration and of overcoming of obstacles which characterize the execution of a new study design—in this case, a design which called for jumping from an influencee to her influential and vice versa.

In a second excerpt from the field memorandum, there will be indicated some of the reasons why we have chosen to report the follow-up interviews with influentials (that is, where the original respondent was the influencee) rather than the follow-up interviews with influencees. Ostensibly, it might seem that the two should be exactly comparable and that one should validate the other; but we shall see that this is not necessarily the case.

Thirdly, we shall select one arena of influence—that of fashions —and report on the "mortality" and on the "representativeness" of the follow-up interviews. That is, we shall account first for why so many designated influentials were not followed up by our field staff, and second we shall look into the extent to which the follow-ups which were actually completed are representative of the total population of opinion leaders who were so designated. However this may be, it should be remembered that we are making no claim to representativeness, as we have stated repeatedly throughout the final section of the text.

Finally we shall append a note on the analysis of a flow-of-influence table. The "who-to-whom" tables which were presented in the text were made up of raw data alone and it is worth exploring the possibilities of a more sophisticated analysis.

# 1. The Evolution of the Follow-up Questionnaire

The Questionnaire, at various points, called for the respondent to provide the names of other people as either influentials (opinion leaders) or influencees. Among the various kinds of "mentions," the following were selected for the follow-up interview—that is, it was decided to try to locate and interview these particular kinds of designatees.[1]

From the First Interview (Wave I):

*"Influentials"*—those persons whom respondents implicated in some recent decision they had made in:

Marketing (Question 12c)

Fashions (Question 20a and b)[2]

Public Affairs (Question 47a)

*"Influencees"*—those persons whom respondents indicated as recent recipients of their advice in connection with decisions in:

Marketing (Question 15)

Fashions (Question 23)

Public Affairs (Question 50)

From the Second Interview (Wave II):

*"Influentials"*—those persons whom respondents implicated in some recent decision they had made in:

Marketing (Sheet B; Question 11)

*"Influencees"*—those persons to whom respondents had recently stated their views in:

Public Affairs (Question 36)

In all of these cases a specific communication had been referred to by the original respondent;[3] that is, she had either heard some-

1. Questions representative of those used for locating follow-ups may be found in sections 2 and 5 of the preceding Appendix.
2. Fashion influentials included those people *seen* wearing or using the new style or product.
3. We also followed up "general influentials" in public affairs (Wave II, Question 35: ". . . someone who keeps up with the news and whom you can trust to let you know what's going on . . ."). We omit them here because their names were not elicited in connection with a specific decision and, consequently, the follow-up interview which is under discussion here was somewhat different; for example, names of the designating respondent were not introduced into the "general influential" interviews. Other "mentions" interviewed in follow-up interviews were the Wave I "specialists": salespersons and beauty parlor operators mentioned in marketing and fashion changes, and

one say something about the subject on which she reported a
change, or she had been asked advice (or given it unasked) in connection with some specifiable subject. These follow-ups (the persons
designated) could and were asked to confirm that the designated
communication had indeed taken place as reported by the original
respondent. Thus, initially, the purpose of the follow-up interview
was to confirm the fact that the alleged contact had taken place.

Evaluation of the earliest (pilot) results as they came into the
field office, however, and examination of the data as to uniformity
suggested that the data were inadequate for clearly defining the
relationships we were after. Instead, we found that there were two
steps to a confirmation analysis, each of which had to be considered
separately: *Step One* consists of ascertaining whether or not the
specific communication has taken place as reported by the original
respondent, and *Step Two* involves discerning whether the specific
communication has actually exerted influence and/or the nature
of the relationship—the direction of the flow of influence—between
the two people. In other words, given that the conversation had
taken place as alleged, what we wanted to know was whether the
follow-up also acknowledged having exerted (or received) the influence indicated or whether the follow-up insisted that the relationship was one of peers or the reverse, perhaps, of that indicated
by the original respondent.

We knew, of course, that these two dimensions existed, but we
did not carefully provide for them in our questionnaire. We would
like to report on the way we went about remedying this. But let
us start at the beginning, at the point where the earliest (pilot)
data convinced us that we had two separate items to confirm.

We knew, first of all, that we could not go to a designated individual, point a finger and ask, "Did you influence (or were you
influenced by) Mrs. A with regard to Z?" Follow-up respondents
could hardly be expected to define and identify a phenomenon
which we ourselves did not fully comprehend and were, as a matter
of fact, studying. Questions had to be formulated which would
select those aspects of interpersonal relationships reflecting influence and which could be phrased in the language of everyday
ideas—i.e., in terms of indices which would be familiar to our respondents. Moreover, there was the problem of tact. We had to
avoid the appearance of soliciting gossip and of suggesting that
the follow-up respondent had been domineering or submissive.

---

teachers and ministers mentioned in politics. These are omitted from discussion here because of the formal nature of their roles and because our text
does not report on these.

With these problems in mind, and contrary to the usual procedure in such studies, the questions to be asked were not frozen when the follow-up interviewing began. Instead the interviewers were instructed as to the above objectives and their ingenuity was called on. Throughout the follow-up interviewing new suggestions were turned up and there was constant consideration of what we wanted to know and what we were getting.

The questionnaire and procedure originally devised was as follows. Interviewers introduced themselves exactly as in the interview with the original respondents, without reference to the designator's name. They went through the original (panel) questionnaire first, paying particular attention to the names of persons mentioned by the follow-up respondent in the area (e.g., fashions, marketing) in which she herself had been named. In an effort to get the follow-up herself to mention the name of the person who had mentioned her, interviewers were told to ask, "Well, with whom do you usually talk about this topic?" and any other general question about conversations the follow-up had with other people.[4] Thus, in a sense, the regular questionnaire was used as a springboard to the confirmation questionnaire.

If this was not accomplished in the regular interview, the confirmation questionnaire (special questions pertaining to relationship with panel member) began with an introduction as casual as possible of the original respondent's name, to ascertain first whether the follow-up was acquainted with the woman who had designated her. (Of course this was not necessary if they were related through kinship.) The printed confirmation questionnaire provided these questions:

(If original respondent is in same family): "Do you and ............ often talk about ............ (the area: marketing, fashion or politics)?"

(If original respondent is not family, but is mentioned earlier in the interview): "You mentioned ............ Do you talk with her rather frequently about ........ (area)?"

(If original respondent is not family and is not mentioned earlier in the interview): "By the way, do you know Mrs. ............? She and I were talking the other day about ........ (area). Do you know her?" (If yes) "Do you ever talk with her about ........................ (area)?"

Then:

1. "Can you think of any recent example where you and she exchanged

---

4. The attempt was made to elicit spontaneous mention of the panel members because it was awkward for the interviewer to introduce the name; too often this aroused the suspicion of the follow-up.

views about............(topic specified by original respondent within the area—
e.g., nail polish in fashion)?"
2. (For influential follow-ups): "Did you happen to suggest that she try
............(brand) or consider ............(opinion)?"
(For influencee follow-ups): "Did she happen to suggest that you try........"
3. (For influential follow-ups): "Did she seek your advice or did you just
happen to suggest it to her?"
(For influencee follow-ups): "Did you seek her advice or did she just happen to suggest it to you?"

Thus in all cases, guided by this questionnaire, interviewers sought
to ascertain whether or not the follow-up and the original respondent had talked about the area, and about the specific topic,
whether the designated exchange had taken place, and at whose
initiative—whether volunteered or sought.

Furthermore, in line with the original quest for ascertaining the
usual relationship between these two people with regard to the
given area, interviewers were told (taken from general instructions):

"The Number One point of all follow-ups is to confirm whether the respondent is one of three things to the original interviewee:
(a) an influential or leader in the area involved
(b) more or less of a follower or influencee in the area involved
(c) whether the original respondent and the follow-up respondent are really
completely equal, i.e., "mutuals.""

The selection of indices of these roles was left, more or less, to the
interviewer's perceptions; they were to be noted and discussed
with the supervisor. With the caution that such words as influence,
advice, leader, and follower were not to be used because of their
manipulative connotations, and with some general talk about leadership traits, such as self-confidence, poise, etc., the interviews were
launched.

During the course of the interviewing many problems and suggestions came up. Recall of the specific conversation did not always
ensue; similar conversations were therefore accepted as substitutes
(e.g., discussion of lipstick instead of nailpolish).[5] Occasionally,
respondents volunteered that their role in the specific conversation
was contrary to their usual role with the designator; or they could
not recall any specific conversation but only the general tone of
their relationship. The most difficult to break was the tendency
for the follow-up respondent to assert that they just talked about
things, with no indication of the roles. Clearly we had to devise
indices of role.

The occasional inability to recall any specific conversation and

---

5. Fortunately, final tabulations reveal that this happened in only about
9 cases.

to assess roles gave rise to the suggestion that we focus first on the product or style or opinion: was the follow-up herself using the product, was she strongly attached to it, had she talked about it, had she talked with the original respondent about it, and which of them used it first. This last point especially—establishing temporal priority—is important as a logical means of discerning influence.

With regard to the influencee follow-ups, we had only little information from the original respondent. We knew the general subject of conversation, but not the pros and cons, nor did we have any clue as to which side of the discussion each party took. We therefore began to ask: "What do you use (or how do you feel about it), what does she use, which of you used it first, does she agree with you, does she have good ideas about such topics . . . ?"

What we were doing, in effect, was sloughing off the soft and general focus of the original approach and achieving some comparability with the questions asked of the original respondents. Since this development occurred during the actual interviewing of the first wave follow-up, we do not have this specifying information uniformly for all the respondents. As a result, however, of the first wave experiences, the following questions were included in the second wave follow-up interview:

FOLLOW-UP INTERVIEW WITH MARKETING INFLUENTIALS

1. Do you ever discuss marketing with........(relation with original respondent was specified, i.e., friends, relatives, neighbors, or co-workers)?
2. What.......(product mentioned by original respondent, i.e., cereal, cleanser, etc.) do you use?
3. Have you exchanged views about........(topic) with........(again relation was specified)? With whom?
4. Do you know Mrs.........(original respondent)?
5. Do you ever happen to talk with her about what's good to buy? (If yes:) On what occasions?
6. Have you talked with her about........(specified brand or product)?
7. (If specific brand not mentioned in Question 2): Do you use........?
8. How long have you been using it?
9. Do you know which of you happened to use it first?
10. Have you had much experience with (specified brand)?
11. Has she?
12. Did you suggest that she try (specified brand or product) or did she suggest that you try it?

FOLLOW-UP INTERVIEW WITH POLITICAL INFLUENCEES

1. Everyone discusses current problems like (insert topic). Have you happened to discuss it with your.......(specify relation of source respondent: friends, relatives, neighbors)?
2. Who are some of your (specify relation of source) with whom you have discussed it?
3. Do you know Mrs.........(original respondent)?

4. Have you had occasion to discuss (this topic) with her?
5. On what occasions?
6. How do you feel about (topic)?
7. Does (or did) she agree with you?
8. Did she suggest (the opinion) to you, or did you happen to suggest it to her?
9. Do you believe she has pretty good ideas about such topics?
10. Do you discuss such topics with her pretty often?

Thus the final questionnaire (asked of the 31 Wave II marketing influentials and the 76 Wave II political influencees) made these discriminations:

(a) Introductory questions about general participation in discussion of the area
(b) Description of the *specific* designated communication:
whether it had taken place
under what conditions or situation
what each person used or believed
(also, in marketing only: who used product first, and who told whom— that is, whether the communication had been made in the direction asserted by the original respondent)
(c) Description of the *usual* opinion climate between the two persons:
evaluation of skill or qualifications of original respondent and of self in the particular area (and in politics only: whether such discussions were usual or just an isolated instance).

There are thus two general sets of information. For all follow-ups we have data on the specific communication: had it taken place and had the follow-up or the original respondent made the suggestion. This was what we had *asked* the original respondent and what we wanted the follow-up to confirm.

Less uniformly there are data pertinent to discerning influence— priority of use, the follow-up's judgment of her skill, and of her designator's skill, and in the case of alleged influencees, whether or not they had acted on the suggestion.

We have reported many of the results of the analysis of this information in Part II, Section One of our text. Our purpose here was to report something of the evolutionary history of the follow-up questionnaire.

## 2. Two Kinds of Follow-up: Influential and Influencee

There is a second aspect of our experience with the follow-up interview which is worth reporting. This concerns the difference between the follow-up interviews with influentials and those with influencees. Ostensibly, one might suppose that they should be opposite sides of a coin: on one side, that is, an original respondent-influencee points out somebody who has influenced her; while on the other side, the influential, now original respondent, points out somebody whom she has influenced. If this were so, we would have reason to expect that the picture of the flow of influence in any area, derived from interviewing influencees and then their influentials, should be a mirror image of the picture obtained by interviewing influentials and then their influencees. If these pictures did not match, we would have reason to expect that something had gone wrong.

But, in the course of our interviewing experience, again we learned something new: we learned that we had no right to expect the two pictures to match.

In going out to interview the influentials designated by our original respondents we were armed with this information: we knew what change the original respondent had made—from coffee A to coffee B, from a long bob to a feather-cut, or from indifference to violent dissatisfaction with the activities of the OPA. We knew that the follow-up was a person whom the original respondent had heard talk about the subject and we knew that this talk, at least according to our original respondents, had something to do with the change reported.

In interviewing influencee follow-ups, however, our information was far less clear-cut. The subject matter of the influential-influencee communication, first of all, was not as well defined. Thus the original respondents had merely been asked, "Have you recently been asked your advice on any brands or products?" or, "Have you recently been asked your advice on any such things (fashions)?" and, if the answer was yes, there followed the question "On what?" The answers to "On what?" were not nearly so specific as was our information about changes where we knew exactly what was rejected and what was adopted.

Secondly, the influencee follow-ups are not quite comparable to the follow-up of influentials because the question "Have you recently been asked your advice . . . ?" tends to imply a crucial, "Mr. Anthony" kind of communication as well as a degree of formality which would cause respondents to overlook, perhaps, the very kind of informal communication in which we were interested. Consequently, interviewers were instructed in the course of the field work to substitute the word "suggestion" for advice, and in addition were permitted to ask "Have you recently *made* a suggestion . . . ?" instead of "Have you recently *been asked* your advice (suggestion) . . . ?" Most unfortunately, there was no record of how the question was asked in each interview—we know only the range of possibilities.[6]

Furthermore, in the case of self-reported suggestions or advice to influencees our original respondent-influential could not, obviously, tell us whether his advice or suggestion had been taken or not. Unlike the designated influentials whose names came up in connection with a specific change made by the original respondent, we could not know until the follow-up interview was actually made whether the influencee had actually taken the advice the influential-respondent told us she had given. As a matter of fact, when we began to talk with alleged influencees, we found that the follow-up sometimes had acted contrary to advice received, sometimes deliberately. (A parallel to this occurred in some few cases of follow-up interviews with influentials where the advice they claimed to have given was different than the change made by the original respondent.)

We might repeat here[7] (this is mentioned in the text, Part II, Chap. II) that occasionally advice-seeking is a gambit used by individuals who are not interested in *taking* advice but in *giving* it. Asking another individual for an opinion or a suggestion is the best way—some of our supposed influencee follow-ups informed us —to be influential yourself.

In addition to advice given that is not followed, there is also the problem of advice taken without being given—or at least without the influential being aware of her influentiality. The case of seeing another woman's fashions and copying them is the most obvious example, but clearly advice may be derived from the most casual everyday conversation without the adviser being aware of her role. This, too, makes for non-comparability of the two kinds of inter-

---

6. Noting the precise wording of the question each time it was asked was not deemed important at the time because the primary emphasis was on getting around the reluctance of respondents to name names. It was hoped that the nature of the relationship would be precisely defined in the follow-up interview.

7. Though the influential is unable to state definitively whether or not the follow-up influencee has, in fact, taken her advice, the follow-up questionnaire, of course, can ascertain that. Thus if this were the only difference between influentials and influencees as original respondents, we should have reason to expect that the *confirmed* follow-up interviews, stemming from either source, would present the same picture of the flow of influence. But as will be evident below, others of the differences (between original respondents as influentials or influencees) cannot be checked on by a follow-up interview, e.g., when the original respondent does not know that she has been influential because her advice has been solicited judiciously or because her dress style has been imitated, or the like.

views: where the original respondent is influencee, she can report on advice she might have taken without the knowledge of the influential, but where the original respondent is reporting herself as influential clearly she cannot know if something she may have said has been put to use. Thus the original respondent as influential can err both by overestimating or by underestimating her influentiality.

For all these reasons, our initial expectation that the two sorts of follow-ups (with influentials and influencees) would be exactly comparable was frustrated. We therefore shall not present—as we had planned—tables comparing the follow-up influentials' relations with their original respondent-influencees to similar tables of follow-up influencees and their original respondent-influentials. We shall note here only that the degree of comparability, despite all the differences mentioned above, is not as low as might be expected.

Finally, it should be noted that we have elected throughout the text to report only those flow-of-influence tables where the original respondent is influencee, since these have received the higher degree of confirmation and since our analysis of the character of the follow-up interview with influentials so designated indicates its much greater utility.[8]

On the other hand, however, in those sections of the text where we define opinion leaders by self-designation, we have no alternative but to employ the questions where the original respondent indicates that she has been influential.

## 3. The Follow-up Mortality

We report here on the fate of the follow-up interviewing attempt. As we have indicated in the text, a sizable proportion of the people we set out to interview—that is, the people whose names were mentioned in connection with an interchange which we followed-up—were not actually interviewed. For this reason, we have insisted repeatedly that our flow-of-influence data cannot be treated as

8. The chapter on confirmation (Part II, Chapter II) in Tables 6 and 7 compares influencees and influentials as follow-ups. Note that follow-up influentials confirmed the fact that the conversation had actually taken place more often than did influencees and that, in the realms of marketing and fashions, influentials acknowledge the role attributed to them more often than do influencees. The difference does not emerge in the realm of public affairs due to the insistence of a substantial proportion of public affairs influentials that they had not been unilaterally influential but that there had been a mutual exchange of influence; it is not clear to us why modesty presents itself so strongly only at this point. Our argument in this Appendix does not lead to the prediction that the influential follow-ups should necessarily yield the higher confirmation rate, though perhaps one could make a case for it.

"representative" in any sense, since we must assume that some bias was introduced by virtue of our unsuccessful efforts to interview all designated follow-ups; what's more, we have pointed out that the actual number of cases interviewed in each realm was quite small. Nevertheless, it will be of interest to report where our intentions were frustrated; that is revealed in the following table, which is drawn from the area of fashions but is fairly typical of the other realms as well. This table is for designated *influentials* only.

**Table CI—Accounting for the Fate of the Designated Fashion Influentials**

| Interviewing Fate | Number | Per Cent |
|---|---|---|
| Interviewed[9] | 186 | 41% |
| Did not attempt to reach | | |
|    Respondent did not know person[10] | 71 | 16 |
|    Incomplete Information[11] | 28 | 6 |
|    Out-of-town residents | 94 | 21 |
| Attempted but could not reach | | |
|    Moved out-of-town; died; hospitalized | 7 | 2 |
|    Temporarily out-of-town | 13 | 3 |
| Reached but refused to be interviewed | 12 | 3 |
| Trial interviews; clerical errors | 41 | 8 |
|      Total | (452) | (100%) |

# 4. Representativeness of the Follow-up Interviews

Although we have avoided claiming any sort of "representative-ness" for these fashion follow-ups, nonetheless we can, to a limited extent, report on the degree to which they are and are not similar to the universe of designated influentials from which they come. We can base our analysis on the testimony of the original respondent about the individual who influenced her: thus we shall be able to compare the ages, for example, of those designated influentials actually followed-up with the ages of the total of all influentials who were designated. Let us continue in the realm of fashions, where it will be seen from the previous table that there are a

---

9. In the text we have reported on only 162 of these 186, since 24 of these fashion influentials (13%) were men, eleven of them husbands. The relatively small number of men influential in the fashion realm—compared, for example, with the overwhelming influence of men in public affairs—led us to base our analysis of the flow of fashion influence on women influentials only.

10. As, for example, in copying a dress style without personally knowing the "model."

11. Where the original respondent does not know her influential's full name, or her address, etc.

total of 452 designated influentials of whom 186 were successfully followed-up.

The fact that we have chosen the fashion realm as illustration forces us, first of all, to distinguish three categories of influential designatees: those with whom the respondent had talked about the new fashion; those whom the respondent had seen wearing or using the fashion; and, finally, those whom the respondent had talked to and had also seen wearing the new fashion. A much greater mortality in interviewing was experienced in attempting to reach the designatees who were advisers by example. Thirty-three per cent of the persons mentioned in this category were unknown to the panel respondent. Table C2 presents the interviewing fate of the three types of designatees.

**Table C2—Proportion of Fashion Influentials Followed-up According to Character of Contact with Influencee**

|  | DESIGNATED INFLUENTIAL WAS: | | |
|---|---|---|---|
|  | Talked to only | Visible Example only | Both talked to & visible example |
| Proportion of Designated Influentials Interviewed | 50% | 33% | 41% |
| Total (= 100%) | (188) | (201) | (63) |

The persons interviewed are more likely to be persons who have influenced the original respondent by word-of-mouth than by example. How much this biases our results is of course indeterminable. If persons who act as visible fashion examples to the respondent are of a different sort than those to whom the respondent talks, then it is reasonable to expect that this introduces a definite bias; since inter-class communication is quite slight, the best way for an upper-class individual to influence a lower-class individual or vice versa is through acting as a visible example.

On the other hand, if we consider such characteristics as socio-economic status, education and age, we do not find very large differences in the proportion of each group followed-up. Table C3 reports the proportion of successful follow-ups in the several categories just mentioned. The table is based, however, not on the total number of designated influentials of, say, varying social status, but rather on the total number of original respondents. Comparing the social status of the original respondents in terms of the extent to which their designatees were followed-up is, of course, only an indirect way of comparing the follow-ups themselves. But since we do not have complete data for the designated influentials whom we failed to follow up, we present these data instead.

**Table C3—*Proportion of Fashion Influentials Followed-up According to Socio-Economic Status, Education and Age of Original Respondent***

| Original Respondent (Influencee) | Proportion of Designated Influentials Interviewed |
|---|---|
| Under 45 years | 46% |
| Over 45 years | 48% |
| High Status (A&B)[12] | 48% |
| Middle status (C) | 52% |
| Low Status (D) | 39% |
| Completed High School | 41% |
| Did Not Complete High School | 51% |
| Total (= 100%) | (452) |

Influentials designated by both older and younger respondents were interviewed in equal proportion; opinion leaders named by lowest (D) status respondents were somewhat underrepresented in the follow-up interviews as were those of highly educated respondents. But, by and large, these differences do not seem very great.

To the degree that age and status groups do not differ significantly in the extent to which their designatees were followed-up, we can entertain the idea that the follow-ups obtained may not be unrepresentative in at least these two important respects.

Designatees who were related by blood or marriage but who were not members of the original respondent's own household, were definitely more difficult to reach and interview than those who were the friends and neighbors of our original respondents. Family relationships cover a greater geographical distance than relationships which are not based on blood or marriage.

**Table C4—*Proportion of Fashion Influentials Followed-up According to Relationship with Influencee***

| Relationships of Designated Influential to Original Respondent | Proportion Designated Influentials Interviewed | Total (= 100%) |
|---|---|---|
| Neighbor | 50% | (26) |
| Friend | 58% | (117) |
| Boss or co-worker | 39% | (36) |
| Parent | 37% | (32) |
| Child | 35% | (40) |
| Other blood relatives | 41% | (56) |
| Husband | 61% | (18) |
| In-laws | 30% | (27) |

12. The measure of social status employed here is the interviewer's intuitive rating into A, B, C, D categories. A and B are here called "high."

Evidence of sampling bias is shown in Table C4. Neighbors and friends are over-represented in the designatees interviewed while non-household relatives of all sorts are definitely under-represented. How much this biases our results is purely conjectural without further information.

Returning to the original respondents once more, we find that there are only insignificant differences in the proportion of completed follow-ups among respondents who are married or single, or who have been married only recently or long ago; nor are there any important differences among respondents with varying communications habits, differing religion, differing political party affiliation, and the like.

## 5. On the Analysis of a Follow-up "Flow" Table

A flow table, as defined in the text, occurs if we cross tabulate a property of an influential against the corresponding property of an influencee. Suppose the property is age, classified into old (o), middle (m), and young (y). Then Table C5, with schematic entries, would be an example

**Table C5—(hypothetical) Schematic Cross Tabulation of Age for 100 Influentials and Their Influencees**

|  |  | INFLUENCEE | | | |
|---|---|---|---|---|---|
|  |  | o | m | y | Totals |
|  | o | 15 | 7 | 8 | 30 |
| INFLUENTIAL | m | 3 | 40 | 7 | 50 |
|  | y | 2 | 3 | 15 | 20 |
|  | Totals | 20 | 50 | 30 | 100 |

The following three aspects are most relevant for analysis and interpretation.

1. Who is older on the average, influential or influencee? The answer can be given by comparing the marginal distributions in the last row and last column respectively. In Table C5, since the influentials are somewhat older, advice flows slightly downward; this we shall call "direction."

2. How much of the advice circulates within the same age strata? This can be seen by focusing on the main diagonal. Seventy per cent of the pairs have both partners in the same age group. It should

be remembered that this figure depends somewhat upon the number of categories into which the property is divided. In general, if there are 5 age classes the proportion of pairs where advice is given within an age group would be smaller. If, therefore, we want to compare two properties in regard to "homogeneity" of flow, we have to use the same number of classes. In the text, age, social status, and the other properties were always grouped into three categories when flow tables were compared.

3. Finally the "range" of the flow can be inspected in the following sense. In Table C5 we have 30 old influentials. Half of them give advice to people younger than themselves. About the same number advise young (8) and middle-aged people. It could however well be that one-step differences are relatively more frequent than the more distant range from old to young.

It is possible to change any one of these aspects without changing one other; but the three together have to adjust to each other. Suppose, for example, we want to construct a flow table where the "range" is smaller. Then we can leave either "direction" or "homogeneity" unchanged, but not both. In the first case Table C6 might ensue and in the second case Table C7.

**Table C6—(hypothetical) How Table C5 Would Change If "Range" Were Decreased and Direction (The Marginals) Were Left Unchanged**

| | | INFLUENCEE | | | |
|---|---|---|---|---|---|
| | | o | m | y | Totals |
| | o | 15 | 12 | 3 | 30 |
| INFLUENTIAL | m | 4 | 34 | 12 | 50 |
| | y | 1 | 4 | 15 | 20 |
| Totals | | 20 | 50 | 30 | 100 |

**Table C7—(hypothetical) A Table Where the Range Is the Same as In Table C6 and the Homogeneity the Same as In Table C5**

| | | INFLUENCEE | | | |
|---|---|---|---|---|---|
| | | o | m | y | Totals |
| | o | 15 | 12 | 3 | 30 |
| INFLUENTIAL | m | 2 | 40 | 8 | 50 |
| | y | 1 | 4 | 15 | 20 |
| Totals | | 18 | 56 | 26 | 100 |

In Table C7 the figures 2 and 8 are not determined by the formulation of the problems and have been left as similar as possible to the corresponding figures in Table C6. It is obvious that all these schematic tables would be affected by the specific indices which one might choose to "measure" direction, homogeneity and flow. The present note does not aim at leading to quantitative results but to exemplify qualitative relations. Only such qualitative inferences were made from flow tables in the course of the text.

# On the Construction of Indices

### INCLUDING A SUBSTANTIVE ADDENDUM ON
### AN INDEX OF POPULAR FICTION CONSUMPTION

IN THIS APPENDIX there are listed all of the indices that appear in the text. We shall single out several for comment. Then, we shall introduce one final index—an index of Popular Fiction Consumption—which does not appear elsewhere in the text, but about which there is an interesting story to tell.

## 1. An Inventory of Indices Appearing in the Text

The specific manner in which each index was formed from a combination of items is discussed in the text itself, or in a footnote, at the point of introduction of the index. Here we shall simply list the indices employed in the text, and allude in abbreviated form to the content of the items that went into the make-up of each.[1]

1. *Opinion Leadership* (self-designated)[2] *either*
   a. An instance of advice-giving in a particular area (e.g., marketing) reported both in June and in August; *or*
   b. One such instance plus self-rating as "more likely" than others to be called on for advice in that area.
2. *Index of Effectiveness* (for rating the overall impact of a given medium on decisions)
   Ratio of "effective exposures" to a particular medium to total exposures to that medium.
3. *The Life-Cycle*
   Age; marital status, number of children.
4. *Social and Economic Status* (three indices were employed alternatively as follows:)
   a. Rent and education.

---

1. With the exception of the Index of Effectiveness all of these indices appear in Part Two, Section 3 of the text. The Effectiveness index appears in Section 2; the Opinion Leader index is introduced in Part Two, Section 1 but reappears throughout Section 3.
2. This is the definition of Marketing, Fashion, Public Affairs and Movie Leadership.

  b. Occupation of breadwinner.
  c. Interviewer's intuitive rating.
5. *Gregariousness*
  Number of friends; number of organizations.
6. *Fashion Interest*
  Opinion concerning importance of being in style; having made a recent change; having purchased or made new dresses in 3 months previous.
7. *The "Export" Index* (for estimating the rate of out-group opinion leadership)
  Extent of deviation, in a given group, from the "average" (sample as a whole) ratio of the rate of leadership to the rate of interest in a particular area (e.g. fashion).
8. *Public Affairs Information*
  Correct answers to questions concerning a local highway scheme and the British elections.
9. *Index of Formulated Opinions*
  Having an opinion (regardless of content) on 10 public affairs opinion questions.
10. *"Local" and "Cosmopolitan" Media Behavior*
  Taking an out-of-town newspaper and reading of news in national magazines.
11. *Index of Importance* (for rating the relative importance of various factors for the determination of opinion leadership.)[3]

# 2. *Four Indices Discussed: Gregariousness, Social Status, "Importance" and Opinion Leadership (self-designated)*

At four points in this study we used somewhat more sophisticated procedures to form indices appropriate for our purpose.

### GREGARIOUSNESS AND SOCIAL STATUS INDICES

The index of social status[4] and index of gregariousness used in the final section were developed by a procedure which used considerably more material than is indicated in the text.

---

3. Discussed below in this Appendix.
4. We refer here to the index used most frequently—that composed of rent and education. At times, we were forced because of the absence of the rent and education data in our follow-up interviews to employ occupation and interviewers' intuitive ratings as substitute measures of social status. Traditional occupational categories were used to divide respondents into business and professional, white collar and wage worker groups. The interviewers' ratings were obtained in response to the following instructions from the field supervisor:
  *A—Level:* The best residential sections. Top 5-10% of the population in living standards. Well-to-do business and professional people.
  *B—Level:* Upper middle-class districts. The next 20% in living standards.

Let us take the index of gregariousness as our main example. The reader will remember that in its final form the gregariousness index divided people according to the number of friendships which they reported and the number of organizations to which they belonged. But we had other information in the questionnaire which was pertinent, too, such as whether the respondent attends social affairs in the afternoon or whether she enjoys meeting new people. All this information was combined and subjected to a so-called latent structure analysis. The idea behind such a procedure is something like this: We would like to order people according to how gregarious they are. In order to do this we can use quite a number of indicators of the type just mentioned. But we have to make sure that these indicators express an underlying one-dimensional order. We are are asking ourselves, in other words, whether we really have the right to assume that people who qualify on five or six of these indicators are more gregarious than those who qualify on only one or two of them. The statistical part of this procedure has been described fully and understandably for the layman in another place.[5] Here it will suffice to state that upon examination these items really did form a one-dimensional test similar, for example, to the traditional IQ tests. Once this has been ascertained it is then not necessary to keep all the original items in the test. As we wanted to divide people only into three groups it was enough to use two of the original items. The reader will remember that we called highly gregarious people those who qualified on both items; the ungregarious ones are those who qualified on neither of the two selected items; and the remainder were put into a middle group.

The meaning of this procedure can be clarified still further with the help of our social status classification. Here again we started with a larger number of items. In addition to rent and education, which were finally retained, we had such items as whether the respondents had a telephone. The idea again is that the status which a person has in a community can express itself in a variety of ways. One person might have a house in a more expensive neighborhood but might not furnish it too well, another person might be more

---

White collar and supervisory occupations; owners of small business, salesmen, some professional, *highly* skilled manual.

*C—Level:* Large groups of moderately skilled or semi-skilled manual working people and lower paid white collar employees. Average and somewhat below average socio-economic status. Necessities of life but few luxuries.

*D—Level:* Poorest one-fourth to one-third of population. Common laborers, domestic employees, many foreign-born. Range from extremely poor to nearly C.

5. "The Conceptual Foundation of Latent Structure Analysis," in Lazarsfeld, ed. (1954).

concerned with the comfort within the house. One person might
gain prestige by having had more than high school education. Another might be a laborer but by spending money on a telephone he
will increase the potential range of his influence. In using such
indicators we do about the same thing which a doctor does when
he tries to diagnose a patient's illness. The more tests that point,
say, to a possibility of cancer, the more sure will the doctor be that
something is wrong with the patient. But again when it comes to
classifying people into a few broad groups along one dimension we
don't need all the indicators. We have selected rent and education
mainly because they correspond to two aspects of a man's life
which, from a common-sense point of view, are known to make
for prestige. But the right to use them as indicators of one underlying characteristic, social status, is derived not from common sense
but from the latent structure analysis which we have carried out
with a whole set of indicators.

### INDEX OF IMPORTANCE

A third index we would like to discuss is of a more complicated
nature. At the end of Part Two we raised the question of the extent
to which the various characteristics like gregariousness, status and
life-cycle are related to opinion leadership. The statistically minded
reader might want to know in some detail what "index of correlation" we used. We will assume that the reader knows that the
correlation of two attributes can be represented by a four-fold table.

ATTRIBUTE II

|  | 1 | 2 |  |
|---|---|---|---|
| 1 | $a_1$ | $a_2$ | A |
| 2 | $b_1$ | $b_2$ | B |
|  | $s_1$ | $s_2$ | N |

ATTRIBUTE I

The usual measure for this interrelationship is given by the following formula:

$$r^2 = \frac{a_1 b_2 - a_2 b_1}{A\,B\,S_1 S_2}.$$

Now very simple algebra shows that this same index can also be given in the following formula:

$$r^2 = 1 - \frac{\dfrac{a_1b_1}{S_1} + \dfrac{a_2b_2}{S_2}}{\dfrac{AB}{N}}$$

In this form, the formula is quite easily extended to our problem. Opinion leadership can either be present or absent (so it can be treated dichotomously as are the Attributes above). But the characterizations of our respondents come in three or four classes (high, middle, low; or, girls, small family wives, large family wives, matrons). We must therefore deal not with four-fold tables but with tables which have six or eight entries, thus:

CHARACTERISTIC X

|  | | High | Middle | Low | |
|---|---|---|---|---|---|
| LEADERSHIP | absent | $a_1$ | $a_2$ | $a_3$ | A |
| | present | $b_1$ | $b_2$ | $b_3$ | B |
| | | $S_1$ | $S_2$ | $S_3$ | N |

Then it is a consistent idea to extend the last formula in the following way:

$$r^2 = 1 - \frac{\dfrac{a_1b_1}{S_1} + \dfrac{a_2b_2}{S_2} + \dfrac{a_3b_3}{S_3}}{\dfrac{AB}{N}}$$

This formula developed by Professor Mosteller can be interpreted in the usual way. The value becomes 1 if opinion leadership is completely determined by the characteristic under investigation. If the latter has no bearing on opinion leadership, then the index would be 0. The numerical values of the index are necessarily small. If, for example, groups of equal size show a difference as large as .60 — .40 — .20 the index value would be only .334. Smaller "corner" groups make for a lowering of the index value. The index figures, therefore, should be used for comparison only.

## INDEX OF OPINION LEADERSHIP

The fourth index which deserves special attention is our index of self-designated opinion leadership. It will be recalled that three items were used to construct this index. First of all there was the question, repeated in June and in August, concerning a recent specific episode of advice-giving, "Have you recently been asked your advice about . . . (marketing, fashion, etc.)?" Secondly, we asked, "Compared with other women in your circle of acquaintances, are you more or less likely than any of them to be asked your advice on . . . (marketing, fashion, etc.)?" The two specific items plus the one general one make up the index.

There are obvious advantages and disadvantages to these questions which we have discussed in the text and which we elaborate on in the previous Appendix. Here, however, we want to report on the extent to which women who reported an advice-giving episode in June reported another episode in August, and the extent to which these specific instances of influentiality correlate with self-appraisal of oneself as more or less likely to be asked advice. We want, in other words, to report the inter-correlations among replies to the three questions.

Of course, comparing respondents for their consistency of reply to the two specific advice-giving questions is not at all the same as testing the reliability of a factual question by asking it on two successive waves. If one asks a person about his nationality or date of birth it is to be expected that his answers will be consistent over a long period of time, but we cannot expect advice-giving to be so continuous an activity that answers will be highly consistent over time. There is no reason to expect that individuals who had been asked their advice "recently" in June need also have had such a "recent" experience in August. Here, at any rate, are the cross-tabulations for fashions and for public affairs:[6]

In both fashions and public affairs only about 40 per cent of those who reported having been influential in June report themselves as influential in August.[7]

---

6. What we shall say for fashions and public affairs holds good for marketing and movie-going as well, except where specifically noted.

7. Examining those who are influential in August, we find that in fashions, about 40 per cent of the August influentials were influential in June (which is about the same proportion of June influentials who remained influential in August). In public affairs, however, that is not at all the case. While 34 per cent of the June influentials remained influential in August, only 19 per cent of the August influentials were recruited from the ranks of the June influentials. A glance at the "marginals" of the two tables will reveal that while

JUNE FASHION ADVISER

|  |  | Yes | No |  |
|---|---|---|---|---|
| AUGUST | Yes | 76 | 106 | 182 |
| FASHION ADVISER | No | 98 | 434 | 532 |
|  |  | 174 | 540 |  |

JUNE PUBLIC AFFAIRS ADVISER

|  |  | Yes | No |  |
|---|---|---|---|---|
| AUGUST PUBLIC | Yes | 22 | 95 | 117 |
| AFFAIRS ADVISER | No | 43 | 555 | 598 |
|  |  | 65 | 650 |  |

But if we have no right to expect a high degree of consistency in the reports of specific, advice-giving episodes, we do perhaps have a right to expect that the individuals who are singled out on the basis of two such episodes ought to be different from women

the number of fashion influentials remained virtually constant in June and in August (174, 182), the number of public affairs influentials almost doubled between June and August. There is a reason for this. In the August interview the wording of the public affairs question was changed somewhat in order to see whether the connotation of "Have you recently been asked your *advice?*" was inhibiting reports of the kind of informal influentiality which we were seeking. Accordingly, only in the public affairs area, the August question was changed to "Have you recently been asked your *views* on national, international or local affairs?" Whereas in June only 9 per cent replied affirmatively, in August, 18 per cent reported some advice-giving episode. But although *more* influentials stepped forward in response to the re-worded question, we have reason to believe that the two questions point out the same *type* of leader. Thus, the correlation between answers to the question, "Compared with other women . . . are you more or less likely to be asked your advice?" is just as high among those who responded affirmatively to the August "views" question as it is among those who responded affirmatively to the June "advice" question.

who report only one episode and these, in turn, should be different
from those who reported no such incidents at all on either interview. And we should expect them to be significantly different on
something like a "potentiality" for influence. The appraisal by
respondents of their general likelihood of being asked for advice
compared with others in their circle should certainly get at this
difference.

**Table D2—Frequency of Advice-Giving and Self-Appraisal of Influentiality**

| "Compared with other women in your circle are you more or less likely to be asked advice about fashion?" | 2-Time Fashion Adviser (June and August) | 1-Time Fashion Adviser (June or August) | Did Not Give Fashion Advice Either Time |
|---|---|---|---|
| More Likely | 72% | 42% | 17% |
| Less Likely | 21 | 51 | 77 |
| Same (volunteered) | 4 | 2 | 2 |
| Don't know; No answer | 3 | 6 | 4 |
| Total (= 100%) | (76) | (204) | (434) |

| "Compared with other women, etc." | 2-Time Public Affairs Adviser (June and August) | 1-Time Public Affairs Adviser (June or August) | Did Not Give Public Affairs Advice Either Time |
|---|---|---|---|
| More Likely | 64% | 44% | 15% |
| Less Likely | 27 | 49 | 77 |
| Same (volunteered) | 9 | 1 | 3 |
| Don't know; No Answer | — | 7 | 6 |
| Total (= 100%) | (22) | (138) | (555) |

These tables reveal a strong correlation between self-appraisal of
of one's own influentiality and the number of actual advice-giving
episodes which the respondent was able to report to our interviewers. The most frequently consulted women in both fashion
and public affairs also see themselves as "more likely"; those who
were unable to relate an advice-giving episode either in June or
in August also consider themselves "less likely"; while the women
who were consulted only once—either in June or in August—clearly
stand in between in the self-appraisal of their own influentiality.

These computations led us to the construction of our index of
self-designated opinion leadership. Cross-tabulation of the three
questions yields six response combinations as follows:

**Table D3—Six Advice-Giving Types**

| | 2-Time Adviser (June and August) | 1-Time Adviser (June or August) | Did Not Give Advice Either Time |
|---|---|---|---|
| "More Likely"[8] | 1 | 3 | 5 |
| "Less Likely" | 2 | 4 | 6 |

8. The few cases who volunteered that their influentiality was about the
"same" as others were, after scrutiny of the interviews, grouped with "more
likely."

The positions of individuals whose responses fell into combinations 1 and 6 are unambiguous. Those whose responses fell into pattern 2 were considered "modest" about themselves while those falling into category 5 were considered "boastful." These categories were accordingly combined with categories 1 and 6 respectively. By examining the social and other characteristics of the individuals in categories 3 and 4—which obviously pose the most difficult problems—it was found that persons in 3 were more like those in 1 and 2, while those in 4 were more like those in 5 and 6. Accordingly, the six response categories were reduced to two groups: the Opinion Leader group of categories 1, 2 and 3; and the Non-Leader group of categories 4, 5 and 6.

For simplicity, we have reported the intercorrelations among the three questions in the index only for the arenas of fashion and public affairs. The intercorrelations for the movie arena are about as high, but it should be noted that in marketing they are somewhat lower. It would seem that advice-giving in marketing may be somewhat more random than in the other areas where the give-and-take of every day conversation frequently thrusts women into an advice-giving role. Thus it may be that the character of influence-flow in this area causes a woman who actually does report some specific instance of advice-giving not to perceive of herself as "more likely" than others to be asked for advice and, similarly, the woman who did not actually give advice may think of herself as just as likely as her neighbor to be sought out. In any event, this is more the case in marketing than in the other three areas.

## 3. A Substantive Addendum: On Gregariousness, Anxiety and the Consumption of Popular Fiction

Before closing the book, we shall introduce one final index: an index of exposure to what we shall call "popular fiction."[9] We asked the women in our sample: (1) whether they read magazines of the "true story" type; (2) whether they read movie magazines; and (3) whether they listened to daytime serials on the radio. For exposure to two or three of these, we rated a respondent 2 on the popular fiction index; for exposure to any one we rated her 1; and if she did not attend to any we rated her 0. We then compared women (1) with varying degrees of gregariousness (measured by

9. Leo Srole proposed this index and the analysis which follows.

the gregariousness index discussed above) and (2) with varying degrees of "anxiety" to see whether their exposure to popular fiction differed in any way. The outcome, we think, is of considerable interest to the mass media researcher and to the student of popular culture.

First of all, we compared the popular fiction scores of women of differing gregariousness. Note that education level—which we know to be related to the items in the popular fiction index—is being held constant.

**Table D4—On Both Education Levels, Women With Lower Gregariousness Report Greater Exposure to Popular Fiction**

| | LOW EDUCATION | | | HIGH EDUCATION | | |
|---|---|---|---|---|---|---|
| | High Greg. | Medium Greg. | Low Greg. | High Greg. | Medium Greg. | Low Greg. |
| Popular Fiction Score | | | | | | |
| 2 | 7% | 15% | 20% | 3% | 7% | 12% |
| 1 | 38 | 43 | 46 | 33 | 41 | 38 |
| 0 | 55 | 42 | 34 | 64 | 52 | 50 |
| Total (= 100%) | (87) | (189) | (136) | (102) | (135) | (60) |

Since we know that gregariousness is related to social status, we ran this table once more, this time holding socio-economic status (instead of education) constant.[10] But the results were the same: on both high and low status levels, the less gregarious women were more likely to be popular fiction fans. The differences are not spectacular but they are completely consistent. Thus, among high status women, 36 per cent of the most gregarious, as compared with 50 per cent of the least gregarious, reported exposure to at least one of the three items in the popular fiction index.

That the inverse relationship between gregariousness and popular fiction cannot be explained by education level or by social status lends support to the obvious interpretation—though this has hardly ever been documented by mass media research—that the popular fiction media serve to some extent as a substitute for socializing activity. "Escapist" is the label that the popular culture theorist has given them.

We do not know, of course, what makes one woman more gregarious than the next—given the same level of social and economic status; perhaps a personality factor accounts for it. As a matter of fact, we have in our study several questions relative to "anxiety"

10. We used interviewers' A, B, C, D ratings of socio-economic status.

(worrying, feeling blue, etc.) which tap one aspect of personality. These mood factors are also related to popular fiction—though they are completely independent of gregariousness.[11]

Our respondents were asked: "In general do you think you worry more or less as compared with other people?" The significant break in the distribution of replies seems to fall between those who replied "less" as against those who replied "the same" or "more." Table D5 relates these responses to the popular fiction index.

**Table D5—Women Who Think They Worry More Than Others Are Also Likely To Have Higher Exposure To Popular Fiction**

| Popular Fiction Score | | COMPARED WITH OTHERS, THINK THEY WORRY | |
|---|---|---|---|
| | | "More" or "Same" | "Less" |
| High | 2 | 13% | 6% |
| Medium | 1 | 42 | 39 |
| Low | 0 | 45 | 55 |
| Total (= 100%) | | (507) | (202) |

There is a slight relationship revealed here between self-image as an anxious person and exposure to popular fiction. The more one conceives of oneself as a worrier, the higher one's exposure to these media. But let us try this again with another one of the mood questions: "Are you ever blue or depressed about things in your life?" This time, we shall reintroduce our measure of gregariousness and shall see that both gregariousness and anxiety are independently related to popular fiction consumption.

**Table D6—Women Who Are Sometimes Blue and Depressed Are More Likely To Be Consumers of Popular Fiction Regardless of the Extent of Their Gregariousness**

| | BLUE OR DEPRESSED? | | | | | |
|---|---|---|---|---|---|---|
| | YES | | | NO | | |
| | High Greg. | Medium Greg. | Low Greg. | High Greg. | Medium Greg. | Low Greg. |
| Popular Fiction Score | | | | | | |
| 2-1 | 44% | 58% | 67% | 34% | 44% | 47% |
| 0 | 56 | 42 | 33 | 66 | 56 | 53 |
| Total (= 100%) | (131) | (220) | (141) | (59) | (102) | (55) |

Comparing the "yes" and the "no" on each level of gregariousness, it is evident that there is a significant relationship between

11. Gregariousness, that is, is not associated with greater or lesser worrying or feeling blue.

feeling "blue or depressed" and the consumption of popular fiction. Table D3 shows, too, that gregariousness is still a factor to reckon with—regardless of amount of anxiety.

We may summarize these findings as follows:

1. Popular fiction consumption is related to social and economic status. While we have not dwelled on this point, it is well established in our data: exposure to popular fiction might be said to be a majority characteristic of lower status groups and a minority pattern among people of upper status.

2. Popular fiction consumption varies inversely with gregariousness even when status level is held constant. Though we have not presented all the data here, this is more marked among upper status groups than among lower.

3. Popular fiction consumption varies directly with an anxiety component in personality; this relationship is quite independent of gregariousness.

In short, the media content which we have labeled popular fiction seems to serve needs and interests which are associated with the sub-culture of lower status groups; with lower levels of social activity; and with anxiety elements in personality.[12]

---

12. Elsewhere, we have called this approach to the mass media the study of "uses and gratifications." See Katz, E. (1953) and McPhee (1953). Because these data do not fit directly into the main theme of our discussion of personal influence, but because they are so intriguing, we have presented them in capsule form here.

# Bibliography

*Bibliographical Note:* The bibliography is arranged alphabetically by author, and wherever an author is cited more than once his various publications are arranged chronologically. All references in the text may be located here simply by matching author and date of the reference with author and date in the bibliography.

Wherever possible, we have preferred to cite the most readily available source for every article rather than the original place of publication. We refer particularly, therefore, to the various "readers" such as Swanson, Newcomb and Hartley (1952) which is an excellent source for much of the small group material and to such mass communications "readers" as Schramm (1949) and Berelson and Janowitz (1950).

Our references in Part I—which, of course, make up the bulk of this bibliography—do not, in general, date later than mid-1953. Since a number of directly pertinent works have appeared since that date, we are listing some of them in this bibliographical note.

Additions to the literature of *small group research* have grown very rapidly. An outstanding new "reader" is Cartwright and Zander (1953) and another whose publication is awaited is Hare, Borgatta and Bales (1955). Comprehensive and highly authoritative reviews of various aspects of the small groups field can be found in Lindzey (1954). The *American Sociological Review* devotes its entire issue of December, 1954 (Vol. 19, No. 6) under the guest-editorship of Fred L. Strodtbeck, to recent work in the small group field.

The field of *mass communications research* has also been enriched by the appearance of Hovland, Janis and Kelley (1953) and of Schramm (1955). The former contains a series of research reports organized within the framework of one of the major research traditions in mass communications; the latter is a "reader" which places particular emphasis on communications process including the part played by interpersonal relations in communications flow, and there is also a section devoted to International Communications Research. International Communications is also the subject of a special issue of the *Public Opinion Quarterly* (Vol. 16, No. 4, Winter 1952-3), under the guest-editorship of Leo Lowenthal. A number of relevant readings, finally, are to be found in Katz, D., Cartwright, et al (1954).

[ 381 ]

Allport, Gordon W. and Leo J. Postman (1940), *The Psychology of Rumor*, New York: Henry Holt.

Asch, S. E. (1940), "Studies in the Principles of Judgments and Attitudes: II. Determination of Judgments by Groups and by Ego-Standards," *Journal of Social Psychology*, Vol. 12, pp. 433-465.

—— (1952A), "Effects of Group Pressures Upon the Modification and Distortion of Judgments," in Swanson, Newcomb and Hartley, eds., *Readings in Social Psychology*, New York: Henry Holt.

—— (1952B), *Social Psychology*, New York: Prentice-Hall.

Back, Kurt W. *et al.* (1950), "A Method of Studying Rumor Transmission," in Festinger *et al.*, *Theory and Experiment in Social Communication*, Ann Arbor, Mich.: Research Center for Group Dynamics, University of Michigan.

Back, Kurt W. (1952), "Influence Through Social Communication," in Swanson, Newcomb and Hartley, eds., *Readings in Social Psychology*, New York: Henry Holt.

Bales, R. F. (1945), "Social Therapy for a Social Disorder—Compulsive Drinking," *Journal of Social Issues*, Vol. 1, No. 3, pp. 14-22.

—— (1952), "Some Uniformities of Behavior in Small Social Systems," in Swanson, Newcomb and Hartley, eds., *Readings in Social Psychology*, New York: Henry Holt.

Barnett, H. G. (1953), *Innovation: The Basis of Cultural Change*, New York: McGraw-Hill.

Bavelas, Alex (1951), "Communications Patterns in Task Oriented Groups," in Lerner and Lasswell, eds., *The Policy Sciences*, Stanford, Calif.: Stanford University Press. Reprinted in Cartwright and Zander (1953).

Benne, K. D. and P. Sheats (1948), "Functional Roles of Group Members," *Journal of Social Issues*, Vol. 4, No. 2, pp. 41-49.

Bennett, Edith (1952), *The Relationship of Group Discussion, Decision, Commitment and Consensus to Individual Action*, unpublished Doctoral Dissertation, University of Michigan. Abstracted in *The American Psychologist*, Vol. 7, p. 315.

Berelson, Bernard R. (1950), "Communication and Public Opinion," in Berelson and Janowitz, eds., *Reader in Public Opinion and Communication*, Glencoe, Illinois: Free Press.

Berelson, Bernard R. and Morris Janowitz, eds. (1950), *Reader in Public Opinion and Communication*, Glencoe, Illinois: Free Press.

—— (1951), *Content Analysis in Communication Research*, Glencoe, Illinois: Free Press.

Berelson, Bernard R., Paul F. Lazarsfeld and William N. McPhee (1954), *Voting: A Study of Opinion Formation During a Presidential Campaign*, Chicago: University of Chicago Press.

Berenda, Ruth W. (1950), *The Influence of the Group on the Judgments of Children*, New York: Columbia University Press.

Blumer, Herbert (1946), "The Mass, the Public, and Public Opinion," in A. M. Lee, ed., *New Outline of the Principles of Sociology*, New York: Barnes and Noble. Reprinted, in part, in Berelson and Janowitz (1950).

Bogart, Leo (1950), "The Spread of News on a Local Event: A Case History," *Public Opinion Quarterly*, Vol. 14, pp. 769-772.

Brunner, Edmund deS. *et al.* (1945), *Farmers of the World*, New York: Columbia University Press.

Bureau of Applied Social Research, Columbia University (1951), unpublished series of studies on Communications Behavior in the Near and Middle East.

Burt, Cynl (1938), *The Young Delinquent*, New York: Appleton-Century.

Bushee, Frederick A. (1945), "Social Organizations in a Small City," *American Journal of Sociology*, Vol. 51, pp. 217-226.

Cantril, Hadley and Gordon Allport (1935), *The Psychology of Radio*, New York: Harper & Brothers.

Carter, L. F. and M. Nixon (1949), "An Investigation of the Relationship Between Four Criteria of Leadership Ability for Three Different Tasks," *Journal of Psychology*, Vol. 27, pp. 245-261.

Cartwright, Dorwin (1949), "Some Principles of Mass Persuasion: Selected Findings of Research on the Sale of U.S. War Bonds," *Human Relations*, Vol. 2, pp. 253-267. Reprinted in Katz, Cartwright et al (1954).

—— (1951), "Achieving Change in People: Some Applications of Group Dynamics Theory," *Human Relations*, Vol. 4, pp. 381-392.

Cartwright, Dorwin and Alvin Zander (1953), *Group Dynamics: Research and Theory*, Evanston, Illinois: Row, Peterson.

Chowdhry, Kamla and Theodore M. Newcomb (1952), "The Relative Abilities of Leaders and Non-Leaders to Estimate Opinions of their Own Groups," *Journal of Abnormal and Social Psychology*, Vol. 47, pp. 51-57. Reprinted in Hare, Borgatta and Bales (1955).

Coch, Lester and John R. P. French, Jr. (1952), "Overcoming Resistance to Change," in Swanson, Newcomb and Hartley, eds., *Readings in Social Psychology*, New York: Henry Holt.

Cooley, C. H. (1909), *Social Organization*, New York: Charles Scribner's Sons.

—— (1950), "The Significance of Communication," in Berelson and Janowitz, eds., *Reader in Public Opinion and Communication*, Glencoe, Illinois: Free Press.

Cooper, Eunice and Marie Jahoda (1947), "The Evasion of Propaganda," *Journal of Psychology*, Vol. 23, pp. 15-25. Reprinted in Katz, Cartwright et al (1954).

Davis, Kingsley (1949), *Human Society*, New York: Macmillan.

Dotson, Floyd (1951), "Patterns of Voluntary Association Among Urban Working Class Families," *American Sociological Review*, Vol. 16, pp. 687-693.

Duncker, Karl (1938), "Experimental Modifications of Children's Food Preferences Through Social Suggestion," *Journal of Abnormal and Social Psychology*, Vol. 33, pp. 489-507.

Eisenstadt, S. N. (1952), "Communication Processes Among Immigrants in Israel," *Public Opinion Quarterly*, Vol. 16, pp. 42-58.

Ennis, Philip H. (1955), *The Changed to Tea, A Study in the Dynamics of Consumer Behavior*, unpublished research report of the Bureau of Applied Social Research, Columbia University.

Faris, Robert E. L. (1953), "Development of the Small Group Research Movement," in Sherif and Wilson, eds., *Group Relations at the Crossroads*, New York: Harper and Brothers.

Ferber, Robert (1955), "On the Reliability of Purchase Influence Studies," *Journal of Marketing*, Vol. 19, pp. 225-232.

Festinger, Leon (1950), "Informal Social Communication," *Psychological Review*, Vol. 57, pp. 271-282.

Festinger, Leon, Stanley Schachter and Kurt Back (1950), *Social Pressures in Informal Groups*, New York: Harper and Brothers. Excerpts in Cartwright and Zander (1953), Chaps. VIII and XVI.

Festinger, Leon and John Thibaut (1952), "Interpersonal Communication in Small Groups," in Swanson, Newcomb and Hartley, eds., *Readings in Social Psychology*, New York: Henry Holt.

Fisher, Sarah C. (1948), *Relationships in Attitudes, Opinions, and Values Among Family Members*, Berkeley, Calif.: University of California Press.

Foskett, John M. (1955), "Social Structure and Social Participation," *American Sociological Review*, Vol. 20, pp. 431-438.

Freidson, Eliot (1953A), "Communications Research and the Concept of the Mass," *American Sociological Review*, Vol. 18, pp. 313-317. Reprinted in Schramm (1955).

—— (1953B), "The Relation of the Social Situation of Contact to the Media in Mass Communication," *Public Opinion Quarterly*, Vol. 17, pp. 230-238.

Gibb, Cecil A. (1947), "The Principles and Traits of Leadership," *Journal of Abnormal and Social Psychology*, Vol. 42, pp. 267-284.

—— (1950), "The Research Background of an Interactional Theory of Leadership," *Australian Journal of Psychology*, Vol. 28, pp. 19-42.

Giddings, Charles H. (1896), *Principles of Sociology*, New York: Macmillan.

Glock, Charles Y. (1953), "The Comparative Study of Communication and Opinion Formation," *Public Opinion Quarterly*, Vol. 15, pp. 512-523. Reprinted in Schramm (1955).

Goldhamer, Herbert (1942), *Some Factors Affecting Participation in Voluntary Associations*, unpublished Doctoral Dissertation, University of Chicago.

Handel, Leo A. (1950), *Hollywood Looks at its Audience*, Urbana, Illinois: University of Illinois Press.

Hare, A. Paul (1952), "Interaction and Consensus in Different Sized Groups," *American Sociological Review*, Vol. 17, pp. 261-267. Reprinted in Cartwright and Zander (1953).

Hare, Paul, Edgar F. Borgatta and Robert F. Bales (1955), *Small Groups: Studies in Social Interaction*, New York: Knopf.

Hartley, Eugene (1951), "Psychological Problems of Multiple Group Membership," in Rohrer and Sherif, eds., *Social Psychology at the Crossroads*, New York: Harper and Brothers.

Hartley, E. L. and R. E. Hartley (1952), *Fundamentals of Social Psychology*, New York: Knopf.

Hites, R. W. and D. T. Campbell (1950), "A Test of the Ability of Fraternity Leaders to Estimate Group Opinion," *Journal of Social Psychology*, Vol. 32, pp. 95-100.

Homans, George C. (1950), *The Human Group*, New York: Harcourt, Brace.

—— (1952), "Group Factors in Worker Productivity," in Swanson, Newcomb and Hartley, eds., *Readings in Social Psychology*, New York: Henry Holt.

Horsfall, A. B. and C. M. Arensberg, "Teamwork and Productivity in a Shoe Factory," *Human Organization*, Vol. 8, pp. 13-28.

Hovland, Carl I., Arthur A. Lumsdaine and Fred D. Sheffield (1949), *Experiments in Mass Communications* (Studies in Social Psychology in World War II, Vol. III), Princeton, N. J.: Princeton University Press.

Hovland, Carl I., Irving L. Janis and Harold H. Kelley (1953),

*Communication and Persuasion,* New Haven, Conn.: Yale University Press.

Huth, Arno G. (1952), "Communications and Economic Development," *International Concilliation,* No. 477, Carnegie Endowment for International Peace.

Hyman, Herbert H. and Paul B. Sheatsley (1952), "Some Reasons Why Information Campaigns Fail," in Swanson, Newcomb and Hartley, eds., *Readings in Social Psychology,* New York: Henry Holt.

Inkeles, Alex (1950), *Public Opinion in Soviet Russia,* Cambridge, Mass.: Harvard University Press.

Jenkins, W. O. (1947), "A Review of Leadership Studies with Particular Reference to Military Problems," *Psychological Bulletin,* Vol. 44, pp. 54-79.

Jennings, Helen H. (1952), "Leadership and Isolation," in Swanson, Newcomb and Hartley, eds., *Readings in Social Psychology,* New York: Henry Holt.

Jones, Maxwell *et al.* (1953), *Social Psychiatry: A Study of Therapeutic Communities,* New York: Basic Books.

Kagan, Henry E. (1952), *Changing the Attitude of Christian Toward Jew,* New York: Columbia University Press.

Katz, Daniel (1949), "Psychological Barriers to Communication," in Wilbur Schramm, ed., *Mass Communications,* Urbana, Illinois: University of Illinois Press.

—— (1951), "Social Psychology and Group Processes," *Annual Review of Psychology,* Vol. 2, pp. 137-172.

Katz, Daniel, Dorwin Cartwright, Samuel Eldersveld and Alfred M. Lee, eds. (1954), *Public Opinion and Propaganda,* New York: Dryden Press.

Katz, Elihu (1953), *The Part Played by People: A New Focus for the Study of Mass Media Effects,* unpublished memorandum of the Bureau of Applied Social Research, Columbia University.

Katz, Elihu and Herbert Menzel (1954), *On the Flow of Scientific Information in the Medical Profession* (2 vols.), unpublished research reports on a pilot study of the Bureau of Applied Social Research, Columbia University.

Kelley, Harold H. (1950), "Communication in Experimentally Created Hierarchies," in Festinger *et al., Theory and Experiment in Social Communication,* Ann Arbor, Michigan: Research Center for Group Dynamics, University of Michigan. Reprinted in Cartwright and Zander (1953).

Kelley, Harold H. and Edmund H. Volkart (1952), "The Resistance to Change of Group Anchored Attitudes," *American Sociological Review*, Vol. 17, pp. 453-465. Reported also in Hovland, Janis and Kelley (1953), Chap. V.

Klapper, Joseph T. (1950), *The Effects of the Mass Media*, New York: Bureau of Applied Social Research, Columbia University.

Komarovsky, Mirra (1940), *The Unemployed Man and his Family*, New York: The Dryden Press.

—— (1946), "The Voluntary Associations of Urban Dwellers," *American Sociological Review*, Vol. 11, pp. 686-698.

Krech, David and Richard S. Crutchfield (1948), *Theory and Problems in Social Psychology*, New York: McGraw-Hill.

Larsen, Otto N. and Richard J. Hill (1954), "Mass Media and Interpersonal Communication in the Diffusion of a News Event," *American Sociological Review*, Vol. 19, pp. 426-433.

Larsen, Otto N. and Melvin L. DeFleur (1954), "The Comparative Role of Children and Adults in Propaganda Diffusion," *American Sociological Review*, Vol. 19, pp. 593-602.

Lazarsfeld, Paul F. (1940), *Radio and the Printed Page*, New York: Duell, Sloan and Pearce.

—— (1941), "Audience Building in Educational Broadcasting," *Journal of Educational Sociology*, Vol. 14.

—— (1942), "The Effects of Radio on Public Opinion," in Douglas Waples, ed., *Print, Radio and Film in a Democracy*, Chicago, Ill.: University of Chicago Press.

—— (1947), "Audience Research in the Movie Field," *Annals of the American Academy of Political and Social Science*.

—— (1948), "Communications Research and the Social Psychologist," in Wayne Dennis, ed., *Current Trends in Social Psychology*, Pittsburgh, Pa.: University of Pittsburgh Press.

Lazarsfeld, Paul F., Bernard Berelson and Hazel Gaudet (1948), *The People's Choice*, New York: Columbia University Press.

Lazarsfeld, Paul F. and Patricia L. Kendall (1948), *Radio Listening in America*, New York: Prentice-Hall.

Lazarsfeld, Paul F. and Robert K. Merton (1949), "Mass Communication, Popular Taste and Organized Social Action," in Wilbur Schramm, ed., *Mass Communications*, Urbana, Ill.: University of Illinois Press.

Lazarsfeld, Paul F. and Patricia L. Kendall (1950), "Problems of Survey Analysis," in Merton and Lazarsfeld, eds., *Continuities in Social Research: Studies in the Scope and Method of "The American Soldier,"* Glencoe, Ill.: Free Press.

Lazarsfeld, Paul F. and Morris Rosenberg, eds. (1955), *The Language of Social Research*, Glencoe, Ill.: Free Press.

Leavitt, Harold J. (1952), "Some Effects of Certain Communications Patterns on Group Performance," in Swanson, Newcomb and Hartley, eds., *Readings in Social Psychology*, New York: Henry Holt.

Lee, Alfred M. and Elizabeth B. Lee (1939), *The Fine Art of Propaganda*, New York: Harcourt, Brace.

Leighton, Alexander (1945), *The Governing of Men*, Princeton, N. J.: Princeton University Press.

Lerner Daniel, Paul Berkman and Lucille Pevsner (forthcoming), *Modernizing the Middle East: Studies in Communication and Social Change* (tentative title).

Levine, Jacob and John Butler (1952), "Lecture vs. Group Decision in Changing Behavior," *Journal of Applied Psychology*, Vol. 36, pp. 29-33. Reprinted in Cartwright and Zander (1953).

Lewin, Kurt and Paul Grabbe (1945), "Conduct, Knowledge and Acceptance of New Values," *Journal of Social Issues*, Vol. 1, No. 3, pp. 53-64. Reprinted in Lewin (1948).

Lewin, Kurt (1948), *Resolving Social Conflicts*, New York: Harper and Brothers.

—— (1951), *Field Theory in Social Science*, New York: Harper and Brothers.

—— (1952), "Group Decision and Social Change," in Swanson, Newcomb and Hartley, eds., *Readings in Social Psychology*, New York: Henry Holt.

Lewis, Helen B. (1952), "An Experiment on the Operation of Prestige Suggestion," in Swanson, Newcomb and Hartley, eds., *Readings in Social Psychology*, New York: Henry Holt.

Lindzey, Gardner (1954), *Handbook of Social Psychology* (2 vols.), Cambridge, Mass.: Addison-Wesley Press.

Lippitt, Ronald, Norman Polansky, Fritz Redl and Sidney Rosen (1952) "The Dynamics of Power," in Swanson, Newcomb and Hartley, eds., *Readings in Social Psychology*, New York: Henry Holt.

Lippitt, Ronald and Ralph K. White (1952), "An Experimental Study of Leadership and Group Life," in Swanson, Newcomb and Hartley, eds., *Readings in Social Psychology*, New York: Henry Holt.

Lipset, Seymour M., James S. Coleman and Martin A. Trow (forthcoming), *Union Democracy* (tentative title), Glencoe, Ill.: Free Press.

Lundberg, G. A. and Virginia Beazley (1948), "Consciousness of Kind in a College Population," *Sociometry*, Vol. 11, pp. 59-74.

Lundberg, G. A., Virginia B. Hertzler and Lenore Dickson (1949),

"Attraction Patterns in a University," *Sociometry*, Vol. 12, pp. 158-169.

Lynd, Robert S. and Helen M. Lynd (1929), *Middletown*, New York: Harcourt, Brace.

—— (1937), *Middletown in Transition*, New York: Harcourt, Brace.

MacIver, Robert M. (1942), *Social Causation*, Boston: Ginn and Co.

McPhee, William N. and Rolf B. Meyersohn (1951), *The Radio Audiences of Lebanon*, unpublished research report of the Bureau of Applied Social Research, Columbia University.

McPhee, William N. (1953), *New Strategies for Research in the Mass Media*, unpublished memorandum of the Bureau of Applied Social Research, Columbia University.

Maisonneuve, J. *et al.* (1952), "Selective Choices and Propinquity," *Sociometry*, Vol. 15, pp. 135-140.

March, James G. (1954), "Group Norms and the Active Minority," *American Sociological Review*, Vol. 19, pp. 733-741.

Mead, Margaret (1937), "Public Opinion Mechanisms Among Primitive Peoples," *Public Opinion Quarterly*, Vol. 1, No. 3, pp. 5-16.

Mead, Margaret, ed. (1953), *Cultural Patterns and Technical Change*, New York: UNESCO.

Merei, Ferenc (1952), "Group Leadership and Institutionalization," in Swanson, Newcomb and Hartley, eds., *Readings in Social Psychology*, New York: Henry Holt.

Merton, Robert K. (1949A), "Patterns of Influence: A Study of Interpersonal Influence and Communications Behavior in a Local Community," in Lazarsfeld and Stanton, eds., *Communications Research 1948-49*, New York: Harper and Brothers.

—— (1949B), *Social Theory and Social Structure*, Glencoe, Ill.: Free Press.

Merton, Robert K. and Alice Kitt (1950), "Contributions to the Theory of Reference Group Behavior," in Merton and Lazarsfeld, eds., *Continuities in Social Research*, Glencoe, Ill.: Free Press.

Merton, Robert K., *et al.* (forthcoming), *Patterns of Social Life: Explorations in the Sociology and Social Psychology of Housing* (tentative title). Under a grant from the Lavanburg Foundation.

Meyersohn, Rolf (1953), *Research in Television: Some Highlights and a Bibliography*, unpublished memorandum of the Bureau of Applied Social Research, Columbia University.

Miller, Delbert C. (1945), "A Research Note on Mass Communication," *American Sociological Review*, Vol. 10, pp. 691-694.

Miller, Neal A. and John Dollard (1941), *Social Learning and Imitation*, New Haven: Yale University Press.

Minnesota, University of, School of Journalism Research Division (1949), *Newspapers and their Readers* (2 vols.), Minneapolis, Minn.: University of Minnesota Press.

Moreno, Jacob L. (1953), *Who Shall Survive?*, Beacon, N. Y.: Beacon House.

Myrdal, Gunnar (1944), *An American Dilemma*, New York: Harper and Brothers.

Newcomb, Theodore M. and G. Svehla (1937), "Intra-family Relationships in Attitude," *Sociometry*, Vol. 1, pp. 180-205.

Newcomb, Theodore M. and Eugene L. Hartley, eds. (1947), *Readings in Social Psychology*, New York, Henry Holt.

Newcomb, Theodore M. (1950), *Social Psychology*, New York: Dryden Press.

—— (1951), "Social Psychological Theory," in Rohrer and Sherif, eds., *Social Psychology at the Crossroads*, New York: Harper and Brothers.

—— (1952), "Attitude Development as a Function of Reference Groups: The Bennington Study," in Swanson, Newcomb and Hartley, eds., *Readings in Social Psychology*, New York: Henry Holt.

Park, Robert E. (1949), "The Natural History of the Newspaper," in Wilbur Schramm, ed., *Mass Communications*, Urbana, Ill.: University of Illinois Press.

Precker, Joseph A. (1952), "Similarity of Valuings as a Factor in Selection of Peers and Near-Authority Figures," *Journal of Abnormal and Social Psychology*, Vol. 47, pp. 406-414.

Public Administration Clearing House (1954), "Experiences of Personnel of U.S. Voluntary Agencies," *Economic Development and Cultural Change*, Vol. 2, pp. 329-349.

Riesman, David, Reuel Denney and Nathan Glazer (1950), *The Lonely Crowd*, New Haven, Conn.: Yale University Press.

Riley, Matilda W. and John W. Riley, Jr. (1951), "A Sociological Approach to Communications Research," *Public Opinion Quarterly*, Vol. 15, pp. 445-460. Reprinted in Schramm (1955).

Riley, Matilda W. (1953), "An Interpersonal Approach to Opinion Research," paper delivered at the 1953 meeting of the American Association for Public Opinion Research.

Robinson, William S. (1941), "Radio Comes to the Farmer," in Lazarsfeld and Stanton, eds., *Radio Research 1941*, New York: Duell, Sloan and Pearce.

Roethlisberger, F. J. and W. J. Dickson (1939), *Management and the Worker*, Cambridge, Mass.: Harvard University Press.

Rogers, Maria (1951), "The Human Group: A Critical Review with Suggestions for Some Alternative Hypotheses," *Sociometry*, Vol. 14, pp. 20-31.

Roseborough, Mary E. (1953), "Experimental Studies of Small Groups," *Psychological Bulletin*, Vol. 50, pp. 275-303.

Rossi, Peter H. (1955), *Why Families Move*, Glencoe, Ill.: Free Press.

Sanford, Fillmore H. (1952), "The Psychology of Military Leadership," in Wayne Dennis, ed., *Psychology in the World Emergency*, Pittsburgh, Pa.: University of Pittsburgh Press.

Schachter, Stanley (1951), "Deviation, Rejection and Communication," *Journal of Abnormal and Social Psychology*, Vol. 46, pp. 190-207. Reprinted in Cartwright and Zander (1953).

Schramm, Wilbur and David M. White (1949), "Age, Education and Economic Status as Factors in Newspaper Reading," *Journalism Quarterly*, Vol. 26, pp. 155-157.

Schramm, Wilbur (1949), *Mass Communications*, Urbana, Ill.: University of Illinois Press.

—— (1955), *The Process and Effects of Mass Communication*, Urbana, Ill.: University of Illinois Press.

Sherif, Muzafer (1952), "Social Factors in Perception," in Swanson, Newcomb and Hartley, eds., *Readings in Social Psychology*, New York: Henry Holt.

Shils, Edward A. and Morris Janowitz (1948), "Cohesion and Disintegration in the Wehrmacht," *Public Opinion Quarterly*, Vol. 12, pp. 300-315; reprinted, in part, in Berelson and Janowitz, eds., *Reader in Public Opinion and Communication*, Glencoe, Ill.: Free Press.

Shils, Edward A. (1950), "Primary Groups in the American Army," in Merton and Lazarsfeld, eds., *Studies in the Scope and Method of "The American Soldier,"* Glencoe, Ill.: Free Press.

—— (1951), "The Study of the Primary Group," in Lerner and Lasswell, eds., *The Policy Sciences*, Stanford, Calif.: Stanford University Press.

Sims, Verner M. and James R. Patrick (1947), "Attitude Toward the Negro of Northern and Southern College Students," in Newcomb and Hartley, eds., *Readings in Social Psychology* (first edition), New York: Henry Holt.

Slater, Philip E. (1955), "Role Differentiation in Small Groups," *American Sociological Review*, Vol. 20, pp. 300-310. Reprinted in Hare, Borgatta and Bales (1955).

Smith, Everett R. (1952), "What Is Socio-Economic Status?" *Printer's Ink*, August 1, 1952.

Smith, Joel, William H. Form and Gregory P. Stone (1954), "Local Intimacy in a Middle-Sized City," *American Journal of Sociology*, Vol. 60, pp. 276-284.

Social Science Research Council (1947), *Public Reaction to the Atomic Bomb and World Affairs*, Ithaca, N. Y.: Cornell University Press.

Speier, Hans (1950), "The Historical Development of Public Opinion," *American Journal of Sociology*, Vol. 55, pp. 376-388.

Stewart, Frank A. (1947), "A Sociometric Study of Influence in Southtown," *Sociometry*, Vol. 10, pp. 11-31, 273-286.

Stogdill, R. M. (1948), "Personal Factors Associated With Leadership: A Survey of the Literature," *Journal of Psychology*, Vol. 25, pp. 35-71.

Stouffer, Samuel A. *et al* (1949), *The American Soldier: Studies in Social Psychology in World War II*, (Vols. 1 and 2), Princeton, N. J.: Princeton University Press.

Strodtbeck, Fred L. (1951), "Husband and Wife Interaction Over Revealed Differences," *American Sociological Review*, Vol. 16, pp. 468-477. Reprinted in Hare, Borgatta and Bales (1955).

Stycos, J. Mayone (1952), "Patterns of Communication in a Rural Greek Village," *Public Opinion Quarterly*, Vol. 16, pp. 59-70.

Suchman, Edward A. (1941), "An Invitation to Music," in Lazarsfeld and Stanton, eds., *Radio Research 1941*, New York: Duell, Sloan and Pearce.

Sullivan, Harry S. (1953), *The Interpersonal Theory of Psychiatry*, New York: Norton.

Swanson, G. E., T. M. Newcomb and E. L. Hartley, eds. (1952), *Readings in Social Psychology* (revised edition), New York: Henry Holt.

Tarde, Gabriel (1901), *L'Opinion et la Foule*, Paris.

Thibaut, John (1950), "An Experimental Study of the Cohesiveness of Underprivileged Groups," *Human Relations*, Vol. 3, pp. 251-278. Reprinted in Cartwright and Zander (1953).

Tolman, Edward C. (1951), "A Psychological Model," in Parsons and Shils, eds., *Toward A General Theory of Action*, Cambridge, Mass.: Harvard University Press.

Warner, W. Lloyd and Paul S. Lunt (1941), *The Social Life of a Modern Community* (Vol. 1, Yankee City Series), New Haven, Conn.: Yale University Press.

Whyte, William Foote (1943), *Street Corner Society*, Chicago, Ill.: University of Chicago Press.

—— (1945), "The Social Role of the Settlement House," *Applied Anthropology*, Vol. 1, pp. 14 ff.

Whyte, William H., Jr. (1954), "The Web of Word-of-Mouth," *Fortune*, November, 1954.

Wiebe, G. D. (1951), "Merchandising Commodities and Citizenship on Television," *Public Opinion Quarterly*, Vol. 15, pp. 679-691.

—— (1952), "Responses to the Televised Kefauver Hearings," *Public Opinion Quarterly*, Vol. 16, pp. 179-200. Reprinted in Katz, Cartwright *et al* (1954).

Wilson, A. T. M., E. L. Trist and Adam Curle (1952), "Transitional Communities and Social Reconnection: A Study of the Civil Resettlement of British Prisoners of War," in Swanson, Newcomb and Hartley, eds., *Readings in Social Psychology*, New York: Henry Holt.

Wirth, Louis (1949), "Consensus and Mass Communication," in Wilbur Schramm, ed., *Mass Communications*, Urbana, Illinois: University of Illinois Press.

# Index of Names

# Index of Subjects

Accounting scheme, in impact analysis 189-191, 197, 217

Age, as component of life-cycle types, 224; and acquaintance with public affairs expert, 140; and influence flow in various realms, 241, 257-258, 292-293, 296, 303, 303-308, 329-330. *See also* Life-cycle position

Alcoholics Anonymous, 67

"Anchorage" of opinion, in interpersonal relations, 44 ff. *See also* Norms, Group

Arapesh, 164

"Assessment" of influence, 166, 169 ff., 174

Audience research, 17, 19-22

Balinese, 164

Books, as movie influence, 193-194; and opinion leadership, 311

Campaigns, Media, 8, 19, 26n., 29, 73, 133; marketing vs. nonmarketing, 19, 24n., 29

Change of opinion, *see* Opinion, Change of

Children, studies of, 26-27, 28n., 52, 69, 91, 103, 106n.; and marketing influence, 115, 214n., 245; and media. *See also* Mass Media

Conformity, benefits of, 50 ff.; group enforcement of, 62, 70, 93; and group cohesiveness, 71-72, 86; and leadership, 52-53, 101-103. *See also* Norms, Group, "Social reality"

Content analysis, 17, 22-23, 312-316

"Cosmopolitan" leaders, 2n., 117, 313-315

Decatur study, design of, xx, 4-6, 10-11; selection of city, 335-339; sample, 339

Education, as component of social-economic status index, 226; and public affairs interest, information, participation, 140, 272; and "popular fiction," 378. *See also* Status, social-economic

"Effect" analysis, in mass media research, 3, 18-20, 23n., 316-320

Effectiveness index, defined, 174; for marketing, 175-178; for movies, 179-180, 212, 215; for fashion, 181-182, 210; and exposure, 183, 195-197

*Emperor's New Clothes, The,* 71n.

"Expert," Public affairs, 140, 279 ff., 315n.
  Movie, 306-307

"Export" of influence index, 254 ff., 322

Exposure to sources of influence, 173-174, 310 ff.; and effectiveness: in marketing, 176-178, 211; in movies, 179-180; in fashion, 180-182, 211; summarized, 183; Multiple, 191-197

Family, The, as primary group, 48, 131; influence of, 38, 50; flow of influence within, 8, 114-115, 140 ff., 213, 244-245, 257-258, 276 ff., 292-293, 329 ff. *See also* Life-cycle position

Fashion changes, Personal vs. media influences on, 180-183, 210

Fashion leaders, 159, 247-270, 331; and Mass media, 310 ff.

Follow-up interview, *see* Interviewing procedures

Friendship ties, formation of, 35, 58, 60-61; as networks for influence flow, 8, 35, 58, 60-61, 69, 85-86, 141, 143; extent of, 131, 227; and movie-going, 299 ff. *See also* Primary group; Gregariousness